This volume offers a unique and valuable insight into the novel in French over the past two centuries. In a series of essays, acknowledged experts discuss a variety of topics including nineteenth-century realism, women and fiction, popular fiction, experiment and innovation, war and the Holocaust, the Francophone novel and postmodern fiction. They offer a challenging reassessment of major figures, while deliberately reading traditional views of literary history against the grain. Theoretical discussion is combined with close reading of texts and exploration of context, comparison with other genres and other literatures, and reference to novels from earlier periods. This companionable introduction includes a chronology and guide to further reading. From it emerges a strong sense of the vitality and energy of the modern French novel, and of the debates surrounding it.

THE CAMBRIDGE
COMPANION TO
THE FRENCH NOVEL
From 1800 to the present

CAMBRIDGE COMPANIONS TO LITERATURE

THE CAMBRIDGE
COMPANION TO
THE FRENCH NOVEL
From 1800 to the present

EDITED BY
TIMOTHY UNWIN
University of Liverpool

CAMBRIDGE
UNIVERSITY PRESS

PUBLISHED BY THE PRESS SYNDICATE OF THE UNIVERSITY OF CAMBRIDGE
The Pitt Building, Trumpington Street, Cambridge CB2 1RP, United Kingdom

CAMBRIDGE UNIVERSITY PRESS
The Edinburgh Building, Cambridge CB2 2RU, United Kingdom
40 West 20th Street, New York, NY 10011–4211, USA
10 Stamford Road, Oakleigh, Melbourne 3166, Australia

First published 1997

Printed in the United Kingdom at the University Press, Cambridge

Typeset in Sabon 10/13 pt.

A catalogue record for this book is available from the British Library

Library of Congress cataloguing in publication data

The Cambridge companion to the French novel: From 1800 to the present / edited
by Timothy Unwin.
p.   cm. – (Cambridge companions to literature)
Includes bibliographical references and index.
ISBN 0 521 49563 6 (hardback) – ISBN 0 521 49914 3 (paperback)
1. French fiction – 20th century – History and criticism.
I. Unwin, Timothy A. II. Series.
PQ671.C296   1997
843'.009–dc21   96-52444 CIP

ISBN 0 521 49563 6 hardback
ISBN 0 521 49914 3 paperback

CE

CONTENTS

STEVEN UNGAR

10 War and the Holocaust   161
DENIS BOAK

11 From serious to popular fiction   179
STEPHEN F. NOREIKO

12 The colonial and postcolonial Francophone novel   194
FRANÇOISE LIONNET

13 The French-Canadian novel   214
DENIS BOAK

14 Gender and sexual identity in the modern French novel   223
JANE WINSTON

15 Postmodern French fiction: practice and theory   242
JOHNNIE GRATTON

    General bibliography   261
    Index   264

NOTES ON CONTRIBUTORS

DENIS BOAK is a Professorial Research Fellow at the University of Western Australia, where he held the Chair of French from 1975 to 1995. Since 1975 he has been the Editor of the journal *Essays in French Literature*. He has published books on Martin du Gard, Malraux, Romains and Sartre.

MARGARET COHEN is Associate Professor of Comparative Literature at New York University. Her publications include *Profane Illumination: Walter Benjamin and the Paris of Surrealist Revolution* (Berkeley, 1993) and *Spectacles of Realism – Body, Gender, Genre* (Minneapolis, 1995) which she co-edited with Christopher Prendergast. She is currently completing *Why Were There No French Women Realists?* which will be forthcoming from Princeton University Press in 1998.

DAVID COWARD is Professor of Modern French Literature at the University of Leeds. He has written studies of Restif de la Bretonne, Marivaux, Duras and Pagnol, translated Maupassant, Sade and Albert Cohen, edited numerous novels by Dumas *père*, and is currently writing a History of French Literature. He is a frequent contributor to *The Times Literary Supplement*.

ALISON FINCH is a Fellow and Tutor in French at Merton College, Oxford. She is the author of *Proust's Additions* (Cambridge, 1977), *Stendhal: La Chartreuse de Parme* (London, 1984), *Concordance de Stendhal* (Leeds, 1991), and a number of essays on post-1800 French literature. She is currently working on nineteenth-century French women's writing.

JOHNNIE GRATTON lectures in French at University College Dublin. He is the author of studies on Breton, Colette, Proust, Barthes and Sarraute, and is co-editor of *Modern French Short Fiction* (Manchester, 1994) and of the forthcoming *La Nouvelle hier et aujourd'hui*.

FRANÇOISE LIONNET teaches French and Comparative Literature at North-western University. She is the author of *Autobiographical Voices: Race, Gender, Self-Portraiture* (Ithaca, 1989) and *Postcolonial Representations: Women, Literature, Identity* (Ithaca, 1995). She is co-editor of 'Post/Colonial

Conditions: Exiles, Migrations, Nomadisms', *Yale French Studies* 82–3 (1993), and 'Postcolonial, Indigenous, and Emergent Feminisms', *Signs* (1995).

JANN MATLOCK is Associate Professor of Romance Languages and Literatures at Harvard University. She is the author of *Scenes of Seduction: Prostitution, Hysteria, and Reading Difference in Nineteenth-Century France* (New York, 1994) and co-editor, with Marjorie Garber and Rebecca L. Walkowitz, of *Media Spectacles* (New York, 1993). She is currently completing a book on vision and aesthetics in nineteenth-century France, entitled *Desires to Censor*, and a collection of essays on the relationship of literary and historical study, *Purloined Longings: Letters from the Archives*.

CHRISTIE MCDONALD is Professor of Romance Languages and Literatures at Harvard University. She is the author of *The Dialogue of Writing* (Waterloo, Ont., 1985), *Dispositions* (Montreal, 1986) and *The Proustian Fabric* (Lincoln, NE 1991).

STEPHEN F. NOREIKO is Lecturer in French at the University of Hull. An expert on popular French language and culture, in particular detective fiction, he has written about various aspects of French, as well as publishing studies on Djian, Perec and Queneau. He is Founder Editor of the *Cahiers* of the Association for French Language Studies.

LAURENCE M. PORTER is Professor of French and Comparative Literature at Michigan State University, where he received the Distinguished Faculty Award in 1995. He has published ninety articles and book chapters on all periods of European, African and Latin American literature. His eight books include *The Crisis of French Symbolism* (New York, 1990), nominated by Cornell University Press for the James Russell Lowell prize.

STEVEN UNGAR, Professor of French and Comparative Literature at The University of Iowa, is the author of *Roland Barthes: The Professor of Desire* (Lincoln, NE 1983) and *Scandal and Aftereffect: Blanchot and France since 1930* (Minneapolis, 1995). He is co-editor (with Betty R. McGraw) of *Signs in Culture: Roland Barthes Today* (Iowa City, 1989) and (with Tom Conley) of *Identity Papers: Contested Nationhood in Twentieth-Century France* (Minneapolis, 1996). He is completing a study on culture and renewal in Popular Front France.

TIMOTHY UNWIN, James Barrow Professor of French at the University of Liverpool, is the author of numerous studies on nineteenth-century French writers. His books include *Constant: 'Adolphe'* (London, 1986), *Art et infini: l'œuvre de jeunesse de Gustave Flaubert* (Amsterdam, 1991) and *Verne: 'Le Tour du monde en quatre-vingts jours'* (Glasgow, 1992).

DAVID H. WALKER is Professor of French at the University of Sheffield. He has written on and edited works by Camus, Genet and Robbe-Grillet. In addition to numerous articles, he has published two books on Gide: *André Gide* (London, 1990) and *Gide: 'Les Nourritures terrestres' and 'La Symphonie pastorale'* (London, 1990). He is also the editor of *Albert Camus: les extrêmes et l'équilibre* (Amsterdam, 1994) and the author of *Outrage and Insight: Modern French Writers and the 'fait divers'* (London, 1995). He has contributed to reference works including the *Dictionary of Literary Biography*, the *International Dictionary of Theatre* and the *New Oxford Companion to Literature in French*.

JANE WINSTON is Assistant Professor of French at Northwestern University where she also teaches in the Women's Studies programme. Her recent publications include 'Forever Feminine: Marguerite Duras and Her Critics' (*New Literary History* 24 (1993), 467–82), 'Marguerite Duras: Marxism, Feminism, Writing' (*Theatre Journal* 47 (1995), 345–65), and 'Autour de la rue Saint-Benoît: An Interview with Dionys Mascolo' (*Contemporary French Culture* 18:2 (1994), 188–207). She is currently completing a book on Duras. Other research interests include feminist, postcolonial and queer theories and contemporary women's writing.

PREFACE

This book seeks to give a broad overview of developments in the French novel over approximately the last two centuries, and to provide the student or general reader with a challenging yet user-friendly work of reference. The modern French novel is a vast subject, the contours of which are constantly being redefined, and the aim here is not to give complete coverage to it or to do justice to every major novelist. Rather, each of the fifteen chapters of this volume presents insights into an area or problem, or an author or group of authors, combining background information with up-to-date critical perspectives and debate. Each of the contributors has been encouraged to offer an individual approach. Some concentrate on close readings of a few texts, others give a broader historical sweep, or introduce a more theoretical dimension; and some offer a variety of different perspectives within the space allotted. However, all are concerned to open up pathways for the reader and to provide a companionable introduction rather than a definitive scholarly statement. Suggestions for further reading will be found after each chapter, and the main bibliography at the end of the volume lists manuals and works which will guide the reader towards a fuller knowledge of the field, or of particular aspects of it.

The contributors to this volume were not only working within strict space limitations; they were also working to tight deadlines. My thanks go out to them all for their cheerful acceptance of, and for the most part adherence to, the constraints which this task imposed. I have enjoyed their enthusiastic co-operation, benefited from their knowledge and wisdom, and enjoyed meeting many of them, either virtually or in my real travels across three continents during the period of composition of this volume.

Special thanks are due to the (mainly anonymous) reviewers of the early plans. Their suggestions were gratefully and liberally incorporated into subsequent plans, and I trust that the final product is much the better for their interventions. I should like also to record sincere thanks to my former colleagues in the French Department at the University of Western Australia, whose intellectual and moral support was invaluable at the inception of this project. While at the University of Western Australia, I was the recipient of a research award which enabled me to take time off teaching to carry out editorial duties and the writing of my own chapter. I would like here to record my thanks to that institution for its generous and vigorous promotion of travel and research.

Two individuals should also be singled out for thanks. Kate Brett of Cambridge University Press was the initiator of this project. Her advice was invaluable, her good humour unfailing, and the volume owes a great deal to her. Linda Bree then took over the editorial task in the final stages, and saw it through to completion with admirable care and wisdom. I trust that the end product is an expression of their editorial skills. Errors and lacunae remain my responsibility.

Finally, I should like to thank Michael, Alice and Anthony Unwin whose enveloping mirth was, and always is, the best antidote to the solemnity resulting from a long task.

Timothy Unwin

1800   Mme de Staël, *De la littérature.*

1802   Birth of Hugo. Mme de Staël, *Delphine.*

1804   Bonaparte crowned Emperor. Birth of George Sand.

1807   Mme de Staël, *Corinne.*

1814   Napoleon's first abdication followed by First Restoration.

1815   The 100 Days. Waterloo. Second Restoration.

1816   Constant, *Adolphe.*

1817   Death of Mme de Staël.

1820   Assassination of the duc de Berry.

1821   Death in exile of Napoleon. Birth of Flaubert.

1823   Mme de Duras, *Ourika.*

1824   Death of Louis XVIII.

1825   Coronation of Charles X.

1830   The July Revolution. Louis-Philippe, roi des Français. Death of Constant. Stendhal, *Le Rouge et le noir.* Relaxation of censorship laws.

1831   Hugo, *Notre-Dame de Paris*. Balzac, *La Peau de chagrin*.

1832   Cholera epidemic. Sand, *Indiana*. Death of Goethe and Walter Scott.

1833   Sand, *Lélia*.

1835   Balzac, *Le Père Goriot*.

1836   First stirrings of popular press.

1837   Queen Victoria to the British throne. Opening of the Paris–Saint Germain railway line.

1839   Stendhal, *La Chartreuse de Parme*.

1840   Birth of Zola.

1842   Death of Stendhal.

1844   Dumas père, *Les Trois Mousquetaires*.

1846   Balzac, *La Cousine Bette*.

1848   Louis-Philippe flees after February Revolution. Louis-Napoléon Bonaparte elected President of the Republic. Marx and Engels, *Communist Party Manifesto*. Death of Chateaubriand.

1849   Sand, *La Petite Fadette*.

1850   Death of Balzac.

1851   (December) Coup d'Etat. Louis-Napoléon becomes Emperor Napoléon III. Second Empire commences.

1856   Flaubert, *Madame Bovary*.

1862   Hugo, *Les Misérables*.

1863   Fromentin, *Dominique*. Start of publication of Littré's *Dictionnaire*. Salon des Refusés.

1867   Marx, *Das Kapital.*

1869   Opening of Suez Canal. Flaubert, *L'Education sentimentale.* Birth of Gide.

1870   Franco-Prussian War. Death of Dumas père.

1871   Peace with Prussia. The Commune.

1872   Verne, *Le Tour du monde en quatre-vingts jours.*

1873   Birth of Colette.

1876   Death of Sand.

1877   Zola, *L'Assommoir.*

1878   Exposition universelle in Paris.

1879   *La Marseillaise* becomes national anthem.

1880   Death of Flaubert.

1881   Birth of Picasso.

1883   Brunetière, *Le Roman naturaliste.* Maupassant, *Une vie.*

1884   Legalisation of divorce in France. Huysmans, *A rebours.* Rachilde, *Monsieur Vénus.*

1885   Zola, *Germinal.* Death of Hugo.

1886   Opening of the Statue of Liberty in New York.

1889   Eiffel Tower completed for the Exposition universelle.

1894   Condemnation of Dreyfus.

1895   First film projection by the Lumière brothers.

1898   Zola, 'J'accuse'.

1900 International Socialist Congress in Paris. Opening of first Métro line. Colette, *Claudine à l'école*. Freud, *The Interpretation of Dreams* (trans. into French 1926).

1902 Gide, *L'Immoraliste*. Death of Zola.

1903 First airborne flight by the Wright brothers. First Prix Goncourt awarded to *Force ennemie* by J.-A. Nau.

1905 Birth of Sartre.

1909 Blériot: first flight across the Channel.

1911 Marie Curie wins Nobel Prize for Chemistry.

1912 The Titanic sinks.

1913 Einstein, *Theory of Relativity*. Alain-Fournier, *Le Grand-Meaulnes*. Martin du Gard, *Jean Barois*. Proust, *Du côté de chez Swann*.

1914 Start of First World War. Gide, *Les Caves du Vatican*.

1915 Absinthe made illegal. Romain Rolland wins Nobel Prize for Literature.

1916 Saussure, *Cours de linguistique générale*. Barbusse, *Le Feu* (winner of Prix Goncourt).

1917 Freud, *Introduction to Psychoanalysis*.

1918 Armistice signed on 11 November.

1919 Treaty of Versailles. Proust, *A l'ombre des jeunes filles en fleur* (winner of Prix Goncourt).

1920 Colette, *Chéri*.

1921 Nobel Prize for Literature to Anatole France. Start of regular radio broadcasts from Eiffel Tower.

1922   Martin du Gard, first volume of *Les Thibault* (final volume 1940).
        James Joyce, *Ulysses.*

1924   Breton, *Manifeste du surréalisme.*

1925   Hitler, *Mein Kampf.*

1926   Gide, *Les Faux-Monnayeurs.*

1927   First speaking films: Greta Garbo plays Anna Karenina. Mauriac,
        Thérèse Desqueyroux. Proust, *Le Temps retrouvé.*

1929   The Wall Street Crash. Colette, *Sido.* Saint-Exupéry, *Courrier Sud.*

1930   Simenon, *Pietr le Letton* (first Maigret novel).

1931   Nizan, *Aden, Arabie.* Saint-Exupéry, *Vol de nuit.*

1932   First television images broadcast in Paris. Céline, *Voyage au bout
        de la nuit.* Mauriac, *Le Nœud de vipères.* Romains, first volume of
        Les Hommes de bonne volonté (final volume 1947).

1933   Malraux, *La Condition humaine.* Mauriac, *Le Romancier et ses
        personnages.*

1934   Jean Renoir, film of *Madame Bovary.*

1937   Exposition universelle in Paris. Spanish Civil War. Martin du Gard
        wins Nobel Prize for Literature.

1938   Nizan, *La Conspiration.* Sartre, *La Nausée.*

1939   Declaration of War on Germany by Britain and France (3
        September).

1942   Camus, *L'Etranger, Le Mythe de Sisyphe.*

1943   Saint-Exupéry, *Le Petit Prince.*

1944   Genet, *Notre-Dame-des-Fleurs.*

1945   Defeat of Germany. Death of Hitler, Mussolini, Roosevelt. First atomic bomb on Hiroshima. Sartre, first volume of *Les Chemins de la liberté* (final volume published 1949).

1946   Beginning of Indochina War. First Cannes Film Festival.

1947   Gide wins Nobel Prize for Literature. Beckett, *Murphy* (French translation). Camus, *La Peste.*

1949   Simone de Beauvoir, *Le Deuxième Sexe.*

1950   Start of Korean War. Duras, *Un barrage contre le Pacifique.* Nationwide television broadcasting begins in France.

1951   Gracq, *Le Rivage des Syrtes* (refuses to accept Prix Goncourt). Death of Gide.

1952   Mauriac wins Nobel Prize for Literature.

1953   Barthes, *Le Degré zéro de l'écriture.* Camara Laye, *L'Enfant noir.*

1954   Algerian War begins.

1955   Chraïbi, *Les Boucs.*

1956   Butor, *L'Emploi du temps.* Camus, *La Chute.* Sarraute, *L'Ere du soupçon.*

1957   Founding of Common Market. Camus wins Nobel Prize for Literature. Butor, *La Modification.* Robbe-Grillet, *La Jalousie.*

1958   Beginning of Fifth Republic. Duras, *Moderato Cantabile.*

1959   Queneau, *Zazie dans le métro.* Sarraute, *Le Planétarium.*

1960   Camus killed in car accident.

1961   Construction of Berlin Wall. Yuri Gagarin first man in space.

1963   Assassination of President Kennedy. Robbe-Grillet, *Pour un nouveau roman.*

1964   Sartre refuses Nobel Prize for Literature.

1968   Student insurrection and general strike in France. Assassination of
       Martin Luther King and of Robert Kennedy. The 'Prague Spring'.
       Modiano, *La Place de l'étoile*.

1969   De Gaulle resigns. Beckett wins Nobel Prize for Literature.

1970   Cixous, *Le Troisième Corps*. Anne Hébert, *Kamouraska*.
       Tournier, *Le Roi des Aulnes* (winner of Prix Goncourt).

1973   End of Vietnam War. Yourcenar, *Souvenirs pieux*.

1975   Emile Ajar (Romain Gary), *La Vie devant soi* (winner of Prix
       Goncourt).

1978   Modiano, *Rue des boutiques obscures*. Perec, *La Vie mode
       d'emploi*.

1979   Antonine Maillet, *Pélagie-la-Charrette* (first Canadian to win Prix
       Goncourt).

1980   Death of Roland Barthes and Jean-Paul Sartre.

1981   François Mitterrand elected President (re-elected 1988).

1984   Duras, *L'Amant* (winner of Prix Goncourt).

1985   Nobel Prize for Literature awarded to Claude Simon. Destruction
       of Berlin Wall.

1992   Daniel Pennac, *Comme un roman*. Passage through French
       parliament of Jacques Toubon's *projet de loi relatif à la langue
       française*.

1995   Jacques Chirac elected President. Andreï Makine, *Le Testament
       français* (first novel to win both the Prix Goncourt and Prix
       Médicis).

1996   Death of François Mitterrand.

NOTE ON LITERARY PRIZES

The 'big six' literary prizes in France have an extremely high profile and are, significantly, all awarded for novels. The best known and most prestigious is the Prix Goncourt, named after the Goncourt brothers Jules and Edmond. It is likely to boost an author's sales figures hugely (Marguerite Duras's *L'Amant*, the 1984 winner, eventually sold 1.5 million copies). First awarded in 1903, the Goncourt has included Proust, Malraux and Tournier among its winners – though noticeably absent from the list are Céline, Camus, Sartre and Yourcenar. Gracq, nominated for the prize in 1951 for *Le Rivage des Syrtes*, refused it. The other major literary prizes are the Grand Prix du Roman de l'Académie Française, the Prix Fémina (awarded by a jury of women, though not necessarily to a female novelist), the Prix Renaudot, the Prix Interallié and the Prix Médicis. In 1995 Andreï Makine's *Le Testament français* became the first novel to win both the Prix Goncourt and the Prix Médicis.

Prizes for Francophone literature outside France include the Grand Prix de la Francophonie de l'Académie Française, and the Grand Prix Littéraire d'Afrique Noire. French-speaking writers who have received the Nobel Prize for Literature include Roger Martin du Gard, André Gide, François Mauriac, Albert Camus, Samuel Beckett and Claude Simon. In 1964 Sartre refused to accept the prize.

NOTE ON PRESENTATION

In order to facilitate the reading of this volume, footnotes have been kept to a minimum and, where possible, references have been included in parentheses in the text itself. Where references are to items listed in the Suggestions for further reading at the end of a chapter, the author's name alone is given, followed directly by the page number(s) in the listed work.

Many novels are referred to briefly in the pages of this volume. In such cases, only the author's name, the title of the novel, and the year of its publication are given. However, in cases where textual references are made, full publication details are given. Quotations given in French are accompanied by a translation unless they clearly present no difficulty to the Anglophone reader. Translations, unless otherwise stated, are those of the authors.

I

TIMOTHY UNWIN

On the novel and the writing of literary history

The literary history of France and the Francophone world has, it has been said, a long tradition of censorship. Emphasis on individual genius has not only produced an exaggerated belief in the French cultural heritage, it has fostered an attitude of submissiveness on the part of the student of literature. Literary history has its covert political agenda, and what gets taught in the classroom and in literary manuals tells us much about the authoritarian tradition in which the discipline has evolved.

These were remarks made by Roland Barthes in a 1969 essay entitled 'Réflexions sur un manuel' ['Reflections on a Manual']. The definition of literature itself, he suggested, might in the end be nothing other than 'ce qui s'enseigne' ['what gets taught'], so that the great canonical figures are inevitably invested with all the authority of the state educational apparatus. And Barthes adds: 'Il y a . . . toute une autre histoire de notre littérature à écrire, une contre-histoire, un envers de cette histoire, qui serait l'histoire de ces censures précisément' ['A quite different history of our literature remains to be written: a counter-history, the other side of that history, and that would be, precisely, the history of what has been censored'].[1] He suggests that, in telling the hitherto untold, any literary history worthy of the name must also be a history of the idea of literature, of the way literature has been interpreted, received, distorted or used as a form of political control. It must ask the hard questions, not only of other histories of literature, but also of itself. What is being occluded or foregrounded, and why?

Barthes's words of caution, and the programme of vigilance which he sets out, will be the starting point in this *Companion*. In a postmodern and self-conscious age, it is no longer possible to write a history of French literature, or indeed of any part of French literature, in the grand old style of the classroom manual. The study of literature cannot simply make authoritative pronouncements, for we live in a climate where every discourse is regarded with suspicion. It must include itself and its own presuppositions within its field of vision. The focus is dual: both on the object of study and on the manner in which the object is, or has been, studied.

As for the modern French novel itself, this is a vast and perhaps ultimately unclassifiable area, since the novel has a notorious capacity to cross the boundary and integrate other genres – or perhaps, indeed, to be integrated by them.[2] Any attempt to give complete coverage would encounter huge obstacles. This manual will, rather, function like a collage of snapshots, some overlapping, others leaving gaps and inviting the reader to complete the picture (whatever that picture may ultimately be). The idea of complete coverage may itself be a tendentious one, implying order, closure, totality and the possibility of establishing a definitive canon. More than any other period in literary history, the late twentieth century revised expectations about what the idea of literature is, what its history is, what its contents and hidden agendas are, and where the dividing line between texts and their theory may lie. Many would now dispute that such a dividing line even exists, suggesting not only that the literary text has finally integrated its theory, but that theory in its turn is becoming the literary text. (The writings of Barthes himself, among others, have clearly established the critic's claim to be a 'creative writer'. See Johnnie Gratton's remarks on this subject in the final chapter, pp. 247–8.) This radical reassessment of what literary history is, or might be, must itself be part of the subject of the present volume. Rather than closing off the area of study, the aim here will be to open it up, to provide a glimpse of its possibilities. The task is not so much to provide the answers as to ask the questions. What is the modern French novel and how do we read it? Where are the parameters of the subject? Where do novel and theory separate, if at all? Can we define a corpus of texts which fit the definition? What do we mean by 'modern', by 'French', and indeed by 'the novel'?

The working definitions here will be simple, although like all working definitions they will also be challenged when the need arises. The word 'modern' is taken, broadly speaking, as covering the period from the early nineteenth century through to the present and to the postmodern. However, since centuries are artificial categories, it would be unwise to set an absolute boundary at the beginning of the subject, and many references will be made in the course of these pages to earlier novels and novelists. Although the organisation of this volume is broadly chronological, the earlier and later chapters corresponding in about equal proportion to the nineteenth and twentieth centuries, the reader should be aware that this is, partly at least, a matter of convenience of presentation, and that many chapters deliberately overlap and cross-refer to earlier or later ones in a self-consciously fragmentary collage. As for the use of the word 'French', it is intended to refer not just to France itself, but to the French novel elsewhere in Europe, Canada, the Caribbean, Africa, the Middle East or South East Asia. Study of Francophone literature outside of France has been a huge growth area in recent years, as the canon has been revised and other literatures in French, or dialects of French, given a fair reading. This process has been helped also by the fact that many Francophone writers have been winners of literary awards in France (see the note about literary prizes at the beginning of this volume), the prestigious Prix Goncourt counting among its ranks, for example, Antonine Maillet (Canada), Tahar Ben Jelloun (Morocco), Patrick Chamoiseau (Martinique) and Amin Maalouf (Lebanon). And although statistically it is true that France itself still produces by far the most French novels (a fact which is reflected in the overall concentration of this volume), the reader will find two chapters on the Francophone novel outside of France, as well as references from time to time in other chapters to Francophone novels. It seems possible that as the study of the French novel develops, the French/Francophone distinction may itself eventually either lose its sharpness or become obsolete. In the present state of the discipline there is still, however, much compartmenta-lising of the two areas.

Yet perhaps it is the definition of 'the novel' which poses the most difficulties at the outset. Given that, in the French tradition in particular, the novel has a history of questioning itself, redefining itself, seeking itself out, challenging its own identity and status as a literary genre, and blending into other genres, when do we decide that a novel is not a novel any longer? Such is the protean capacity of the novel to adapt, that even the styles judged most 'un-novelistic' will inevitably be appropriated by it sooner or later. And given that French novelists are prone to theorise extensively about their own novels and the novels of others – often within the compass of their own fiction – do we include such theorising within our field of vision? Again, the intention here is to open up the field rather than to close it off, and if this leaves gaps, then it is to be hoped that those gaps will function as an invitation to explore this infinite subject further. It would no doubt be tendentious to define the novel merely according to a highbrow canon of 'teachable' classics, although the classics remain by definition important both as cultural and as aesthetic reference-points. The purview here will include the highbrow and the lowbrow, the remembered and the forgotten, the important and the not-so-important, the straight and the not-so-straight, pure narrative and 'genre-blending' works that take the novel to and, in some cases, beyond its own limits. This *Companion* will also include (partly at least) the theory of the novel within its field of vision. Some might wish to argue that the theory of novel is a separate discipline which has little to do with the reading of novels themselves, and that it should be consigned to a separate volume. To separate novel and theory would, however, not only deprive us of many of the insights which theory affords. Such a separation would also be extremely difficult to effect, since there is no precise point at which the gap between the two becomes evident. Many novelists from the early Romantic period onwards include or represent their own narrative strategies within the fiction itself. Stories are constructed, again and again, around the notion that 'reality' may be a fiction, or around its corollary that fiction is the only reality. They embody an implicit statement of the relationship or overlap between the writing and the theory. The theory is there within the so-called 'primary' texts. It seems wholly right and proper, therefore, to include the theory of the novel in a volume on the novel, and this will be done in two obvious ways here: first, by the inclusion of chapters which deal more or less explicitly with theoretical issues and their relation to the novel (the final two chapters of the volume are particularly important in this respect) and, second, by the inclusion of theoretical issues in and alongside discussion of specific novels and novelists.

The reader of this volume will, then, repeatedly come across references, in a wide variety of contexts, to theoretical problems and issues. Questions will be asked about the changing canon of texts; about the under-representation of women writers in the history of the French novel and about the possibility of re-reading the discipline from a feminist perspective; about the problems of representation and mimesis; about self-consciousness and formal experiment; about the role of ideologies and political commitment; about the way in which novels can empower us emotionally or politically; about the constituents of narrative and the philosophy of language implicit in novels; about the links between novels and cinema, television, radio, the *bande dessinée* (or 'graphic novel', a genre which has a higher cultural standing in the Francophone than in the Anglophone world); and – last but by no means least – about standards of aesthetic judgement which lead communities or generations of readers to prefer one text to another. Without this theoretical dimension, there would indeed be no history of the French novel, since so much depends on how novels have been read, construed and (perhaps mis-) interpreted. This is, of course, true of literature in general, and Paul De Man once wrote (a trifle pessimistically perhaps) that 'the specificity of literary language resides in the possibility of misreading and misinterpretation' (*Blindness and Insight*, p. 280). Whether or not we agree with this, it is certain that reading and interpretation – or the reception of the text – are now at the centre of the discipline. This volume is, then, endeavouring to provide an account of the French novel which, following Barthes's precept, also contains the idea of the French novel. The essays here do not set out with the intention of saying everything about each of these areas of focus, operating by preference in the introductory and indeed the companionable mode. As 'companions' to the reader, the authors of this volume offer insights, assessments and knowledge relating to their different specialist areas. Yet at the same time, their picture is provisional. It is there to provide focal points, and it should ideally be completed, altered or ultimately even transformed. The reader is invited not to receive ready-made knowledge but rather to participate in its construction. And of course, the reader will discover not only differences of approach in the various chapters of this volume, but also frequent overlapping concerns in the picture that is presented.

What makes us read novels? What kind of view of the world, vision or philosophy, can they offer which we might not find elsewhere? What knowledge, pleasure, insights or experience do we get from them? In a 1976 essay entitled 'Sur la lecture', Barthes distinguished three types, or modes, of reading.[3] The first was what he called the 'desiring' mode in which there is an almost fetishistic pleasure in the words themselves. The second is the mode of 'suspense', where we are carried forward by the narrative (or by what is known as its hermeneutic code) to the point where we almost forget the actual words of the text as we unravel the story. And the third is the 'productive' mode, where our relationship with the text is active, initiating in us the desire to write. To these three categories or modes (which might also be present in our reading of other genres) one might add the additional mode of enquiry. We read novels to find out about people, societies, ideas, places. The provision of knowledge is on occasions such a powerful component of fiction that novels themselves become the best source for our enquiries. Engels wrote in 1888 that he had learned more from Balzac than from all the professional historians, economists and statisticians put together.[4] As a tool of historical research, novels can be invaluable – yet they can also be extremely misleading. Flaubert's 1869 L'Education sentimentale, which is occasionally quoted in history books to illuminate the events of 1848 in Paris, is itself an ironic send-up not only of the writing of history, but of the very 'idea of history'. Hot property for the historian!

If we see the attractions of the novel in terms of the four modes outlined above – Barthes's three categories of desire, suspense and production, and the additional one of enquiry – then we might conclude from this that their co-existence is itself one of the main sources of the novel's success as a genre. Poetry may fulfil our desire to relate to the word. Drama and film may provide suspense. Autobiography may encourage us to write for ourselves. Historical or documentary writings and films will operate in the mode of enquiry. But the novel touches on all of these at some time. It moves between the different modes, showing greater variety and flexibility than any other genre. It can be anything from poetic to discursive, descriptive to theoretical, intimate to analytic, encyclopaedic to confessional, and the links between narrative and autobiography are themselves an area of intense interest (as witnessed by Philippe Lejeune's seminal 1975 study, *Le Pacte autobiographique*). The narrative point of view can be omniscient or subjective, or anything in between, varying in infinite blends between what Genette (*Figures III*, pp. 206–11) has called 'external focalisation' (focus on a character's behaviour from outside) and 'internal focalisation' (focus on the world from within a character's mind or feelings). Yet the novel maintains in most cases a peculiarly powerful relationship with the real, partly because its form is extensive and because it operates typically in a mode of verbal profusion (unlike poetry which, typically, is intensive and operates in a mode of verbal economy). It often speaks of a world which is recognisable, indeed verifiable, to the point where there is possible confusion of the fictional and the real (Balzac is an obvious and major example of this, and he thrives on the pact of truth which he initiates with his reader ('all is true', we are told). So at the same time as it offers textual pleasure or hermeneutic satisfaction, the novel also goes beyond the fictional and provides facts or information. Although fiction is clearly, as John Searle and others have argued, a form of pretence,[5] it is one of the properties of fiction to blur the division between its 'fictional' and its 'serious' statements. When Jules Verne's *Le Tour du monde en quatre-vingts jours* was being serialised in *Le Temps* in the latter stages of 1872, real-life bets actually took place as to whether Phileas Fogg was going to make it back to London in the allotted time, and travel companies approached Verne in an attempt to get themselves written favourably into the story. Fiction and reality have a strange relationship. This peculiar power of the novel to engage the real is both its greatest strength and, arguably, its area of greatest difficulty. It can lead us to ask questions which, properly speaking, are 'unfair' or not in the domain of the novel (such as when we use a text naïvely in pursuit of historical insights). It is, of course, the author's absolute right to omit as well as to include, yet at some other level, readers might feel 'cheated' by this procedure. Questions such as 'how does Emma Bovary avoid getting pregnant?' might seem real enough to many readers, yet they of course receive no answer within the novel and – like the great unanswered question about Lady Macbeth's children – ultimately lead nowhere. This may be a disappointment to some. Fiction seems to offer truth, and ends up as precisely what it was at the outset: a fiction, an invention, perhaps even a lie.

Here we touch on one of those paradoxes which abound in the writing and the reading of novels. In order to speak the truth, the novelist has to invent and pretend. So even as it makes statements about verifiable realities, the novel willingly exposes the lie of its own discourse. If the novel is to aspire to a higher truth, it must of course reveal its pretence. And yet, it requires that pretence in the first place if it is to exist as a novel. This recalls the famous 'Cretan liar' paradox of Antiquity, in which a speaker claimed: 'All Cretans are liars. I am a Cretan.' To establish any truth-value in such a statement is virtually impossible since, for the speaker to maintain both that Cretans are liars and that he is a Cretan is irreconcilable. If he is a Cretan, then he must be a liar, and therefore in all likelihood not the Cretan he mendaciously claims to be. But if he is *not* a Cretan, it seems also that he is lying (since he is pretending to be one), so maybe he *is* a Cretan after all! Fiction, and the reading of it, is riddled with similar paradoxes, and often the novel finds its way out of the conundrum by unmasking its own charade, stepping back and perceiving itself within its vision. The first great French novelist, Rabelais, did precisely this, and his work is a self-consciously brilliant example of linguistic virtuosity and showmanship, exuberantly revelling at every turn in the gigantically preposterous nature of its medium. Rabelais proclaims at the dawn of the modern era that the writing of narrative is in a sense a flawed activity which must undermine or exaggerate its own procedures if it is to aspire to any truth at all. Its condition is thus both inescapable and impossible, yet it is precisely in this knowledge of its 'fall from grace' that the novel finds its voice. Rabelais's message will not be lost on later comic writers, such as Voltaire, whose *Candide* (1759) is also a joyful send-up of the whole notion of fiction. Voltaire revels precisely in the fictional, in the absurd twists and turns of plot, the contrived coincidences, the exaggerated descriptions of battles and disasters, in order to get beyond fiction itself and convey a philosophical message. Diderot, on the other hand, pursues the experiment in a different direction. In *Jacques le fataliste* (1773) he plays mockingly with the reader's expectations, threatening at every turn to break the contract of fictional pretence (which he is thereby underlining) and destroy the whole story, yet he constructs the story itself precisely on such tenuous premises. Such processes are particularly apparent, too, in many modern comic novels, Raymond Queneau being a notable exponent of this 'parody of fiction' within the fiction itself. A contemporary québécois novelist, Réjean Ducharme, using some of the same techniques as Queneau (phonetic spellings for example) makes the fragility of the medium into a central element of his novelistic vision, for example in *Dévadé* (1990) where he presents a compassionate yet topsy-turvy view of the world through a down-and-out narrator.

Another reason for this tendency of the novel to undermine its own procedures may be that the genre poses an inherent problem of 'accept-ability'. We might focus on this problem initially by looking at Aristotle's famous distinction, in the *Poetics,* between the historian and the poet. 'The difference between the historian and the poet is', he wrote, 'that one tells of what has happened, the other of the kinds of things that might happen'.[6] The novelist is, in a sense, like Aristotle's historian, using extended narrative, precise denotation, detailed description, the evocation of verifi-able realities and facts. The organisation of narrative depends to a large extent on this cumulative power and extensiveness, whereas the tragic poet, in Aristotle's view, aspires to a realm of higher truth, or of paradigms of truth. Whatever we may think of Aristotle's view of the narrator of history, the novel too has traditionally had to contend with the fact that it is organised not only, to use a term borrowed from Linguistics, on a 'vertical' axis of paradigms, analogies and structural patterns, but also on the 'horizontal' axis, the verbal extension of those structures (on this see Roger Fowler, pp. 1–25). In a famous article which was to influence the structuralist and post-structuralist movements in France, Roman Jakobson talked of this opposition as being between 'metaphor' and 'metonymy' (see Jakobson in the Suggestions for further reading). Metaphor, he argued, was a system of relationships by analogy, a structural patterning on the vertical axis. (A phrase such as 'the fire of passion' brings into a relationship of analogy – or similarity – two separate concepts, and therefore constitutes a metaphor.) Metonymy, on the other hand is a system of relationships of contiguity, a progressive and linear development on the horizontal axis. (The sentence 'let's have a butcher's' ('let's have a look') in cockney rhyming slang is a classic example of metonymic contiguity and substitu-tion, 'butcher's' being short for 'butcher's hook', and 'hook' rhyming with 'look'.) Narrative, although obviously relying heavily on systems of meta-phoric relationships, also depends largely for its unfolding on metonymic progression. It is linear extension, expansion, profusion, progression through time. Genette was later to argue picturesquely, and perhaps some-what ruefully, that the categories of metaphor and metonymy had become too influential (*Figures III*, p. 25). Be that as it may, the idea of metonymic progression, extension through verbal contiguity, helps us to see more clearly that one of the very organisational strategies of the novel is at the heart of its traditional problem of acceptability. Metonymic progression introduces an element of arbitrariness into the structure (the word 'butcher's' bears no obvious relation to the word 'look'). The point of arrival may be far removed from the point of departure. And the novel is, by its very nature, aesthetically untidy. Novelists from Rabelais onwards, seeking to make a virtue of necessity, have exploited this untidiness in various ways. Proust must be considered the outstanding figure in this respect, *A la recherche du temps perdu* (published from 1913 onwards) being a deliberately sprawling, sometimes seemingly random text which 'belatedly' finds its unity – a unity which was there at the outset within its very multiplicity – turning into itself, into the novel that had to be written if the narrator was to find sense and meaning in his existence.

For a long time the novel carried the stigma not only of aesthetic untidiness but also of vulgarity. It was considered a lower form of art, dealing with the banal and the humdrum rather than aspiring, like tragedy or like poetry, to a higher vision of the human condition. In one striking passage in Gide's 1926 *Les Faux-Monnayeurs,* the central character who is himself a would-be novelist expresses the nostalgia for a more transcendent form of art such as tragedy. 'Parfois il me paraît', he says, 'que je n'admire en littérature rien tant que, par exemple, dans Racine, la discussion entre Mithridate et ses fils; où l'on sait parfaitement bien que jamais un père et des fils n'ont pu parler de la sorte, et où néanmoins . . . tous les pères et tous les fils peuvent se reconnaître' (*Les Faux-Monnayeurs* (Paris: Folio, 1990), p. 184) ['Sometimes it seems to me that I admire nothing more in literature than, for example, the discussion in Racine between Mithridate and his sons, where you know perfectly well that fathers and sons have never spoken in that way, and yet where all fathers and sons can recognise themselves.'] Now this view of 'universal man' in the writings of classical France may have been discredited, but the point about the novel is valid: a novelist does not always have the luxury of being able to represent universal, or even general, matrices of human conduct. Though it may *illustrate* general truths or have some didactic function, narrative invariably has to function in the mode of particularity. Characters in the novel rarely have the mythical and transcendent status of characters in tragedy. They are too closely identified by their individual situation, and tragedy in the novel, in so far as it exists, becomes the tragedy of the banal. Emma Bovary, on her death bed, vomits and writhes in agony, unlike Racine's Phèdre who elegantly swallows her poison and makes a graceful dying speech. And many heroes and heroines of novels are not even dignified with anything so grand as death. Their miserable existence continues, or peters out, and the novel functions in the mode expressed by Gide in *Les Faux-Monnayeurs:* 'pourrait être continué' ['could be continued']. Adolphe, the eponymous narrator of Constant's famous novel (1816) dies only a moral death after his disastrous relationship with Ellénore, and he lives on, significantly, to tell the story and experience his own wretchedness down to the last dregs. Pierre in Maupassant's *Pierre et Jean* (1888) departs on a transatlantic steamer as a doctor, presumably to return a few weeks later to the same family crisis which has, to all intents and purposes, destroyed him. And the hero of Butor's *La Modification* (1957) returns to Paris and the wife he had decided to leave, with a vague plan to write his own story. That story – like Proust's – can have no end, for the end is its own beginning.

The novel is, then, precise, extensive and detailed, tending towards the depiction of the ordinary. It individualises and demystifies. It is small wonder that it was considered an indecorous form of art in the classical age. As Gérard Genette reminds us (*Seuils*, p. 42), Madame de La Fayette did not even sign the first editions of *La Princesse de Clèves* (1678), perhaps because the plebeian nature of the genre was unbecoming to her aristocratic status. Yet by the standards of seventeenth-century prose fiction which had a tendency towards the prolix, *La Princesse de Clèves* seems to be a classically sparse novel, concentrating on the tragic and inescapable predicament of a single character. And yet, even here, the extensive and profuse nature of prose fiction becomes apparent. The initial descriptions of the court and the individuals in it anchor the narrative in a context which becomes plausible. The narrator, who appears to be an inside observer of the scene she describes, adopts a tone of familiarity. The device is one that will be used again and again in the novel, since it is precisely such a tone which lends authenticity to the account. A narrator speaks, suggesting thereby some first-hand experience of events. Later first-person narratives such as *Manon Lescaut* (1731) will again use this device in order to establish the authority and plausibility of their account. What is striking, of course, is not so much that this simple technique is used, but that it should be deemed necessary in the first place. In order to establish their credentials as serious literature, early modern novels place an almost exaggerated reliance on this notion of 'authenticity'. The eighteenth century sees the invention and repeated use of the topos of the lost manuscript. The fiction is thus passed off as being a real document, and worthy of consideration on those grounds alone. The huge success of the epistolary novel in the eighteenth century (culminating in Rousseau's *La Nouvelle Héloïse* (1761) and more especially Laclos's *Les Liaisons danger-euses* (1782)) owes something to this device. Letters are presented as not just one document, but as a whole series of interrelated documents, and they have the added advantage that the same story is told from multiple points of view. The reader will find as much in the gaps and the omissions as in the ironic variations of testimony.

The epistolary novel provides us with a glimpse of two fascinating problems associated with the novel in general. On the one hand, it is the perfect illustration of the novel's requirement for authenticity or acceptability. On the other hand, it takes us in exactly the opposite direction, away from the representation of life, whatever that may be, and into the whole problem of hermeneutics, reading strategies, interpretation. Letters are not only written, they are read, and the letter-novel puts the 'reader' (fictional or otherwise) and the process of reading at the heart of the text. Yet to what extent is the reading or interpretation of the novel an inherent part of the text itself? If a text includes its reader in some way, as does the letter novel, does it also impose correct readings and censure incorrect ones? When is a reading not a true reading any longer? Can we agree with the claim made by E. D. Hirsch in *Validity in Interpretation* that authorial intention is the norm of interpretation and precludes the anarchy of possibilities? In Plato's *Apology for Socrates,* there is a passage which evokes this problem in a striking way, and that passage is worth reflecting on. Quoting Socrates, who had in vain sought wisdom among the politicians, the craftsmen, the philosophers, the poets and others, Plato writes this:

> After I had finished with the politicians I turned to the poets, dramatic, lyric, and all the rest, in the belief that here I should expose myself as a comparative ignoramus. I used to pick up what I thought were some of their most perfect works and question them closely about the meaning of what they had written, in the hope of incidentally enlarging my own knowledge. Well, gentlemen, I hesitate to tell you the truth, but it must be told. It is hardly an exaggeration to say that any of the bystanders could have explained those poems better than their actual authors. So I soon made up my mind about the poets too: I decided that it was not wisdom that enabled them to write their poetry, but a kind of instinct or inspiration, such as you find in seers and prophets who deliver all their sublime messages without knowing in the least what they mean.[7]

In a sense, the Platonic dialogue foreshadows a great deal of modern critical theory, which tells us to trust the tale, not the teller. Though an author may be able to speak of her or his intended meaning, this does not account for the actual meanings of the text for others. It is one of the characteristics of the novel that it often foreshadows and builds in this 'otherness' of the reader – as in the example of the letter-novel – and yet this must imply an openness to many possible interpretations, and a certain scepticism with regard to itself and what it has to say. The idea that there is a clear and possibly single 'meaning' to the text, and that this must be the meaning which the author intended, has – notwithstanding the view of Hirsch and others – come in for some harsh scrutiny over the last half-century. The debate about authorial intention was properly launched in a famous article by Wimsatt and Beardsley entitled 'The Intentional Fallacy'.[8] The argument is essentially a simple one, which says that the text has to be looked at in terms of its actual significance for the reader, not its intended significance by the author who may after all have written something which he or she did not intend to write. To look at the text in terms of some putative intention, the argument goes, is in some sense to refuse a reading of what is actually there. And even if the intention of the author were available to us, Wimsatt and Beardsley claim, it is not desirable since it is very clearly something which is outside the text itself. Like Socrates, then, we the reader must have a privileged place in the text, since we become part of its signifying process. What we read into it, or out of it, is as much our business as the author's. This does not entitle us, of course, to engage in purely fanciful readings (at least, not if our readings are to be submitted to the judgement of others). Clearly there are misreadings and wrong read-ings, as any reader of novels in a foreign language knows. But the challenge that modern criticism has laid down to the absolute authority of the author shifts the whole emphasis of the text onto reading itself as a signifying process. Without the reader's participation, the text does not truly live. Each generation brings to the reading of literature its own preoccupations, concerns and methods, and texts take on new significance in the light of these. As Barthes once put it, submission to authorial authority closes off the text: 'donner un auteur à un texte, c'est imposer à ce texte un cran d'arrêt, c'est le pourvoir d'un signifié dernier, c'est fermer l'écriture' ['to give the text an author is to give the text a stopping point, to provide it with a final signifier, and to close off writing'].[9] To give a privileged status to the reader in a text is to open it out and to read it as plurality. The introduction to Barthes's hugely influential *S/Z* puts it nicely: 'Interpréter un texte, ce n'est pas lui donner un sens . . . c'est au contraire apprécier de quel pluriel il est fait' (*S/Z*, p. 11) ['To interpret a text is not a matter of giving it a meaning; rather, it is a matter of understanding the plurality of which it is made up']. Thus do we return to the notion of openness which was the starting point of this chapter. Just as novels self-consciously question their own procedures and messages, so too do criticism and theory engage in the unending debate about what novels can mean, what significances we can derive from them.

I have suggested that theory and criticism, as the mirror in which the French novel views and rewrites itself, are an integral part of the discipline.

The French novel is quintessentially self-scrutinising, and the long series of writer-critics throughout its history is testimony to the extraordinary vitality of the critical consciousness which informs the writing of novels in France and the Francophone world. Some will argue that the self-consciousness of the French novel is narcissistic, a sign of its own impending death. The argument is an important one, not least because there have been strong reactions against self-consciousness within the French tradition itself. In novels of war and extreme situations, it is usually the case that the relationship between language and reality is not the primary concern, since these deal with much more fundamental issues such as death or survival in the face of atrocity. A bomb is a bomb by any other name, and descriptions of the horrors of war take us beyond language and confront us with the spectacle of man's hostility to man. Yet, even in novels of war or terrorism, there is a strong intellectual and reflective tradition in the French novel. Malraux's *La Condition humaine* (1933) (analysed by Steven Ungar in chapter 9 of this volume) is surely one of the great novels of our century, examining as it does the quest for dignity and meaning by the individual engaged in conflict, and providing a tragic vision of the human condition which takes the genre beyond the banal with which it is so often associated. Following on from Malraux, Sartre, Beauvoir and Camus among others were all able to use the writing of novels as a powerful tool of ideological exploration. And much more recently, Jorge Semprun has taken reflection on the atrocities of war to new heights. He has explored very precisely and very poignantly, in texts as recent as *L'Ecriture ou la vie* (1994) the question of the relationship between writing and the horror of Buchenwald. There may be, in Adorno's famous phrase, no poetry after Auschwitz. Yet Semprun, a Spaniard who has chosen to write in the French language, shows movingly that it is not possible anyway to escape from writing, for that would be precisely to run away from the horrible truth.

Self-consciousness in the novel, far from being a sign of sterility and impending doom of the genre, is a source of great vitality, experiment and creativity. From Rabelais's giants to Stendhal's self-parodying narrator, to self-referential novels from Proust onwards, self-consciousness pushes the novelist to seek out the limits of the genre and go beyond what was previously possible. Thus the French novel is constantly breaking out of its limits and finding new forms of expression, as Perec's *La Vie mode d'emploi*, winner of the 1978 Prix Médicis, triumphantly demonstrates (that colossal and hugely influential novel is discussed in chapters 8 and 15 of the present volume). As it evolves, the genre blends into others, bringing its particular qualities into a different medium. There is hardly a French

TIMOTHY UNWIN

novelist of the last twenty or thirty years who has not also at some time written plays or poetry, written for radio or television, been adapted to *bandes dessinées* and other media. The immense source of inspiration of the novel for film-makers is also apparent, and the links between page and celluloid are forever being made, not least by the novelists themselves. As we move into the twenty-first century, electronic publication is already proving to be a further area of innovation and experiment, hypertextuality affording the means to find multiple routes through the text. The French novel is changing and evolving. It is the point of convergence, and of divergence, of many different genres. But it is alive and well, and likely to be with us for some time to come.

NOTES

1 R. Barthes, 'Réflexions sur un manuel', in *Le Bruissement de la langue*, pp. 49–56, 51.
2 For a challenging discussion of this issue, see the item by J. Culler listed in the Suggestions for further reading.
3 Reprinted in *Le Bruissement de la langue*, pp. 37–47.
4 See F. Engels and K. Marx, *On Literature* (Moscow: Progress Publications, 1976).
5 In *Expression and Meaning*. See especially chapter 3, 'The Logical Status of Fictional Discourse', pp. 58–75.
6 Aristotle, *Poetics*, in T. S. Dorsch (ed.), *Classical Literary Criticism* (Harmondsworth: Penguin, 1965), p. 43.
7 Plato, 'The Apology', in *The Last Days of Socrates*, ed. H. Tredennick, (Harmondsworth: Penguin, 1969), p. 51.
8 Originally published in 1946, the article was reprinted in W. K. Wimsatt, *The Verbal Icon*, pp. 3–18.
9 R. Barthes, 'La Mort de l'auteur' (1968), reprinted in *Le Bruissement de la langue*, pp. 61–7, 65.

SUGGESTIONS FOR FURTHER READING

Barthes, R., *S/Z* (Paris: Seuil, 1970)
Le Bruissement de la langue (Paris: Seuil, 1984)
Culler, J., 'At the Boundaries: Barthes and Derrida', in Herbert L. Sussmann (ed.), *At the Boundaries* (Boston: Northeastern University Press, 1984), pp. 23–41
De Man, P., *Blindness and Insight: Essays in the Rhetoric of Contemporary Criticism* (London: Methuen, 1983; first published 1971)
Fish, S., *Is There a Text in This Class?* (Cambridge, MA: Harvard University Press, 1980)
Fowler, R., *Linguistics and the Novel* (London and New York: Methuen, 1977)
Genette, G., *Figures III* (Paris: Seuil, 1972)
Seuils (Paris: Seuil, 1987)
Hirsch, E. D., *Validity in Interpretation* (New Haven: Yale University Press, 1967)

Jakobson, R., 'Deux aspects du langage et deux types d'aphasies', in *Essais de linguistique générale* (Paris: Minuit, 1963), pp. 43–7

Lejeune, P., *Le Pacte autobiographique* (Paris: Seuil, 1975)

Pennac, D., *Comme un roman* (Paris: Gallimard, 1992)

Searle, J., *Expression and Meaning* (Cambridge: Cambridge University Press, 1979)

Wimsatt, W. K., *The Verbal Icon* (Lexington: University Press of Kentucky, 1954)

2

JANN MATLOCK

Novels of testimony and the 'invention' of the modern French novel

In 1801, in the preface to *Atala*, the first runaway bestseller of the new century, François-René de Chateaubriand offered an account of his text's evolution in the traumatic decade of the French Revolution. *Atala* was not a novel at all, he claimed, but a segment of an epic on Native Americans planned before the Revolution. He called this fragment of his writings from a trip to the United States in 1791 a 'sort of poem' (*Œuvres romanesques et voyages*, ed. Maurice Regard (Paris: Gallimard, 1969), vol. I, p. 17) modelled on works of classical antiquity. Transformed in form and purpose by the events of the Revolution and Terror, this little book no longer figured as part of an epic, but was now offered up as a pre-publication teaser for its author's monumental historical and philosophical treatise, *Le Génie du christianisme* (1802) to which he claimed it now belonged.

For more than a century, *Atala* and its pair, *René* (1802), have served as the inaugural texts in a critical history of the modern French novel. By means of these fictions, and especially of *René*, Chateaubriand has been credited with inventing the 'Romantic novel', the 'autobiographical novel', even Romanticism itself. Immensely popular and critically appreciated for decades, these two works did indeed sound a clarion call at the dawn of the new century. They were marked by an indelible sense that the overturned 'natural order' could not be reinstated (see *Œuvres romanesques*, vol. I, p. 17). For a young aristocrat like Chateaubriand, aged 31 in 1789, the Revolution had changed not just his financial or social expectations, but the entire vista of the future.

Given such an outlook, it is not surprising that for Chateaubriand, epic novels about distant lands seemed less necessary than works exhorting the French to rethink their values and goals. Published shortly after Chateaubriand returned from exile in May 1800 to Consulate France, his fictions on the French colony in Louisiana were poised precariously on a frontier between fiction and non-fiction in yet another moment of radical change – just as Napoleon was about to declare himself Emperor, dashing the last of the Revolution's hopes. Though most of the events in Chateaubriand's fictions are set far from France in the early eighteenth century, they were deeply imprinted by the traumas of the revolutionary era.

Fast on the heels of these works came a series of novels that similarly confronted the changes in French society through their characters' individual perceptions. By the 1830s, some of these novels become touchstones for what 'good' novels could be, and several would continue to be elevated, well into the next century, for their implosion of 'truth' and 'morality' into the novel form, as masterworks of literature. Unlike late eighteenth-century 'gothic', 'libertine' and 'sentimental' novels, these works were not born with a label. Yet by the July Monarchy, critics had begun to group them according to a thematic trait. What Benjamin Constant called in 1816 the 'moral malady of the century' was baptised by Sainte-Beuve in his 1833 preface to the re-edition of Senancour's *Obermann* as the *mal du siècle*. By 1849, Sainte-Beuve would declare such a malady a thing of the past and rename it the 'malady of René'.[1]

Well aware of the contagion set off by his second novel, Chateaubriand complained in 1836 that if *René* did not exist, he would not write it again, and if he could destroy it, he would do so. The burgeoning numbers of would-be Renés horrified the ageing statesman. He had, he said, exposed a weakness of his century in René; but it was crazy for other novelists to have wanted to universalise those afflictions (*Mémoires d'outre-tombe*, ed. Levaillant and Moulinier (Paris: Gallimard, 1951), vol. I, p. 462). Despite Chateaubriand's insistence that an entire literature could not emerge from a malady of the soul, some would argue even today that he made such a literature possible. What, then, was this 'mal de René' and how did it relate to the horrors that led to these works about an exiled Frenchman? Was there a literature of these 'maladies' as Sainte-Beuve claimed? How did that literature participate in other literary, social, and political events of its era?

Read as a pair, the two novels depicting René have much in common. Both are extremely short by comparison with most novels of their era – fewer than a hundred pages in most modern editions. Both works use the common eighteenth-century device of a confession by one character framed by the discourse of another. In *Atala*, the Native American Chactas tells his story to René, and that story is passed down from father to child until the the narrator himself reports it. In *René*, the confession is that of the European to his adopted father Chactas and to a missionary, le père Souël; it is recorded by an anonymous third-person narrator who claims posthumous knowledge of the fate of all the individuals in the text. Both texts provide an account of the reactions of the interlocutors to the confessions made to them and, ultimately, the narrator's further comments on those exchanges. Both have at their centre a monologue about a secret grief, the story of a lost, dead beloved. Both monologues recount that woman's secret, framed now in terms of her death and the agony it has caused the man telling her story. Both women are given their own confessional moments embedded in the confessions of the men who loved them. Both passions are depicted by the tellers as impossible: Chactas's wife has vowed to her mother to remain a virgin; René's beloved is his own sister. Both women take themselves away: Atala through suicide, Amélie through refuge and eventually death in a convent. Both men trace their current circumstances to this troubled past event, and both remain racked by the weight of these secrets. Everyone involved – Chactas, René and the priest – is represented as perishing in the historical massacre of 1725, leaving only stories passed down to a narrator.

Often read as a throwback to the values of the eighteenth-century novel, *Atala* was nevertheless the more overwhelming contemporary success of the two novels. *René* enjoyed far less commercial success but, like the French translation (1776) of Goethe's *Die Leiden des jungen Werthers*, spawned a generation of moody youths who, in Chateaubriand's own words, dreamed themselves 'the most unhappy of men' (*Mémoires d'outre-tombe*, vol. I, p. 462). What Margaret Waller has called 'Being René, Buying Atala' characterised the different expectations channelled through these novels for generations to come, expectations that contributed to views of the earlier novel as outdated while the latter gained a reputation as the founding text of the modern French canon (see Waller, 'Being René, Buying Atala', pp. 157–8; Schor, *Breaking the Chain*, p. 145). Though *Atala* was imagined by its author and his contemporaries as the source of female hysteria, and *René* the avatar of a new, dignified literature – legendarily appreciated by men – of male suffering, these two novels nonetheless have an interdependency underlined by their connection to the same non-fiction work and their separate publication as a pair after 1805. Linked in terms of setting and character, similar in length, form and theme, the novels jointly represent a character who is not just a suffering confessee but also the interlocutor through whom others are able to testify to their own losses.

Atala and *René* mirror one another and function as a double set of Chinese boxes, each having an internal complexity of narrative frames, yet both caught in a larger framework of their supposed transcription by a traveller to the New World in the 1790s. Neither fiction gains its complexity from *plot* as such – Chateaubriand even flaunted the absence of 'adventures' in *Atala* (*Œuvres romanesques*, vol. I, p. 18) – but rather from the way secrets are shared and the results of that sharing. In the earlier novel, such confessions still have a purpose in keeping with Saint Augustine's influential definition of the spiritual act: the confessee manages to make truth in himself (*facire veritatem*) through self-examination, but also to gain access to enlightenment (*venire ad lucem*), discovering God through self-submission.[2] Confessing her vow made to her dying Christian mother, Atala is relieved of her sins by the attending priest who attributes her mistake to her savage upbringing and the lapses of her mother's confessor. Telling his story years later to René, Chactas redeems the passionate errors that induced Atala's suicide through repeating the Christian vows he hopes will reunite him with her for eternity. In *René*, however, neither Amélie's partial, overheard confession nor the protagonist's explanation for his incurable melancholia procures salvation for their speaker. Indeed, the priestly interlocutor's harsh response to René's confession seems added to dissuade Christian readers from following the young man's example – even if the narrator offers a more humane confessor in Chactas. What in each novel has been read as a 'moral' emerges as less identifiable than many critics have contended. Though we read these testimonies as if privy to the exact words of a transcript, they are all passed down to us second, third or even fourth hand. Potentially falsified by such a transfer, both confessions obtain from (albeit fictional) circumstances where their speakers have every reason to manipulate their listeners by means of what they choose to reveal and how they unveil it.

Any reading of these novels needs to consider the way narrative tension is constructed around suspenseful revelations of the secrets of the men and those of the women they loved. What do these men want from the telling of these women's secrets, one must ask, and what do they achieve by exchanging those secrets between men? The entire set of novels associated with the 'mal de René' encourages broader examination of this question (see Waller, *The Male Malady*), for the *mal du siècle* procured much of its narrative power through recourse to an old currency from the eighteenth century – the suffering, expiring heroine who, in these new works, was no longer permitted to tell her own side of the story through letters purportedly transcribed directly from originals, but was instead 'told'. Variations of such uses of women's stories appear in many of these novels, but we would lose sight of the complexities of the early nineteenth-century novel if we looked only at those structurally exploiting male confessions or those revolving thematically around women's suffering. While Chateaubriand's novels offer two variations on a similar narrative strategy, his contemporaries would offer further narrative mechanisms and further thematic twists. What Chateaubriand's novels share, however, with other novels associated with the *mal du siècle* is the relationship to their own times and to perceptions formulated by the narrator at the conclusion to *Atala*'s epilogue. There, the narrator tells how he encountered René's daughter mourning her dead child as she wandered with her husband and other refugees from the slaughter of the Natchez, and how he learned of the demise of all those whose legends he had collected from her people. Unlike these errant exiles though, the narrator must content himself with relaying only stories, for, as he writes, he wanders 'at the mercy of men, and less happy in [his] exile', for he has not even managed to 'bring away the bones of [his] fathers' (*Œuvres romanesques*, vol. I, p. 99).

Such passages have encouraged reading this narrator as Chateaubriand himself, exiled from a France in which his own 'fathers' have been mercilessly slaughtered like the Natchez by the French. One need not read Chateaubriand's personal biography into either of these characters in order to imagine, however, how this text becomes, like those bones carried by the Natchez survivors, a reliquary for the remains of a no-longer reachable past. As forms of witnessing for a previous generation's grief, Chateaubriand's texts convey reproaches of the Revolution far more severe than those levied on René by le père Souël. If an entire generation of men saw themselves in René and not in Chactas, it is perhaps because the world of the the early 1800s offered little hope to warriors, Christians or crippled sages. As Chateaubriand's biography demonstrated, that world offered more to those who aspired to the pantheon of literary passion and to those who traded on the stories of ancestral bones.

Such an account of René's influence makes Chateaubriand's melancholic hero a model for a kind of 'autobiographical novel' (labelled the *roman personnel* after Joachim Merlant's exhaustive study of 1904).[3] Associating *roman personnel* with an individual's 'true' interior experience, Merlant promoted such novels as the highest forms of fiction, investing them with a moral purpose derived from the supposedly autobiographical nature of the experiences recounted there. Such an account had the virtue of attributing to these novels certain formal similarities – their frequent reliance on embedded confessions in a frame narration – as well as certain thematic impulses: a turn away from 'events' toward interior self-examination, a concern with thwarted relationships and particularly with men's percep-tions of those relationships, and anxiety about the changes from an aristocratic to a bourgeois society. Merlant's generic account of the *roman personnel* depended, however, on notions of authorship and intentionality that few critics would accept today. What he valued in *Obermann*, *Valérie* and *Adolphe* was the way their authors managed to use the novel form to tell their own personal story. Seeing these novels as the heirs to an autobiographical tradition inaugurated by Rousseau's 1782 *Confessions*, Merlant sought to expose the 'real story' beneath the fictions. Unveiling the way 'real life' made its way into the novel was a favourite pastime of critics well into the twentieth century, and although one cannot reproach Merlant for engaging in the critical moves of his era, we must acknowledge that his generic rubric for these novels derived from a cult of 'authorship' questioned by critics such as Barthes and Foucault in the 1960s. What happens when we try to read the *roman personnel* as a genre in the age of what Barthes called 'the death of the author'?[4] If the personal can no longer be imagined as deriving from extratextual evidence in which one might recognise the author's similarity to the protagonist, can such novels be linked, let alone represent a genre?

Philippe Lejeune has insisted on the mutual exclusivity of autobiography and the novel, arguing that the former operates according to a pact of truthfulness between the speaking (writing) subject and the reader (Lejeune, pp. 311–41). Such observations point to important differences in the ways texts stage their readers' expectations, for if readers believe, for example, that *Adolphe* contains the true story of Constant's relationship with Staël, they read it differently from readers who expect to find there the story of his relationship with Anna Lindsay or Charlotte de Hardenberg. More significantly, if readers believe the novel to demand that it be read as a fiction, unconnected to accounts of its author's life, they interpret it differently yet again. That many of these novels were indeed read, by both contemporaries and critics, as elaborating an alternative account of their author's personal story is as much the legacy of this literary tradition as the stories told in the novels themselves.

Foucault has suggested that instead of seeking the author in a text one might ask other questions, among them, 'What matter who is speaking?' (Foucault, p. 160). The questions about the myriad voices channelled through texts offer an alternative to valuing the so-called *roman personnel* only for its autobiographical 'personal confessions'. What characterises these novels, as even Merlant's exaggerated sense of their moral worth reminds us, is their ability to convince readers of the truth-value of the pain relayed by their protagonists. Regardless of whether these novels use a framed confession, virtually every candidate for this rubric is obsessed with bearing witness, if not specifically through its characters' confessions, then through the kind of story narrated there and the terms of its exchange. These novels therefore constitute less a genre than a *mentalité*, representing the trauma of the new century and the search for terms to express it. Their formal innovations, though inviting critical fascination and, in some cases, canonical acclaim, attest less to an overhaul of the novel than to a fervent exploration of ways of giving testimony about the anxieties of a troubled historical era. Rather than viewing these works as as masterpieces for their exploration of a universal 'self' with value for all readers, I would suggest that the novels of the *mal du siècle* have a unique way of exploiting the tensions between fiction and history, fictive self and autobiographical self, true testimony and withheld stories – and that they do so specifically in response to the anxieties of the early nineteenth century and to new uses, in this period, of writing and self-writing.

Between *René*'s first appearance and Chateaubriand's decision in 1805 to separate *Atala* and *René* into an independent book, three innovative novels – Staël's *Delphine* (1802), Krüdener's *Valérie* (1803) and Senancour's *Obermann* (1804) – laid out alternative ways of conceptualising the malaise of their era. Though Staël is today better known for her monumental second novel, *Corinne* (1807), and Krüdener's novel was out of print for nearly a century after 1898, both were read in the early nineteenth century with an interest that the more canonised *Obermann* would not enjoy until the 1830s. Unlike Chateaubriand's fictions, all three novels used an epistolary form, though Senancour provided only his protagonist's letters and none of the responses, achieving an effect resembling that of a private journal. Also unlike Chateaubriand's novels, all three novels were set in contemporary Europe: *Delphine* in France between 1790 and 1792, *Valérie* between Stockholm and Italy in a period vaguely contemporary with the decade before its publication, and *Obermann* over a ten-year period which is not situated historically but whose references to exile in Switzerland encourage parallels with its aristocratic author's own exile in the 1790s. What these three novels have in common, making them important models for literary accounts of a changed conception of the self, are their characters' elaborate explorations of their own individual psyches in a world that no longer offers the consolation of Christianity. All three offer an account of a failed love affair through the eyes of a male character who has been unable, either constitutionally or for social reasons beyond his control, to find happiness with his beloved. Though indebted to the *roman sentimental* for this theme, these novels nevertheless break with the feminine tradition in their handling of it. At times *Delphine* reads like a *roman noir* with its twists of plot where a persecuted heroine is rejected by her beloved in favour of a more 'feminine' woman, enters a convent, is delivered from her vows by the Revolution, attempts again to unite with her now widowed lover and finally commits suicide after he is shot as an *émigré*. *Obermann*'s Swiss setting and journal-like epistolary form merge aspects of Saint-Preux's experiences in Rousseau's *Julie* with metaphysical concerns formulated in the *Rêveries d'un promeneur solitaire* (1782). *Valérie* was the first to make specific reference to Chateaubriand whose *René* it cites in its introductory frame. Furthermore, while the tradition of the *roman sentimental* freely explores its female characters' feelings, the last two novels limit our perception of their female characters' circumstances even more than did *René* by comparison to *Atala*. Though the novel bears her name, Valérie is not one of the correspondents but rather the *subject* of their correspondence. Like René's sister Amélie, she gets an opportunity to speak through a letter transcribed by the protagonist, but that letter does not reveal whether she shared Gustave's ill-fated love. Senancour's elision of the female character goes even further: Obermann's beloved may well be a woman with a secret, but we have little clue what it is, and can only barely piece together an outline of the couple's troubles through Obermann's letters to his male friend.

Like *Obermann*, *Valérie* has frequently been read for its autobiographical elements. Critics have given as much attention to the way Krüdener transformed the events of her personal life into this *récit* as to the workings of the novel itself. Does it matter, one must ask, that the Russian-born wife of the French ambassador to Denmark was pursued by a young man who shot himself because of his passion for her? I think it does, though not because, as has been often argued (e.g. Merlant, p. 190), such a work shows how Krüdener *wanted* to see her past, but because this novel suggests how such a past was placed on public display. Like many works concerned in this chapter, *Valérie* is framed by a preface claiming it is constituted from real letters and journal fragments collected by someone who learned of the real passion of 'Gustave', whose name – like the places and time – that publisher has ostensibly changed to protect the secret-sharer. That confidante – indeed, the repressed 'confessee' of all the materials published under the cover of the novel *Valérie* – was the very person who had been the innocent cause of his unhappiness (*Valérie*, ed. Michel Mercier (Paris: Klincksieck, 1974), p. 21). And like Krüdener herself, who allowed the story of her unhappy association with Alexandre Stackhiev to be known in order the better to market her novelisation of it, this publisher claims to have filled in lacunae, added 'necessary details' and imitated 'the simple and passionate language of Gustave' to give continuity to his fragmentary writings (pp. 22–3).

Despite its autobiographical sources, this text remains palpably and insistently a *novel*, for its very 'autobiographical' intertexts are caught up in the manipulations of fiction. We will not find the 'real' Krüdener in this text any more than we will find Valérie's own views in the self-absorbed and delirious writings of Gustave. Instead, we find an obsession with what remains of wrecked lives – Gustave's fantasy of his letters, saved by Ernst, as 'a monument that will live more than I' (p. 150), his request that the count name one of Valérie's sons after him so that 'the sweet feeling of maternity mix with his memory' and finally, the publisher's pretension to have only minimally transformed the real fragments of this passion. Like the exchanged letters in the body of the work that seem never to have been received by the addressee, the framing preface fails to connect Gustave's life either to its time or to the life of the person transmitting it. Valérie emerges there, as in the letters, as a ghost at the centre of this game of autobiographical hide-and-seek, even as she lurks behind the novel's preface-writer as the source of all the information in the book, and therefore as the manipulator of anything we are allowed to know. Disavowed, like the fictional nature of the work itself, Valérie takes on a power which Krüdener's text does not assume. She becomes a stand-in for exterior events that could have rendered someone like Gustave so incapable of mastering his destiny.

While *Delphine* has been criticised for failing to exploit its revolutionary setting, *Obermann* has been praised for its refusal to associate its self-explorations with a specific historical moment.[5] Such appraisals neglect the difficulty, for the Revolution's heirs, of finding adequate narrative terms for their historical circumstances. One could neither turn to traditional genres, now tainted by their association with a decadent ancien régime, nor find literary models in a revolutionary era that had provided far more political than literary discourse. Staël's magisterial *De la littérature* (1800), like her *De l'Allemagne* (1810), attempted to conceptualise how past literature could offer models for the future. That Napoleon would exile Staël in 1803 for her subversive views and order the destruction of the latter work demonstrates the political consequences of such aesthetic inquiries in early nineteenth-century France. Staël's republicanism and proto-feminism have frequently served as a justification for prolonging her isolation from other *mal du siècle* novelists. Differentiated from other works of her generation for their divergence from the confessional framework of *René* and the more blatantly autobiographical associations of *Obermann*, Staël's *Delphine* and *Corinne ou l'Italie* might be better read for the spin of social conscience they put on the illness afflicting the novelistic characters of those frequenting her salon at Coppet – including Constant, Krüdener and Chateaubriand.

Like *Atala*, *René*, *Valérie* and *Obermann*, *Corinne* turns on a secret and the way its revelation transforms its characters' lives. But unlike any of these works, which give substantial play to the male characters' accounts of their experiences through extended 'recorded' monologues or epistolary self-exploration, *Corinne* uses a third person anonymous omniscient narrator to provide an overview of its main characters' experiences. At the centre of *Corinne* we become privy to two extended monologues, each about the entire length of René's confession: the first that of Oswald, Lord Nelvil, delivered orally to his lover Corinne during their travels, the second that of Corinne herself, conveyed in manuscript form to Oswald and read by him simultaneously to our reading of it in the novel. Though Staël's work embraces a different structure from earlier confessional novels, *Corinne* nevertheless similarly traffics in self-writing to develop her characters and their conflicts. Furthermore, in a unique move among the novels of the era, *Corinne* gives equal weight to the confession of each individual.

Despite its generally hostile and misogynous reception by the press of the Napoleonic France from which she was exiled, *Corinne* came to be one of the most popular novels of its era. Transpiring in Italy, England and France between 1794 and 1803, *Corinne* provides subtle commentary on the political landscape of the period leading to Napoleon's quashing of republican ideals. *Corinne ou l'Italie* announces in its title a choice: we are reading either about a woman named Corinne, or else about Italy itself. The woman Corinne therefore comes to stand allegorically for the country overrun by Napoleon's armies in the late 1790s and early 1800s. Napoleon had himself crowned King of Rome in 1805, the year after he upstaged the stunned Pope who had come to Paris from Rome to coronate the new Emperor, and crowned himself. That Staël's novel begins with a coronation – not of a usurping Emperor but of a female poet – could not have failed to impress European readers with its rejection of Napoleon's pretensions to power.

Like Staël herself, the heroine of *Corinne* believes deeply in the power of art and literature to transform society in political as well as aesthetic ways. As the male protagonist Oswald and his friend the Count arrive in Rome, Corinne is crowned at the Capitol as Italy's 'most famous woman', renowned for her painting and poetry. 'To foreigners we say, "Look at her: she is the image of our beautiful Italy; she is what we would be but for the ignorance, the envy, the discord, and the apathy to which our fate has condemned us"' (*Corinne ou l'Italie*, ed. Simone Balayé (Paris: Gallimard, 1985), p. 57). The Prince's words register potently in the spirits of the foreigners who have just arrived in the Italy Corinne is designated as representing. In a matter of chapters, Corinne will transform that country for one of them, Oswald, becoming not only his tour guide but his lover. The overall narrative thus becomes as much an account of the glories of Italy's past as of the future of these two individuals. Alternatively a tour guide – *Corinne* was even classed among travelogues at the Bibliothèque Nationale during the nineteenth century (see Marie-Claire Vallois, *Fictions féminines: Madame de Staël et les voix de la Sibylle* (Stanford: Stanford University Press, 1987), p. 133) – and an allegory of Europe's possible routes to salvation against Napoleon, the novel never loses sight of its relation to the confessional tradition of its literary predecessors.

The confessions at the heart of *Corinne* unveil secrets that finally destroy the hopes the novel invests in this couple. Oswald reveals how he has come to Italy to assuage his grief after his father's death. Corinne provides the beleaguered son with his father's posthumous consent to his marriage – though not to her, for she reveals not only that her younger half-sister Lucile was the father's choice, but also that she had herself been rejected as a possible bride. Corinne's willingness to provide Oswald with the truth costs her far more than his love, ultimately silencing her poetry and inducing her death. In the conclusion, Corinne and Oswald again exchange letters, this time sharing no secrets, but instead revealing the depth of Oswald's failure to understand the impact of his choices, and allowing a more visible narrator to emerge, impatient with the example she declares Lord Nelvil provided 'of the most orderly and pure domestic life': 'But did he forgive himself for his past conduct? Did the approval of society console him? Was he happy with an ordinary fate after what he had lost? I do not know and do not wish, in this regard, either to blame or absolve him' (*Corinne*, p. 587).

What does it mean for the female artist Corinne to waste away at abandonment by her lover? How does this novel's withholding of a conclusion about Oswald's behaviour ultimately shed light on its moral and political role as a literary work? What testimony to the crises of the post-revolutionary era has been transmitted here in a novel superficially about betrayed love and filial duty? To answer these questions, one needs to emphasise two intertwined stories which serve as the principal under-currents of Staël's novel: the first, a story of the power of art in Republican ideology and of the salvationary goals ascribed to it by Staël and her heroine Corinne; the second, a story of the rights of women so vocally championed by the early revolutionaries and so brutally reneged upon by the Napoleonic Code. Though women would permanently retain their power to inherit property and temporarily, until 1816, continue to claim a right to divorce, the 1804 Civil Code restricted their expectations in ways particularly disappointing to those who, like Staël, had projected future possibilities far beyond those they claimed with their pens. The Napoleonic Empire's restitution of the patriarchal family left few outlets for women's political expression. While women reclaimed public space through the novel, as did Staël and Duras, gaining a podium to express their values and demands, their public displays, like those of the character Corinne, seemed only to compromise their goals and desires. One must therefore read *Corinne* as a political allegory of such disappointments, and as a forceful attack on the Napoleonic regime that stripped women like Corinne of their power.[6] By writing Corinne's betrayal by the aristocratic Oswald so explicitly into her testimony about the dashed hopes of the Republican era, Staël made a statement about the powers of art that outlasted her protagonists. She inscribed Corinne into a story of mourning and unresolved trauma that exposed as delusionary and retrograde the traditions to which Oswald belonged. The 'mal de René' had been unveiled as self-serving and destructive, belonging to a generation of men who could not recognise the value of women's testimony. Staël would ensure, by engendering a generation of powerful female voices, that Corinne's art continued to haunt those who had lost sight of the Revolution's dreams.

Adolphe has often been read as the retort by Staël's lover Constant to *Corinne*, yet one would be wrongheaded to read either novel as strictly autobiographical (see Paul Delbouille's edition of *Adolphe* (Paris: Les Belles Lettres, 1977), pp. 36–7). Far less explicitly grounded in an historical moment than Staël's works, *Adolphe* nevertheless remains recognisably about the same kind of dashed hopes analysed by every novel we have considered. As do its predecessors, *Adolphe* purports to unveil the suffering of a male protagonist through his own embedded confession. Like *René*, *Adolphe* is often given the stature of a founding text, usually of a uniquely 'modern' subjectivity, constructed by critics as a peculiar self-awareness that fails to redeem its speaker and as a radically different relationship to the past than in previous novels.[7] What separates *Adolphe* formally from these earlier texts is the relationship of the frame-writer to the suffering hero. Unlike all of the confessing characters in these earlier novels, Adolphe does not provide his confession to someone from whom he seeks understanding, but rather relays it inadvertently, by losing a strongbox containing writings. An 'editor' prefaces their publication with the explanation that he assumed they belonged to a suffering traveller he met in Italy. Unable to return the box to its owner, the editor has instead shared them with someone who revealed himself to have known both of the individuals concerned in the confessional text. Although we are never privy to the outcome of Adolphe's story, we are nevertheless invited to imagine he is no longer in a position to oppose its publication, and that the editor and friend are therefore in their rights to appropriate and offer comment on his misplaced documents.

The difference in the circumstances through which this text is supposedly placed at our disposal transforms substantially our relationship to the narration. Whereas in earlier works, we were given proximity to the speaker by being situated as interlocutor and confessor to his (or her) ills, here we are made voyeur to circumstances even more unverifiable than the events confessed by an individual to a confidant. The distance established here might well be compared to that of some modern novels which invite us to spy on individuals presumed real by the narrative discourse, but fabricated as potentially unreal by a cultural institution that shrugs off pretensions to verity. And yet, *Adolphe* invites even greater awareness of its complicated stakes, for it pretends, through its frame and Constant's prefaces, to educate an audience in need of 'real' examples for conduct.

In an early preface to the novel, Constant explained his goals in terms already prefiguring Sainte-Beuve's language of the *mal du siècle*: 'I wanted to paint in Adolphe one of the principal moral maladies of our century: that fatigue, that uncertainty, that lack of strength, that perpetual analysis that puts an afterthought against all feelings and corrupts them at birth' (*Adolphe*, ed. J.-H. Bornecque (Paris: Garnier, 1963), p. 304). While Constant's various prefaces prescribe a moralistic stance towards Adolphe, whose voice is not heard until his publishers have their say, the two other relayers of Adolphe's confession inscribe this text even more firmly in their interpretive vista by getting, literally, the last words. The example of Adolphe is to be made 'instructive', according to the friend who now shares further letters about the fate of Adolphe (p. 148). According to the 'editor', Adolphe's story will be offered up as 'a rather true story of the misery of the human heart' (p. 149). Small wonder that Adolphe complains in his own *récit*, 'people were telling my story' (p. 125). Yet the story told here is no more Adolphe's story alone than the stories of Chactas, René, Obermann, Gustave and Oswald remain only their own stories. As in all these transmissions of male suffering, a woman's story remains to be told if the man's present dilemma is to be understood. While *Obermann* and *Valérie* repress that story, *Adolphe*, like Chateaubriand's and Staël's works, purports to let us hear the woman's voice, through a letter transcribed by Adolphe into his own confessional text. Yet that letter, which Ellénore requested her lover to burn unread, symbolises the contortions through which the writings of others are put. The entire work, including the words of the editor and his correspondent, expresses betrayal of the silenced, with documents and letters being purloined into usefulness by archivists unconcerned with the repercussions of their publication.

Adolphe therefore succeeds in thematising through its formal structure the problematic status of the so-called autobiographical novel. Purporting to relate the intimate recesses of the human soul, such a work gains its power from its potential truth value – from being possibly the disguised

confession of its real-life author – even as it shirks that truth by appropriating the novel's guise. But *Adolphe* shirks more than truth by pretending to be, as its subtitle declared, only an 'anecdote found in the papers
of an unknown man': it also dodges the very historicity of its time, place
and characters. For, as Adolphe's confession quickly demonstrates, this
individual has a name, origins, a history, and, like all men in these early
nineteenth-century novels, a secret weighing on him with the force of a
political scandal.

Adolphe's narrator tells his own story, unveiling his betrayal of the
woman who loved him, and her subsequent suffering and death. Like
Staël's Oswald, Adolphe finds himself constrained by his aristocratic birth
to social expectations that come into conflict with his liaison with a woman
dispossessed of her country and social standing. Unlike Corinne, who chose
to leave England for her mother's native Italy, Ellénore has been torn from
her origins by Poland's tragic fate, and plunged into a precarious social
situation at the side of a count seeking to re-establish his own interests. The
young Adolphe pursues Ellénore in a tradition of libertinism espoused by
his father, and quickly finds himself both unable to sustain the cold-
blooded disinterest of the seducer and shackled by his allegiance to social
mores. Though Adolphe's father has counselled him to follow his pleasure,
he calls his son away from the arms of the woman who has given up for
him her children and status. Unlike Oswald, who is depicted as desperately
in love with the heroine, if fickle in the face of his father's will and society's
opprobrium, Adolphe describes himself as incapable of returning the love
offered to him. Rather than denying his guilt over not loving – a position
that his first person retrospection might certainly have afforded him –
Adolphe makes his story into a confession of hypocrisy and deception. Like
René, to whom he has often been compared, Adolphe aspires to revelations
of his own feckless compromise of his beloved, all the more terrifying since
he has chosen to make a woman love him whom he could have loved in
return. 'The laws of society are stronger than the wills of men', writes
Adolphe as he announces to Ellénore that he no longer loves her (p. 88).
Ellénore serves for Adolphe from this moment forward as a spectre of all
the successes he could have claimed, as though in the body of this
'inappropriate' mate were enunciated all the curses that Napoleon's empire
cast on those of aristocratic birth and political aspirations.

This novel reduces history to a shadow over the hopes of the young of a
certain generation in Poland, over the insecurities of yet another in France,
and to the exile engulfing shattered dreams. The novel's foundation on its
exiled aristocrat's loss of personal possessions – specifically, of the archive
of his own life – magnifies its statement about the impossibility of achieving

a history that is not based upon cataclysmic loss. It is as if this novel constructs a past through 'love' for lack of a past through political or social rapports, as Adolphe suggests of his early liaison with Ellénore: 'All other feelings need the past: love creates, as if by enchantment, a past with which it surrounds us . . . As long as it exists, it spreads its light on the era that preceded it as well as on the one that must follow it' (pp. 51–2).

But though the novel inscribes the inevitable from the outset through its protagonist's allegiance to social conventions, one remains struck by the nuances given to such a content by the exchanged letters of its frame and the letters represented in its central confession. Ellénore's death is precipitated, we learn from Adolphe's confession, by someone to whom he had confided in a letter his intention to break with her. The tragic consequences of such a misappropriated letter cast a peculiar light on the process of reappropriating documents which is central to Adolphe's narration. Yet despite the novel's undermining of the truth-value of both letters and confessional documents, it provides the last word to those who have received and used such documents for their own devices. Though Ellénore will speak last in Adolphe's text, her own words are denatured by the very betrayal of her stated intentions that her letter be burned unread and by Adolphe's admission that he has excerpted that letter, choosing what he wants to be known of it. The last word, though, goes to the recipient of the lost strongbox who chooses to withhold the new evidence provided him by his correspondent on the fate of Adolphe, preferring to delegate his own meaning to this life of remorse.

But what meaning is ultimately given here to a fate that seems more explicitly sordid than that of either René, alone on his rock of exile, or Oswald, in his life of bleak English domesticity? The answer lies perhaps less in the editor's disavowal of the instructive value of this confession, than in the antagonism of Constant's peers towards his fictional work. Despite its relative success over several editions in the early years of the Restoration, *Adolphe* did not gain critical favour until the end of the nineteenth century. The attitude of Constant's peers may have related to Parisian anxiety over the author's political aspirations, to suggestions that 'real' people might have been portrayed in Ellénore, and to concerns, especially after Napoleon's fall in 1814, about aristocratic ascendancy in France. I think the truth lies rather in another anxiety – anxiety about the kind of woman Adolphe asks to be condemned for betraying. While Corinne remained aristocratic, if too free in her affections, and talented, if too desirous of public devotion, Ellénore's shaky reputation warned Restoration and July Monarchy fathers of the dangers of encouraging 'honour' in their male offspring. With the increasing rejection of arranged marriages, bourgeois and aristocratic families found themselves unable to direct the futures of sons whose hopes had already been narrowed by social upheavals. Libertinism was seen as corrupt, but no new system of values had been put in place to ensure women's freedom from servitude and men's freedom from social constraints on their affections (see Waller, *The Male Malady*, pp. 95–8). Yet the value such a text might have for us today is less archival than the novel's attentions to the exemplarity of its 'found' documents might suggest, for these texts appear to shift the burden of their historical moment onto confessions of men's inabilities to adjust themselves to women's new social roles. There would be no story to tell here without Ellénore's death, nor any 'letter' to purloin without her lover's silence. Constant's anxiety over a counterfeit version of this novel, expressed in the preface to the third edition, replicates uncannily an anxiety this work embraces about its relation to the ability of language to give expression to subjectivity. For all discourse here is potentially counterfeit; all letters may be turned to ends other than those to which they were destined. The emptiness they ultimately express can only be filled through a retrospective murmuring of secret knowledge, itself somehow not quite history, nevertheless trying its chance at restoring the pacts through which subjectivity is constituted, if not given meaning.

The confessional novel of the early nineteenth century proliferates in the late Restoration and early July Monarchy in ways suggesting the ascendancy of a new literary model, born of the combined efforts of Chateaubriand, Senancour, Staël, Krüdener and Constant. Following the publication of Duras's *Ourika* and *Edouard*, and the scandal through which she ultimately withheld *Olivier* in the face of Stendhal's mockery and publication of *Armance* (see Waller, *The Male Malady*, pp. 114–35), a series of works appeared which further explore the *mal du siècle* through portrayals of impotent manhood. Sainte-Beuve's *Joseph Delorme* and *Volupté*, Balzac's *Le Lys dans la vallée*, Musset's *Confession d'un enfant du siècle*, Dumas fils's *La Dame aux camélias* and Fromentin's *Dominique* replicate structurally as well as thematically the intimate confessional discourse we saw in *René*, *Atala* and *Adolphe*. It would be shortsighted, however, to speak of these novels as a genre, as have many who sought to give unity to this set of works by insisting on the 'truth' value of their accounts of subjectivity. The popularity of Chateaubriand's and Staël's works made them models for success-seeking novelists of subsequent generations, just as critical interest in the *mal du siècle* novelists during the July Monarchy led novelists to explore the meaning of such a 'malady' for the new bourgeois generation of 1830. Given the success of these themes and narrative conventions, we should not be surprised how much confessional discourse permeates July Monarchy social novels, among them Eugène Sue's *Mystères de Paris* where characters repeatedly tell their histories to an intriguing social reformist, or the idealistic fiction of George Sand, whose *Lélia* gave a new twist to the *mal du siècle* by attributing it to women as well as men (see Waller, *The Male Malady*, pp. 136–75), or even the so-called 'realism' of a Balzac who exploited the structures of intimate confession in works such as 'Sarrasine' and *La Peau de chagrin*, and the themes of the *mal du siècle* in novels such as *Le Lys dans la vallée* and *Illusions perdues*.

The historian Alain Corbin has called the nineteenth century 'the century of confession', pointing not only to the boom in published 'journaux intimes' dating from the early nineteenth century but also to an impulse toward an 'accountability for one's life', 'a desire for inner illumination', and 'a dread of loss' that could no longer be articulated in the traditional structures of Catholic confession. According to Corbin, the long interior monologues marking the novels we have considered here as well as the private writings (potentially for public consumption) under the rubric of *journaux intimes* have a peculiar way of simultaneously permitting a control over the 'appearances of the self' and a dissimulation of the self to the Other (see Alain Corbin, 'Les Coulisses', in *Histoire de la vie privée*, ed. Michelle Perrot (Paris: Seuil, 1987), vol. IV, pp. 503, 456–7). The private act of writing, whether of a journal or a fictionalised confession, promotes the introspections of self-examination at the same time as it (paradoxically) lays claim to secrecy.

The most significant secrets such writing keeps, however, relate to the accidents of history. As Béatrice Didier has noted, the published private journals of the late eighteenth and early nineteenth centuries maintain their most privileged silence at the level of the historical event. Louis XVI's journal offers no account of the political upheavals of 14 July 1789; likewise, Constant's journal gives much more space to his emotional turmoils with Staël than to his political engagements. If the journal ultimately reduces, in Didier's words, a headache to the same importance as a war or a revolution, it does so not to deny the significance of the historical event, but rather as a gesture giving magnified significance to the journal's refuge of interiority (Didier, pp. 64–6).

I have repeatedly insisted here on the way the confessional discourse of these *mal du siècle* novels distances their protagonists from the ruptures into which their historical time has thrust them. While none of these novels can be reduced to an allegory of disenfranchisement from a historical past, each nevertheless engages that past as something only tenuously manipulable within the exterior world of political and social events. Control over the world seems to extend, in these novels, only to control over how one's story is relayed. And even that control, as we have seen in our reading of *Adolphe*, emerges as a fragile one, always subject to manipulations beyond the power of those who write and transmit private experience.

With the French Revolution and its tragic aftermath, the stakes for cultural memory changed radically, for – as the revolutionaries themselves well knew – culture is manipulable to transform perceptions of political events (see Hunt, *The Family Romance of the French Revolution*). The novelists we have considered in this chapter were both avatars and victims of the cultural manipulation of historical events. Through their demands for a new kind of literature that could better bespeak the traumas of a transformed world, they found the voices they appropriated to do so continually misread as their own. Shoshana Felman and Dori Laub have formulated an account of a 'literature of testimony' to characterise the writing that attempts to come to terms with the devastation of the Holocaust. The confessional discourses enveloped in the early nineteenth-century novel were struggling to make sense of many similar cataclysmic traumas. 'The accident which pursues the witness' (Felman, p. 23) remains always as unspeakable as it is inescapable. Characterising the *mal du siècle* novels is a 'breakage' with known forms of telling, with traditional conceptions of novelistic form, and even with conventional appropriations of the historical event. Such a breakage repeatedly suggests that secrets are being maintained here that haunt even as they silence their speakers (see Felman, p. 25). Literature has become, for the survivors of the French Revolution as for those of the Holocaust, the site of a stammering that elicits only more telling, that goes on mourning something it has difficulty enunciating as a historical loss, but to which it testifies in forms that must be invented anew for each subject wrenched from familiar stories and expectations (Felman, p. 56).

If history is, as Hegel argued, not just what happened but how it is told, the novels of the generation that came of age in 1789 lay claim to the history of the disruptions of their world through formal innovations in the making of narratives. That these texts must always be unveiled as only fictions and not, as many critics have wished, the true accounts of the selves that made them, does not lessen their capacity to testify to the tragedies that racked a generation. If it is possible to call these texts the first 'modern' novels, then it is less because they champion a changing world, than because they mourn so poignantly the one in which their authors, readers and characters held tight to the trauma of memory, making sense of history as a story told about loss.

NOTES

1 B. Constant, *Adolphe*, ed. J. H. Bornecque (Paris: Garnier, 1963), p. 304 ; C.-A. Sainte-Beuve, preface to E. P. de Senancour, *Obermann* (Paris: Ledoux, 1833; second edn), vol. I, p. v ; *Chateaubriand et son groupe littéraire sous l'Empire* (Paris : Garnier, 1948 (first edn 1849)), vol. I, p. 314.

2 See M. Foucault's account of Augustinian confession in *Technologies of the Self*, ed. L. H. Martin et al. (Amherst: University of Massachussetts Press, 1988), pp. 16–49; and 'Les Techniques de soi', in *Dits et écrits, 1954–1988* (Paris: Gallimard, 1994), vol. IV, pp. 783–813.

3 The expression *roman personnel* seems to date from an 1888 essay by Ferdinand Brunetière, 'La littérature personnelle', republished in *Questions de critique* (Paris: Calmann-Lévy, 1897), pp. 211–52; it is reformulated by Merlant in 1904, and by J. Hytier in *Les Romans de l'individu* (Paris: Les Arts et le livre, 1928).

4 For a translation of Barthes's famous article, see 'The Death of the Author', in *Image/Music/Text*, trans. S. Heath (New York: Farrar, Straus and Giroux, 1977), pp. 142–8. Foucault's article is listed in the Suggestions for further reading for this chapter.

5 See A. Sorel, *Les Grands Ecrivains français* (Paris: Hachette, 1890), p. 100, as well as S. Balayé on *Delphine*'s supposed shirking of the values of the French Revolution ('*Delphine*, roman des Lumières: pour une lecture politique', in *Madame de Staël* (Geneva: Droz, 1994), pp. 185–98). On *Obermann*, see Merlant, p. 150.

6 See D. Kadish, 'Narrating the French Revolution: The Example of *Corinne*', in *Germaine de Staël: Crossing the Borders*, ed. M. Gutwirth et al. (New Brunswick: Rutgers University Press, 1991), pp. 113–21.

7 See G. Poulet, *Etudes sur le temps humain* (Paris: Rocher, 1952), vol. I, p. 273. Poulet defines the modernity of this novel as its presentation for the first time of a past that is veritably over but on which being is nevertheless based. For discussion of *Adolphe*'s relationship as narrator to his past, see T. Unwin, *Constant: 'Adolphe'* (London: Grant and Cutler, 1986), pp. 76–83, and M. N. Evans, '*Adolphe*'s Appeal to the Reader', *Romanic Review* 73 (1982), 303–13.

SUGGESTIONS FOR FURTHER READING

Didier, B., *Le Journal intime* (Paris: Presses Universitaires de France, 1976)

Felman, S. and D. Laub, *Testimony: Crises of Witnessing in Literature, Psychoanalysis and History* (New York: Routledge, 1992)

Foucault, M., 'What is an Author?', in *Language, Counter-Memory, Practice: Selected Essays and Interviews by Michel Foucault*, ed. D. Bouchard (Ithaca: Cornell University Press, 1977), pp. 113–38

Hoog, A., 'Who Invented the *Mal du siècle*?', *Yale French Studies* 13 (1954), 42–51

Hunt, L., *The Family Romance of the French Revolution* (Berkeley: University of California Press, 1994)

Kadish, D., *Politicising Gender: Narrative Strategies in the Aftermath of the French Revolution* (New Brunswick: Rutgers University Press, 1991)

Lejeune, P., *Le Pacte autobiographique* (Paris: Seuil, 1975)

Merlant, J., *Le Roman personnel de Rousseau à Fromentin* (Paris: Hachette, 1904)

Schor, N., *Breaking the Chain: Women, Theory and French Realist Fiction* (New York, Columbia University Press, 1985)

'*Triste Amérique: Atala* and the Postrevolutionary Construction of Woman', in *Rebel Daughters: Women and the French Revolution*, ed. S. E. Melzer and L. W. Rabine (New York: Oxford University Press, 1992), pp. 139–56

Waller, M., 'Being René, Buying Atala: Alienated Subjects and Decorative Objects in Postrevolutionary France', in *Rebel Daughters: Women and the French Revolution* (see previous entry), pp. 157–77

The Male Malady: Fictions of Impotence in the French Romantic Novel (New Brunswick: Rutgers University Press, 1993)

3

ALISON FINCH

Reality and its representation in the nineteenth-century novel

As Timothy Unwin points out in the opening chapter, one of the aims of this volume is to discuss not only 'great' French novels, but also fiction which has been marginalised by the literary-critical establishment – women's novels, thrillers, novels written in former French colonies. It is clear what kinds of prejudice may have operated in this marginalisation: sexism, snobbery, racism. But in the process of highlighting these prejudices, and reassessing the marginalised works, we need to remember that it may not be solely bias that has promoted some novels and allowed others to sink into the background. Is it purely misogyny that makes most readers prefer Stendhal's *Le Rouge et le noir* (1830) to the novel which in part inspired it, *Edouard* (1825) by the talented Mme de Duras? Is it purely middle-class ideology that makes them prefer Zola's *L'Assommoir* (1877) to Sue's shocking novels about the Paris working class (1842–57)? This argument – that it is bias which creates such preferences – becomes especially difficult to maintain when we realise that there was no sharp dividing-line in the nineteenth century between popular and 'great' novels; like Dickens in England, Balzac, Hugo and Zola were themselves popular novelists, and benefited from the new developments which led to the rise of the bestseller: the enormous growth in the novel-reading public, the marketing of cheaply produced novels, and the rise of periodicals which allowed serialisation of fiction (Flaubert's *Madame Bovary* (1856) was first published serially).

So if certain novels by Stendhal, Balzac, Flaubert and Zola are still considered the best ones written in nineteenth-century France, this is because, more consistently than their contemporaries, they are able to think beyond the stereotypes of their period and indeed of ours. They move between the dramatic, the tragic and the comic without being dominated by the popular equivalents of these modes: melodrama, sentimentality, and farce or brittle wit. As well as having comedy, they have irony, a quality often lacking in popular minor works. Finally, these novelists are still valued highly because they are able to combine the illusion of reality with imaginative boldness, and because their language is more inventive and their novel-structures more skilful than those of their contemporaries. To deny these merits would be just as serious a falsification of the nineteenth-century 'picture' as to dismiss other kinds of writing out-of-hand. These other kinds are interesting. But 'interesting' is not the same as 'valuable'. This chapter aims to show why Stendhal, Balzac, Hugo, Flaubert and Zola are still judged exceptionally aesthetically successful, both inside and outside France. (Chapter 5, 'Popular fiction in the nineteenth century', also raises points about both the differences and the overlaps between popular and 'literary' novels.) Of these five novelists, Hugo is the most difficult case. He is more often sentimental and melodramatic than the others, and his novels are rarely read now in their entirety, or studied at university. But, at their best, their political insight, plotting and style are powerful.

The novelists named above have often been bracketed together as 'realists', or later, in the case of Zola and others, 'naturalists'.[1] The term 'realist' is not one that can be maintained once we start to think about what 'reality' in a work of literature can possibly be.[2] But the label is a useful point of entry into certain aspects of the best-known nineteenth-century novelists. In particular, it helps us locate the new attitudes which encouraged the extraordinary achievements of the novel, and contributed to the corresponding decline of drama, in nineteenth-century France.

Nineteenth-century novelists were shaped by eighteenth-century ideas. Stendhal, for example, was already seventeen by the turn of the century and had done most of his formative theoretical reading in the eighteenth-century 'philosophes'. Voltaire, Diderot, Rousseau and Montesquieu had from varying angles undermined the assumption that social organisation was a God-given structure which could never be changed, and had stressed that cultural values were relative. Thus the discrepancy between rich and poor was not one that had to be accepted for all time; and even Christianity – even belief in God – might be varieties of thought rather than absolute truths. Environment and circumstance, rather than immutable rules, shaped character, custom and laws. These ideas helped create a political atmosphere which made the French Revolution possible; the Revolution itself, and its aftermath, provided a startling demonstration that society could be changed. The poor and humble could assert their right to be elevated; history offered a lesson in mutability.

Many nineteenth-century thinkers, such as Mme de Staël and Taine, took up these ideas and elaborated them (sometimes making them cruder than they were in the writings of the eighteenth-century 'philosophes'). But what we see in the major nineteenth-century novelists is perhaps not always the direct influence of contemporary thinkers – thinkers who were often less intelligent and imaginative than they; what we see is first, the absorption and reshaping of the ideas of the four famous eighteenth-century 'philosophes', who were all also creative writers themselves; second, we see in these novelists their own experience of politics; and third, we see conflicting responses to the development of French literature during the seventeenth and eighteenth centuries.

All the major nineteenth-century novelists, and many of the minor ones, at some point set out theories of what literature can be. These theories, sometimes amounting to 'manifestos', vary in their degree of sophistication, and even the more penetrating ones do not do justice to the complexity of the works they describe or prophesy. Nevertheless, it is important to pick out their core ideas, if only to register the fact that these were among the main influences on literary criticism of the period. Among the earliest are Stendhal's pamphlets *Racine et Shakespeare* (1823, 1825) and Hugo's preface to his play *Cromwell* (1827). These ostensibly discuss drama but also tell us much about the nineteenth-century novel. Thus Stendhal, reacting against seventeenth-century drama and its eighteenth-century imitators, argues for the value of prose as against verse (which he dismissively calls 'beaux vers'), and stresses the importance of historical and geographical breadth; he gives as one reason for this that you cannot depict the gradual growth of a conspiracy or popular movement if your time-scale is constricted (*Racine et Shakespeare*, p. 76). Stendhal is too sweeping here: in the seventeenth century, Corneille's *Cinna* and Racine's *Bérénice* used a restricted time-scale in order to suggest what led up to, precisely, a conspiracy and a popular movement respectively. But the point to register is that already in the 1820s Stendhal is making a deliberate connection between new literary form and the politically mutable.

Hugo, still more forcibly, presents as caricatural a picture as he dares of almost all past European literature in order to assert that a new aesthetic, suited to modern times, must experiment with verse-form and must juxtapose the lowly, banal and grotesque with the lofty, dignified and beautiful; our conceptions of 'beauty' will thereby change. Like Stendhal, Hugo implies a political dimension to this: the de-hierarchising of aesthetic categories goes hand in hand with a de-hierarchising of social attitudes. Later, describing in verse his own 'revolutionary' stress on humble vocabulary and subject-matter, he makes a specific link with the French Revolution, referring to the red caps worn by the revolutionaries: 'Je mis un bonnet rouge au vieux dictionnaire. / Plus de mot sénateur! Plus de mot roturier!' ('Réponse à un acte d'accusation' (1834/1856), in *Les Contem-*

plations, book 1, no. 7) ['I gave the dictionary a red cap. No more "senator" or "commoner" words!'].

In the early decades of the century, then, Stendhal and Hugo explicitly or implicitly set the stage for the following aspects of the modern novel. First, a firmer stress on politics and on the historical specificity of given circumstances (history in literature is no longer to be 'generalised', as in seventeenth-century tragedy, nor glamorised, as in much of Walter Scott). Second, new choices of hero (proletarians can become worthwhile and tragic heroes, as in Stendhal's *Le Rouge et le noir*, Hugo's *Les Misérables* and Zola's best novels); and a new use of banal consciousnesses through which to reflect the narrative (as in Flaubert). Third, a more serious and prolonged attention than hitherto to 'humble' but revealing physical details – details which give important insights into the relationship between circumstance and individual (Balzac will endow with significance lowly objects like chair-legs and lowly sensations like the smell of boarding-houses).

Later theories take up these points and develop them. In 1842, Balzac, in the foreword to the *Comédie humaine* (his collected fiction), launches a comparison between humans and animals with the remark that differences between animals are attributable to the different 'milieux' in which they develop. And, like Stendhal, he sketches out points of comparison between literature and History. It is in the middle of this decade, too, that 'realism' appears as an aesthetic category, explicitly linked with a socialist interest in the working class (through the painter Courbet's defence of his art); and, some ten years later, the novelists Champfleury and Duranty write polemics on behalf of 'Realism' in both art and literature, again often associated with socialist politics: the former publishes a collection of articles called *Le Réalisme* (1857), and the latter co-edits the short-lived review *Réalisme* (1856–7).

Flaubert writes no polemic of this kind; in fact, he is at pains to dissociate himself from 'Realism' as such; but, like Stendhal, he suggests that verse has had its day and that prose is now the mode to be developed. In a letter of 1852 to Louise Colet, he writes: 'La prose est née d'hier, voilà ce qu'il faut se dire. Le vers est la forme par excellence des littératures anciennes. Toutes les combinaisons prosodiques ont été faites, mais celles de la prose, tant s'en faut' (*Correspondance*, vol. II, p. 79). ['Prose was born just yesterday, we must remind ourselves of that. Verse is the essential form of ancient literatures. All combinations of poetic form have been carried out, but as for those of prose, far from it.'] Since prose had normally been thought of as the poor relation of verse, this view too implies a move away from linguistic hierarchies. We need not agree with Flaubert and Stendhal about the 'death' of verse. Even if poetry indeed moves increasingly in the direction of free verse and the prose poem, many brilliant poets will continue to observe and exploit the rules of French prosody, and the work of two of the greatest of these, Mallarmé and Valéry, lies ahead. But what is important is that even here we find a revaluation of the 'humble' or 'ordinary'.

Zola, in *Le Roman expérimental* (1880), stresses causality and the effects not just of heredity ('le milieu intérieur') but also of environment ('le milieu extérieur'); and now the social and political interest is still more overt and programmatic than with the mid-century polemicists: when the laws of 'milieux' are understood, man will have only to act on this understanding in order to arrive at the 'meilleur état social' and resolve 'tous les problèmes du socialisme' (*Le Roman expérimental*, pp. 1181, 1188). Finally, Maupassant, in 'Le Roman' (1888, the preface to *Pierre et Jean*), claims that the novelist must avoid the exceptional and must write about states of mind and feeling 'à l'état normal' (p. 20): this essay is more apolitical than those of some of his predecessors, but it implies once more a refusal of 'high History' and a promulgation of 'History from below', the history of the everyday.

To sum up: we must not crudely see all these writers as 'left-wing' in their beliefs (and Balzac, as is well known, was a Royalist); but nineteenth-century French novelists' theories do, with surprising frequency, associate modern aesthetics with attacks on 'rank' and on 'nobility' in many different areas.

Of course, there is more in the theoretical writings than I have described so far, and, especially, there is a great deal more in the fiction. I shall discuss other perspectives later. But let us first see how the interest in environment, in cause and effect, and in the sociology of the 'lowly', is embodied in the novels themselves; and let us remember that it is not only fiction which is profoundly marked by these new emphases. The nineteenth century in France is the century in which not just the novel, but lyric poetry also, flowers. And poetry too, as the century goes on, not only plays with the borderline between verse and prose in the ways already mentioned, but, increasingly, creates a dialectic between the ugly and the sublime. Poets' experiments with form, diction and subject-matter are the counterpart of the new areas being highlighted by their novel-writing contemporaries.

In his survey of representation in Western literature from Homer to the twentieth century, Erich Auerbach singles out Stendhal as the first imaginative writer to create in his works a modern sense of history ('In the Hôtel de la Mole', *Mimesis*, pp. 454–92). Auerbach discusses *Le Rouge et le noir*, citing the atmosphere in the Mole salon as his chief example. In the seventeenth and eighteenth centuries, upper-class salons had been places of lively exchange and intellectual debate. But since the Revolution, the aristocracy is terrified of anything that looks like a radical idea – terrified, indeed, of anything that looks like an idea at all. As a result, the atmosphere in the salons is deadly dull; so Mathilde de la Mole is bored. She is thus ready to fall in love with Julien. Auerbach's analysis shows in its broad outlines, then, that a specific historical moment is not just part of a backcloth to the main characters' feelings. It permeates and even creates the feelings. And we can see this relationship between history and psychology at work on many levels in *Le Rouge et le noir*. It is not simply because Mathilde is bored that she falls in love with Julien. It is also because she knows proletarians like him have recently guillotined aristocrats like her, and this idea excites her. Julien's swings of feeling towards Mathilde and, initially, Mme de Rênal are again inseparable from his awareness that these women are wealthy aristocrats, in 'le camp ennemi' (p. 305), and that he is a struggling peasant who is, however, as good as they are. So, when Mathilde begs Julien to punish her for her pride and says she will be his slave, the words 'orgueil' and 'esclave' are not to be taken merely as those of any impetuous and infatuated young woman (p. 559). They have depths of social irony which cannot be fully understood without some knowledge of the reversals of the Revolution and of the immediate post-Revolutionary decades.

With Balzac, similarly, it would be a misreading to separate the dilemmas and feelings of the characters from the historical situation in which they are embedded. Hulot of *La Cousine Bette* (1847) is thought of by many readers as some archetypal incarnation of Lust. But he is not so much an archetype as a particular personality shaped by a particular historical situation. He has been faithful to his wife for twelve years, but now, bored by the inaction he is forced to endure after Napoleon's fall, this former military man 's'était mis en service actif auprès des femmes' (*La Cousine Bette*, p. 35) ['had taken up active service with women']. Bette too would not be the scheming avenger she becomes if not for Napoleon's fall. Before this, she has been self-sufficient: she has had a managerial role in a firm which makes embroidery for Napoleonic uniforms – Napoleon is fond of such finery. But the Napoleonic regime is replaced by that of the Bourbons, which makes cuts in both government departments and the military, and hence reduces the demand for the finery. Bette loses her entrepreneurial courage, and becomes impoverished and dependent on the Hulots. They tease her and steal the young man who is her only object of affection; this is one of the main motors of the plot. In *Le Père Goriot* (1834), Goriot has been able to make his fortune as a pasta-maker because of the shortage of bread at the time of the Revolution (it was this shortage which, famously, provoked Marie-Antoinette's uncomprehending comment 'Qu'ils mangent de la brioche' and, at least in popular mythology, sparked the Revolution). The doubly exploitative relationship Goriot has with his daughters – he expects love in exchange for money, they accept the money without giving the love – is thus rooted in a clearly outlined historical situation. And in all Balzac's novels, the implication is not simply – say – 'Here is a character making his way in society', but 'Here is a character making his way in a specifically nineteenth-century Paris where we see at work a specifically nineteenth-century form of capitalism'; not simply, 'Here are the problems faced by an apprentice writer who wants to make a name for himself' but, as in *Illusions perdues* (1837–43), 'Here are the problems faced by an apprentice writer who, because of the new mass market for books and newspapers in nineteenth-century France, faces the choice between remaining true to his talent or prostituting it. And here, furthermore, are the opportunities this mass market opens up to the same writer's brother-in-law, a paper-manufacturer who invents the cheap, lightweight paper now required by printers and publishers, but who, because of the cut-throat competitiveness of nineteenth-century business, loses both his invention and the prospects it seemed to offer.'

So both Balzac and Stendhal have a keen perception of historical uniqueness; and because class and money were understood as crucial issues in post-Revolutionary France, both writers show, with unprecedented complexity, the function of these in their characters' lives. Money, and differing class-conditions, also preoccupy those novelists who pinpoint historical causes less subtly than Stendhal and Balzac. Hugo, in *Les Misérables* (1862), puts figures on his characters' expenditure and shows what the possession or loss of small amounts of money can mean. Unemployed one winter, Jean Valjean steals a loaf of bread for his dependants (a sister and her seven children); he is caught, imprisoned for an eventual total of nineteen years, and never sees the sister and children again. This novel, throughout, creates a sense of compassion for the underclasses unique in French literature and probably impossible to conceive in such depth without the burning eighteenth- and nineteenth-century consciousness of the arbitrary nature of social conditions.

Flaubert is much slyer in his depiction of politics and history. Sometimes they seem to be deliberately sidelined, as when Frédéric and Rosanette, in *L'Education sentimentale* (1869), spend a day in the country just as revolution is erupting in Paris; but there is irony here, of course; and rank and money ineluctably enter into the dreams both of Frédéric and of the heroine of *Madame Bovary* (1857). Ostensibly, Emma Bovary commits suicide because her illusions have collapsed and because she has a Romantic notion of death; but these causes are shot through with class and financial issues. The illusions were those of a middle-class woman yearning for a relationship with a 'gentleman', and the debts which trigger the suicide were contracted because of stereotyped aspirations to dress and to live beyond lower middle-class means.

Finally, with Zola, it is hardly necessary to emphasise the importance of class and money; they could almost be thought of as acting creatures in his novels, and in *Germinal* (1885), indeed, he does 'animalise' capitalism, describing it as a crouching monster. Again we have a perhaps less obvious pinpointing of dates and historical moments than in Stendhal and Balzac. But the stratum into which one is born, and one's relationship with Capital (which manipulates the bourgeoisie and nakedly exploits the working class), are the core of Zola's two best novels *L'Assommoir* and *Germinal*. Other factors may be at work in the characters' lives, but these factors will always be interwoven with questions of rank and poverty.

How else does the interest in history and environment shape these novels? The two most influential thinkers of modern times, Marx and Freud, both stress the importance of understanding the past in order to change the present. Both were formed by the nineteenth century, the century of historicism. Just as we can see certain emphases of Marx's foreshadowed in the political thought and even the literary practice of the early nineteenth century, so also Freud's study of childhood did not spring from nothing. Childhood – the 'history' of each individual – becomes increasingly important in European thought from the late eighteenth century onwards. In 1762 Rousseau published *Emile*, a work on the upbringing and education of children which not only had a deep impact on theories of child-rearing, but was to influence many novels of the nineteenth century. Childhood is reassessed in the nineteenth century: it is now assimilated to artistic creativity, for it is the time when impressions and imagination are at their freshest. The great novelists' main focus is of course still on adults acting in an adult world; but they will often give us one key, at least, to the behaviour of these adults in a few telling sentences which pinpoint central dramas of their early years. Julien Sorel as a child and adolescent has been the 'objet des mépris de tous à la maison' ['the object of everyone's scorn at home']; in public games, 'il était toujours battu' (p. 233) ['he was always beaten']. This quietly imparted information goes some way to explaining the fear of humiliation which governs many of his responses, and which – most notably – makes him want to kill both Mathilde and Mme de Rênal when they express extremes of contempt for him. (When Mathilde relegates him to the status of 'little nobody' after their first night together, Julien seizes a sword (pp. 546–7); when Mme de Rênal writes the letter that again presents him as a despicable nobody, he makes the journey to Verrières to shoot her.) Hugo, for his part, shows how the personality of the child Cosette is all but destroyed by the neglectful and cruel treatment meted out by the family supposedly taking care of her (*Les Misérables*, book 4, ch. 3).

Quite apart from wide questions of history and class, and the formative role of childhood, these novelists are also acutely interested in the power of immediate surroundings: thus Balzac will often imply or state that such-and-such a turn of events could not have taken place anywhere but: in the capital; or in a large provincial town; or in a village where everyone knows of everyone else's movements. This interest in present circumstance also informs, say, Flaubert's novels. We must not see Emma Bovary as too much a victim of her provincial surroundings; to do so would be to miss the ironies surrounding her personality; yet one reading of *Madame Bovary* is undoubtedly as a wickedly amusing account of the particular constrictions prevalent in nineteenth-century provincial life. And if Flaubert sets *L'Education sentimentale* in Paris, and gives Frédéric an inheritance, it is in part to show what happens to a hero who – unlike Emma – has the advantages of being male, moneyed and in the capital. Even if what is finally shown is that fundamentally the same happens, contrasts are set up en route which are in a nineteenth-century mode rather than an eighteenth-century mode – contrasts which are suggested through a greatly increased use of physical detail.

For this, perhaps more than anything, is what readers have picked out over the years as exemplifying the so-called 'realist' novel: its intensive evocation of clothes, of hair-style, of furnishings, of weather . . . It is what distinguishes the nineteenth-century novel from the seventeenth-century novel and, less clearly but still markedly, from the eighteenth-century novel. (Any page from *La Princesse de Clèves* (1678) or *Les Liaisons dangereuses* (1782) will show this relative bareness, which was not an involuntary omission but a consciously assumed theoretical position developed in the seventeenth century.) The wide-ranging interest in physical detail is also what distinguishes the nineteenth-century novel from some of the boldest experimental fiction of the twentieth century: writers like Sarraute and Robbe-Grillet have distanced themselves from what they see as a comforting fictional world which allows us to 'label' characters and their appearance, and where objects or landscapes become controllable because they are always endowed with a human significance. This is a simplification, as I shall show later. However, it would be absurd to deny that whereas in most pre-1800 fiction we scarcely know what characters look like, beyond the fact that they are said to be beautiful, badly formed, etc., Hugo does make us imagine his hunchback's eyebrows, teeth and chest (*Notre-Dame de Paris* (1831), p. 51). And, whilst the seventeenth- and eighteenth-century novel will probably, in a dignified generalisation, state that the time of day is morning or evening, or that a given building is magnificent, comfortable or poor, Zola tells us the exact hour his miners get up and how the mine is constructed, down to the bolts on which the iron mine-cages come to rest (*Germinal*, pp. 17, 29). We are *not* being given 'exhaustive detail', 'every detail', as readers sometimes claim; but we are being invited to pay more attention to what has hitherto been thought of as undignified.

I mentioned earlier that this new focus on the 'lowly' leads to new choices of hero, who are often now proletarian or middle-class. There are no absolute chronological divisions here: previous comic or picaresque novels frequently had lower-class heroes or heroines (as in the eighteenth-century *Le Paysan parvenu* (1734–5) by Marivaux); conversely, the nineteenth-century novel may still choose heroes of aristocratic family, like Balzac's Rastignac or Stendhal's Fabrice del Dongo, in *La Chartreuse de Parme* (1839). But even where nineteenth-century heroes are upper-class, there is still often a clear intention to question both their aristocratic and their heroic stature. Rastignac's impoverishment, and naïve desire to succeed, put him in undignified situations, and the end of *Le Père Goriot* removes any prestige that might still tenuously attach to him: his challenge to Paris, 'A nous deux maintenant!' ['It's the two of us now!'], is described as 'ces mots grandioses' ['these grandiose words'] (p. 254). Fabrice is not in fact the marquis del Dongo's son, and, far from being publicly 'heroic', finds himself wondering what heroism is. And in any case, the description of the battle of Waterloo, in its key position near the beginning of *La Chartreuse de Parme*, has already swept away ideas of Fabrice as a glorious hero, or of battle as the criterion for heroism. This description has been called the first modern account of warfare in its refusal to glamorise military prowess and its powerfully understated evocation of the chaos and physical horror of the battlefield. (On this, see the opening remarks in Denis Boak's chapter, 'War and the Holocaust'.) There are some antecedents, for example Voltaire's ironic description of battle in *Candide* (1759). But Stendhal's Waterloo is crucial in its undermining of a key component of the epic – an undermining that must take place if the novel is to treat non-glorious lives and events seriously.

So aristocrats like Rastignac and Fabrice have lost their heroic stature; and other nineteenth-century characters like Julien or Frédéric have been thought of by many critics as anti-heroes. That is to say, they are still heroes in the sense of being the central figures of the narrative, but they do not possess the high social or moral status we associate with the heroes of tragedy. Hence, it has been argued, the dominating modern literary mode – the novel – lacks not only a sense of the epic but also a sense of the tragic. Whether this is actually so will be examined in the last part of this chapter. Meanwhile, it is true that although these nineteenth-century heroes do strive and suffer, and do sometimes have an exceptional dynamism and intelligence, their situation and presentation differ markedly from those of earlier epic or tragic heroes.

They may yearn to be such heroes, however; and here is a rich and seemingly inexhaustible tension in the nineteenth-century novel. It has been said that all the best-known nineteenth-century novels could be called *Illusions perdues* or *L'Education sentimentale*. For they portray a clash between, on the one hand, their heroes' fantastical or stereotyped longings – often shaped by the clichés of popular literature – and, on the other hand, the sober analyses of motive and desire suggested by the authors themselves. The soaring-up of the heroes' imagination, the puncturing of this by the surrounding narrative – expansion accompanied by deflation with an often bathetic physical detail – this narrative procedure has played its part in the perception of the nineteenth-century novel as more 'down-to earth', 'realistic' than some of its predecessors or successors (Alison Fairlie gives well-chosen examples in *Flaubert: Madame Bovary*, pp. 15–17).

Finally, the sense of 'reality' is created too by the extraordinarily well-concatenated plots, which can again give an illusion of cause-and-effect operating in an unassailably tight process. Certainly, in comparison to deliberately casual eighteenth-century narratives like *Tristram Shandy* and those twentieth-century novels which experiment with chronological order, the structure of the best nineteenth-century novels is engineered to resemble that of a thought-through historical chronicle. 'Because' and 'therefore' hover as the key hidden conjunctions in Hugo, in Zola, even in Flaubert, the novelist who is often thought of as the grandfather of the twentieth-century experimental novel. 'This happened because that happened; as a result, this further event took place.' And sometimes, of course, the causal conjunctions are not hidden but highlighted, as with Balzac's famous 'Voici pourquoi'.

But how far are we justified in stressing these sides of the nineteenth-century novel – the sides which the novelists' best-known theories seem to promulgate, either explicitly or implicitly?

Everything described so far bears out the common image of these novelists as more 'realistic' than earlier writers, or than their Romantic contemporaries. But this cannot be the only reason they are considered great writers. Their novels are ambiguous, metaphorical, symbolic and internally patterned in ways which both encompass and go beyond any narrowly defined 'realism'. And if we re-read the less publicised parts of their theoretical statements, or look at comments in their other works, we find that they themselves see these more ambiguous, open sides as just as much part of their enterprise: indeed, in the case of Flaubert, much *more* their enterprise.

Thus Stendhal in *Racine et Shakespeare* spends almost as long discussing the nature of aesthetic illusion as in promoting new areas for literature. And in his autobiographical *Vie de Henry Brulard* (1835) he asserts that it is crucial *not* to describe key moments in detail – for then too little is left to the reader's capacity to dream and imagine. Balzac, in his foreword to the *Comédie humaine*, follows his comparison of man to animal with an immediate statement that man is different from animal – in what? In his sheer mobility, in the difficulty of defining him, in that human socialisation which is subject not just to laws of cause-and-effect but to chance, 'des hasards'; everything is a more complex business for humans than for animals, including gender-definition (the lioness is simply the female of the lion, whereas 'dans la Société la femme ne se trouve pas toujours être la femelle du mâle' (pp. 8–9) ['in Society woman is not always simply the female to the male]. And the rest of the 'Avant-propos' is full of words stressing complication, dissimilarity, changeability, hiddenness; Balzac's own search for motive will, he says, be exploratory rather than definitive. He even throws doubt on how far his work really can be compared to a history: the novelist is freer than the historian, and the novel is an 'auguste mensonge' (p. 15) ['an august lie']. And in generalisations scattered throughout the *Comédie humaine*, Balzac invokes not only historical necessity but also, with wonder and curiosity, the diversity and unpredictability of the mind: for example, the artist's need to dream and the more general human longing for play and aesthetic pleasure.

Flaubert too stresses that the work of art must suggest, rather than state; that experience and feeling are so complex and shifting that language can scarcely render them. The most compassionate moment in *Madame Bovary*, and the one when the narrator most openly affirms a shared humanity with both Emma and the reader, makes just this point: Emma expresses her feelings to Rodolphe in such a clichéd form that he does not see they are true, 'puisque personne, jamais, ne peut donner l'exacte mesure de ses besoins, ni de ses conceptions, ni de ses douleurs, et que la parole humaine est comme un chaudron fêlé où nous battons des mélodies à faire danser les ours, quand on voudrait attendrir les étoiles' (p. 196) ['since no one can ever give the exact measure of their needs, nor of their thoughts or sorrows, and human language is like a cracked cauldron on which we beat out melodies for bears to dance to, when we would like to move the stars to pity']. We have here again, then, not that reproduction of the concrete stressed in one view of the nineteenth-century novel, but a focus on intangibility, on hiatus, and on the fact that language can never be seen as a transparent tool which simply 'copies' the 'real'.

How does this interest in suggestion, in unpredictability and in imagination mark the novels themselves? First of all, some of the very features we might pick out as embodying the 'realism' of these works in fact transmit an open, multilayered sense of the possible as much as of the actual. This is the case with the well-engineered plots and the creation of apparently strong chains of cause-and-effect. For if a cause is laid bare, then one response may be, 'I can now see that if the cause had been different, the outcome could have been different too'; in other words, variability as well as necessity is evoked.[3] The forward-moving, teleological temporality of many of these novels may also be interpreted in different ways. Let us take the most extreme example. Stendhal creates the fastest narrative pace of all: he does so through a nimble insertion of unexpected asides which whet the appetite without diluting the thrust of the sentence; through a use of common hyperbole (after an apparent rupture with Mathilde, 'Julien était décidément l'un des hommes les plus malheureux' (*Le Rouge et le noir*, p. 568) ['Julien was decidedly one of the unhappiest of men']); and with phrases which speed up the time-scale of the story (Fabrice is showering Gina with kisses: 'Au même instant, on entendit le bruit de la voiture du comte qui entrait dans la cour, et presque en même temps lui-même parut dans le salon' (*La Chartreuse de Parme*, p. 190) ['At the same moment, the count's carriage could be heard entering the courtyard, and almost at the same time he himself appeared in the drawing-room']). This narrative impetus could not be more different from the slow or fragmented pace of many twentieth-century novels; in its rapidity, it looks at first sight 'historical' and goal-directed; but is it? It is, rather, narrative speed *in excelsis*; it does not imitate anything, but is a new aesthetic experience in itself.

What about those famous 'descriptions' in Balzac and others? The most famous is that of Mme Vauquer's pension in *Le Père Goriot*. This is often cited as a 'typically' Balzacian, hence 'typically' nineteenth-century, passage, in its focus on the detail of furnishings and in particular, perhaps, in its climactic affirmation of the continuity between individual and environment: 'toute sa personne explique la pension, comme la pension implique sa personne' (p. 30) ['her whole person explains the boarding-house, just as the boarding-house implies her person']. But this description often breaks off into alliteration, personification and even rhyme: it takes on a life of its own. It becomes metaphorical. Similarly, Hugo pauses in his chronicle of Jean Valjean's early life and imprisonment to write not just a few sentences but a whole chapter in an entirely metaphorical mode. He describes the plight of the wretched, or of 'wretches' ('les misérables' can mean both), through an image of the man who has fallen off a ship and must, with increasing helplessness, contend with the waves, finally to sink and drown ('L'onde et l'ombre', book 2, ch. 8). Here too, the description is densely alliterated and assonantal: 'Les flots déchirés et déchiquetés par le vent l'environnent hideusement . . . il sent qu'il devient abîme, il fait partie de l'écume . . . Il assiste, agonisant, à l'immense démence de la mer' (p. 101) ['The waves torn and shredded by the wind surround him hideously . . . He feels himself becoming the abyss, he is part of the spume . . . He witnesses in his death-throes the immense madness of the sea']. It should not be thought that this language is fine and allusive mainly because Hugo is a poet as well as a novelist; the other four are masters of phonetic patterning and of figurative writing. To take one example from many, Zola's description of Goujet's forge in *L'Assommoir* evokes, just as much as a 'real' working environment, an ambiguous, quasi-magical scene where machines become giants and the noise of the overhead connecting belts becomes the flight of night birds (pp. 193–4). This passage also, like Hugo's, is alliterative and assonantal. Naturally, these novelists' use of phonetic patterning and of metaphor varies: Stendhal is the most restrained, Flaubert the most luxuriant. But all depend on linguistic and imaginative play to disturb, to delight and, above all, to create a shifting, mobile world where identity can change and 'reality' begins to dissolve. And through it they also – especially Hugo and Zola – restore to the novel that mythical and epic dimension which at first sight we might have thought lost.

The five novelists we are looking at are also humorous and ironic writers. If the humour or irony is of a physical kind, it will inevitably convey that 'down-to-earthness' which for most readers is a crucial aspect of the nineteenth-century novel, as when characters fall off their horses in Stendhal, or Emma's thoughts about Léon are compared to the pigeons on the inn roof whose feet are in the gutters (*Madame Bovary*, p. 110). Humour and irony also help to give a sense of 'realism' by deflating characters' illusions and by stripping away pretension, showing greed or vanity for what they are. But, equally, humour and irony take the reader off into another world, an exaggerated world which can be as preposterous as it is 'realistic'. When Rastignac appears to the Vauquer boarders dressed up and ready for the social fray, Vautrin gives a virtuoso soliloquy suggesting the young man's need to find a wife and the necessity for that wife to be an all-purpose commodity; so bold are his comparisons that we end up not just with a searingly unsentimental picture of the state of marriage in nineteenth-century France, but with an image of a comically monstrous being (the wife). She is simultaneously a boat-like container with compartments, a chemist's store and a fairground exhibit accompanied by a band that cannot play in tune (*Le Père Goriot*, p. 137). Writers like Balzac and Zola owe as much to Rabelais as to any contemporary theories emanating from the sciences, and Gervaise's 'epic of dirty linen' is not only in part deterministic but also, at many moments, comical and fantastical in its sheer appallingness.

We should notice, also, what these novelists are doing with their characters' speech. More than ever before, they individualise this speech, showing the characters' often helpless reliance on crude or empty phrases. This is at one level a contribution to a new 'realism': the inflections of ordinary language, of everyday cliché, are apparently being reproduced before our very eyes. But of course, this speech is itself exaggerated and stylised; and the platitudes or vulgarisms often contribute to the comic incongruity of given scenes. Thus Zola's style in *L'Assommoir* often appears to espouse brilliantly the very thought-processes of characters who can perceive reality only through their colloquialisms; at such moments, this style seems 'undignified', 'low'. But by becoming part of the narrative, and part of a humorous yet humane vision, it achieves a comic sublimity of its own; one outstanding example is the wedding episode. Similarly, when characters strive for linguistic originality (like Crevel in *Bette*, or the students in *Goriot* with their tedious '-rama' jokes), certainly a 'realist' attention is being paid to bathetic detail. But at the same time there is a carnivalesque celebration of the need for expression – even, or perhaps especially, when that expression 'comes out wrong'.

If, more widely, the humour or irony are so far-reaching that they undermine the reader's own belief in the novel, we have a form of playing that is as old as the novel itself – one which creates the illusion of reality only to snatch it away dizzyingly.[4] Such are the interventions of Stendhal's narrators; the questioning of the influence of fiction in *Madame Bovary*; and, more radically, the very structure of *L'Education sentimentale*. For this is more like an anti-*éducation sentimentale*. Frédéric's aimlessness parodies all fictions whose heroes are young men learning about the world and making their way in it. And the ending seems to wipe out the whole novel. Frédéric and his friend conclude that a failed visit to a brothel, which took place before the action of the novel even starts, was the best experience they've had. The best? Then everything described in the pages we have been reading was even more of a failure – so where is the substance of the novel? Of course, this is to some extent only Frédéric's feeble view. There *is* substance: Flaubert suggests social and aesthetic issues which simply pass Frédéric by. And a profounder substance resides in the reader's exhilarating sensation of the gaff being constantly blown. This novel lifts the lid on cosy assumptions – including our own wish to find in the novel energetic heroes and firm teleology. *L'Education sentimentale* is more tonic, and even preposterous, than is sometimes assumed. But its ironies exemplify the intellectual and aesthetic sophistication of the best nineteenth-century novels – a sophistication which readers hunting out 'realism' sometimes miss.

Such readers may also miss these novelists' interest in the ambiguity of desire. Far from creating monolithic, firm characters, they draw attention to the mobility of drives. Balzac and Flaubert in particular often dissolve gender boundaries. Balzac creates the powerful gay character Vautrin and suggests bisexuality in others (for example, in the relationship between Valérie and Bette); and his similes can amusingly suggest temporary changes of gender. Rastignac, out walking with Delphine and alert to new sexual and social opportunities, is compared not to the male animal one might expect but to an ardent female date-tree waiting impatiently to be fertilised (*Le Père Goriot*, p. 148). Flaubert explodes Emma's stereotyped images of 'men' and Rodolphe's stereotyped images of 'women', and suggests the ambiguities of Emma's own sexuality: with Léon especially, she is said to be more like the man and he the woman.

Finally, these novelists, for all their recreation of 'the ordinary', are, like other great writers, interested in 'extraordinary' states of mind, such as madness. Coupeau ends in a lunatic asylum and Gervaise (also madly?) imitates his tics (*L'Assommoir*, pp. 487–94). Bianchon, the brilliant doctor of the *Comédie humaine,* is especially enticed by the prospect of curing not a physical illness but a mental one – the cause of the mysterious nervous tremor which afflicts Adeline at the end of *Bette* (p. 418). The poet Ferrante Palla – Stendhal's only fictitious writer of genius – is said to be mad; and words and phrases like 'folie', 'égaré', 'hors de lui' have been calculated by one critic to occur on average every two pages in *Le Rouge et le noir* and *La Chartreuse de Parme* (S. Felman, in *La 'Folie' dans l'œuvre romanesque de Stendhal*). Madness, in these novelists, is sometimes seen as threatening or laughable, deviating too far from various norms to be anything other than 'crazy'; but it is equally often implied to be valuable and visionary in its querying of those norms.

The complex depiction of madness brings us back to the novelists' puncturing of Romantic dreams. This too is complex. They do puncture the dreams. But while doing so, they make us feel them in our bones; they make us enjoy them as part of the human need to create, and make us, at some level, mourn their failure. There *is* tragedy of 'older' kinds in the post-1800 French novel (as with Julien's execution, for instance). But it is in this blend of the foolish and the splendid that we find a peculiarly modern, uneasy tragedy.

Proust's *A la recherche du temps perdu* (1913–27) is often thought of as the first truly modernist novel. But Proust, like his predecessors, endows the ordinary with significance; analyses class structure; highlights political crises; gives new value to prose; builds up and deflates dreams not only at the level of the 'story' but in his very sentence-structure. And, in comments on Balzac, Stendhal, Flaubert and Zola, Proust brings out their visionary qualities and their skill with form, discussing their imagery and the structural patterning to be found in, say, the symbolic recurrence of height in Stendhal.[5] Some later twentieth-century novelists – like the Sartre of *La Nausée* (1939) – claim that they are reacting against the nineteenth-century novel. But they in fact owe a great deal both to its promotion of the lowly and to its ambiguous or 'poetic' aspects; and one of them, at least, has been honest enough to admit this. The *nouveau romancier* Butor is witheringly scornful of the idea that the modern novel is really 'anti-Balzac', and rightly argues that 'il est peu d'inventions actuelles qui ne puissent y [i.e. in *La Comédie humaine*] trouver leur annonce et leur justification' (in 'Balzac et la réalité', pp. 79, 93) ['few contemporary creations can claim not to have been anticipated and justified by it'].

So, yes – there is an attempt in the nineteenth century to make readers believe they are seeing new and more 'real' kinds of 'reality'; and that attempt is often interestingly linked with a socialist or at least a liberal political outlook. But the best nineteenth-century novelists are also keenly aware of the tensions between 'reality' and its 'representation'; they question the meaning both of 'reality' and of 'representation', and their works are comic and tragic celebrations of these tensions.

NOTES

1 For further discussion and definition of 'realism' and 'naturalism' as terms attaching to specific theories, good starting points are the relevant entries in *The New Oxford Companion to Literature in French*, ed. P. France (see General bibliography). See also the brief but wise remarks on 'realism' in A. Fairlie, *Flaubert: Madame Bovary*.

2 C. Prendergast highlights the fact that language can never copy 'reality'; as a code, it can only symbolise it. See his *The Order of Mimesis* (in General bibliography).

3 F. Marceau is good on this side of Balzac in his *Balzac et son monde*; trans. D. Coltman, *Balzac and his World*.
4 See on this subject R. Alter, *Partial Magic: The Novel as a Self-conscious Genre* (in General bibliography).
5 For this kind of patterning in Flaubert (in whom it is the most noticeable), see A. Fairlie's book on *Madame Bovary* and 'Some Patterns of Suggestion in *L'Education sentimentale*', in her *Imagination and Language*.

SUGGESTIONS FOR FURTHER READING

Primary works

Balzac, 'Avant-propos' to the *Comédie humaine* (Paris: Gallimard, Bibliothèque de la Pléiade, 1976), vol. I, pp. 7–20
    La Cousine Bette (Paris: Librairie Générale Française, 1963)
    Le Père Goriot (Paris: Garnier-Flammarion, 1966)
Flaubert, *Correspondance* (Paris: Gallimard, Bibliothèque de la Pléiade, 1973–91)
    L'Education sentimentale (Paris: Garnier, 1964) (Classiques Garnier)
    Madame Bovary (Paris: Bordas, 1990) (Classiques Garnier)
Hugo, *Les Misérables* (Paris: Gallimard, Bibliothèque de la Pléiade, 1951)
    Notre-Dame de Paris – 1482 (Paris: Gallimard, Bibliothèque de la Pléiade, 1975)
Maupassant, 'Le Roman', preface to *Pierre et Jean* (Paris: Albin Michel, 1984)
Stendhal, *La Chartreuse de Parme* (Paris: Gallimard, Bibliothèque de la Pléiade, 1952)
    Racine et Shakespeare (Paris: Garnier-Flammarion, 1970)
    Le Rouge et le noir (Paris: Gallimard, Bibliothèque de la Pléiade, 1952)
Zola, *L'Assommoir* (Paris: Fasquelle, 1967)
    Germinal (Paris: Fasquelle, 1973)
    Le Roman expérimental, in *Œuvres complètes*, vol. X (Lausanne: Cercle du Livre Précieux, 1968)

Secondary works

(See also entries in the General bibliography at the end of this volume under Alter, Ambrière, Auerbach, Bersani, Brooks, France, Girard, Prendergast, Raimond.)
Butor, M., 'Balzac et la réalité', *Répertoire* (Paris: Minuit, 1960–82), vol. I, pp. 79–93
Fairlie, A., *Flaubert: Madame Bovary* (London: Edward Arnold, 1962)
    'Some Patterns of Suggestion in *L'Education sentimentale*', in *Imagination and Language* (Cambridge: Cambridge University Press, 1981), pp. 379–407
Felman, S., *La 'Folie' dans l'œuvre romanesque de Stendhal* (Paris: Corti, 1971)
Marceau, F., *Balzac et son monde*; trans. D. Coltman, *Balzac and his World* (London: W. H. Allen, 1967)

4

MARGARET COHEN

Women and fiction in the nineteenth century

Staël, Sand, Rachilde: we now remember women's contribution to the nineteenth-century French novel as a few exceptional figures leaving their mark on a genre dominated by men. But women were in fact the most acclaimed practitioners of the novel when the century opened and integral to the novel's development during what critics have long considered its 'golden age'. If their importance has subsequently been forgotten, it is the result of literary battles which this chapter describes. The nineteenth-century novel takes shape in struggles between the sentimental form which reigns at the beginning of the century and newly-emerging realism which will come to supplant it. Throughout these struggles, female novelists overwhelmingly prefer sentimental codes.

The history of the nineteenth-century novel has long been written from the standpoint of the victorious realist aesthetic. This chapter brushes such literary history against the grain. It isolates four phases in women's contribution to the nineteenth-century novel that are inseparable from the prestige and decline of the sentimental form. From the Revolution to 1830, the most important novels are sentimental novels written by women. During the years 1830–1850, realism takes shape in a struggle to displace the sentimental novel, but the contest has no clear winner. The years 1850–80 correspond to the triumph of the realist aesthetic and women writers' disappearance from the vanguard of the novel. At the century's end, women writers once more emerge as important presences in the novel, and their contributions now cover the spectrum of possible novelistic forms (sentimental, realist, decadent).

'Women figure with greatest distinction among modern novelists', wrote Marie-Joseph de Chénier in his 1816 survey of 'the state and progress of French literature' since the French Revolution.[1] Chénier's opinion was characteristic of its time. During the first decades of the nineteenth century, women were the most respected as well as the most commercially successful novelists. 'The novels of Madame de Staël, Madame Cottin, the author of *Adèle de Sénange* [Madame de Flahaut] and perhaps others [women], surpass the novels currently being written . . . by men in number, variety and appeal': thus wrote the literary critic, journalist, and member of the French Academy, Charles-Marie de Féletz.[2] 'Nowadays, without wanting to denigrate the merit of men, is there one of them who surpasses Madame de Genlis, Madame de Staël, Madame Cottin, Madame Flahaut?' asked the bookseller and publisher Alexandre-Nicolas Pigoreau, a man with his pulse on the works promising the best economic return.[3]

When early nineteenth-century critics run through the most important contemporary novels, frequently mentioned titles include Germaine de Staël's *Delphine* (1802) and *Corinne* (1807); Sophie Cottin's *Claire d'Albe* (1799), *Amélie Mansfield* (1802) and *Mathilde* (1805), Adélaïde de Flahaut's (later Souza) *Adèle de Sénange* (1805) and *Eugène de Rothelin* (1808); Stéphanie Félicité de Genlis's *La Duchesse de la Vallière* (1804); Isabelle de Montolieu's *Caroline de Lichtfield* (1786); Juliane de Krüdener's *Valérie* (1804); and Claire de Duras's *Ourika* (1823). These novels were also popular successes. Krüdener's *Valérie*, for example, saw three editions in 1804, the year of its appearance; and Cottin's *Œuvres* were reissued over ten times during the Restoration. Duras took a different path to fame, by surrounding her novels with an aura of luxury. A high-ranking aristocrat, Duras initially read her narratives aloud to the Parisian social and cultural élite and had them privately printed in limited editions. This scarcity created a public demand which Duras then satisfied by publishing her novels anonymously, although her identity was generally known.

If twentieth-century literary histories mention women writers' dominance in the novel during the first part of the nineteenth century, it is to dismiss their works' aesthetic claims. Thus Richard Bolster: 'The first decades of the nineteenth century were a good moment for the insipid works of Madame Cottin, Madame de Souza, Madame de Duras and so many others'.[4] But the most celebrated novels of the early nineteenth century belonged to the well-established subgenre of the sentimental novel which was characterised by its own coherent aesthetic. In the post-Revolutionary years, this aesthetic was significantly inflected by France's recent Revolutionary trauma. The inventors of realism would, moreover, appropriate much from the post-Revolutionary sentimental novel even as they aggressively denigrated the form.

The post-Revolutionary sentimental novel is structured around a conflict between two equally valuable moral imperatives: first, the imperative to build and sustain the collective social order which these novels represent as duty to the family ; and second, the natural imperative to happiness; the imperative to pursue individual freedom and be true to what these novels call the 'heart'. This subgenre thus conforms to the definition of tragedy Hegel offered in his *Aesthetics* composed around the same time. 'The original essence of tragedy consists then in the fact that within such a conflict each of the opposed sides, if taken by itself, has *justification*; while each can establish the true and positive content of its own aim and character only by denying and infringing the equally justified power of the other.'[5]

In struggling with the relation between collective good and individual freedom, the sentimental novel addresses a fundamental problem in the political theory and practice of its time. In the late eighteenth and early nineteenth centuries, the new social élites conceptualise an alternative to absolutism in liberal terms. French liberalism rests on an uneasy tension between a negative notion of rights (rights to be free from government intervention) that French thinkers take from their Anglo-American counterparts, and a positive notion of rights (rights to participate in government) inherited from a Continental tradition. The early nineteenth-century sentimental novel represents individual freedom (negative rights) and collective welfare (positive rights) as impossible to reconcile in response to recent historical traumas. The difficulty of accommodating these two versions of rights had, after all, been spectacularly played out in the Revolution's bloody failure to preserve either individual freedom or public safety.

The literary conventions of the post-Revolutionary sentimental novel work to intensify its constitutive conflict. These novels unfold predominantly within the narrow confines of an aristocratic family and the place of family residence, although sometimes, as in Staël's *Corinne* or Krüdener's *Valérie*, the characters travel for pleasure. This narrow plot focus is true whether the novel is set in the present (*Corinne*, *Valérie*) or is historical (Genlis's *La Duchesse de la Vallière*). Critics evaluating the post-Revolutionary sentimental novel from the standpoint of realism take this aspect of the subgenre to task. But the narrow plot focus must be understood as part of the sentimental novel's effort to pare away any distraction from the starkness of its constitutive conflict; as equivalent to the unities of time, space and action important in classical French tragedy.

The effort to highlight the tragic conflict as starkly as possible also explains why the sentimental novel does not evoke material appearance with the rich description found in realism. Physical aspect and social specificity are downplayed in order to foreground the workings of the psyche, what these novels term the 'suffering' that renders a character 'interesting'. 'Interesting' in the sentimental sense means worthy of compassion and sympathy. Contemporary critics called this downplaying of material appearance the 'light touch'. It was accompanied by an anti-materialist philosophy which emerges most pointedly in Genlis's 1806 *Alphonsine ou la tendresse maternelle*. In this novel, Genlis tells the story of a child raised by her mother in a cave without light for twelve years. When mother and daughter are finally rescued, the mother educates her daughter in the correct use of the sense of sight which is Platonic. Vision is the gateway to intangible intellectual and emotional pleasures and the privileged object of visual contemplation is nature.

In the post-Revolutionary sentimental novel, a protagonist's gender makes little difference in his or her fate. Heroes and heroines alike suffer the tensions caused by their dual allegiances to collective welfare and individual freedom. For both, this conflict is often emplotted as a tyrannical parent or relative who rules with crushing authority over the child's choice of beloved, whether the parent is dead or alive. In Staël's *Corinne*, Oswald and Corinne surrender their chances for personal happiness to the will of Oswald's dead father, while Souza's *Eugène de Rothelin* ends more happily, with the children being able to reconcile estranged families through their love. At the same time, these novels do not violate conventional gender expectations and there is hence some difference in how male and female characters imagine personal happiness. While female characters frame love as communion of the souls, male characters give it an explicitly sexual dimension. So, too, the sufferings of the male protagonist are more likely to be represented as pathological than the sufferings of the female protagonist. They become a kind of 'male malady', as they contrast with the 'new orthodoxy of virile and militarist masculinity set in place by Napoleon' (Margaret Waller, p. 3).

Women's pre-eminence in the novel during the post-Revolutionary decades may seem surprising, given the political and economic discrimination women suffered at this time. Women were second-class citizens in French society throughout the nineteenth century, granted formal equality but treated as minors in multiple social arenas, including politics, the legal system, the professions, and economic relations. At the beginning of the nineteenth century, however, the novel was low in the hierarchy of literary genres, ranking behind drama and poetry. It was therefore accessible to those writers who might lack the benefit of formal education and who could not compete for the top honours in French literature. The history of the genre also facilitated its availability to women writers. Under the ancien régime, women had played an important role in the development of the modern novel, from the work that has long been hailed as its invention, La Fayette's *La Princesse de Clèves* (1678).

Between 1830 and 1850 the novel undergoes a significant cultural transvaluation. It shifts from polite entertainment to an ambitious literary form claiming to offer a historically accurate panorama of post-Revolutionary social life. 'All reality seems henceforth to have fallen into the possession of this omnipotent genius', was how one contemporary reviewer expressed the novel's new aesthetic and cultural stature.[6]

The novel's transvaluation was the work of ambitious writers who were drawn to the genre as a medium in which to pass serious social and cultural judgements. Victor Hugo fills *Notre-Dame de Paris* (1831) with mini-essays on the work of art in the age of mechanical reproduction, on class struggle, and on architectural history, while George Sand's *Indiana* (1832) offers a brutal indictment of the institution of marriage. In *Le Rouge et le noir* (1830), Stendhal claims to portray contemporary French society with unflinching and unprecedented accuracy, and Balzac's *Comédie humaine* offers 'the history forgotten by so many historians, the history of manners'.[7] Writers become interested in the novel's serious aesthetic and social potential in part for specifically literary reasons: as a result of the failure of the Romantic drama to live up to its aesthetic promise. They also turn to the novel because of the cultural climate in which they are writing. During the July Monarchy, the institutions of literary production are remarkably open to what the period calls 'the social': a knot of practices including politics, economic processes and the unobtrusive rituals of everyday life. Of all literary genres, the novel has historically been the most concerned with this cluster of subject-matter.

'Quel sera le roi du roman?' ['What will be the king of the novel?'] asked the renowned critic Gustave Planche in 1834.[8] His statement makes explicit the question preoccupying novelists in the 1830s and 1840s. At this time, new practices of the novel vied with each other for cultural legitimation and there was intense polemic around this competition. 'At the moment, writers . . . struggle against each other and sometimes cut each other down in the ideas they put forth', wrote Gaschon de Molènes of the 'bizarre confusion' reigning in the contemporary novel.[9] While Balzac sets his *Illusions perdues* during the Restoration, the novel describes a climate of literary struggle even more characteristic of the 1830s when it was written.

Almost all writers engaged in these battles around the novel start from the previously dominant sentimental conventions which they appropriate and transform. Given the important presence of women writers in the sentimental subgenre, it is not surprising that July Monarchy writers use a rhetoric of gender to stake out their positions in the battle. The novelists whom we today remember as the inventors of realism (Stendhal, Balzac,

Charles de Bernard, Félix Davin) portray themselves as performing the rejuvenating if harsh masculinisation of a washed-out, feminised form. 'He dared to paint love in Paris', Stendhal proclaims of *Le Rouge et le noir*'s originality. 'No one had attempted it before him', in particular not Madame de Genlis. And if 'all women in France read novels', Stendhal predicts that they will all be shocked by his unflattering portrayal of modern love.[10]

The realists' claims to masculinise the novel in fact correspond to substantial modifications these writers work on the sentimental novel's codes. Realist writers dismantle the sentimental novel's enclosed universe of private, emotional suffering with the help of 'objective' professional discourses – notably the discourses of history, the nascent social sciences, and the natural sciences – and the professions at this time were the province of men. Thus, Balzac and Stendhal refuse the 'light touch' of the sentimental novel. Instead they employ a descriptive rhetoric privileging the material detail which shares much with descriptions found in contemporary sociology (as well as owing something to Walter Scott). Or thus, the pathologised female body so important in nineteenth-century science was central in realism too. As critics like Roland Barthes and Naomi Schor have argued, there is much slippage in realist narrative construction between the novel's inquiry into the hidden truth of social relations and a male protagonist's investigations into transgressive feminine sexuality.

The pathologised heroine is related to another modification realist authors work on the sentimental novel: to introduce a gender divide in the respective careers of its heroes and heroines. In best bourgeois fashion, the realist hero no longer passively suffers the constraints of his situation, but rather actively sets out to make his way in the world. Heroines, in contrast, remain suffering, as their sexuality, their money, and their social position become the tools the hero manipulates, more or less skilfully, in his rise (*Le Père Goriot*, *Illusions perdues*, *Le Lys dans la vallée*, *Le Rouge et le noir*). Sometimes, however, a realist heroine may turn the tables, successfully trafficking in her sexuality herself (*La Cousine Bette*).

As Stendhal's assertions about *Le Rouge et le* noir indicate, the realist transformation of the sentimental novel extends to the realist authors' new way of conceptualising social relations. The realist novel does away with the absolutes and principles of the sentimental tradition. Might now makes right and the winner in social struggle is s/he who best recognises how to play the game. In realist polemic, to tell this truth is to speak with masculine frankness to a male audience. When contemporary critics attacked the world of *La Comédie humaine* for being amoral, Balzac responded 'J'écris pour les hommes et non pour les jeunes filles' ['I write for men, not girls'].[11]

At the same time, the realist claim to masculinise the novel is misleading. It masks the substantial debt of nascent realism to the post-Revolutionary sentimental subgenre. Far from offering a radically new depiction of social relations, realist authors accept the sentimental novel's tragic vision of the relation between individual and collective but transform it in one crucial way. In the realist novel, the protagonists are not destroyed by the contradiction between individual freedom and collective good, but rather learn from it what realism portrays as the fundamental social skills of manipulation and compromise. If the heroes of Balzac start by discovering the sentimental gap between duty to the collective and duty to the heart, they then proceed, in most unsentimental fashion, to make it the basis of their success.

The realist transformation of the sentimental tradition is evident from comparing Cottin's *Claire d'Albe* (1799) to Balzac's *Le Lys dans la vallée* (1836). In both novels, a young man becomes involved in a Platonic, adulterous love triangle with a noble young woman married to an older man. In Cottin's novel, Claire dies to mark the impossibility of reconciling the collective good with individual freedom and the novel ends with its hero, Frédéric, vowing he will soon follow her. In Balzac's rewriting of *Claire d'Albe*, in contrast, the hopeless adulterous triangle teaches the hero, Félix, how to defer immediate gratification and manipulate other characters to obtain his ends. The hero of Stendhal's *Le Rouge et le noir* follows a similar trajectory. Julien's first affair with Madame de Rênal teaches him the mastery, self-control and skills at deception he will then employ in his meteoric rise in Parisian society.

The transformation of the tragic collision into sentimental education occurs in the case of Balzac's female protagonists as well, although the female protagonist's arena of action is limited to sex and love. Thus, in *La Muse du département*, Balzac describes the adulterous sufferings of an unsatisfied, provincial bluestocking raised on too many novels, Dinah de la Baudraye. Rather than dying from her betrayal of her husband, however, Dinah undergoes a sentimental re-education in the ruses and compromises that constitute the lot of a woman in love. This novel also makes evident the difference in careers open to men and women of talent in Balzac's universe. There is never any possibility that Dinah's experiences will transform her into an intellectual à la George Sand. Rather, her story ends when she returns to the family and to marriage.

As such a domestication of the intellectual heroine indicates, the realists' use of anti-feminine rhetoric to delineate the importance of their own project extends to negative portrayals of female authors. In these portrayals, realist novelists make use of a cultural construct that was a site of more general ideological controversy during the July Monarchy. Women writers were important members of the intellectual landscape of the time. If their presence was amply remarked, reactions to it extended beyond discussions over the merits of individual writers to lively argument over the merits of 'la femme auteur'. 'La femme auteur' provoked such contestation because she foregrounded issues of great sensitivity in the contemporary social formation, where the bourgeoisie was in the process of consolidating its hegemony. As a public woman, the woman writer transgressed a fundamental tenet of bourgeois ideology: the equation of the public/private opposition with the difference between man and woman.

George Sand was universally recognised as the most important female novelist of the time. Indeed for many readers, professionals and amateurs alike, she was quite simply the period's most important novelist. But Sand also had a host of respected *consœurs*. They ranged from Angélique Arnaud, an active Saint-Simonian (the Saint-Simonians were the first French socialists), to the Countess Merlin, a highly placed aristocrat who ran a prestigious literary salon; from the Baronne Aloïse de Carlowitz, a scholar who won prizes from the French Academy for her translations of the German Romantics, to Caroline Marbouty, a self-made woman of letters now remembered for her brief friendship with Balzac, as she accompanied him on an 1836 trip to Italy posing as his male secretary, Marcel.

If we take novels by July Monarchy women as a group, we notice a remarkable alignment of gender and genre. This alignment is negative: with only one exception (Delphine de Girardin), women writers steer clear of the polemic and conventions characterising realism. Women do write novels on similar subject-matter, post-Revolutionary social relations, and some of them have substantial literary ambitions. But women writers represent nineteenth-century society in a coherent novelistic subgenre that I have elsewhere termed the 'sentimental social novel' (see my *Why Were There No French Women Realists?* listed in the Suggestions for further reading).

Like more well-known forms of the social novel, the sentimental social novel seeks to put art in the service of social change. But it represents social suffering with conventions drawn from the sentimental rather than the realist lineage. Some sentimental social novels were, moreover, explicitly hostile to realism. Thus, the villain of Jenny Bastide's 1832 *La Cour d'assises* is a scheming, ambitious parvenu named Julien after Stendhal's hero in *Le Rouge et le noir*. Determined to succeed at all costs, he makes a good career for himself but destroys the novel's Corinne-like heroine,

Laurentine, on the way. The sentimental social novel was also written by men – in contrast to women, male novelists of the time were distributed across the generic spectrum.

The sentimental social novel is close to the post-Revolutionary sentimental novel in many respects. It handles social and physical setting with the sentimental novel's light touch, analysing the sufferings of characters caught in situations of contradiction. In contrast to the earlier sentimental novel, however, the novels of the July Monarchy use the sentimental double bind to explore a variety of social conflicts. In contrast to the earlier sentimental novel, too, the sentimental social novel frames its tales as exemplifying the sufferings of a group rather than as the tragic story of private individuals. 'Dans la vie que la civilisation chrétienne a faite aux femmes, deux genres de devoirs leur sont imposés, qui semblent au premier aspect difficiles à concilier', writes Sophie Pannier at the opening of *Un Secret dans le mariage* ['In the life which Christian civilisation has made for women, two types of duty are imposed on them which at first glance seem difficult to reconcile'] (Paris: 1844, vol. I, p. 40). In Pannier's novel, these two types of duty are a woman's responsibility to reveal her life in its entirety to the husband who is her master, and the social importance placed on feminine modesty.

When sentimental social novelists position their writings in contemporary literary struggles, they too use a rhetoric of gender. They feminise the sentimental novel's attention to private suffering and claim to extend it to diverse situations across the social spectrum. So, Hortense Allart proclaims the importance of her sentimental social novel, *Settimia* (1836), by locating it in a lineage of women writers running from the early nineteenth century to the present. She writes: 'Madame de Staël a peint des femmes mourant pour les préjugés; notre époque, plus avancée, peint des femmes qui bravent les préjugés' (Hortense Allart, *Settimia* (Paris, 1836), vol. I, p. ix) ['Madame de Staël painted women dying for prejudices; our own period, more advanced, paints women who bravely defy prejudices'].

Women's socially motivated suffering was not the only subject of the sentimental social novel. The subgenre also represented the sufferings of those barred from the ranks of wealth and privilege, notably the proletarian (Clémence Robert's *René l'ouvrier*, Auguste Luchet's *Le Nom de famille* (1842)), and the petit bourgeois (Emile Souvestre's *Riche et pauvre* (1836)). There were also a few novels on the problems of belief, slavery and capital punishment. Victor Hugo's *Le Dernier Jour d'un condamné* [1829] is an early example of the social turn taken by the sentimental novel.

If sentimental social novels by men were evenly distributed across this range of subject matter, sentimental social novels by women were overwhelmingly concerned with women's issues. These issues included women's status as second class citizens, their restriction to the private sphere, and their sufferings in unhappy and indissoluble marriages. Flora Tristan's *Méphis ou le prolétaire* (1838), Angélique Arnaud's *Clémence* (1841) and Caroline Marbouty's *Une fausse position* (1844) tell of women's difficulties supporting themselves outside the ordinary route of maternity within marriage. Bastide's *La Cour d'assises* (1832), Carlowitz's *Le Pair de France ou le divorce* (1835) and Allart's *Settimia* (1836) are novels which explore the advantages and disadvantages of reinstating the divorce law instituted during the Revolution but abolished under the Restoration. 'These ladies . . . will carry on so much they will end up making husbands interesting', wrote Auguste Bussière in 1843. 'Doubtless, marriage is a tyranny, and the tyrant must be slaughtered . . . But as a result of slaughters of this kind, honest hearts, sensitive and gentle minds will eventually tire of seeing the sad head of what was formerly the family eternally dragged to be strung up by the levellers of community.'[12]

Returning to the archive to rescue forgotten literature, we confront the vexed question of aesthetic value. Were these works good? Perhaps they deserve to be forgotten? These are responses a revisionist literary historian often hears. I would, however, suggest that one measure of aesthetic value is the fit between a work's literary conventions and its ideological project. In the case of the post-Revolutionary sentimental novel, the fit is good: its conventions help the conflict between individual freedom and collective welfare to stand out in starkest possible fashion. The same cannot be said of the sentimental social novel, however. This subgenre confronts the problem of adapting the sentimental novel's neo-classical devices (light touch, narrow milieu, uniformity of diction, restricted number of characters, etc.) to the panoramic representation of social life that is fundamental to the novel's claims to cultural and literary authority in the July Monarchy.

As a consequence, many sentimental social novels run into aesthetic difficulties. Carlowitz's *Le Pair de France*, for example, opens the sentimental plot onto the broad social spectrum by including a profusion of protagonists all caught in insoluble conflicts exemplifying the evils caused by the abolition of divorce. The result is an episodic three-volume work with a diffuse plot line that has none of the post-Revolutionary sentimental novel's tragic majesty.

The most aesthetically successful sentimental social novels either stick closely to the post-Revolutionary sentimental novel, telling one simple but powerful story of suffering, or frankly exploit the contradictions between the sentimental novel's literary conventions and the novel's new social and cultural ambitions. Sand's novels excel at such exploitation. Indeed, Sand's virtuosity in playing with the contradictions facing the sentimental social novel constitutes one of her *œuvre*'s most impressive aspects, although it is not apparent today, since we have forgotten both the post-Revolutionary sentimental novel and the sentimental social novel.

Sand's cleverness in exploiting the contradictions between sentimental aesthetics and the novel's new panoramic ambitions is evident from her first novel, *Indiana*, that turned her into a literary celebrity overnight. Like Carlowitz, Sand here confronts the problem of opening up the sentimental form onto the sufferings of women across the social spectrum. Rather than accumulating characters and plot lines, however, Sand solves the problem by giving her heroine, Indiana, a 'milk sister', Noun. The lower-class Noun is Indiana's servant and her closest friend, until both maid and mistress become embroiled in unhappy love affairs with the same ambitious man. In the creation of Noun, Sand not only finds an economical way to represent socially differentiated experience but challenges the notion of the family so important to aristocratic and bourgeois ideology, as well as to the post-Revolutionary sentimental novel. For the family, Sand substitutes a suffering sisterhood of women across class and possibly colour. Both Noun and Indiana are 'créoles', an ambiguous term at the time that could mean either a white settler born in the colonies or a colonial subject of mixed race.

Female novelists' overwhelming lack of interest in the conventions of realism may have resulted from the confluence of two orders of factors. July Monarchy women making a bid for literary prestige had strong impetus to continue the sentimental form. As we have seen, women wrote in a climate where there was considerable debate around if and how women should participate in the public sphere. Using sentimental conventions, women novelists authorised their literary interventions by invoking a respectable historical precedent. The post-Revolutionary sentimental novel was only the latest avatar of a well-acknowledged tradition of women's contribution to the French novel which had predominantly taken the sentimental form.

Women writers' allegiance to the sentimental tradition may also have derived from their lack of enthusiasm for the realist position in itself. If realism's representation of social truth was deeply bound up in a masculine investigation of transgressive, feminine sexuality, this aspect of the subgenre would need to be modified for it to focus principally on other aspects of women's lives. In addition, the realist claims to cultural authority were inseparable from a work of gendering denigrating the nexus of femininity and the novel and casting the novel and/or novelist as male. This was not a position attractive to women writers, given the extent to which a woman's gender was at issue when she entered the public arena of letters. While men wrote as universal subjects, women of the time wrote first and foremost as women, as 'femmes auteurs'.

Between 1850 and 1880, women writers' importance in the novel declines. Sand remains a literary celebrity and there are other women who publish respected and/or commercially successful novels during the Second Empire, including Louise Colet, the Countess Dash, Juliette Adam née Lambert, Pauline Caro and Madame Augustus Craven. But Sand's Second Empire works are not as aesthetically innovative or sophisticated as her July Monarchy production and are no longer in the thick of mid nineteenth-century ferment around the genre. Indeed, there are no women writers in the vanguard of the novel at this time; there is no Second Empire Staël or Sand.

Since little work has been done on female novelists of the second half of the nineteenth century (even less than on female novelists of the first half), the reasons for women's declining contribution to the novel are not yet clearly understood. This decline may well be related to the triumph of the realist aesthetic. Following the débâcle of 1848 (and in part, in response to it), the sentimental social novel loses out to realism which will dominate until it starts to be dismantled by decadent and symbolist writers at the century's end. The decline in women's contribution to the novel may also be related to the fact that the novel is now a high literary form while the Second Empire is a time of backlash in women's rights. This backlash contrasts both with the disorganised ferment around gender in the 1830s and 1840s and the liberal, reformist feminism of the Third Republic.

The representation of women in realist fiction during its heyday continues the July Monarchy preoccupation with transgressive feminine sexuality (naturalism belongs to the realist lineage and we may include it in this literary historical moment). Indeed, the preoccupation is, if anything, intensified, sometimes entirely displacing the other constitutive plot line of July Monarchy realism: the vicissitudes of an ambitious young hero. Even more than in the earlier part of the century, transgressive feminine sexuality crosses class difference, from the lurid fantasies of the idle *bourgeoise* who has read too many novels, like Flaubert's Madame Bovary, to the hysterical satanism of the aristocratic Madame Chantelouve in Husymans's *Là-bas*; and from the virile sexuality of working-class women like the servant in the Goncourt brothers' *Germinie Lacerteux*, to the treacherous, consuming prostitute who reaches her paroxysm in Zola's *Nana*, with her powerful and destructive sexuality which swallows up entire fortunes and families.

The realist–naturalist fascination with dangerous femininity sometimes extends from feminine sexuality to other forms of feminine psycho-social pathology, as is the case of Zola's alcoholic Gervaise in *L'Assommoir*.

The most well-known novels and tales written by women in the years 1850–1880 'continue in a dignified manner the tradition which has remained uninterrupted across centuries', which is to say the sentimental lineage.[13] If these works maintain the sentimental focus on suffering generated by contradiction, they turn away from the sentimental social novel's conceptualisation of suffering as a collective social problem, preferring a representation of suffering closer to that prevalent early in the century. They use sentimental conventions to tell the stories of private individuals torn between duty to the collective and duty to the self, although these individuals are now most frequently bourgeois. In her 1870 *Saine et sauve*, Juliette Adam employs the epistolary form that was already outmoded by 1830 to explore the conflicting allegiances of two young bourgeois women, one of whom is travelling in a search of what she calls 'melancholy', fleeing society and fashion, while the other stays at home to build a model worker's colony. Pauline Caro's acclaimed debut novel, *Le Péché de Madeleine*, first published in *La Revue des Deux Mondes* in 1864, emplots the conflict between collective good and individual freedom as a love triangle. It tells the story of Madeleine who loves her cousin's fiancé with all her heart, and who sacrifices this mutually shared love to her sense of family obligation. The popular novels by women of the time also follow sentimental conventions. This is the case, for example, of the works of Madame Augustus Craven, exemplified by her best-selling *Fleurange*.

Novels by women from the heyday of realism do, however, absorb the realist aesthetic in one important way. The realist interest in material aspect has filled out the light touch, particularly when it comes to natural or exotic landscapes as well as to a character's physical appearance and dress. Judith Gautier's *Le Dragon impérial*, first published in 1868 in serial form, provides a good example of such increased attention to the material. While Gautier's plot line is sentimental, her descriptions extend well beyond anything found in historical novels by women earlier in the century such as Genlis's *La Duchesse de la Vallière* or Sand's *Consuelo*. 'Salammbô without the heaviness' was how her father, Théophile Gautier, characterised *Le Dragon impérial*, whose exotic detailing was admired by the Parnassian poets.[14]

Despite women's declining contribution to the novel during the 1850s–70s, there is one arena of fiction where a woman reigns. This arena is the burgeoning field of children's literature where women have played an important role throughout the century. During the Restoration, Pauline

Guizot, notably, writes pedagogical novels as well as pedagogical treatises. In the July Monarchy, important children's works include the novels of the journalist Eugénie Foa as well as *Le Livre des mères et des enfants* (1840) by the noted poet Marceline Desbordes-Valmore, and the *Contes d'une vieille fille à ses neveux* (1832) by the journalist, novelist, poet and *salonnière* Delphine de Girardin. But none of these works attains anything like the extraordinary success of the fiction of Sophie Rostopchine, Comtesse de Ségur, who starts to write children's fiction in the 1850s (*La Santé des enfants*, 1855; *Les Petites Filles modèles*, 1858; *Les Malheurs de Sophie*, 1859; *Mémoires d'un âne*, 1860; etc.) Robert de Montesquiou later called her 'the Balzac of childhood', and his judgement is suggestive. Ségur's stories mix their didactic instruction with acute social observation and satire, and, like Balzac, Ségur repeats characters from story to story. Like Balzacian realism, too, these stories put forth a model of social integration as compromise and adaptation.

From 1880 onwards, women once more emerge as major players in the French novel. 'Let's have the courage and frankness to admit it from the first page of this book: the success of contemporary feminine literature has been massive, it has surprised us all, it has humiliated us a bit', wrote Jules Bertaut in the opening to his 1909 survey of recent novels by women. 'Mademoiselle de Scudéry and Madame de Lafayette may have reigned in the seventeenth century, Madame Marcelle Tinayre and Madame de Noailles shine at the dawn of the twentieth century, here are two incontestable truths.'[15] That Bertaut can point to women writers' recent success with such surprise indicates not only women's renewed importance in the novel, but also the erasure of women's contribution to the genre in the middle part of the nineteenth century. Women's pre-eminence in the post-Revolutionary period, George Sand's importance as the most energetic talent spawned by the Revolution of 1830, have been forgotten.

Bertaut describes a success that belongs to the turn of the twentieth century, with the novels of Gérard d'Houville [Madame Henri de Régnier], Marcelle Tinayre, the Comtesse de Noailles, Myriam Harry, Gabrielle Reval, Colette Yver, Lucy Delarue-Mardrus, Colette, Camille Marbo, Camille Perty, Claude Freval, Renée-Tony d'Ulmès, Renée Vivien, Louise-Marie Compain and Liane de Pougy. We can, however, already see the beginnings of women's re-emergence to prominence in the novel as the nineteenth century draws to a close. This re-emergence runs across the spectrum from popular to élite literature. Importantly, however, novels by women from the 1880s and 1890s are no longer overwhelmingly concentrated in the sentimental lineage, as they were earlier in the century.

If we do not have sufficient literary historical knowledge to account for women's declining contribution to the novel in the years 1850–80, nor can we yet explain why they re-emerge to prominence when they do. It may well be important that the last decades of the nineteenth century are, as Bertaut observes, a time of active gains in women's rights, particularly in education and the professions. Given women writers' troubled relation to realist conventions in the middle of the century, it may also be significant that women's renewed novelistic contribution coincides with the waning of realism's prestige.

The woman dominating the late nineteenth-century popular novel is Gyp (Sibylle-Gabrielle de Martel de Janville), who begins to collect her witty, slick dialogues exposing the foibles of middle- and upper-class life in novel form in the early 1880s. Gyp's works are firmly within the parameters of realism. They emphasise social observation and material detail; employ socially nuanced diction; drive their narratives forward with an exploration of hidden sexual practices; and put forth a world-view based on compromise. With one important difference, however: they refuse the naturalised understanding of sexual difference that underwrites realism's imbrication of feminine sexuality and narrative truth. Rather, they expose sexual difference as socially constructed in a number of different ways. Gyp's novels are replete, for example, with acute and satirical demonstrations of how feminine fashion creates beauty, as Gyp shows the allure of the female body to be produced rather than natural. Or thus, she assigns the conventional masculine attributes of realist heroes to her heroines and vice versa, as a contemporary reviewer of her *Bijou* (1896) noted with some dissatisfaction. 'Dominate, dominate, dominate constantly, dominate always, dominate without letting anyone escape her ascendancy', wrote Emile Faguet of the heroine who gave the novel its name.[16]

But sentimental conventions are alive and well in the popular works of Daniel Le Sueur (Madame Henri Lapauze), Brada (the Countess de Puliga), Georges de Peyrebrunne (Georgina Elisabeth de Peyrebrun) and Madame Henry Greville (Alice Durand), who was also the first woman to be awarded the Légion d'Honneur for literature, in 1899. 'Es-tu bien sûre de l'aimer, Lucie? bien sûre? Prends garde de te tromper, ton erreur serait irréparable', a mother anxiously cautions her daughter in the opening lines of *Lucie Rodey* (Madame Henry Greville, *Lucie Rodey* (Paris, 1881)) ['Are you sure you love him, Lucie? Quite sure? Be careful you are not fooling yourself, your mistake would irreparable']. Disregarding her mother, the daughter embarks on marriage, and thereby sets the stage for her unhappy experience of the conflict between individual freedom and duty to the social collective. Like most other late nineteenth-century sentimental novels, however, *Lucie Rodey* does not end in impasse but rather has absorbed the realist lesson of reconciliation to the actual.

A similar generic range characterises late nineteenth-century novels by women on the high end of the literary spectrum. We can date women's re-emergence to prominence in the aesthetic vanguard to 1884, the year when Rachilde (Marguerite Eymery Vallette) made her literary reputation with the publication of *Monsieur Vénus*. Appearing in Belgium, the work also earned her a sentence of two years of prison and a two thousand franc fine if she ever crossed the Belgian border. Rachilde was a member of the symbolist literary circle that met in the Café de l'Avenir around Verlaine, and *Monsieur Vénus* has been called the first symbolist novel.

In *Monsieur Vénus*, Rachilde employs key conventions of realism (social specificity, attention to material appearance, imbrication of narrative and sexuality) in order to attack the realist slippage between the truth of social relations and the mysteries of feminine sexuality. Rachilde wages her attack through regendering Zola's *Nana*. The golden beast of *Monsieur Vénus* is a plump working-class boy, Jacques Silvert, a fine artificial flower maker and a poor aspiring artist of ambiguous sexual identity: 'les cuisses, un peu moins fortes que des cuisses de femme, possédaient pourtant une rondeur solide qui effaçaient leur sexe' (*Monsieur Vénus* (Paris: Flammarion, 1977) p. 55) ['the thighs, though less thick than a woman's, were still round enough to make his sex uncertain']. The decadent aristocrat he drives mad is a young woman, Raoule de Vénérande, determined to be his lover [*amant*] rather than his mistress [*maîtresse*] (p. 90). And in the course of their relation, the two will demonstrate sexual difference to be a mutable, treacherous, and artificial construct that is unfit to guarantee truth of any kind.

Other *fin-de-siècle* women with high literary ambitions do, however, continue the sentimental lineage. Thus, Jean Bertheroy (Berthe LeBarillier), known principally for her historical novels, fuses a sentimental plot with the symbolist exploration of exotic and anti-referential figuration in *La Danseuse de Pompeii* (1899). In best sentimental fashion, this novel tells the story of the double bind facing Hyacinthe, a pure young man dedicated to Apollo and disillusioned by the debauch of Pompeii, who falls in love with the dancer, Nonia, a descendant of Hugo's Esmerelda but lacking her sexual chastity. In its outcome, *La Danseuse de Pompeii* modifies the sentimental tradition in similar fashion to late nineteenth-century popular novels. While Hyacinthe dies unable to reconcile the conflict between the ideal and the material, Nonia emerges from it with renewed dedication to her chosen way of life. The novel ends with an ecstatic image of Nonia alone on a mountain top: 'Elle dansa dans l'ivresse de sa jeune ardeur retrouvée, dans l'allégresse nouvelle de sa vie; elle dansa soulevée d'un indicible élan' (Jean Bertheroy, *La Danseuse de Pompeii* (Paris: Ollendorf, 1899), p. 335) ['She danced in the intoxication of her young passion that she had found again, she danced in the new cheerfulness of her life, she danced, lifted up in an indescribable rush'].

The novelist whom contemporary critics considered the most important woman writing at the dawn of the new century, Marcelle Tinayre, also takes sentimental conventions as her starting point (Tinayre's most celebrated novels are *La Maison du péché* (1902) and *La Rebelle* (1906)). Employing the sentimental plot of contradiction, with, however, an ending of compromise rather than impasse, Tinayre uses it to explore the conflicts facing women in an era of liberal feminist reform. Her first novel, *Avant l'amour* (1897), narrates the adolescence of a rebellious, impoverished, illegitimate and intelligent orphan, Marianne, caught between conventional feminine dreams of happiness in love and the desire to make her own way in the world. In Tinayre's work, that is to say, the make-up of the sentimental conflict has shifted significantly from the earlier part of the century. Love is no longer the expression of individual freedom but rather is associated with the norms of the social collective, while individual freedom has become aligned with a somewhat undeveloped yearning for self-sufficiency and independence.

The plot of Tinayre's novel principally turns around Marianne's complicated relation to Maxime, the son of her conventional bourgeois godparents. And if the struggle between realism and the sentimental novel has been important in shaping women's relation to fiction across the nineteenth century, Tinayre's portrayal of this relation makes clear that it has not entirely been resolved. When Marianne initially meets Maxime, she finds him repellent because he seems an ambitious realist hero, determined to succeed. 'Il semblait incapable d'émotion. Personne ne pouvait dire l'avoir vu pleurer. Epris d'un petit livre qu'il relisait sans cesse et que je trouvai un jour – *Le Rouge et le noir* d'Henri Beyle – il affectait d'admirer les impassibles, les audacieux, les hommes d'action.' ['He appeared incapable of emotion. No one could say they had ever seen him cry. In love with a little book that he re-read constantly and that I found one day – *Le Rouge et le noir* by Henri Beyle – he affected admiration for impassive, daring men, men of action']. After some experience in the world, however, Maxime goes from being a bourgeois man of ambition to an 'implacable adversaire' of bourgeois society, and his partially unrequited love for Marianne puts the finishing touches on his transformation. 'Il leva un visage contracté que la douleur transfigurait en une beauté inconnue, un front creusé, des lèvres ouvertes et palpitantes, des yeux pleins de lumières et de pleurs . . . – O

Marianne chérie! J'ai tant souffert. Et je souffre!' ['He raised a tensed face which sorrow was transfiguring into unknown beauty, a lined forehead, lips that were open and trembling, eyes full of light and of tears . . . – Oh Marianne darling! I have suffered so much. And I am still suffering!'] (Marcelle Tinayre, *Avant l'amour* (Paris: Calmann-Lévy, 1897), pp. 18, 117, 319).

NOTES

1 M.-J. de Chénier, *Tableau historique de l'état et des progrès de la littérature française depuis 1789* (Paris: Maradan, 1816), p. ii.
2 C.-H. de Féletz, *Mélanges de philosophie, d'histoire et de littérature* (Paris: Grimbert, 1828–30), vol. IV, p. 102.
3 A.-N. Pigoreau, *Troisième supplément à la petite bibliographie biographico-romancière* (Paris: Pigoreau, 1822), p. v.
4 R. Bolster, Introduction to *Documents littéraires de l'époque romantique* (Paris: Minard, Lettres Modernes, 1983), p. 30.
5 G. W. F. Hegel, *Aesthetics*, trans. T. M. Knox (Oxford: Clarendon Press, 1974), vol. II, p. 1169.
6 H. Fortoul, cited in M. Iknayan, *The Idea of the Novel in France* (Geneva: Droz, 1961), p. 67.
7 Balzac, 'Avant-propos', *La Comédie humaine* (Paris: Gallimard, Bibliothèque de la Pléiade, 1976), vol. I, p. 11.
8 G. Planche, 'Les Royautés littéraires. Lettre à M. Hugo', *Revue des Deux Mondes*: 3.1 (1834), 533.
9 G. de Molènes, 'Le Roman actuel', *Revue des Deux Mondes*, 28 (1841), 1020.
10 Stendhal, 'Appendice sur *Le Rouge et noir* [sic]' (Paris: Garnier, 1957), p. 527.
11 L. de Surville, *Balzac, sa vie et ses œuvres d'après sa correspondance* (Paris: Librairie Nouvelle, 1858), p. 178.
12 A. Bussière, 'Les Romans de femmes', *Revue de Paris*, October 1843, p. 349.
13 M. Topin, *Romanciers contemporains* (Paris: Didier et Cie, 1881), p. 303.
14 See J. Richardson, *Judith Gautier* (New York: Franklin Watts, 1987), p. 64.
15 J. Bertaut, *La Littérature féminine d'aujourd'hui* (Paris: Librairie des Annales, 1909), pp. 1, 3.
16 E. Faguet, review of *Bijou* in *Cosmopolis*, 6 October 1896, 170, 172. Cited in W. Silverman, *The Notorious Life of Gyp* (New York: Oxford University Press, 1995), p. 258.

SUGGESTIONS FOR FURTHER READING

Apter, E., *Feminizing the Fetish* (Ithaca: Cornell University Press, 1991)
Cohen, M., *Why Were There No French Women Realists?* (Princeton: Princeton University Press, forthcoming)
Cohen, M. and C. Prendergast (eds.), *Spectacles of Realism: Body, Gender, Genre* (Minneapolis: University of Minnesota Press, 1995)
Goldberger, A. H. (ed.), *Woman as Mediatrix: Essays on Nineteenth-Century European Women Writers* (New York: Greenwood Press, 1987)

Gutwirth, M., *Madame de Staël, Novelist* (Urbana: University of Illinois Press, 1978)

Miller, N., *Subject to Change: Reading Feminist Writing* (New York: Columbia University Press, 1988)

Sartori, E. and D. Zimmerman (eds.), *French Women Writers: A Bio-Bibliographical Source Book* (New York: Greenwood Press, 1991)

Schor, N. *George Sand and Idealism* (New York: Columbia University Press, 1993)
    Breaking the Chain: Women, Theory and French Realist Fiction (New York: Columbia University Press, 1985)

Waller, M., *The Male Malady* (New Brunswick: Rutgers University Press, 1993)

5

DAVID COWARD

Popular fiction in the nineteenth century

'Popular' literature is valued because it gives direct access to the collective heartbeat. Cultural historians, formalists (who seek out its structures) and psycho-sociologists look to it to reveal the permanence of the communal experience. But literature which is popular has properties which, though definable, are too elusive to take any single shape. Cinderella, Robin Hood and Robinson Crusoe are all popular in different ways. The first is a folk myth sired by a Darwinian process of survival. The second is a folk hero shaped by anonymous hands out of a real life. The third is a character in a book written by an individual. Nineteenth-century France was familiar with all three types. 'Bonhomme Misère' – Poverty – survived in the cheap tracts hawked by pedlars known as *littérature de colportage*; Napoleon was turned into a new Charlemagne; and d'Artagnan was a legend in his creator's lifetime. But after 1800, popular literature began to acquire a new common denominator: it was transmitted by the printed page. No longer expressed by word of myth, it resumed its career in created fictions.

For three centuries, the chapbooks of the *bibliothèque bleue* (so called because they were bound in blue paper) continued to be more heard than read. They stood half way between the old oral tradition and a new written culture based on fixed forms and an organised system of transmission. Popular fiction in the nineteenth century was a by-product of the processes of urbanisation. The pressure for change came from below. Some upward movement is discernible in the late eighteenth century, but the Revolution of 1789 altered the image of the people who were henceforth a force to be reckoned with, to be revered or feared. Politicians would seek to court them, the Church to educate them, and intellectuals to improve them, while for business they were a potentially rich market. By 1900, 83 per cent of French men and women could read and write. They had grown accustomed to dealing with new ideas and they lived under a parliamentary regime. In this long process of democratisation, opinion and information were essential agents of change.

More and cheaper books were sold. Between 1812 and 1814, four to five thousand titles were published annually, a figure which rose to seven to eight thousand over the next thirty years, and stabilised at twelve or thirteen thousand between 1855 and 1914. In 1830, when manual workers earned 3 francs a day, an octavo volume sold for 7,50 francs. In 1838, Charpentier switched to the duodecimo format at 3 francs. Michel Lévy introduced the volume at 1 franc in 1855. By the 1880s, competition had driven this figure down further and the book selling for 13 sous (65 centimes) became standard within a decade. The growth of newspapers was even more dramatic. In 1824, the combined circulation of the Paris periodicals was 60,000, a figure which trebled by 1848. In 1865, using the new rotary press, *Le Petit Journal*, priced 1 sou, had a print-run of 256,000 and by 1886 it reached 1 million. In 1914, Parisians were buying 5 million newspapers every day.

New and increasingly aggressive methods were devised to take books to readers. During the Restoration, the idea of the *bibliothèque populaire* was floated and the Church set up the *Société des Bons Livres* in 1824. The aim of both was to counter the effects of *colportage* (the *bibliothèque bleue* survived until 1863) and the spread of cheap fiction, but neither prospered until the 1860s. Meanwhile, capitalist enterprise showed the way. Until 1855, when they were overtaken by cheaper alternatives, commercial lending libraries (the *cabinets de lecture*) hired out books – of which between 60 and 90 per cent were fiction – at 10 centimes per volume. In 1836, newspaper proprietors began taking advertising, cut their cover price and started to serialise novels, for the formula 'La suite au prochain numéro' boosted circulation dramatically. Novels published in episodes (*romans feuilletons*) dominated the 1840s, and thereafter nearly all fiction of all kinds was first published in instalments. After 1848, some magazines printed nothing but fiction, while most novels first appeared in periodic parts (the *livraison* and later the more ambitious *fascicule*), often illustrated, which were to be the major outlet for novelists after 1870.

However popular fiction is defined (by content, orientation or unreliable 'quality' criteria), the form it took in nineteenth-century France was a function of rising literacy, changing social patterns and the growth of the publishing industry. Readers remained unsophisticated and were happy with genre fictions produced mainly by middle-class authors who, with their dreams of literary glory dashed, paid their bills with tales written to order: working-class novelists were rare until the end of the century. Progress was slow and only by the end of the 1860s does the statistical record indicate the emergence of a mass market. If this market was supply-led, what was the nature of the demand and how did it evolve?

1800–1830

The French Revolution had discredited aristocratic taste and promoted cruder forms of expression which thereafter remained a part of the broader, less exclusive remit of literature. Excess found a natural home in the theatre. But though melodrama, as spectacle, was more accessible to a popular audience than the book, the novel continued to develop, drawing on the new but not abandoning the old. The extension of eighteenth-century sensibility, the violence and horror of the *roman noir*, and an interest in outsiders (exiles, *pícaros* and victims of injustice) all survived into the Empire and beyond. Women novelists (Mme de Guénard de Méré, Mme de Souza), usually with aristocratic connections and their sights on the literate public, wrote in unrosy terms of marriage, divorce and free love. Sophie Cottin (1770–1807) specialised in heroines (*Claire d'Albe* (1799), *Malvina* (1800)) riven by passion which conflicted with social constraints, ground also covered in a dozen statuesque novels by Sophie Gay (1776–1852). Like other women writers, Mme Gay followed the trend and took to the historical novel, relocating the same issues in other centuries or the more recent past: *Un Mariage sous l'Empire* (1832) dealt with the social and personal consequences of Napoleon's social engineering.

The licentiousness of the Directoire retreated before the puritanism of the 1800s but survived in milder forms. Aimed to titillate (the degree of bawdy may be judged by their titles), these risqué novels were usually the work of men (e.g. *Clémentine, orpheline androgyne*, by J.-P.-R Cuisin (b. 1777)) but not exclusively so. Between 1799 and 1824, the Comtesse de Choiseul-Meuse kept up a steady output of indelicate novels which included *Julie, ou j'ai sauvé ma rose* (1807). But the most enduring of the breed was the prolific Paul de Kock (1794–1871). His pictures of Parisian life amused France for half a century and, after 1843, he was one of the few novelists who successfully made the transition from the novel to the *feuilleton*. He wrote of *concièrges*, artisans, and amiable *rentiers* who pursue accommodating *grisettes*. Mildly bawdy rather than erotic, love here is never passionate but a kind of jousting. The tension derives from accidents and minor transgressions of the conservative middle-class moral code. Kock's tolerant, amused view of the world never went entirely out of fashion and, though often dismissed as fodder for 'concierges, cooks and ladies maids', his best novels (say, *Gustave ou le mauvais sujet* (1821)) appealed to a wide range of tastes and social classes and are still worth reading today for their realism and genuine humour. Kock was admired and, after 1830, much imitated. Two novelists, however, set bench-marks.

Pigault-Lebrun (1753–1835) developed a brand of below-stairs realism and social observation combined with dramatic adventures recounted at high speed. His first novel, *L'Enfant du carnaval* (1796), mixes autobiography, adventure and a virulent denunciation of the Terror. *Les Barons de Felsheim* (1798) and a stream of regularly reprinted novels pitted beleaguered lower-class heroes against foreign agents, convicts and evil men of right and left who oppress the vulnerable. For two generations, Pigault was read by the lower middle classes, servants, office-clerks, *modistes* and students. But while Pigault's cheerful realism was a reaction against both the sentimental and gothic trends, François-Guillaume Ducray-Duminil (1761–1819) (*Victor, ou l'Enfant de la forêt* (1796), *Cœlina, ou l'Enfant du mystère* (1798)) uncompromisingly followed Mrs Radcliffe, author of *The Romance of the Forest* (1791) and *The Mysteries of Udolpho* (1794). His heroes (who included children) face a world of brutes and knaves against a gothic backdrop spiced with injections of the supernatural. Innocence always emerges triumphant and vice and evil are invariably punished. Both Pigault-Lebrun and Ducray-Duminil found imitators into the 1860s and between them gave popular fiction an armoury of enduring clichés: murder, poison, foundlings, stratagems and spoils.

Until 1815, the novel avoided direct political comment, was fixated on love and eagerly embraced gothic themes and atmospheres. After the return of the Bourbons, it grew nostalgic for the old aristocracy and the 'noble' values of honour and duty. The lower middle classes moved up at the expense of the comfortable bourgeoisie which had gained most from the Revolution, and Pigault's resilient 'enfant du peuple' turned into a more sharply challenging figure. Such realignments were further reflected in the vogue for history. Between 1815 and 1832, a quarter of all novels were set in the past, a sign of a need to come to terms with change which had been a permanent feature of the French landscape since 1789. But it was also an early indication of the popularity of imported authors. Walter Scott may have packaged tradition and modernity in a manner which satisfied both bourgeois and aristocratic ideologies, and also, by 1829, provided a weapon for the liberal offensive. But for most readers Scott's novels, like those of Fenimore Cooper, were page-turners. Their high standing is reflected in the catalogues of the *cabinets de lecture* which kept readers of the 1820s supplied with authors old and new. There, Mme de Genlis and Mme Riccoboni rubbed shoulders with Mme Cottin, Mme de Souza, Mrs Radcliffe and of course Pigault-Lebrun and Ducray-Duminil.

By 1830, 'popular' fiction, though not yet available to a mass audience, had thrown down a challenge to the established cultural hegemony. Basic themes, moods, narrative strategies and stereotypes were firmly in place. It was already as responsive to foreign influences as it would be in subsequent generations which welcomed Harriet Beecher Stowe's *Uncle Tom's Cabin* in 1852, the countless *Robinsonnades* derived from Johann Wyss's *Robinson suisse* (1812), and Conan Doyle who, in the 1890s, helped redirect the embryonic *roman policier*. By the time France acquired a new king in 1830, the popular novel was stirring, revealing clear signs of the vigour and flexibility to come.

1830–1848

Until the rise of the *roman feuilleton* after 1836, popular fiction remained a hostage to the *cabinets de lecture* which dominated the market. It also minded its manners, for while the new regime was more liberal, it remained watchful. The *roman gai* in the manner of Kock was one safe area. Emile Cabanon's *Le Roman pour cuisinières* (1834) satisfied a clear demand for earthy dreams of love. Maximilien Perrin (1794–1879: sixty novels to 1856), a star of the *cabinets de lecture*, specialised in suggestive, anecdotal fictions, while Auguste Ricard (1799–1841) emerged as Kock's main rival for readers with a taste for slightly scabrous humour: the publication of *Monsieur Mayeux* (1831) was heralded by an unprecedented publicity campaign of posters and caricatures. Sentiment and adventure were also non-controversial, but most novels were *romans de mœurs* set in elegant drawing-rooms where dramas of money and adultery were played out. The staple conflict between noble hearts and cruel predators was resolved by duel, murder, suicide, madness and retribution. Patricians were admired, but there was no forgiveness for the nobleman who abused his rank to prey upon orphaned heiresses, widows and decent men fallen on bad times. The money-lender was now promoted to banker and, when not abusing trust and lining his pockets, expressed a high ideal of public service. The popularity of new middle-class types (the selfless doctor who attends the poor) improved the image of capitalism by an injection of practical philanthropy. The lower orders provided a respectful background against which the villainy and generosity of their betters could be judged. Though much was made of love, duty and honour, the motor of most society novels was money.

Sex, after a brief revival, made a poor showing. The late eighteenth century had marked the high point of the libertine novel. Controls were tightened throughout the Empire and the Restoration, but after 1830 restrictions were relaxed until the official overview of the book trade was strengthened in 1835. The Garnier brothers had taken advantage of the situation to publish licentious texts, though the modesty of their operation indicates that the demand for pornography was specialised rather than general. They continued to supply this small market discreetly and, after 1848, stepped up production until 1853 when, having decided to abandon this side of their business, they were prosecuted for obscenity. Popular novels were thereafter to deal sensationally with sex (rape, abortion) but never overtly. The evidence suggests that the cause was not the anti-obscenity measures but enduring popular conservatism.

In any case, there were ample opportunities for sexual thrills in safer contexts. The taste for local colour combined with France's new colonial ambitions revived the sensual exoticism of the perennial Bernardin de Saint-Pierre. Dumas's *Georges* (1843) revisited Mauritius and Soulié chose the West Indies for *Le Bananier* (1843). But it was Joseph Méry (1798–1867) who opened the largest windows on foreign parts. Of his forty novels, the most successful were his well-documented tales set in far-flung places. His 'Indian' trilogy began with *Héva* (1840) which packaged a story of impossible love with local colour (tigers), natural history (baobabs) and anthropology (religious practices), and put forward a specific view of colonial development: the future of mankind lay in mixed marriages which alone would secure the union of the races.

But for most readers, the exotic was less a place than a province of the mind: it was to be found close to home, in the gothic, in social fictions and, increasingly, in the past. The new literary Romantics took readily to history though only Hugo's *Notre-Dame de Paris* (1831) held the kind of mass appeal which was to triumph in the 1840s in the *roman feuilleton*. In the hands of the *feuilletonistes*, fiction began to widen its hold on the popular imagination. Frédéric Soulié (1800–47) wrote sombre, sensational novels (*Les Deux cadavres* (1832)) before turning to a sequence of *Romans historiques du Languedoc*. But he was to find stupendous fame as a mainstay of the *Journal des Débats* which serialised *Les Mémoires du diable* (1837–8). Taking the Faustian bargain with the Devil as his starting point, Soulié blended the fantastic with tales of murder, rape and macabre mayhem culled from newspaper reports. Charles Bernard (1804–50) had also begun as a historical chronicler before turning out highly coloured novels of contemporary life featuring more or less innocent convicts, adulteresses, aristocratic persecutors and pure victims.

Alexandre Dumas (1802–70) also wrote of convicts, prisons and vengeance (*Le Comte de Monte Cristo* (1844–6)), but was no less famous for reviving the swash-buckling derring-do of the *roman de cape et d'épée*. He divided humanity into roundheads (Richelieu, Mazarin, Colbert) and cavaliers (Monte Cristo, d'Artagnan and himself), the first symbolising the creeping bureaucracy of modern life and the second individualism, male friendship and freedom. Dumas was not merely a master story-teller, but carried an indirect political charge. He gave ordinary French men and women a highly tendentious view of their history which he used as a stick to beat the present. His huge readership identified closely with his dashing heroes who reject the shabby delays of real life and solve all problems with a thrust of a flashing blade. Dumas politicised good and evil and mytholo-gised the hero.

It has been estimated that he wrote 650 novels and plays featuring 4,056 main characters, 8,872 minor characters and 24,339 walk-on parts. It is a measure of the monstrous scale of the *roman feuilleton* in the 1840s which is further illustrated by Dumas's main rival, Eugène Sue (1804–57). Sue invented the French sea-faring story (*Atar-Gull* (1831)), then moved on to the *roman de mœurs* (*Mathilde* (1841)) and the historical novel (*Jean Cavalier* (1840)). But his growing socialist sympathies added a new dimension to his *feuilletons*. *Les Mystères de Paris* (1842–3) is a vast, unplanned narrative which Sue (who readily incorporated suggestions made by readers) was happy to extend for as long as demand held up. Rodophe de Géroldstein is a Prince in disguise who, to expiate a crime against his father, wanders through the violent, crime-ridden, precarious lives of the Paris poor righting wrongs, rescuing the innocent and punishing the wicked. *Le Juif errant* (1844–5) relates at inordinate length how the descendants of the Wandering Jew reassemble the family fortune dispersed by the Jesuits. Sue's political influence was more direct than that of Dumas. His reservations about capitalism and his championing of the underprivi-leged advanced the cause of socialism significantly, though Marx disap-proved of him as a paternalistic conservative who made social justice the business not of just laws but of private enterprise. He lacked the ability of Hugo or Dumas to create myths (Jean Valjean and d'Artagnan live on) and he has dated badly. But Sue, an early media star, raised the political consciousness of several generations and is one of the few popular novelists who have helped to change the world.

In 1848, novels in book or serialised form were still too expensive to reach the mass of the people who bought nine million chapbooks from hawkers and pedlars in 1847. Nevertheless, between 1830 and 1848, popular fiction took significant steps towards a wider public by allying itself to the newspaper. It consolidated its hold on the gothic, the fantastic and above all history, and established itself in a number of new areas, notably the exotic at home and abroad. The lower classes, no longer portrayed simply as dangerous criminals or helpless victims, had begun to come of age.

1848–1870

During the July Monarchy, novelists, while remaining snobbishly attached to aristocratic values, had exploited the dramatic potential of the new, upwardly mobile middle class. Throughout the Second Empire, they continued to pay homage to patrician tone but responded even more positively to accelerating social change. The growth of the enterprise culture furnished new stereotypes (the banker was now a capitalist) and new situations (the fortune made or lost by speculation and fraud), while class realignments led to endless variations on the marriage of noble name with middle-class money and the purloined inheritance (always restored). Scientific positivism and technological progress replaced the Philosopher/ Sage by the Rationalist and the Inventor, and the Hero lost ground to a more defensive individualism. The rural exodus stimulated an early interest in the regional novel (George Sand (1804–76), Emile Souvestre (1806–50)) which was to gain ground after 1870. Rising urbanisation also confirmed the vein of post-Sue social romanticism: the historical novels of Clémence Robert (1797–1873) kept one foot in the present and breathed socialist and Republican ideals, while Hugo's Jean Valjean (*Les Misérables* (1862)) showed that even the most marginalised citizen can be redeemed. The growth of the City also made the human problems of poverty (sentimenta-lised or otherwise sanitised according to the requirements of taste) a marketable subject for fiction. Thus Henri Murger (1822–61), with *Scènes de la vie de bohème* (1851) and *Les Buveurs d'eau* (1853–4), fixed the image of the struggling artist and the impoverished student oppressed by a philistine society. The courtesan who sacrifices all to love was definitively established in *La Dame aux camélias* (1848) by Dumas fils (1824–95). Sex was relegated to the safe area of the *demi-monde* (by Dumas and Adolphe Belot) or legitimised as honest bawdy.

But although the novel of contemporary manners gained ground, its stereotypes and preoccupations remained rooted in a strict hierarchy of class values. Idealised lives of the gentry exerted a considerable fascination. Haughty aristocrats of both sexes safeguarded tradition; younger sons abused trust to finance their pleasures; poetic young women were torn between love and duty; handsome young men, with hearts nobler, alas, than their birth, staked all for love; wily lawyers oiled wheels; and retainers remained loyal. Drama was supplied by passion, betrayal and the social barrier. Settings (rich interiors and manicured parks) offered readers easier access to the high life than to many heroes. In *Mademoiselle de La Seiglière* (1848), Jules Sandeau (1811–83) does not allow Bernard to marry Hélène though he has a nobler heart than the better born but arrogant Raoul. If

Maxime, hero of *Le Roman d'un jeune homme pauvre* (1858) by Octave Feuillet (1821–90), wins Marguerite, it is because he is socially suitable, being poor only in the sense that his family's fortunes were lost by unwise speculation. The same terrain was covered by writers as diverse as Virginie Ancelot (1792–1875) who defended love against the new predators, or the edifying Hector Malot (1830–1907), who prescribed religion and honour as solutions to the problems of thwarted passion. Others portrayed women in a harsher light. The sensitive hero of Ernest Feydeau's *Fanny* (1858) describes himself as a 'forçat de l'amour' ['a slave to love'], for Fanny toys with his affections and we leave him pondering suicide.

These genteel fictions all show the old society standing firm and admitting the new money only on its own terms. But other kinds of novels, while underwriting social and moral conservatism, crossed class boundaries in a number of areas. Proto-feminists such as Clémence Robert or Marie Aycard (1794–1854) demanded a better deal for women and justice for girls who were seduced and abandoned. But male authors remained unconvinced and continued to portray women according to a manipulative formula which most female readers seemed prepared to accept. There were three basic archetypes: the wife and mother (admirable and unthreatening to men), the pure, inaccessible virgin/goddess (a source of male idealism and poetry) and the *femme fatale* who, from the courtesan to the *mangeuse d'hommes*, was a danger to a society predicated on money, marriage and respectability. But in other kinds of fiction, outsiders and upstarts were measured by different standards.

At a time when urban crime began to soar, Emile Gaboriau (1832–73) judged individuals in legal terms. His novels (beginning with *L'Affaire Lerouge* (1866)) drew on the enduring notoriety of Vidocq (*Mémoires* (1828)) and coincided with the rise of the 'presse à un sou', or penny press, aimed at a working-class readership. Gaboriau's hero, le père Tabaret (called 'Tirauclair') and his disciple, Lecocq, are the ancestors of the French detective, though their methods depend less on detection than on their analysis of the psychology of the criminal. But though Gaboriau, founder of the *roman judiciaire*, is more significant historically, he did not match the astounding success of the Vicomte Ponson du Terrail (1829–71), the undisputed master of the Second Empire *feuilleton* and author of 101 sprawling novels. Carelessly written at a furious pace (at one point he was writing five serials simultaneously, the equivalent of 10,000 pages a year), they are remarkable for the way in which they involved the public. Ponson was the creator of Joseph Fipart, *alias* Rocambole, who begins as a thief, expiates his crimes through a series of redeeming trials, and returns, a master of disguise, a formidable mix of criminal and avenger. Ponson adopted suggestions sent in by readers who corrected his many mistakes and asked him to kill off unpleasant characters, though it was the editor of *La Patrie* who ordered him to resuscitate Rocambole whom he had ill-advisedly allowed to die in *Les Chevaliers du clair de lune* (1862). Ponson resorted shamelessly to established stereotypes and clichés – brothers who are enemies, honest workmen falsely accused, virginal heroines who must be saved, secret societies, powerful narcotics, secret passages – but from 1859 until 1870 he thrilled his readers with the *Drames de Paris*, a vast cycle of 'rocambolesque' adventure novels.

A similar brand of individualism marks the various kinds of exotic novel which, intruding into the territory of the fantastic, ranged from tales of vampires (Ponson, Pierre Féval) to the first romances of Jules Verne (1828–1905) which promoted the new figure of the scientist and explorer for whom class mattered less than boldness. *Cinq semaines en ballon* (1863) inaugurated a series of yarns which involved marvellous machines and journeys around the world, inside the earth, to the poles and beyond the stars. Edmond About (1828–84) wrote conventional sentimental fiction and social novels on the theme of partnership between capital and labour, from *Maître Pierre* (1858) to *Le Roman d'un brave homme* (1880) which taught generations of schoolchildren (who were given it as a prize) how to be good workers, good employers and good citizens. However, About is best remembered now for *Le Roi des montagnes* (1857), an exciting tale of capture by Greek bandits. This kind of adventure story (savages, precipices, hairsbreadth escapes) was the stock-in-trade of Gustave Aimard (1818–83). He wrote first about pirates but became immensely popular for transposing Fenimore Cooper into French. Most of his fifty-two novels (beginning with *Les Trappeurs de l'Arkansas* (1858)) were set in what was known as 'le Far West' and feature high adventure, scalping and uplifting moral messages which included a definite stance on colonialism. Red Indians – noble but inferior – have been corrupted by contact with Europeans and, to correct past mistakes, Aimard called for large-scale emigrations of decent French families to California. The vogue for Aimard continued into the twentieth century and reflected the new myth of America as a land of wealth and opportunity.

Meanwhile, the historical novel increased its hold over readers and accounted for about half the *feuilletons* published during Second Empire. Dumas and Hugo, still active, were joined by Amédée Achard (1814–75), the prolix Emmanuel Gonzalès (*Les Sept Baisers de Buckingham* (1858)) and especially Paul Féval (1816–87) who had mounted a serious challenge to Sue with *Les Mystères de Londres* in 1844. As popular as About and Feuillet, and second only to Ponson, he made his name with *Le Bossu*

(1857) which tells how, during the Regency, the dashing Lagardère disguises himself as a hunchback and tracks down the murderer of the Duc de Nevers. Féval inserted his characters neatly into history, as Dumas had done, and in his Breton cycle introduced legends into the *roman feuilleton*. A former secretary to Gaboriau, he attempted crime fiction with great success in *Les Habits noirs* (1863), based on a real gang which had terrorised Paris in the 1840s. Féval, author of some 200 titles, was one of the rare authors to make an impact through the new municipal *bibliothèques populaires*. Students, apprentices, workmen, middle-class men and ladies of fashion all clamoured for well-crafted action novels. Even better written were the often semi-documentary 'romans nationaux' of Erckman-Chatrian (pseudonym of Emile Erckman (1822–99) and Alexandre Chatrian (1826–90)). Usually set in Alsace-Lorraine, their understated tales bring to life France's past (*Histoire d'un conscrit de 1813* (1864), *Waterloo* (1865)) from the point of view of the ordinary Frenchman. Their modest protagonists are very different from the swash-bucklers of Dumas and Féval and they anticipate the decline of the hero after 1870.

For despite the popularity of outsiders like Rocambole, Lagardère and the intrepid heroes of About and Aimard, the pressures to conform to the moral and social code were strong. The tendency is particularly marked in books intended for the young who in, the 1850s, were identified as a valuable new public. Serials and collections were aimed at girls, boys, schools and families. By the 1860s, Hetzel dominated the market, recruiting authors of high standing like Erckman-Chatrian and Jules Verne for his successful periodical, *Le Magasin d'éducation et de récréation,* which placed the emphasis on the 'instructive and dramatic' tale. The score of novels written between 1856 and 1869 by the Comtesse de Ségur (1799–1874), a pillar of Hachette's 'Bibliothèque rose', have narrative drive and an eye for the comic, but the Comtesse schooled the new generation very firmly.

To a large extent, popular fiction was self-regulated, largely because the authorities now kept a close watch on its progress. Free of official interference to about 1820, it was thereafter subject to the kind of controls designed to contain *colportage*. The late Restoration was notoriously illiberal: it imprisoned Victor Ducange (1783–1833) for publishing *Valentine, ou le Pasteur d'Uzès* (1820) which had denounced the brutal repression of opponents of the Bourbon Restoration, known as the White Terror, in the Midi in 1815. Among *cabinet de lecture* books labelled 'dangerous' for either their liberal opinions or 'obscene' content were Pigault's *Enfant du Carnaval*, Raban's *Mon cousin Mathieu* and various titles by Cuisin. Left largely to police itself during the July Monarchy, it increasingly drew the eye of the authorities after 1852. Some action was taken on political grounds: Sue was allowed to serialise *Les Mystères du peuple* (1849–57) but not to publish it as a book. But in the main, breaches of the sexual code drew the strongest official fire. The Goncourts, Flaubert and Baudelaire were not the only casualties. In 1853, one of the Garnier brothers was jailed for publishing obscene books. In 1855, Xavier de Montépin was taken to court for *Les Filles de Plâtre* as was Adolphe Belot (1829–90) when *Le Figaro* refused to continue serialising *Mademoiselle Guiraud, ma femme* (1870). Popular novelists were alert to the dangers and, since they wrote for money not art (like Maupassant, who in 1879 narrowly escaped prosecution for publishing an obscene poem), were careful to avoid offending. There were occasional lapses, as when Oscar Méténier, author of *Madame la Boule* (1890) was found guilty of outraging public morality. But writers who sought notoriety by venturing into the taboo area of sex were careful not to overstep the mark. By the end of the century, the boundaries of acceptability had been pushed back, but popular novelists rarely adopted the frank approach.

By 1870, the gap between serious fiction and popular novels (available in increasingly cheap forms) had widened dramatically. But popular fiction itself was separating into discrete constituencies. The middle-brow *roman de mœurs* was solidly crafted, intellectually pretentious and often over-written, its literary ambitions a reflection of its social snobbery. On the other hand, the *feuilleton* was hastily written but, when not overburdened with clichés, more inventive and dynamic, more concerned with action than with analysing feelings or maintaining the bourgeois code.

1870–1890

After 1870, the clichés of popular fiction become institutionalised across the whole range. The action novel featured ghosts, secret passages, spiritualism, catatonic trances and pass words. In the novel of manners, virtue is persecuted and honour is constantly under threat: the decent bourgeois is opposed by unscrupulous rivals and class prejudice, aristocratic families are under siege from vulgar money, the honest workman fights against betrayal or the poverty that is his fate, and women, torn between love and duty, are martyred in droves. It is a world of extreme values (love/hate, good/evil, greed/altruism) and starkly drawn character-types (good woman/courtesan, good bourgeois/swindler, good workman/thief). The new stock characters were modernised versions of older stereotypes. The avenger now reunites separated lovers or warring families, the betrayer becomes the unscrupulous rival, the dandy a gentleman-crook, the good cleric a sinister intriguer and the *femme fatale* a schemer, the bourgeois a considerate employer but more often a swindler or war-profiteer or land speculator. Orphans still go in search of an identity and inheritances are vigorously contested. Men fall in love with class enemies and the link between seduction and money strengthens further. To tuberculosis, the standard literary disease, are added madness and neurasthenia, and a proper dénouement exposes wickedness, thus allowing villains to be punished, fortunes to be restored to their rightful owners, class differences to yield to love, courtesans to be redeemed by good men, and rakes to reform. Few popular novels could afford to deny these conventions.

After 1870, there was a vogue for the military novel which turned jingoistic in the *roman revanchard* of, for instance, Pierre Decourcelle (1856–1926). In calling for revenge ('revanche') for the loss of Alsace-Lorraine in the Franco-Prussian war, such fictions were narrowly conservative and reflected a more general retreat into defensive positions. Freemasons, Germans and Jews received a bad press, while industrialists and financiers improved their image. Jules Boulabert (1830–87) was one the rare novelists to defend the Communards. Jules Vallès (1832–85) was another (*L'Insurgé* (1882)). Vallès also took up trade-union issues (*Les Blouses* (1880)) which were to have a higher profile in the 1890s. Challenges to the dominant conservatism were mounted from time to time by the anticlerical left (Michel Morphy (1863–1928), Léo Taxil (1854–1907)), while in the 1880s Vallès's autobiographical Jacques Vingtras trilogy carries a distinct revolutionary charge. Women novelists raised contentious issues, such as divorce, and Marie-Louise Gagneur (1837–1902) made the case for improving the lot of working women and drew attention to legal inequalities: *Les Droits du mari* (1876) dramatised the murder, legal under the Code Civil, of an adulterous wife by her husband.

Anti-liberal, anti-republican novelists like René de Pont-Jest (1830–1894) were at home in the mainstream *roman de mœurs* which turned in on itself, wallowing in sentiment and happy endings. Readers were spoiled for choice. Xavier de Montépin (1823–1902), a favourite of the Second Empire, came into his own again (*La Porteuse de pain* (1885)). Emile Richebourg (1833–98), another survivor, scored his greatest success with *L'Enfant du faubourg* (1876) and continued to make a new generation of middle-class women weep thereafter. Jules Mary (1850–1922) published some eighty novels in various inks but specialised in melodramatic sentiment aimed specifically at 'les honnêtes gens' who learned that honour can inspire even humble hearts (*Roger-la-Honte* (1887)). The same middle-class public was drawn to Charles Mérouvel (1832–1920) (*Chaste et flétrie*, 1894) and Georges Ohnet (1848–1918) whose series *Les Batailles de la vie* (33 vols.) includes *Le Maître de Forges* (1882) and *Serge Panine* (1881), the best sellers of the decade. In such hands, the society novel, well-constructed, snobbish in tone and mawkish in manner, often spiced with elements of the *roman judiciaire*, continued to dominate fiction between 1870 and 1890.

While the centre of gravity of popular fiction remained Paris, the elegance associated with country estates and, from the publishers' point of view, the growing provincial readership, helped boost an interest in regionalism. Regional writers such as Ferdinand Fabre (1827–98) and Léon Cladel (1835–92) stressed traditional country values of permanence and submission to the elemental, often mystical forces of nature. Simple lives were described in a variety of tones, from the sentimental to the caricatural, but normally from the condescending perspective of the townsman. A more personal note was struck by *Le Petit Chose* (1869) of Alphonse Daudet (1840–97), a vein of personal reminiscence also mined by Paul Arène (1843–96) in *Jean des Figues* (1868). Both took Provence to a Parisian readership, though not without cost. Daudet's Tartarin and *Maurin des Maures* (the larger-than-life creation of Jean Aicard (1848–1921)) helped shape the popular image of *mériodional* boastfulness. In the hands of the regional writers, traditional France was a safe place.

The conservative mood was reinforced by the Church which remained committed to resisting the forces of irreligion. The *Société des Bons Livres* was founded in 1824 and, from various provincial centres, had produced 5,000 improving titles by 1875. It rose as *colportage* fell and it fed moral uplift into periodicals (*L'Ouvrier* (1861) and especially *Les Veillées des Chaumières* (1877)), *livraisons* and collections which showed honesty rewarded and drunkards reclaimed by *curés,* though they were not above including hair-raising accounts of the tortures of those persecuted by enemies of Catholicism. The spiritual needs of the faithful, soldiers, invalids and the young were supplied by both women (Marie Emery (1816–89), Victorine Monniot (1825–80)) and men like Paul Verdun (b.1861) who also took the opportunity to denounce international finance, Jews and freemasons.

The conformist spirit which marks the fiction of the early Third Republic was not seriously incommoded by working-class novelists like Alexis Bouvier (1836–92) or the republican, anticlerical Benjamin Gastineau (b.1832). On the contrary it was reinforced on a number of fronts. Novels for children were no less didactic and heavily moralistic, as in the case of Zénaïde Fleuriot (1829–90) who wrote eighty-three novels, mostly for

Hachette's juvenile collections. Even *Sans famille* (1878), the enduring classic children's book by Hector Malot, which tells how the foundling Rémi finds a place in society, was fundamentally reassuring. The same comfortable message was underlined in the *roman judiciaire* by the heirs of Gaboriau: Fortuné de Boisgobé (1821–91), Pierre Zaccone (1817–95) and Eugène Chavette (1827–1902). Although judicial errors abound to the point of casting doubt on the competence of the legal system, the obligatory happy ending invariably restored order, created a healthy fear of the police, respect for authority and made it plain that power lay not with the individual avenger but with the state.

In the 1880s, popular fiction, unhampered by imagination or invention, seemed shackled by traditional forms and preoccupations. Closing the door on new ideas and experiment, it offered models of goodness and charity and underwrote conservative retrenchment. However, publishers made systematic efforts to expand the market, launching publicity campaigns for new *feuilletons,* creating more Collections, and attempting to take their wares into country areas. The spread of education after Jules Ferry's reforms contributed significantly to expanding the readership which grew younger and, in time, demanded a more varied diet.

1890–1914

With the unfolding of the Belle Epoque, the self-satisfied tone gave ground to a new spirit of modest anarchy. While the *roman de mœurs* remained safe in the hands of novelists like René Boyslève (1867–1926) and Henri Bordeaux (1870–1963), it acquired a more daring image with the prolific Gyp (1850–1932), who specialised in the liberated young woman, and her main rival Rachilde (1860–1953), who investigated morbid sexuality in line with the interest in the fashionable 'pathological' study (for further discussion of Rachilde, see the next chapter, pp. 101–7) and the psychological novels of Paul Bourget (1852–1935). Marcel Prévost (1862–1941) also analysed women, to the point of scandal. Marcelle Tinayre (1872–1948) raised sentimental and moral problems from a feminist perspective while the Claudine novels of Colette (1873–1954) provided role models for the non-conforming modern girl.

The appetite for stronger meat is further reflected in the growth of xenophobic depictions of Germans, Jews and international financiers, the grim social study in the Naturalist style, the resounding success of *Le Journal d'une femme de chambre* (1900) in which Octave Mirbeau (1850–1917) exposed the shams of high society, and in a shift in the interest taken in foreign parts which now moved away from the thrilling

Africa of Louis Noir, the American romances of Gustave Aimard and the travelogues of Pierre Loti, towards a harder anticolonial and antimilitarist stance. While Claude Farrère (1876–1957) wrote blandly of the Far East, harder-edged authors expressed reservations about France's overseas empire, from Hector France (1840–1908), who wrote critically of his Algerian service, to Henri Daguerche (*Le Kilomètre 83* (1913)), who questioned official policies in Indochina. But none was as ferocious as Georges Darien (1862–1921) who denounced brutality in North Africa (*Biribi*, 1890) and the class bias of the army (*L'Epaulette*, 1905).

A comparable shift is visible in the regional novel which began to lose its genteel image as peasants and country people began to tell their own stories. The hero of *Jacquou le croquant* (1899) is a rebel used by Eugène Le Roy (1836–1907) to advance the case for socialism. Emile Guillaumin (1873–1953), less politically committed, expressed a strong sense of social injustice in *La Vie d'un simple* (1904), a dignified chronicle of country life. Guillaumin was one of a growing band of struggling, self-taught or newly educated writers who wrote directly of working-class experience and punctured middle-class assumptions.

A similar retreat from reassuring stereotypes occurred in the *roman judiciaire* which, rejuvenated by the vogue for Sherlock Holmes and the well-publicised use of new scientific police methods, began its transformation into the *roman policier*. Gaston Leroux (1868–1927), author of *Le Mystère de la chambre jaune* (1907), the most famous of the 'sealed-chamber' stories, now launched the journalist-sleuth Rouletabille on a very long career. Maurice Leblanc (1864–1941) gave Arsène Lupin, the amateur cracksman, the first of many outings in 1904. The new hero (like Leroux's *Fantôme de l'Opéra* (1910)) was frequently an individualist contemptuous of authority, whose relationship with the law was ambiguous. There was no doubt, however, about the standing of Fantomas, the evil genius created by Marcel Allain (1886–1969) and Pierre Souvestre (1874–1914), who by 1914 had achieved cult status. He stood outside the law, a figure of mystery and menace who symbolised the retreat from the quietism in which popular fiction had long slumbered.

Fantomas, like Judex, the masked avenger created by Arthur Bernède (1871–1937), was a version of the dashing Romantic hero who, since the 1850s, had been sacrificed to sentiment and respectability. There were signs of his revival elsewhere. Dumas had never quite gone out of fashion and after his death sales of his historical novels soared and were much imitated, notably by Paul Malahin and Jules Lermina. Indeed, the last author to make his name as a *feuilletoniste* was Michel Zévaco (1860–1918), who brought the sixteenth century to life. His cycle of novels, *Les Pardaillan*, which began appearing in 1902, was a saga of revenge and betrayal and the huge fees it earned him were a clear indication of the reviving fortunes of the spectacular hero.

The new spirit also spread to books for children. Authors who could interest and educate remained in demand: Mme Alfred Fouillée's ('G. Bruno') *Le Tour de France par deux enfants* (1877) had sold 6 million copies by 1900. But while some novelists like Paul (1860–1918) and Victor (1866–1942) Margueritte could still patronise the young (e.g. *Poum* (1897)), Jules Ferry's schoolchildren preferred more exciting and less didactic fare. The first comics appeared in the 1890s and Paul d'Ivoi (1856–1915) scored a huge success with an around-the-world story, *Les Cinq sous de Lavarède,* in 1894. Children were at last allowed to exist as individuals in their own right and the world of the child was explored autobiographically by Anatole France (from *Le Livre de mon ami* (1885) to *Le Petit Pierre* (1919)) and Jules Renard (1864–1910) (*Poil de Carotte* (1894)), hauntingly by Alain-Fournier (*Le Grand Meaulnes* (1913)), and imaginatively by Louis Pergaud (1882–1915) in *La Guerre des boutons* (1912).

But children increasingly graduated to kinds of fiction not expressly written for them. If they now appropriated crime fiction and the 'Far West', they had long been at home with the fantastic. Throughout the century the *roman d'anticipation* combined time-shifts with a serious reflection on mankind and society. What had been a thoughtful, satirical, socialist trickle aimed at adults (Jean-Baptiste Cousin de Grainville's *Le Dernier Homme* (1805), Geoffroy's *Napoléon et la conquête du monde* (1836), Etienne Cabet's socialist fantasy, *Voyage en Icarie* (1842)) gathered ground with Jules Verne, whose enduring popularity began in the 1860s, and turned finally into a flood of adventure yarns which replaced traditional children's fantasies with the miracles of science. Rosny aîné (1856–1940) journeyed into pre-history (*Les Xipéhuz* (1887), *La Guerre du feu* (1911)), Camille Flammarion (*Uranie* (1889)) took up space travel as did Jean de la Hire (*Prisonniers de la planète Mars* (1908)). The 'science' novel, which strayed into Egyptology and seized on death-rays, vampires and the oneiric possibilities of the new psychiatry, captured the juvenile market. Here were individualism and private enterprise transposed into an apolitical, classless setting. Here too the old Romantic hero weighed down by fate emerges as master of his destiny. But such tales also sounded a warning. Dr Cornelius, brainchild of Gustave Lerouge (1867–1939), was one of many deranged geniuses who set out to rule the word. The mad scientist thus linked arms with the master criminal. Men of stern purpose might halt them, but their real power undermined the old settled world-view and reflected the uncertainties of the new century which, in the aftermath of the Dreyfus affair, stood on the verge of a new age of conflict at home and abroad.

By 1914, the printed word was not so much available as unavoidable. The general readership was huge and it grazed willingly on the inexpensive 'roman à treize sous' and the ubiquitous *feuilleton*. Popular fiction had separated into recognisable subgenres: the genteel *roman de mœurs*, the historical novel, romantic sentiment, risqué fiction, the adventure yarn, the *roman de la science*, detection, and the socially contentious novel. Readers too divided into distinct but overlapping categories which are perhaps best thought of as loose 'followings'. The following for sentiment, though predominantly female, crossed age, sex and class lines, while Pardaillon or Rouletabille thrilled and stirred adolescents old and young in cottage and castle. Fantomas fascinated Apollinaire, Cocteau and Cendrars. A whole new generation cut its literary teeth on popular novels. Pagnol read Gustave Aimard alongside Virgil. In *Les Mots* (Paris: Gallimard, 1964, pp. 57–60), Sartre recalled that his 'premières rencontres avec la Beauté' derived not from the 'phrases balancées de Chateaubriand' but from the 'boîtes magiques' opened by Paul d'Ivoi, Arnold Galopin and Jean de la Hire.

Such boundary-crossing allegiances were not new. True, in 1839 Sainte-Beuve dismissed the kind of 'industrial' literature which later softened Emma Bovary's brain, and many others subsequently endorsed his stance. But Thackeray recommended Charles Bernard to English readers as a wholesome alternative to Balzac who had begun his career with pot-boilers and was thought to be not very different from Sue. Stendhal chose Pigault to take to his desert island and Kock delighted writers as different as Chateaubriand and Vallès. Lamartine and Hugo held Dumas in high regard, and Mérimée admired Ponson. Moreover, 'literary' novelists were influenced by their better-selling rivals. Balzac's *La Peau de chagrin* (1831) is an early instance of how popular themes (in this case, the fantastic) entered serious fiction, and there is a case for arguing that the success of Naturalism stemmed from the decision by self-consciously literary writers such as Zola and Maupassant to take the fight to the *roman feuilleton* by challenging it on its own sombre ground.

But for all its diversity of types, themes and growing sophistication, popular fiction never outgrew the taste, established during the French Revolution, for the *mélodrame* and the *roman noir*. Its natural habitat was the elementary and classless human response to two extreme stimuli, violence and pathos, suitably packaged to be thrilling but unthreatening. It projected a sanitised transcript of life which was easier to read than everyday reality. Here, people were visibly good or bad and their actions unambiguously right or wrong. Stock characters endlessly repeated their roles in stereotyped situations until the formulaic dénouement resolved the invariably manichean conflict by showing the triumph of virtue over vice. For popular literature provided reassurance: reading meant travelling along a familiar road which, however dangerous, led inescapably to a return to a safe moral order. If the literary novel disturbed, experimented, reflected reality and pursued human truths through individual destinies, popular fiction recycled its own clichés, reflected only itself and traded in the more comfortable collective illusions. It was a literature not of discovery but of recognition.

Paradoxically, such fictions were 'popular' only in a restricted sense. They rarely spoke of the people to the people. Most novelists were middle class and they took as their norms the manners and values of the higher social strata. They were also pale imitators of their literary betters, yet many were competent artificers who made few concessions, in terms of syntax, vocabulary or cultural references, to the Common Man, whose time had not yet come. Of course, they stand accused of being the tools of capitalism, and their novels of being manufactured products aimed at the lowest profitable denominator. But they discharged the essential function of popular literature – to save Red Riding Hood and kill the wolf – by expressing the inner yearnings and protecting the social identity of the reader. Readers loved and avenged vicariously, but they also found confirmation both of the Christian message of Heaven, Hell and redemption and of the necessary (but untenable) propositions that in this life justice is done, wickedness is punished, all are equal and that the weak can triumph over the strong. Popular fiction was a source of personal and collective reassurance. It gave a content to the notion of 'le peuple', defined France for the French and helped citizens of all classes to know who they were. It may have been an economically engineered product, but it discharged the time-honoured duty of popular culture by underpinning and directing the unambiguous, self-confident, communifying spirit without which no nation can function.

SUGGESTIONS FOR FURTHER READING

Histoire de l'édition française, sous la direction de H.-J. Martin et R. Chartier, 4 vols. (Paris: Promodis, 1983–6), vol. III: *Le Temps des éditeurs*
'Le Roman feuilleton', *Europe,* no. 542, June 1974

Martin-Olivier, Y., *Histoire du roman populaire en France de 1840 à 1980* (Paris: Albin Michel, 1980)

Mollier, J.-Y., *Michel et Calmann Lévy, ou la naissance de l'édition moderne 1836–1891* (Paris: Calmann Lévy, 1984)

L'Argent et les lettres: Histoire du capitalisme d'édition 1880–1920 (Paris: Fayard, 1988)

Nathan, M., *Anthologie du roman populaire, 1836–1918* (Paris, Union Générale d'Editions, collection 10/18, 1985)

Parent-Lardeur, F., *Les Cabinets de lecture. La Lecture publique à Paris sous la Restauration* (Paris: Payot, 1982)

Todd, C., *A Century of Best-Sellers (1890–1990)* (Lewiston, Queenston and Lampeter: Edwin Mellen, 1994)

6

LAURENCE M. PORTER

Decadence and the *fin-de-siècle* novel

From a historical standpoint, the metaphor of 'decadence' implies that art and society must age, decline, and die like a human body. Prestigious dramatisations by Baudelaire (for example in 'La Géante' of *Les Fleurs du mal*, 1857) and Laforgue, as later by Eliot, Toynbee and Spengler, perpetuated this notion. One cannot limit considerations of decadence to the novel or to France: decadence was an international intellectual current that left its mark on historiography, philosophy, poetry, drama, prose fiction and the visual arts throughout Western Europe and England.

In history, the degeneracy of French society seemed to have been foreshadowed by the decline and fall of the ancient Roman and Byzantine Empires. In these empires, moral decay had led to military defeats that recalled the humiliating rout of the French armies in the recent Franco-Prussian War (1870), and the three-month takeover of Paris by the revolutionary Commune in 1871. The self-selected title of 'Second Empire' (1851–70) for the government of Louis Napoléon, himself a pale reflection of Napoleon I, invited comparisons with Imperial Rome. Afterwards, France tried to live down its shame. The spectacular Basilica of the Sacré-Cœur (constructed between 1875 and 1914) stands today on Montmartre as a monument of national expiation and as an expression of the will to moral renewal after 1870.

Philosophy contributed to the idea of decadence the popularised forms of the pessimistic philosophies of Schopenhauer and Hartmann, leading to the creation of fictional characters engulfed in *delectatio morbosa* (morbid delectation).[1] The priest in Chateaubriand's *René* (1801) had already so identified *le mal du siècle*. But whereas the Romantic *mal du siècle* involved brooding over one's fate, the decadents also contemplated committing destructive and self-destructive acts from sheer boredom. In 'Au lecteur', the initial poem of *Les Fleurs du mal*, Baudelaire anticipated this spiritual malady with his allegorical figure of *ennui* (world-weariness), 'qui rêve d'échafauds en fumant son houka' ['who dreams of scaffolds while

93

smoking his opium pipe']. To live was to be commonplace; to refuse to live seemed to promise distinction. Shortly before he and the beautiful Sara take poison, the eponymous hero of Villiers de l'Isle-Adam's symbolist drama *Axël* (1890) says that living is pointless because their servants can do it for them. Hope seemed naïve. Selfishly (meaning that they suggested no alternative form of social commitment), and fearing disappointment, the decadents rejected procreation and the family. Hubert d'Entragues, the writer-protagonist of Rémy de Gourmont's *Sixtine, roman de la vie cérébrale* (1890), puts it succinctly: 'Du moment qu'on ne cherche que la jouissance, il est bien indifférent quel mécanisme la donne ... [Mon principe] est court, strict, et je le voudrais universel: Pas d'enfants' (pp. 266–7) ['If you're seeking only physical pleasure, it scarcely matters which mechanism produces it. My guiding principle is brief, strict, and I would like to see it shared by everyone: No children']. The logical consequence of such imaginings, in writers such as Laforgue, was fantasies of race suicide through the refusal to reproduce.[2]

Nonetheless, the 'decadent' period in Europe coincided with 'la Belle Epoque' (1880–1914), a historical era of unusual peace, prosperity and progress. Self-conscious literary and artistic decadence in France was part of an extraordinary flowering of literary and artistic creativity that lasted until the First World War. Moreover, a vast French colonial expansion in Africa and South East Asia followed the consolidation of the Third French Republic (1870–1940).[3] One still can feel the optimism of that age reflected in the Eiffel Tower, erected in 1889 to celebrate the hundredth anniversary of the French Revolution. In the same year a huge industrial exhibition glorified material progress. Society felt strong enough to be self-critical. At times, of course, the boundary between criticism and corruption blurs when the latter seems to have been depicted too complaisantly.

In French literature, the decadent movement had been prepared by the influence of the gothic novel from England (starting with Horace Walpole's *The Castle of Otranto*, 1764) and by that of Edgar Allan Poe translated and praised by Baudelaire.[4] The gothic tends to present decay as an external spectacle; Poe often presents it as a subjective experience; the decadents present decay as a condition actively, wilfully sought. As a negative version of the picaresque (one that ends in the protagonist's degeneration instead of success), the episodic structure of the decadent novel reflects a frustrated quest for a bad goal. Unsympathetic observers usually characterise literary decadence as emphasising the morbid and the macabre; crimes remain unpunished; no uplifting moral message emerges. Such amorality is held to reveal a general social decay. The hedonistic, morally degenerate protagonists in decadent works seem to delight in defying nature, and they appear to be speaking for the author.

European decadence passed through two main phases. The first, which one might call 'high decadence', was transient in the careers of the greatest 'decadent' writers: Huysmans, D'Annunzio and Wilde. These figures were versatile. Huysmans wrote distinguished correspondence; he and Wilde wrote outstanding critical essays; Wilde and D'Annunzio were expert in the formally demanding media of poetry and theatre. Good recent Huysmans critics usually avoid applying the term 'decadent' to him because his devout Catholic writing superseded his decadent phase and lasted twice as long.

In France, 'high decadence' had been anticipated by the symbolist poets Baudelaire and Verlaine, and by two of the later novels of Gustave Flaubert (*Salammbô* (1862) and *La Tentation de saint Antoine* (1874)). In retrospect, the point of departure for the international decadent movement in literature was the early Joris-Karl Huysmans in *A rebours* (1884) and secondarily in *Là-bas* (1891). *A rebours* became the acknowledged masterpiece of the international decadent movement, inspiring works such as Oscar Wilde's *The Picture of Dorian Gray* (1890) and Gabriele D'Annunzio's *Il piacere* (1889), *Il trionfo della morte* (1894) and *Il fuoco* (1900). Huysmans himself was not conscious of founding a tradition. In 1903, his retrospective preface to *A rebours* characterised the novel as a transition between his earlier Naturalism (with working-class characters, whose actions were largely determined by their heredity and their environment) and his later conversion to Catholicism. He admits to having written instinctively, with no fixed plan.[5] The hyperaesthesia (acute sensitivity to sense impressions) of his protagonist reminds one of Poe's Roderick Usher or William Wilson. But the intervening half-century had added a dimension to the morbidly sensitive hero created by Goethe (in *The Sorrows of Young Werther* (1774)) and the gothic.

The dominant ostensible motif of *A rebours* is the decomposition of society and the cult of artificiality that serves des Esseintes, the last scion of a dying aristocratic family, to replace an inadequate reality. From his perspective, initially his tasteful refuge would prove that the poetic soul could escape from the physical, rational world into a realm of unrestrained imagination. The text describes at length the luxurious décor in which he has sequestered himself, and illustrates his cult of aestheticism by listing his likes and dislikes. As a formless enumeration of topics and a catalogue of aesthetic enthusiasms, Huysmans's *A rebours* echoes Flaubert's *Bouvard et Pécuchet*, reviving the ancient encyclopaedic genre Northrop Frye called the 'anatomy', rooted in Menippean satire. (See Frye's *Anatomy of Criticism*, 1957). As Huysmans explained in his retrospective preface, his purpose in *A rebours* had been 'de secouer les préjugés, de briser les limites du roman, d'y faire entrer l'art, la science, l'histoire, de ne plus se servir, en un mot, de cette forme que comme d'un cadre pour y insérer de plus sérieux travaux' (p. 62) ['to shake off prejudices, to break apart the limits of the novel, to introduce art, science, and history into it; in a word, no longer to use that form except as a frame into which more important undertakings might be inserted']. Huysmans returned to the anatomy form in 1898 with the non-decadent *La Cathédrale*, a compendium on Christian symbolism.

Des Esseintes provided a prestigious model for future decadent heroes. In current diagnostic parlance, he suffers from a personality disorder: he is a schizoid personality torn between yearnings for relatedness and for withdrawal. Huysmans was consciously aware of the unconscious, as a subject for scientific investigation. To prepare his portrait of a mentally ill hero, he had read contemporary studies of psychopathology. His sources described the photophobia of certain neurotics, their hallucinatory episodes involving sounds and odours, and the cures recommended at the time. All these elements were systematically integrated into the story of des Esseintes. Inspired by his Naturalist heritage, in the opening pages Huysmans comments directly on the hereditary and environmental causes of his hero's physical and emotional disorders.

Des Esseintes's defective relations with his parents, as Huysmans portrays them, engender the opposite extreme reactions of promiscuity – where sexual perversion represents an attempt to defy the family by refusing to reproduce it – and withdrawal to a house designed as an intimate shelter. In the depths of his retreat, 'il vivait sur lui-même, se nourrissait de sa propre substance, pareil à ces bêtes engourdis, tapies dans un trou, pendant l'hiver' (p. 147) ['he was living off himself, nourishing himself with his own substance, like those numbed animals huddled in a hole during winter']. The regressive temptation of the snug harbour, of the warm, secluded room, persists in Huysmans's work from beginning to end, from 'La Retraite de Monsieur Bougran' through all his later novels. But at length 'cette solitude si ardemment enviée et enfin acquise avait abouti à une détresse affreuse' (p. 201) ['this solitude so ardently desired and finally achieved had ended in fearsome distress']. The total retreat and oblivion of autistic psychosis, unconsciously imaged as return to the womb, entails the threat of the annihilation of the self.[6]

Des Esseintes's repressed needs for relatedness are so intense that he can imagine no love relationship that would not lead either to being devoured by the love object or to devouring it. Unlike most later decadent heroes, however, who never emerge from their final refuge, des Esseintes moves from deep regression through four ever more adventurous forays into the outside world. First he opens a window; later, he goes out to shop for house plants, although he tries to find plants that appear as artificial as possible; next he attempts a journey to London, ending in a Paris pub which evokes London; finally, he leaves his retreat altogether on his doctor's orders. One can predict that he will ultimately embrace a compromise of ritualised, structured object-relationships within the framework of a semi-monastic Catholicism. The cult of art, which preserved a tenuous relatedness with other people while safely distancing the hero from them, will be replaced by a cult of religious observance, which serves the same purpose but in a more widely acceptable way. With the hindsight provided by Huysmans's later novels and particularly by his own 1903 preface to a new edition of *A rebours*, one might say that his protagonist des Esseintes is fitfully, involuntarily living out the initial stages of a return to religion through art. A programme for such a conversion had been drawn up eighty years before in Chateaubriand's *Le Génie du Christianisme* (1802). Husymans's next novel, *Là-bas* (1891), however, openly opposes Naturalism for having obliterated the distinction between art and world. As far as I know, excepting autobiographical accounts and confessions, *Là-bas* is the first novel about writing a book in which that book is quoted *in extenso* (one-third of the text consists of a biography of the horrific, paedophilic mass-murderer Gilles de Retz, previously a captain for Jeanne d'Arc). Many of the protagonist Durtal's experiences are motivated by his desire to learn about the supernatural. Events in the inner narrative uncannily anticipate events in the outer one. As in Wilde or D'Annunzio, such introversion suggests that the outside world is a preliminary sketch for the work of art, and that the latter is more highly organised than the external world because its vision integrates the rational and material with the supernatural and the unconscious. Such early decadent literature anticipates modern psycho-analytic thought.[7]

The most common mainspring of the plot in decadent fiction is the myth of woman as a bestial, irrational, instinctively destructive being. In other countries, compare Wagner's operas such as *Tannhäuser* (1845) and *Parsifal* (1882), or Henrik Ibsen's plays, whose protagonists were inspired by the fiercely independent, vindictive women of the ancient Norse and Icelandic sagas. This myth of the atavistic destructiveness of women was also widespread in French popular culture (abroad, compare such classics of popular culture as H. Rider Haggard's *She* (1886)). It was nourished by historical figures such as Théroigne de Méricourt, the sanguinary heroine who tried to create a woman's army during the Revolution. Commentators ascribed the moral and demographic weakness of France, proven by the defeat of 1870, to 'the emancipation of women, the legalisation of divorce (1884), and the emasculation of men'.[8] Women became the scapegoats for a perceived decline in morality. In decadent fiction written by men, relations with women often are presented as a contest of wills. Then, the triumph of the male decadent is sexually to enslave and finally destroy the woman, forestalling her destructive influence. Such is the plot of Pierre Louÿs's best work, *Aphrodite. Mœurs antiques* (1896).

One finds a dramatic fictional rendering of the female monster in Zola's naturalistic *Nana* (1880), which adds an apocalyptic note. Nana is a showgirl and prostitute from the working classes, a Blue Angel writ large. Many wealthy men humiliate and ruin themselves for her favours. Near the end of his novel, Zola sums up:

> Comme ces monstres antiques dont le domaine redouté était couvert d'ossements, elle posait les pieds sur des crânes; et des catastrophes l'entouraient . . . Son œuvre de ruine et de mort était faite, la mouche envolée de l'ordure des faubourgs, apportant le ferment des pourritures sociales, avait empoisonné ces hommes, rien qu'à se poser sur eux. (*Œuvres complètes* (Paris: Bernouard, 1928), vol. XXVIII, p. 418)

> [Like those monsters of antiquity whose dread domain was covered with bones, she trod on skulls; disasters surrounded her . . . Her mission of ruination and death was accomplished, by this fly that had flown from the filth of the suburbs bringing rot to society. She had poisoned those men merely by alighting on them.]

The middle two sentences omitted from this passage add to the image of the devouring woman a note of class conflict and social justice lacking in decadent novels per se. Nana had done well to afflict the idle, corrupt rich. Like many decadent novelists, however, Zola in turn concludes misogynistically by inflicting a horrible physical punishment on the flamboyantly sexual woman. Those who live by the body must die by the body. In the last scene of *Nana* the heroine perishes from smallpox. Her body becomes a purulent, seething mass (p. 436).

A remarkably similar misogynistic description occurs in Huysmans's *A rebours*. In Gustave Moreau's painting, Huysmans's protagonist finds 'cette Salomé, surhumaine et étrange, qu'il avait rêvée . . . la Bête monstrueuse, indifférente, irresponsable, insensible, empoisonnante, de même que l'Hélène antique, tout ce qui l'approche, tout ce qui la voit, tout ce qu'elle touche' (p. 126) ['the realisation of that superhuman, alien Salomé of whom he had dreamed . . . the Beast, monstrous, indifferent, irresponsible, poisoning, like the Helen of Antiquity, everything that drew near her, that saw her, that she touched']. An unpublished variant (pp. 123/324) identified her with 'the eternal feminine'. We are far from Goethe's condescending but favourable representation of Marguerite and Helen as embodiments of the eternal feminine in *Faust II* (1832), as an inspiration drawing us (males) onwards towards spiritual perfection.

The French *fin-de-siècle* novelists usually responded to the society of their times in one of two contrasting ways, attack or withdrawal. Like the Old Testament Prophets, socially committed authors such as Emile Zola and Paul Bourget whole-heartedly denounced the economic, political and moral corruption of their age. Their protagonists' criminality and depravity were intended to represent symptoms of a widespread social decline. (In the previous generation, Balzac, Stendhal, and Flaubert also were social satirists, but seemed to offer no hope of reform; Hugo advocated reform, but his protagonists were virtuous victims, and he counted on an eventual divine intervention to help reformers.) In contrast, the decadent authors' attitudes towards their protagonists were profoundly ambivalent. Remember that plot reflects an author's rhetoric, for it serves as an implicit evaluation of moral choices. Decadent authors lead their protagonists to a disastrous out-come, where the latter are burned out or physically destroyed. Events seem to condemn their aberrant behaviour after it has been the focus of the plot. At times, of course, moral boundaries blur when the depiction of depravity, ostensibly denounced, nevertheless appears complaisant and complicitous.

The decadent authors' ambivalence can be explained by an analogy. The British critic T. E. Hulme tellingly labelled Romanticism as 'spilt religion'. He referred to religious sentiments that had lost their institutional home in an organised church. Unable to accept traditional religious beliefs, disappointed by them, many Romantic writers nevertheless longed for them: they compensated by trying to apprehend the supernatural directly, to found a personal religion, or to transcend institutional boundaries by advocating religious syncretism, where all religions were one. Thus they could be outside the church yet still part of it, through a vague spiritual kinship. Alternatively, the emotionally disturbed priests in much Romantic literature allow their authors vicariously to explore the hypothesis 'what if I joined the church?' One thinks of Lamartine's eponymous Jocelyn, Hugo's Claude Frollo in *Notre-Dame de Paris* (1831), and Stendhal's Fabrice in *La Chartreuse de Parme* (1839), together with Diderot's anticipatory Mother Superior in *La Religieuse* (composed 1760) and Gide's tortured Protestant minister in the belated *Symphonie pastorale* (1919).

Comparable to the nostalgic 'spilt religion' of Romanticism, literary decadence reflects a nostalgic 'spilt aristocracy'. The protagonists of decadent novelists proper such as Joris-Karl Huysmans, Rachilde (pseudonym for Marguerite Eymery) and Octave Mirbeau flirt with and sometimes embrace moral corruption as a facet of an aristocratic ideal whose prime values are originality, style, aesthetic elegance, contempt for nature and self-control. The last two values are inherited from the 'Neoclassic Stoic' of figures such as the painter David and the poet Vigny, who glorified the sublimity of a willing sacrifice of one's life to honour one's values. Like Vigny, the decadent authors appear to feel nostalgia for the lost social hierarchy of the ancien régime, the former monarchy. In the Middle Ages, the 'basis of legitimacy' for the aristocracy, its raison d'être, justifying special authority and privileges, was public service, particularly in law enforcement and defence. For example, a marquis outranked a count because the former took greater risks: a marquis administered a county on the marches, on the borders of a country where the enemy would first attack. Artists and writers benefited secondarily from aristocratic privileges when wealth trickled down to them from their aristocratic patrons. In their fantasy life, the former could even imagine themselves, an intelligentsia, as equivalent to the non-combatant 'noblesse de robe', commoners ennobled for fulfilling important administrative and judicial functions. After the Revolution, support from patrons was rarely available. Writers now had to appeal to a less élite, much larger audience, composed of persons with tastes as undiscriminating as those of Flaubert's Emma Bovary. To be sure, the Revolution had dreamed in vain of making every French citizen literate; only half the conscripts could read and write as late as 1832, and throughout the century only 1 per cent of French children completed the *baccalauréat*. But the Industrial Revolution made inexpensive fiction available for the first time to the general public. The commercial success of the *roman-feuilleton* after 1830, the development in 1836 of inked rollers for printing, and a further expansion of newspapers and magazines between 1860 and 1885 (a four-fold increase in titles, and a four-fold increase in circulation per title) created a vast new public. (See chapter 5 for a fuller account of the rise of popular fiction in nineteenth-century France.) Meanwhile short stories replaced serialised novels as the leading sales draw for subscribers. Flaubert, Zola and Huysmans among others decried the resulting vulgarisation of taste.[9]

As an organised but short-lived literary movement, associated with symbolism and presented in 'little magazines' such as *Le Chat Noir*, decadence effected a transition between aestheticism and sensationalism by reserving the first for élitist periodicals of limited circulation. The later, sensationalising phase of literary decadence is represented by lesser writers who repeat themselves, dwelling on sado-pornographic subjects and publishing well into the twentieth century. The two features that above all link these two periods of decadence are the contemplative solipsism exemplified by Remy de Gourmont's *Sixtine, roman de la vie cérébrale* (1890), with its motto 'Le monde . . . je l'ai créé avec mes sens' (p. 13) ['The world is something I've created with my senses'], and the concept of the gratuitous act.

The *acte gratuit* refers primarily to the impulsive, apparently unmotivated murder that does not materially benefit its perpetrator. Hearing this expression, students of French literature probably would think first of Gide's Lafcadio pushing an innocuous stranger from a train in *Les Caves du Vatican* (1914), or of Camus's *L'Etranger* (1942) shooting an Arab on the beach (David H. Walker discusses these works in chapter 8, pp. 129–30 and 136–7). The idea of the *acte gratuit* appears, however, to have originated in an earlier source: the author perhaps most influential on French literature during the latter half of the nineteenth century, Edgar Allan Poe. His 'Imp of the Perverse', 'The Black Cat', and 'The Tell-tale Heart' (translated by Baudelaire in the *Nouvelles Histoires extraordinaires*, 1857) all relate such murders. The irrational impulse to aggression appears in France a bit later in Baudelaire's milder prose poem 'Le Mauvais Vitrier'. Jean Lorrain's *Monsieur de Phocas* (1901) takes up Poe's model. Lorrain's eponymous character, fascinated and repelled by the gnomelike, sadistic Englishman M. Ethal, finally kills him so that it looks like suicide, but then retreats for ever to Asia, leaving behind his account of a flirtation with the abyss. One can find other examples of the *acte gratuit* in Octave Mirbeau's *Contes cruels* (1885–99), notably in 'Divagations sur le meurtre'. Note in passing the utility of this concept in gender stereotyping, according to which women commit impulsive acts because of their inherent traits of hysteria and primitive, irrational thinking; where men are concerned, the phrase 'gratuitous act' detaches the same behaviour from the actor, and transforms it from a stigma into an object of detached philosophical contemplation. Such contemplation in and of itself attempts to prove the intellectual superiority of the impulsive male who, like a moral Narcissus, reflects on his own impulsiveness. However, Rachilde gives the *acte gratuit* a homophobic turn in the last chapter of *La Marquise de Sade* (1887): the eponymous character finds no real grandeur left in crime until she discovers male transvestites during her nocturnal slumming. She then dreams of murdering one of these 'useless' beings for thrills. Rachilde also innovates elsewhere by transposing the *acte gratuit* from murder to sexual contact. In *L'Animale* (1893), the heroine has an affair with the father's pitiable, physically repellent law clerk just because the man is available, and desires her. She seems motivated by the perverse exercise of pure freedom; in the relationship, she seeks neither material advantage, prestige, physical gratification, nor even relief from boredom.

Influenced by the examples of Flaubert's *Salammbô* or *La Tentation de saint Antoine* and Huysmans's *A rebours* or *Là-bas* critics today often create the impression that decadent writers defied their public not only by their choice of message, but through their treatment of the medium – through their style. From this perspective, decadent literature is considered artistically as well as morally flawed: written in a turgid, overly refined style that abuses rare words (such as lists of gemstones, and exotic places and plants); indulges in long, tangled sentences; and bores readers with static descriptions. Decadent prose is supposed to be characterised by aestheticism, shown in descriptions of rare and precious objects (unavailable to and unappreciated by ordinary people) harmoniously arranged in luxurious interiors, and by tortuous, complicated sentences. Later perfected by Proust, such sentences themselves become autonomous works of art. From a narratological viewpoint, the frequent digressive descriptions, in decadent prose, stall the story. They imply a refusal to please the mass public eager for fictional action (compare the importunate questioning of Baudelaire's naïve audience in 'Le Voyage': 'et puis, et puis encore?' ['And then? What happened next?']). They seem to spurn the demands of society.

In practice, however, and in contrast to Huysmans or Flaubert, the later decadent novels of Rachilde and her circle ordinarily employ short, clear sentences and simple plot lines. It is true that their frequent evocations of rare and precious objects suggest (as did Balzac's cluttered antique shop in *La Peau de chagrin*, 1830–1) nostalgia for a lost heritage of aristocratic culture. But decadent literature expresses its ambivalence towards the new mass public particularly by splitting into two contrasting modes. The *recherché*, precious style mainly appears in the poems and prose sketches abundant in the many 'little magazines' of the time, closely associated with and derivative of symbolism. These, unlike the decadent novels, are reserved for an élite audience.

A traditional view in literary history would be that after Huysmans, the penny dreadfuls of 'low (or 'decadent') decadence', exemplified by the novelists Lorrain, Louÿs, Mirbeau and Rachilde, openly embraced materialism and the worship of pleasure, flouting public morals while pandering to public taste through melodramatic depictions of sex and sadism, making a spectacle of their depravity. Such an ambivalent characterisation might plausibly fit the attitudes of a displaced, unappreciated intelligentsia, writers who both longed for and scorned broader recognition. What was scandalous in their writing? One can peruse many decadent novels without finding explicit descriptions of sexual acts, nor even the names of the sexual organs. The realists and naturalists had already gone as far as the decadents in 'soft' (suggested, not explicit) pornographic depictions of adultery, rape, incest and homosexuality. But decadent writers add scenes of necrophilia and sexual activity under the influence of opiates, although they avoid overt paedophilia and bestiality. What was particularly subversive in their writings was a dramatisation of polymorphous perversity: they refused to privilege any particular source of sexual pleasure (see the memorable scene where Rachilde's *La Jongleuse* (1900) masturbates by embracing a large vase, in the presence of her scandalised suitor).

What shocks one most today in decadent fiction is its horrific, detailed dramatisations of sadism. Most memorable among these are Octave Mirbeau's revolting scenes of ingenious torture in *Le Jardin de supplices* (1898). He does distance himself through exoticism. The setting is Imperial China, where the ironically named Englishwoman Clara (a name suggesting Enlightenment rationality and lucidity) takes her lover, the narrator, on a tour of the prison. Once a week, the inmates are put on display and fed by the public with rotten meat. Lingering executions are made into a spectacle.[10] At the conclusion, the strong-willed Clara falls unconscious in a terrible seizure, like an exaggerated orgasm. Addicted to vicarious sadism, she undergoes the same experience every week, proving, it would seem, the neurological inferiority of even the most independent woman. Apparently, the military valour that led the ideal aristocrat into battle at the head of his troops has been replaced in the decadent novel by an unflinching contemplation of hideous physical and emotional cruelty, and participation in sexual behaviour not sanctioned by society: cross-dressing, adultery, prostitution, paedophilia, incest, homosexuality, bestiality and sado-masochism. Decadent protagonists seem to regard such behaviour as an expression of the triumph of their will over both nature and social convention, and initially they seem to be speaking for their authors. The latter, however, ruefully detach themselves from their characters by showing that the quest for moral autonomy leads to disastrous outcomes such as Clara's. Moreover, decadent authors sometimes suggest that the quest for social distinction may enslave one in some of the same ways as does submission to social conventions: by making one self-conscious, it robs one of pleasure, and it limits one's choices. As the heroine of Rachilde's *Monsieur Vénus* declares, 'Etre Sapho ce serait être tout le monde!' (Rachilde, *Monsieur Vénus* (Paris: Flammarion, 1977), p. 85) ['Being a lesbian would mean being just like everyone else!']. Finally, the hedonistic, materialistic worship of the body leads characters to an early suicide: Rachilde's *La Jongleuse* slits her own throat by faking a knife-juggling accident at the onset of middle age; her *L'Animale* (1893) throws herself from a rooftop when she has been irreparably mutilated by her rabid cat. The tacked-on quality of these latter two endings, like that of the Marquis de Sade's earlier *Justine, ou les malheurs de la vertu* (1787, 1791; the virtuous victim is struck by lightning), betrays the incoherence of a decadent moral vision. At other times Rachilde is more successful in linking plausible plots with psychological plausibility. As Flaubert's unfortunate Madame Bovary must finally confront in adultery 'all the platitudes of marriage', so the controlling heroine of *Monsieur Vénus* ultimately must helplessly suffer the tortures of jealousy, when her feminised male slave falls in love with another man.

The decadents also had a more serious, socially committed side that went beyond mere defiance. In literary revues of the time, such as *Le Chat Noir* (1882–95) or *Le Mercure de France* (1890–1965) during its early years (founded by Rachilde, her husband Alfred Vallette, and others, and edited by Vallette until 1935), they lucidly advocated what one might call a libertarian position. For example, they opposed compulsory military service and urged the decriminalisation of free sexual self-expression. Rachilde, moreover, by offering an example of the successful, independent, creative woman in the tradition of Mme de Staël and George Sand, helped lay the groundwork for the future liberation of women. She did perpetuate decadent myths of women as amoral, ravening monsters; and she proclaimed more than once that she herself was no feminist. Yet several of her novels dramatise a feminine protest against gender inequity in important ways that are only now being recognised (see in this respect Margaret Cohen's remarks about Rachilde earlier in this volume, p. 69). Implicitly, she asserts the value and autonomy of women, appropriates the male imagination by depicting male protagonists from their own viewpoints, and deconstructs the socially and culturally imposed distinctions between the two genders.

First, she validates the girl child despite her economic insignificance. Until the Romantic period in France, the idea of childhood had been bound to that of economic dependence, not personal development. Previously, stories of the early self had been justified only by didactic (as in Augustine and Montaigne) or apologetic (as in Rousseau) aims. In the early chapters of his *Mémoires d'Outre-Tombe* (1849–50), Chateaubriand was one of the first to treat early childhood for its own sake. George Sand soon followed with *Histoire de ma vie* (1854–5). Since women at the time were debarred from most leadership roles in society, it was more difficult for them than for men to justify treating their formative years spent in the family, since these were to prepare for no broader roles. Lacking opportunities to experience *Bildung* (the largely self-directed insertion of the self into society), women also found it difficult to qualify to write memoirs (the insertion of the self into history). Nevertheless, the first half of Rachilde's early novel, *La Marquise de Sade*, seems autobiographical. Rachilde's father, like her heroine Mary Barbe's, was a career military officer. The first six chapters satirise peacetime garrison life and sensitively describe how sexism deforms the personality of a growing girl. The latter half, unfortunately, degenerates into a rather incoherent, episodic account of Mary Barbe's sadism and vampirism, and of the sexual abuse briefly inflicted on her by her uncle, whom she then blackmails.

Second, Rachilde appropriates the male imagination in situations outside the family and outside heterosexual relationships (most strikingly in *La Tour d'amour* (1899) and in *Le Prisonnier* (co-authored with André David, 1928). The first novel depicts a necrophilic lighthouse keeper who sexually desecrates the corpses of female shipwreck victims. Along with *Monsieur Vénus*, it is perhaps her best work. It creates a typically decadent setting of claustrophobic intensity, progressive social alienation and growing horror. The keeper's new assistant gradually discovers his superior's secret and finds a woman's severed, pickled head. The second uses a first-person male narrator to portray an emerging gay consciousness, anticipating Marguerite Yourcenar's magisterial *Mémoires d'Hadrien* (1954) (Rachilde also admired the Roman emperor).

The idea of decadence has masked Rachilde's occasional psychological richness in character portrayal, and her pioneering reflections on language. Obviously, several of her novels' titles in the 1880s call gender identity into question (*Monsieur Vénus*, *La Marquise de Sade*, *Madame Adonis*). The stereotypes of domination and submission in love relationships are systematically exchanged between their accustomed genders. In *Monsieur Vénus*, for example, Jacques Silvert

> devint sa chose . . . Car Jacques aimait Raoule avec un vrai cœur de femme. Il l'aimait par reconnaissance, par soumission, par un besoin latent de voluptés inconnues . . . Il menait, lui, l'existence oisive des orientales murées dans leur sérail . . . Elle multipliait autour de lui les occasions de se féminiser. (pp. 107–8)

> [became her thing . . . for Jacques loved Raoule with a truly womanly heart. He loved her from gratitude, from submissiveness, from a latent need for unknown ecstasies . . . *He* led the indolent existence of oriental women walled up in their harem . . . *She* provided as many opportunities as she could for him to become more feminine.]

Jacques starts cross-dressing, begins applying feminine forms of adjectives to himself (e.g. 'agaçante'), and becomes impotent. At length he feels desire for Raoule's male friend, Raittolbe, and tries to seduce him. Admittedly, the social significance of such role reversals is greatly diminished by Raoule's overwhelming advantage of great wealth and aristocratic caste. Jacques is a poor working-class man whom she buys. But their psychological import is enhanced by a complexity that distinguishes Rachilde's protagonists from the one-dimensional *debauchés* of most decadent novels. The emotional depth of her interpersonal relations makes gender reversal seem more plausible than it would be in a mere thriller with flat characters. And more subversive: the contempt of Raoule's aristocratic male friends for the lowly Jacques is overwhelmed by their unexpected, instinctual, almost irresistible physical attraction to him (p. 173) – Raittolbe himself had felt it so strongly that he was about to commit suicide from shame until Raoule intervened. Rachilde thus threatens all men with the spectre of latent homosexuality, adopting it as a weapon for gender warfare. Raoule's own lucid cynicism ('la chair fraîche et saine est l'unique puissance de ce monde' (p. 102) ['fresh, healthy flesh is the sole power that rules this world']) alternates with her desperate jealousy as well as with concerns for Jacques's welfare. At times she feels guilty for corrupting him, and begins half-hearted attempts at his rehabilitation. But she ends by furiously arranging Jacques's death in a duel after his attempted betrayal of her with Raittolbe. Only then does she revert to her role as an outwardly impassive, amoral monster, assuming behaviour that outside the context of gender reversal would seem gruesomely comical. In a covert reminiscence of Poe's 'Bérénice', she extracts the hair, teeth and nails from Jacques's corpse. These body parts are then inserted into a life-size mechanical doll that can move its mouth to simulate kisses. Alternately dressed in men's and in women's clothes, Raoule visits and embraces it every evening in a sealed room. Here Rachilde surpasses the phallocratic cliché of woman as pleasure machine, not only by gender reversal, but also by combining the fetishism of detail with the global fetishism of the automaton. (Along with such familiar examples as Olimpia in E. T. A. Hoffmann's 'Der Sandmann' (1809) or Villiers de l'Isle-Adam's *L'Eve future* (1886), let us recall Mme de Staël's little-known, light-hearted play *Le Mannequin* (1811).)

Monsieur Vénus goes beyond the message to consider and problematise the medium. The novel contains serious discussions between the eponymous character and her male military admirer, Raittolbe, concerning how a dominant woman can transform language to characterise herself and her sexual relationship with a weak male.[11] She repeatedly refers to herself with masculine endings (amoureux, jaloux; see especially chapter 5). The exploration of how language inexorably reinforces gender stereotypes anticipates Monique Wittig's *Les Guérillères* of eighty-five years later (1969) (see Jane Winston's discussion of Wittig in chapter 14, pp. 232–3).

Despite Rachilde's achievements, at length she emphatically endorsed the myth of woman's inferiority in *Pourquoi je ne suis pas féministe* (1928). Justifying the cross-dressing of her youth with practical reasons, she explained that in 1885, she had sought written permission (required at the time) from the chief of police. As a journalist, she needed to travel where women didn't ordinarily go. Besides, she couldn't afford women's fashions. As soon as she married, she said, she conformed to traditional dress. She denied any desire to vote or be involved with politics. Unlike men, she added, women are sensualists, not idealists in love. They are fundamentally envious and jealous, because they want to dominate. 'Les femmes sont *les frères inférieurs* de l'homme, simplement parce qu'elles ont des misères physiques les éloignant de *la suite dans les idées* que peuvent concevoir tous les hommes en général, même les moins intelligents' (p. 10; emphasis in original) ['Women are men's lesser brethren, simply because their physical afflictions prevent them from having that coherence of thought that even the least intelligent of men can achieve']. They can be great performing artists, or excellent speculators, because those occupations rely on play and caprice, but obviously they are unfit for public affairs. Women's minds are like sponges, Rachilde continued; when squeezed, they express only what has been put into them; they are neither fountains nor distilleries. She contrasted her grandmother, a devoted wife revered in her community, with her mother, who had political and philosophical pretensions, and ended in the madhouse (pp. 20–4). Well-educated women are the death of family life, Rachilde added; and sexually aware women who deprive their fiancés of the pleasure of initiating them, discourage marriage (pp. 40–2). Demanding equality for women, she concluded, will continue to depopulate and weaken France. Like Camille Paglia or Phyllis Schaffly after her, Rachilde came to realise that the easiest way to get attention is to become a traitor to one's class.[12]

A famous episode in popular culture at the *fin-de-siècle* confirmed the power of the period's self-contradictory image of woman as a frail monster. The common denominator of these two mythic attributes was a lack of rationality. Irrationality became a life and death issue on 16 March 1914, when Henriette Caillaux entered the office of Gaston Calmette, the conservative editor of a prominent newspaper, *Le Figaro*. That paper's editorials had been libelling her husband Joseph, leader of the Radical (i.e. centrist) Party, and endangering his political future. Worse yet, Calmette had just published an intimate letter written by Caillaux thirteen years before to the mistress who would become his first wife. It showed evidence of political double-dealing. Mme Caillaux pumped six shots into Calmette. Later, she admitted the shooting but protested her innocence of premeditated murder. She masterfully exploited male delusions about women, portraying herself as a delicate, hypersensitive neurotic driven to distraction by an invasion of her sexual privacy. The prosecution tried unsuccessfully to prove that she was guilty (intention being the crucial element of the crime) because she had acted from political ambition, like a man. In response, the defence lawyer Labori stressed that his client had killed not out of any masculine need for political revenge but out of a wholly, if irrationally, feminine desire to preserve her sexual reputation. By a vote of 11–1, the jury agreed that Henriette's act had been unpremeditated, involuntary manslaughter; she went free.

To characterise the novel of decadence and the *fin de siècle* in one word other than 'perverse', one might choose 'asocial' ('antisocial' suggests an abrasive contact with society which does not seem the major goal of decadent fiction). The implied authors maintain a great affective distance from their characters. In nearly all decadent novels, the point of view is surprisingly uniform: there are few open-ended debates (although one finds many didactic ones), and few episodic observers (whereas there are many in Balzac). The democratic, carnivalesque proliferation of views in satire is missing. Voluntary seclusion and enclosure, often accompanied by torpor and quasi-hibernation, is the dominant metaphor of decadence, from Baudelaire and *A rebours* to Rachilde's *L'Animale, Monsieur Vénus and La Tour d'amour*. These characters seek a retreat to the womb. They see no possibilities for relating to others than their sexual partner. They eschew social commitment and responsibility.[13]

Even before literary decadence became known, the major literary reaction to it had been anticipated. One could already detect in realist and naturalist writers the origins of the Catholic Renaissance of the first half of the twentieth century, a revival of profound religious conviction in works by Péguy, Claudel, Mauriac, Bernanos and others. Flaubert's *Trois Contes* (1877) are a triptych about saints, and he said that he wrote 'Un cœur simple' under the inspiration of Sand. Huysmans, Villiers and even Zola also finally profess one form or another of spiritualism. A widespread, determined misprision of Baudelaire, Verlaine and, above all, Rimbaud as mystics greatly nurtured this development in the twentieth century. Catholic dogma provided writers of *l'entre-deux-guerres* a sheltering framework within which their protagonists could explore the possibilities for solidarity, possibilities to be fully tested only later, by Existentialism.

NOTES

1 Orthodox Catholic theology recognised three successive stages of sin: the surprise of the senses (one becomes innocently aware of an alluring but forbidden object), morbid delectation (one begins to contemplate the transgression in question), and the consent of the will (one actively tries to sin).

2 Compare the sour attitude of our contemporary, the British poet Philip Larkin, in 'This Be The Verse':

> Man hands on misery to man;
> It deepens like a coastal shelf;
> Get out as early as you can,
> And don't have any kids yourself.

3 To many observers such as Georges Clemenceau, the future leader of the French Republic, such prosperity seemed morally unsound. In his famous debates with Jules Ferry concerning whether France should seek colonial expansion in Africa and South East Asia, he reminded his opponent that it was no more justified to call Black Africans, Arabs and Asians 'inferior races' than it had been justified for the Prussians to call the French an 'inferior race' after France's humiliating defeat in the 1870 Franco-Prussian war.

4 See M. Summers's classic *The Gothic Quest: A History of the Gothic Novel* (New York: Russell and Russell, 1964, rev. edn.) and E. R. Napier, *The Failure of Gothic: Problems of Disjunction in an Eighteenth-century Literary Form* (Oxford: Clarendon Press, 1987). On Poe, see G. Clarke (ed.), *Edgar Allan Poe: Critical Assessments* (Mountfield: Helm, 1991), 4 vols., and P. F. Quinn, *The French Face of Edgar Poe* (Carbondale: Southern Illinois University Press, 1957).

5 J.-K. Huysmans, *A rebours*, ed. R. Fortassier (Paris: Bibliothèque Nationale, 1981), p. 54. For an English translation, see *Against the Grain* (New York: Dover, 1969).

6 A fuller psychoanalytical treatment of Huysmans's hero is presented in L. M. Porter, 'Huysmans's *A rebours*: The Psychodynamics of Regression', *The American Imago* 44 (1987), 51–65.

7 See L. M. Porter, 'Literary Structure and the Concept of Decadence: Huysmans, D'Annunzio, and Wilde', *Centennial Review*, 22 (1978), 188–200.

8 See E. Berenson, *The Trial of Madame Caillaux* (Berkeley: University of California Press, 1992), p. 11.

9 Pierre Bourdieu has argued (e.g. *Les Règles de l'art: genèse et structure du champ littéraire* (Paris: Seuil, 1992)) that the dissemination of standard French was a way of consolidating existing hierarchies by relegating linguistic minorities to a hopeless position of inferiority, lacking in 'cultural capital'. But the writers themselves, such as Flaubert in *Bouvard et Pécuchet* (1881), saw their cultural superiority threatened. By becoming blatantly 'decadent', they could profit commercially while recouping their aristocratic symbolic capital (status and prestige). See J. B. Thompson's excellent introduction to Bourdieu, *Language and Symbolic Power* (Cambridge, MA: Harvard University Press, 1991), pp. 1–34.

10 In a clear reminiscence of Schopenhauer, and an anticipation of Freud's 'death instinct', the narrator observes that the judges, soldiers and priests who pursue the work of death everywhere are emblematic of the forces directing the entire earth.

11 For a fuller discussion see M. Hawthorne, '*Monsieur Vénus*: a critique of gender roles', *Nineteenth-Century French Studies* 16 (1987–88), 162–79.

12 See, for example, C. Paglia, *Sexual Personae* (New Haven: Yale University Press, 1990): 'If civilization had been left in female hands, we would still be living in grass huts' (p. 38).

13 Some may be surprised by the absence of Barbey d'Aurevilly from this chapter. To consider Barbey a decadent writer would, however, be to propagate a widespread critical confusion between subject (what a story is about) and theme (the evaluation of the subject). To write about incest, for example, is not necessarily to endorse it. The accounts of decadent narrators are characterised by an amoral aestheticism and by a sense of complicity with the crimes committed against the human dignity of oneself or others. Barbey's narrators are more detached.

SUGGESTIONS FOR FURTHER READING

Fins de siècle, Colloque de Tours, 4–6 juin 1985 (Bordeaux: Presses Universitaires de Bordeaux, 1990)

Fins de siècle, Société française de littérature générale et comparée, Congrès 1987 (Toulouse: Presses Universitaires du Mirail, 1989)

L'Esprit de décadence, Colloque de Nantes, 21–24 avril 1976, 2 vols. (Paris: Minard, 1980)

Bernart, I., 'Décadence et style décadent,' *L'Information Littéraire* 28 (1976), 23–7

Bronfen, E., *Over Her Dead Body: Death, Femininity and the Aesthetic* (Manchester: Manchester University Press, 1992)

Calinescu, M., *Five Faces of Modernity: Modernism, Avant-Garde, Decadence, Kitsch, Postmodernism* (Durham: Duke University Press, rev. edn 1987)

Carter, A. E., *The Idea of Decadence in French Literature* (Toronto: University of Toronto Press, 1958)

Citti, P., *Contre la décadence: l'histoire de l'imagination française dans le roman 1890–1914* (Paris: Presses Universitaires de France, 1987)

Dijkstra, B., *Idols of Perversity: Fantasies of Female Evil in Fin-de-siècle Culture* (London and New York: Oxford University Press, 1986)

Marquèze-Pouey, L., *Le mouvement décadent en France* (Paris: Presses Universitaires de France, 1986)

Nordau, M., *Degeneration* (New York: Appleton, 1912)

Pierrot, J., *L'Imaginaire décadent (1880–1900)* (Paris: Presses Universitaires de France, 1977)

Praz, M., *The Romantic Agony* (London: Oxford University Press, 1970, second edn)

Spackman, B., *Decadent Genealogies: The Rhetoric of Sickness from Baudelaire to D'Annunzio* (Ithaca: Cornell University Press, 1989)

7

CHRISTIE McDONALD

The Proustian revolution

When Marcel Proust cites Racine or Saint Simon, Flaubert and Baudelaire in *A la recherche du temps perdu*, he embeds the literature and language of the past into the present of a narrative laced with criticism. Creating a new context from which to speak of literature and reading, he rejected the notion of a canon as that which imposes a universalising style on heterogeneous thought. Yet the search for what is most unique for the writer produced a work considered now to be one of the most canonical.

As the narrator of *A la recherche du temps perdu* looks back on the great works of the nineteenth century, he notes incompletion: Balzac's *Comédie humaine*, Hugo's *La Légende des siècles*, Michelet's *La Bible de l'humanité*, all were completed through prefaces serendipitously written after the fact. Like Wagner and Ruskin, these authors discovered unity in retrospect, creation occurring in discrete fragments whose relation remained unsuspected, unbound by any thesis until a 'retrospective illumination' swept them into a whole. Proust sets a different course for his work, mapping out the project of a book unified from its very inception, although it would be exceeded endlessly by the process of writing. Searching the Judeo-Christian tradition for the secret of creation, he looked to philosophy, music and painting to help transform the reading of literature into writing.

In *A la recherche du temps perdu*, Proust charts the way writing transforms the particulars of feeling and thought into form, retroactively conferring the recognition of aesthetic truth through an epiphanic vision. Bridging the worlds of life and literature through first-person narrative, the novel segues from the dominant thinking patterns of two centuries: the nineteenth century in which fragmentary thought is translated through narrative into totality, and the twentieth century in which meaning unravels into a process of infinite referral. Questioning the status of his life and work, the narrator of the novel leads the reader through exquisitely orchestrated reflections on the relationship between truth and signification, the senses and intelligence, as well as memory, time and space. It has often

III

been said that Proust produced only one work during his lifetime, all previous writing a warm-up to the great novel.

Proust began to formulate his project while translating works by the art critic and essayist John Ruskin. He noted that while Ruskin skips from one idea to another without apparent order, his writing obeys a hidden scheme whose order is revealed at the end of the work. Proust later espoused this teleological movement, in which the end is gestured at from the outset, conferring a unity that allows the artist to become himself.

In the fragments gathered under the title *Contre Sainte-Beuve*, Proust rejects Sainte-Beuve's psychobiographical analysis of a writer's life to explain art, and he balances the importance of affect for his own project against the analytic or intellectual function of thought, located between literature and philosophy. At the 'origin' was a project composed of many styles: criticism, parody, theory and narrative. 'Faut-il faire un roman, une étude philosophique, suis-je romancier?' ['Should it be a novel? a philosophical study? am I a novelist?'] he questioned in a notebook from 1908 (*Contre Sainte-Beuve*, 1908, 61). Proust chose the novel and transformed the philosophical question 'how to think' along with the more existential 'how to become what one is' into the literary venture of 'how one becomes a writer'. As he asked who is the subject which 'is', which 'functions' socially and politically in the world, and which 'writes', he began to break away from the opposition between perception and reflection, and understood that the dualism of binary thinking would be altered through what he called 'le redressement de l'oblique discours intérieur' (*Recherche* IV: 458) ['the rectification of an oblique interior discourse' (*Remembrance* III: 926)]. (References are given throughout this chapter to both the original and the English translation of Proust's novel: see suggestions for further reading for details.) Thought would not be *either* philosophical *or* literary, perceptive *or* reflective, conscious *or* unconscious, just as the two walks (by way of Swann's or Guermantes's) so opposed in the beginning of the novel ultimately become connected. In *A la recherche du temps perdu* the paths of literature and philosophy, as ways of making the world intelligible and giving meaning to it, intertwine to become inseparable.

Proust proclaimed the unity of the first and last sections of *A la recherche du temps perdu*, pointing to their simultaneous creation: 'Le dernier chapitre du dernier volume a été écrit tout de suite après le premier chapitre du premier volume. Tout l'"entre-deux" a été écrit ensuite' (Letter to Paul Souday, *Correspondance* 3, p. 72) ['The last chapter of the last volume was written right after the first chapter of the first volume. Everything in between was written after that']. He worked out a number of the key episodes of the novel: awakening disoriented in space and time, the sense of fluidity between dreamlife and consciousness, the experience of jotting down perceptions, and most importantly, two experiences of involuntary memory that furnished the support or 'inner' structure of the work: the first flush of joy when memories irrupt into consciousness as the narrator drinks tea and tastes the madeleine, then feels uneven paving stones underfoot, and hears a spoon drop on his plate. Mysteriously calling forth feelings of elation, of 'pure life conserved pure' (*Contre Sainte-Beuve*, ed. Fallois pp. 53–5), these very experiences begin and end the novel in symmetry. In *Combray*, the scene of the madeleine summons total recall of childhood amnesia; in *Le Temps retrouvé*, the same such memories replay the experience of involuntary memory, preliminaries or rites of passage through Proust's ontology to his aesthetics.

Proust published *Du côté de chez Swann*, the first volume of *A la recherche du temps perdu*, on the eve of the First World War in 1913. The genesis of the novel alternated between a binary and ternary structure: at first in three volumes (*Swann*, *Le Côté de Guermantes* and *Le Temps retrouvé*), but crossed by the structural duality which opposed lost time to time found of the first two volumes to the last. It is difficult to recreate the sense of the initial triptych or even the equilibrium of the diptych because the last section of the novel remained far less developed than what was written subsequently. During and after the war years a proliferation of writing brought about the addition of interim volumes, *Le Côté de Guermantes* I and II, *Sodome et Gomorrhe* I and II, *La Prisonnière*, *La Fugitive (Albertine disparue)*, *Le Temps retrouvé*. In them, the sense of closure and revelation so clear at the outset of the project becomes clouded by the *Bildungsroman*, the apprenticeship of life and love.

The burgeoning inner volumes concern the narrator, Marcel, whose love for and jealousy of Albertine comes to occupy the centre of the later volumes of the novel. With the focus on jealousy, a shift in tone occurs marking the narrator's desperate attempt and failure to enclose meaning within the frame of the original project. This panoramic view suggests that both the genesis of the writing and the structure of the text posit the conditions for the work of art to emerge, only then to exceed them in a compelling way. Changing the project from within, a new 'style' emerges in the search for the self in time which, through associative sequences and repetitions without end, displaces the notion of absolute truth.

Proust develops a principle of individuation as the basis of memory and art, as that which both demands and resists generalisation. Truth resides in the reconstruction of events 'without precedent' where nothing ever repeats itself exactly. By probing the way in which associations seem to guide thought; by translating the simultaneity of associations into the necessarily successive, temporal sequences of writing, Proust attempted to find the general laws of thought out of the singularity of particular sensations and particular situations. He wished to tease from experience some general quality resembling a scientific law and still maintain what is unique. This effort makes of association the unanalysed domain of thought and the premise upon which Proust constructed his sense of literature. He developed a literary theory of knowledge on the margins of rationalism, overtly opposed to positivism, which became implanted affecting thought thereafter.

At the end of the nineteenth century Freud developed the basic rule of 'free association' as the clinical method of psychoanalysis; Ferdinand de Saussure founded semiology from linguistics as a general system of signs, based on the association between signifier and signified; James Joyce wrote *Ulysses*; while Proust was incorporating association into the literary text as an operation fundamental to language and thought. Without apparent influence upon one another, each struggled with the way in which associations integrate irrationality into a paradigmatic organisation of thought and provoke change in the order of knowledge.

Proust took off from a notion of association which initially, like Freud's, was tied to mechanistic determinism. Freud developed the technique of 'free association' for psychoanalysis between 1892 and 1898, the basic rule of evenly poised attention on the part of the analyst and a form of uncensored thought (characterised as free fall – the literal meaning of the German expression *Einfall*) on the part of the analysand in which the (seeming) accidents of association become intelligible through a rigorously determined structure of the psyche. Proust's narrator seeks to establish the truth of being through the way in which associations signify within the heterogeneity of time and space, testing what is contingent, what determined.

In order to account for change, Proust takes up the question of connections (necessary or accidental) as he seeks a form of association located in memory that moves from a subjective origin within the individual to a universalising principle. He describes the heterogeneous experience of the world through perception and time in its relation to language. By contrasting what is most unique to the individual with general laws of thought and habit, he activates a creative force. Although he moves the narrative away from historical associationism, he nevertheless assumes the problems raised by that history: the question asked by Hume, why associative connections appear to be *necessary* connections, and Kant's interrogation of the way in which causal relations emerge from a subjective origin to take on universal validity.

By doubting the fundamental spatio-temporal coordinates of thought,

Proust asks a Cartesian question: whether by mixing perceptions, associations may not result in 'misconceptions' and deceive. It is less the truth factor, or calculation of errors, that ultimately interests him than the way in which thought defines itself with respect to sensation and time. Proust wrote literature from the contingencies of his private sphere, describing the passage from life to art through the point of view of the narrator: impressions of the people he frequents and the places he inhabits.

He was a non-metaphysician moving out from a metaphysical model, an ironist who wanted to created life anew through the word (see Richard Rorty). As a novelist, he was a master at depicting the moments when the contingent turns into a given: in love, Albertine appears to be only one among many young women until a kind of crystallisation takes place, and the narrator's love becomes excruciatingly fixed on her, obsessively coupled with jealousy; in art, how a Manet or Baudelaire passed from being considered revolutionary to having classical status with the passage of time; in thought, how singularity connects, however obliquely, to universalism.

As it is set out in fragments of a preface to *Contre Sainte-Beuve*, the project is totalising, and totality corresponds to a principle of intelligibility. Recounting through the novel the discovery of the narrator's vocation as a writer, the total work emerges as it creates and embodies its own conception: a project in which the end as the beginning demands the hermeneutic completion of understanding and meaning in writing. Yet like a rip-tide, incompletion and uncertainty find expression within an associative mode of thought that brings perspectival shifts through sequenced impressions: 'On raisonne, c'est-à-dire on vagabonde, chaque fois qu'on n'a pas la force de s'astreindre à faire passer une impression par tous les états successifs qui aboutiront à sa fixation, à l'expression' (*Recherche* IV: 461) ['A writer reasons, that is to say he goes astray, only when he has not the strength to force himself to make an impression pass through all the successive states which culminate in its fixation, its expression' (*Remembrance* III: 916)].

What both fascinates the narrator and makes him wary is that association is a thought process in which no truth can ever be fixed. Always unfinished, association cannot be reduced to a theoretical systematisation, based on the intelligibility of the affect, or the abandonment of all meaning in the anarchy of empirical discovery. It allows the reader to locate the resistance to rational thought, and rational philosophy first articulated in *Contre Sainte-Beuve* in relation to the conception of the work of art. The destabilisation of habit and certainty puts everything into question: rationality, causality, the order of discourse and analogical thinking. However, the doubt and incompleteness opened up in such questioning was framed by Proust's initial project which, while always different, would always be the same.

Proust claimed a 'severe construction' to his work through the way in which memory organises experience in relation to matter; it provides the founding principle for the translation of memory into artistic creation. Unlike the kind of voluntary memory conjured by the intellect, involuntary memory – in a tradition going to back to Schopenhauer and Schelling (see Anne Henry, *Marcel Proust* and *Proust romancier*) – arrives without warning in the superimposition of past and present and brings to the narrator a feeling of joy and certainty. Involuntary memory goes beyond the limits of intelligence and reason: the narrator recovers not only a moment from the past, but much more: 'Rien qu'un moment du passé? Beaucoup plus, peut-être; quelque chose qui, commun à la fois au passé et au présent, est beaucoup plus essentiel qu'eux deux' (*Recherche* IV: 450) ['Perhaps very much more: something that, common both to the past and to the present, is much more essential than either of them' (*Remembrance* III: 905)]. As an experience without precedent, involuntary memory produces a miracle of creation, for it is both a particular experience of the individual and an absolute in the truth it invents.

Tracking the dislocations between life and art, determinism and freedom, Proust excludes biography as the basis for art in *Contre Sainte-Beuve*, yet the narrator of *A la recherche du temps perdu* only emerges through the self-reflection of first-person narrative. He refuses the determinism of history (Taine's linkage of 'race, milieu, moment') only to find deterministic patterns in love and jealousy. And, while returning to an idealist model for art inspired by Schopenhauer's conception of music, the narrator nevertheless scrutinises life in society with the care of a connoisseur. Such are the complexities of an art which dwells in the land of paradox, reproducing the very elements denied to its origin.

As the narrator discovers, neither love nor society renders knowledge of others, nor does it ensure creative power. The jealous lover is an interpreter for whom the signs of love, like the objects of the world, are like hieroglyphs to be deciphered. Reconstituting the unity of the other – in this instance, Albertine – implies grasp of a truth not yet revealed: is she or is she not of Gomorrah? The narrator does not directly question the sexuality of his own desire, even though fascination with Albertine's and Charlus's sexual identity reconstitutes impossible knowledge as an expression of desire. Jealousy provokes instability in the hermeneutic function for Swann confronted with Odette, as for Marcel with Albertine. Jealousy repeats the ternary structure inherent in all love: from indifference to desire, in which it reaches full expression and then subsides again in indifference. In every case, the narrator associates indifference with certainty and desire with distress. Love seems locked into laws that dictate that there is no desire without anguish nor certainty without indifference. Swann's story, inserted into the second volume of *Du côté de chez Swann,* is the only third-person narrative. It occurs prior to the narrator's account of his life and serves as its negative forerunner. Swann is the person the narrator might have been, or might become, a source for much of the reflection for his own book. But Swann makes a misguided analogy between love and art, in the resemblance he sees between Odette and Botticelli's Zephora, for example, because such comparisons cannot make of him an artist. What separates love and the work of art is that art presupposes a revelation where love demands analysis and interpretation.

In *A la recherche du temps perdu* the narrator creates his literary landscape in relation to music and painting from impressions linked by association in which memories and feelings combine and recombine disjunctively in thought. Many of the characters are defined by a relationship to art: Bergotte the writer, Elstir the painter, Vinteuil the musician, La Berma the actress; as are the interpreters of music like Morel on the violin, or Albertine at the pianola; there are also art appreciators, the Guermantes or the Verdurin; and literary tastes like the grandmother's for Mme de Sévigné. The narrator translates the experience of the arts – in the models of music and painting – in order to recreate and analyse the itinerary leading to the 'discovery': his 'vocation' as a writer. In *Le Temps retrouvé* he asserts that 'Le devoir et la tâche d'un écrivain sont ceux d'un traducteur' (*Recherche* IV: 469) ['the function and the task of a writer are those of a translator' (*Remembrance* III: 926)]. As quintessential artist, he is to write the book of the self that will bring together private obsession with art and the laws of thought. Proust conferred the image of the book upon the life, even though the life was not to explain the book. Because 'chaque lecteur est quand il lit le propre lecteur de soi-même' (*Recherche* IV: 489) ['every reader is, while he is reading, the reader of his own self' (*Remembrance* III: 949)], the narrator likens time to a library in which one recovers the past by requesting a book and remembers specific episodes by finding lost pages. These images serve as catalysts for discovery because they make the self intelligible to itself. The passage from ontology to aesthetics may be found in the relationship of involuntary memory to metaphor and music, as idealised models for creation.

Music guides the artist away from the pitfalls of idolatry and intellectualism. It establishes a process of growth in art (from fragments of Vinteuil's sonata to the great septet) conceived as translation that leads beyond the threshold of mundane social relations. The little phrase from Vinteuil's sonata becomes in this way the 'national anthem' of love between Swann and Odette, irrupting into the present with each hearing. It plays a role analogous to involuntary memory for the narrator and Swann, with this difference: Swann, the failed artist, cannot carry the experience of memory through music into literary creation.

Vinteuil is the model of the musician whose music is fragmented into the different moments of performance in the same way that the painter Elstir's paintings are scattered about in galleries and private houses. Of the arts, only music, without thematic message, takes on the 'inflection of being' as the first universal form. Like an idea in need of transcription, or some invisible creature whose previously unknown language is now understood, with immediate recognition, music alone returns without ever having been heard. In the 'intermittencies' of music, the sonata forms a 'continuous line with brief calls', whereas the septet melds into an 'indivisible structure' whose internal logic parallels the structure of *A la recherche du temps perdu* (see Jean-Jacques Nattiez).

Questioning throughout how experience relates to the models of art, the narrator discovers his vocation as a writer at the end of the novel through the determination to write a book that is neither the book that one is reading, nor any book that one may read. Similar in that to Mallarmé's conception of 'le livre', this book maintains a status between the ideal and the real, unrealised in the form of extant books.

The passage into art through writing occurs because of the exemplary status granted to the narrator through the uniquely absolute truth of involuntary memory. Creation becomes translation of memory. Commanded by the image of the book, translation allows newness to emerge paradoxically from something presumed to be already there: 'Des impressions obscures . . . cachaient non une sensation d'autrefois mais une vérité nouvelle' (*Recherche* IV: 456) ['Certain obscure impressions . . . concealed within them not a sensation dating from an earlier time, but *a new truth*' (*Remembrance* III: 912, emphasis added)]. The discovery of this 'new truth' constitutes the core of Proust's book project. Truth is there to be found by the writer: 'Ce livre essentiel, le seul livre vrai, un grand écrivain n'a pas, dans le sens courant, à l'inventer puisqu'il existe déjà en chacun de nous, mais à le traduire' (*Recherche* IV: 469) ['The essential, the only true book, though in the ordinary sense of the word it does not have to be 'invented' by a great writer – for it exists already in each one of us – has to be *translated* by him' (*Remembrance* III: 926, my emphasis)].

The myth of interiority is, however, flawed in the attribution of the translation of experience for the interpretation of signs. Though the narrator-theoretician may view his own life abstractly as the translation of a book internal to him, nowhere does this original manifest itself in the writing. Translation brings forth the language of a unique self in relation to the other through time and memory. The book towards which all this tends is a fable about literature as the translation of an 'inner' world of thought. Not because a simple one-to-one relation may be established between a word and a feeling or thought. Though Proust senses that Ruskin like Carlyle held such a belief: the poet was a sort of scribe of nature writing out something of its secret to which the artist should add nothing. For Proust as for Walter Benjamin, whose unrealised project was to translate Proust, the relationship of the translator to the original is one of survival: of one in the other through writing.

The aesthetic theory of metaphor forges a most important connection:

La vérité ne commencera qu'au moment où l'écrivain prendra deux objets différents, posera leur rapport, analogue dans le monde de l'art à celui qu'est le rapport unique de la loi causale dans le monde de la science, et les enfermera dans les anneaux nécessaires d'un beau style. Même, ainsi que la vie, quand, en rapprochant une qualité commune à deux sensations, il dégagera leur essence commune en les réunissant l'une et l'autre pour les soustraire aux contingences du temps, dans une métaphore. (*Recherche* IV: 468)

['Truth will be attained by him only when he takes two different objects, states the connection between them – a connection analogous in the world of art to the unique connection which in the world of science is provided by the law of causality – and encloses them in the necessary links of a well-wrought style; truth – and life too – can be attained by us only when, by comparing a quality common to two sensations, we succeed in extracting their common essence and in reuniting them to each other, liberated from the contingencies of time, within a metaphor.' (*Remembrance* III: 925)]

Elstir provides an example of such a metaphor in his paintings, transplanting flowers in nature to this 'inner garden': 'de sorte qu'on peut dire que c'était une variété nouvelle dont ce peintre, comme un ingénieux horticulteur, avait enrichi la famille des roses' (*Recherche* III: 334) ['so that one might say that [in this case, the roses] were a new variety with which this painter, like a skilful horticulturist, had enriched the rose family' (*Remembrance* II: 975)]. The narrator believes this feat to be transferable to writing: 'Mais j'y pouvais discerner que le charme de chacune consistait en une sorte de métamorphose des choses représentées, analogue à celle qu'en poésie on nomme métaphore' (*Recherche* II: 191) ['I was able to discern from these that the charm of each of them lay in a sort of metamorphosis of the objects represented, analogous to what in poetry we call metaphor' (*Remembrance* 1: 893)]. Articulated in abstract terms, Elstir's painting renders metaphor an intellectual act, equivalent to renaming.

The problem, as Proust suggested in his preface to Paul Morand's *Tendre Stocks,* was that the criterion of singularity in the work of art remains at odds with the concept of a unified style: how to reconcile radical newness with universal truth. For Proust made clear that style was not a question of technique, but of vision. He chose Flaubert as a model for style, a writer in whose work he found the lack of a single beautiful metaphor. The difficulty of passing from ideal to realised form admits to no ready formula. While Proust called all figures of analogy metaphor, most of the metaphors in the novel fall within a sequence of extended comparisons. Involuntary memory appears to function as pure metaphor devoid of metonymy (that is, relations of proximity) – and yet metaphor is constructed from terms that have already been related in spatio-temporal contiguity. The passage from the 'joy of certainty' activated by involuntary memory leads to metaphor, and in the overall structure completes the spiritual journey for the writer-hero by ending the search with theoretical closure. Gérard Genette has analysed how metaphor comes out of metonymy (Genette, *Figures III*), how the 'sense-signal' in the madeleine becomes the equivalent of the context to which it is associated. So that if metaphor finds lost time, metonymy revives it. (For comments on Jakobson's earlier and highly influential discussion of metaphor and metonymy, see chapter 1 of this volume, pp. 8–9.)

Later writers look to this interplay between memory and truth as the basis for art and comment upon it: Sartre kills the affective truth of memory in a passage of *La Nausée* where cold tea signals a dead love affair (Jean-Paul Sartre, *La Nausée* (Paris: Gallimard, 1938), p. 215), yet Roquentin responds to a melody played on a phonograph by a maid named Madeleine: an invitation to leave the contingency of existence for the redemptive world of art. Robbe-Grillet rejects metaphor as the retrieval of the distance between being and things in his theory of the new novel (see his 'Nature, humanisme, tragédie', in *Pour un nouveau roman* (Paris: Minuit, 1963), pp. 55–84), yet his novels rely upon habits of reading that associate them. Sarraute relegates Proust and Joyce to the status of historical monuments, to be visited only by respectful school children, suggesting a period of literary history is closed. Yet the effect of *A la recherche du temps perdu* is to juxtapose history with an extra-temporal vision in which Proust's vigilance about the relationship of signs and truth changes the focus, as Gilles Deleuze suggested: 'What is essential in *The Search* is not memory and time, but the sign and truth. What is essential is not to remember, but to learn' (Gilles Deleuze, pp. 89–90). Contrary to

Sarraute's prediction, the endless quest for truth through signs marks twentieth-century writing with a form of fragmentation in the novel that Milan Kundera has called 'the wisdom of uncertainty'. If Proust's contemporaries could only dimly see the revolution that he was inaugurating – the bold construction of an edifice within which speculation about the literary vocation takes narrative form – late twentieth-century readers can follow the literary map. When one re-reads the novel in relation not only to the finished structure, but with respect to the genesis of the writing, this revolution shows itelf to be less the sense of a break or rupture with tradition, than the repetition and reinterpretation of impressions through difference. Proust encapsulated the passage from the nineteenth to the twentieth century with the displacement of the figure for the book from the grandeur of a religious monument to a more intimate and resourceful image: 'Epinglant ici un feuillet supplémentaire, je bâtirais mon livre, je n'ose pas dire ambitieusement comme une cathédrale, mais tout simplement comme une robe' (*Recherche* IV: 610) ['Pinning here and there an extra page, I should construct my book, I dare not say ambitiously like a cathedral, but quite simply like a dress' (*Remembrance* III: 1090)].

Proust's novel asks a fundamental question. If one can never know the truth behind phenomena, but only relations among things, what then is the nature of truth? If there are no absolutes, what bond can function in place of universal laws in the modern world? The ideal transfer from involuntary memory to metaphor involves the workings of thought which remain at a remove from the social world. Still the two operate in parallel throughout the novel, although the relationship to the world is often one of disillusionment, as when the boy dreams about and finally gets to see the actress La Berma in *Phèdre,* only to feel let down. And when aesthetic concerns touch on ethics, forms of moral evaluation are situated within a context enabling the narrator to follow their social trajectories.

The Dreyfus case provided Proust with an event whose literary transformation within the novel linked ethics to the aesthetic theory of the novel. Alfred Dreyfus, a Jew and a French military officer, was accused and convicted of treason. France divided between the Anti-Dreyfusards – royalists, militarists and nationalists – and the Dreyfusards who were republican, socialist and anticlerical. Only much later was it discovered that Dreyfus had been convicted on the basis of documents forged by Colonel Henry. Not until 1906 was Dreyfus reinstated to his rank in the army and ultimately acquitted. It was an event that imposed choice and judgement upon individuals, cleaving France and setting the stage for many issues that remain unresolved at the end of the twentieth century. What is the role of nationalism in the definition and development of the individual? Where is the borderline between necessary distinctions in social and ethnic categories and racism? Where does diplomacy and tact stop and compromise begin?

Proust deals directly with the Dreyfus trials in *Jean Santeuil*. His character Jean believes that 'la vérité est quelque chose qui existe réellement en soi, en dehors de toute opinion . . . ' (*Jean Santeuil*, p. 650) ['truth is really something that existed in itself and had nothing to do with opinion . . . ' (*Jean Santueil*, trans. Gerard Hopkins, pp. 351–2)]. An avowed Dreyfusard, the novelist will later portray those who opposed his position in *A la recherche du temps perdu*, confiding in a letter: 'Ne me croyez surtout pas devenu anti-dreyfusard. J'écris sous la dictée de mes personnages et il se trouve que beaucoup de ce volume-ci, le sont' (*Correspondance 6*, p. 236, cited in *Recherche* II: 450n) ['Do not believe that I have become anti-Dreyfusard. I write at the dictate of my characters and it happens that many of them in this volume are anti-Dreyfusard']. On the maternal side, his grandmother expresses benevolent ambivalence, while his mother reserves an undecided silence. As for who the most antisemitic person in the family is, versions of *Combray* vacillate between the grandfather and the maternal grand uncle. The narrator chronicles reactions to the case, inscribing something impossible at any given moment in time: a shift in position. The brunt of the antisemitic jokes thus migrates from Bloch to Swann, and what is important is that the ability to change voluntarily signals an exercise of freedom that counters the nationalist, antisemitic philosophy prevalent at the time, in which everything (in both individual and collective life) was said to be determined.

By suggesting that even overtly political themes become comprehensible only when passed through the stages of 'experience', Proust takes a more political stand than he is usually given credit for. The remark 'aucune action extérieure à soi n'a d'importance' ['no form of action exterior to oneself has any importance'] (*Contre Saint-Beuve*, 1908, p. 101) did not suggest a radical form of quietism. Proust plunges into the predicament of human thought: the freedom to think beyond the determined. He analyses the moral positions of his characters as a scribe of society, its ironic philosopher or critic, in terms of the futility of judging them.

It is against the notion of determinism that Proust portrays the lack of consensus and the possibility for change where it is least suspected: Saint-Loup, whose background would have led him to be anti-Dreyfusard, elected Dreyfusism and then switched back, choosing what heredity might otherwise have dictated. The narrator runs through a series of characters stating each of their positions (down to the Guermante's maître d'hôtel) –

who is for and who is against Dreyfus – exhibiting the way in which households can divide against themselves politically.

The novel presents social and political attitudes reshuffling like a kaleidoscope with fragments of colour. The parodic freedom glimpsed in the actions of a Mme de Guermantes (an anti-Dreyfusard believing in the innocence of Dreyfus who exercises her options by refusing invitations) finds its serious counterpart in the choices of the Prince and Princesse de Guermantes who each become Dreyfusard unbeknownst to the other. The compelling question for the characters as for the narrator is one of responsibility in the exercise of freedom of choice.

In *Contre Sainte-Beuve*, Proust had proclaimed not only that a book renders a self separate from the one in the world, but that 'notre personnalité sociale est une création de la pensée des autres' (*Recherche* I: 19) ['our social personality is a creation of the thoughts of other people' (*Remembrance* I: 20)]. The disintegration and reformation of social positions, make the search for a structure grounded in some truth, as well as a process in the world through which to work it out, all the more imperative: finding the basis for a higher order in art. The social and political frame for the development of an ethics of the subject deflects empirical moralism, and its aesthetic corollary, 'la fausseté même de l'art prétendu réaliste' (*Recherche* IV: 460) ['the falseness of so-called realist art' (*Remembrance* IV: 460)], in affirming how the contingency of fiction reveals truth.

If the dominant new genre of the twentieth century may said to be literary criticism, Proust criticism spans its growth from the early work of Jacques Rivière, François Mauriac and Albert Thibaudet. After publication in 1927 of *A la recherche du temps perdu*, a spate of mostly admiring biographical and anecdotic criticism appeared by people who knew Proust. Although there was much interest in finding out who the life models for his characters were, almost nothing was said at the time about his homosexuality. Stylistic studies appeared in the works of Curtius and later Spitzer. *Jean Santeuil* appeared in 1952; *Contre Sainte-Beuve* and an edition of *A la recherche du temps perdu* were published in 1954; questions arose about the evolution of these works and the premises upon which editorial decisions were based. When Proust's niece, Suzy Mante-Proust, sold the manuscripts to the Bibliothèque Nationale in 1962, it became apparent that the chronology of the writing did not correspond to the finished work (see Milly, p. 28). So too with *A la recherche du temps perdu*. The Proust papers came into the public domain in 1987, a year that marked the end of readings largely from the Clarac and Ferré edition of 1954, an edition based on the uncorrected typescripts that had not taken account of changes indicated by Proust himself. 1987 began a new era of reading Proust as well, with the publication of several new editions and many sketches or early drafts included in the Pléiade edition. The two sides of Proust's thought are reproduced in these publications – one tending toward a notion of totality and ultimate meaning, the other toward the unravelling of meaning in the infinite movement of piecing together fragmentary knowledge.

Within Proust criticism, three general critical approaches have dominated since the 1940s: phenomenological criticism prior to the mid-1960s concentrated on the phenomenology of mind within the project, the relationship of subject to object with analysis of consciousness and time; within literary studies in the 1960s and 1970s, the period of poetic structuralism, critics focused on semiological analyses, exploring the levels of linguistic patterning within the text; 'genetic' criticism followed in the 1980s, with the greater access to previously unavailable material, bringing to light problems of uncertainty, similar to the kind claimed for the finished text within deconstructive criticism.

The transition within Proustian studies from phenomenology to rhetorical analyses, to genetic criticism, opens the way for exploration of the ways in which the mechanisms of thought (be they philosophical or artistic) deal with the sub-theoretical level present in all theorising. For Proust, the rational notion of totality and the concept of an all-encompassing theory are at some level synonymous. By putting in place a practice for which there is no adequate speculative theory, Proust's texts raise a key question of how literature may lead to a redefinition of thought which is neither solely rational nor irrational, singular nor universal.

SUGGESTIONS FOR FURTHER READING

Works by Proust

A la recherche du temps perdu, 4 vols., ed. J.-Y. Tadié (Paris: Gallimard, Bibliothèque de la Pléiade, 1987–9)

Remembrance of Things Past, trans. C. K. Scott Moncrieff and T. Kilmartin (New York: Random House, 1981)

Albertine disparue, ed. N. Mauriac and E. Wolff (Paris: Grasset, 1987)

Chroniques (Paris: Gallimard, 1927)

Contre Sainte-Beuve, ed. B. de Fallois (Paris: Gallimard, 1954)

Contre Sainte-Beuve, ed. P. Clarac with Y. Sandre (Paris: Gallimard, Bibliothèque de la Pléiade, 1971)

Correspondance, ed. P. Kolb, 17 vols. (Paris: Plon, 1970–   )

Jean Santeuil, ed. B. de Fallois (Paris: Gallimard, 1952)

Jean Santeuil, trans. G. Hopkins with a preface by André Maurois (New York: Simon and Schuster, 1956)

Critical studies

Bales, R., *Proust: 'A la recherche du temps perdu'* (London: Grant and Cutler, 1995)

Beckett, S., *Proust* (New York: Grove Press, 1931)

Bersani, L., *Marcel Proust: The Fictions of Life and Art* (Oxford: Oxford University Press, 1965)

Bowie, M., *Freud, Proust and Lacan: Theory as Fiction* (Cambridge: Cambridge University Press, 1987)

Compagnon, A., *Proust entre deux siècles* (Paris: Seuil, 1989)

Deleuze, G., *Proust et les signes* (Paris: Presses Universitaires de France, 1964)

Descombes, V., *Proust: philosophie du roman* (Paris: Minuit, 1987)

Fraisse, L., *Le Processus de la création chez Marcel Proust: le fragment expérimental* (Paris: José Corti, 1988)

   L'Esthétique de Marcel Proust (Paris: SEDES, 1995)

Genette, G., *Figures* (Paris: Seuil, 1966)

   Figures III (Paris: Seuil, 1972)

Henry, A., *Marcel Proust. Théories pour une esthétique* (Paris: Klincksieck, 1981)

   Proust romancier: le tombeau égyptien (Paris: Flammarion, 1983)

Kristeva, J., *Le temps sensible. Proust et l'expérience littéraire* (Paris: Gallimard, 1994)

Leroy, G. (ed.), *Les Ecrivains et l'Affaire Dreyfus* (Paris: Presses Universitaires de France, 1983)

McDonald, C., *The Proustian Fabric: Associations of Memory* (Lincoln: University of Nebraska Press, 1991)

Milly, J., *Proust et le style* (Geneva: Slaktine Reprints, 1991)

Nattiez, J., *Proust musicien* (Paris: Christian Bourgois, 1984)

Poulet, G., *L'espace proustien* (Paris: Gallimard, 1963)

Richard, J. P., *Proust et le monde sensible* (Paris: Seuil, 1974)

Rorty, R., *Contingency, Irony, and Solidarity* (Cambridge: Cambridge University Press, 1989)

Spitzer, L., 'Le style de Marcel Proust', in *Le style de Marcel Proust* (Paris: Gallimard, 1970), pp. 397–473

Sprinker, M., *History and Ideology in Proust. 'A la recherche du temps perdu' and the Third French Republic* (Cambridge: Cambridge University Press, 1994)

Tadié, J.-Y., *Proust* (Paris: Les Dossiers Belfond, 1983)

8

DAVID H. WALKER

Formal experiment and innovation

The two decades spanning the end of the nineteenth and the beginning of the twentieth centuries were a period of intense crisis for the novel. On the one hand, it was not clear what more could be done with the form after the achievements of Balzac, Stendhal, Flaubert and Zola. Balzac had created a world rivalling 'l'état civil' for his era, and Zola's project for systematic, scientifically documented studies of all sectors of society, had been all but consummated by its principal begetter. The realistic portrayal of everyday life could be extended into ever more marginal or sensational sectors such as those explored by the Goncourt brothers (*Germinie Lacerteux*, 1864) and less memorable exponents; but this was merely following in Zola's footsteps, without the creative conviction or epic gifts that, until the anticlimax of *Les Quatre Evangiles*, compelled the assent of his readers. In *Pierre et Jean* (1888) and its prefatory essay, 'Le Roman', Maupassant sought to revitalise realism by drawing attention to the illusions of the mind that influence the formation of stories, but the picture conveyed by the naturalist novel was beginning to be perceived as the least significant feature of reality. In a reaction against the positivist doctrines which had come to dominate the century and informed both realism and naturalism, the symbolists, inspired by Mallarmé, sought a higher set of truths, above and beyond documentary fact and the limited scope of physical observation. The mechanisms of cause and effect, the acme of rational explanation and the backbone of plotting in the traditional novel, seemed reductive and hardly relevant in the *fin-de-siècle* scheme of things. The novel thus came to seem incompatible with the pursuit of finer, less easily graspable ideals and intuitions, and poetry became the elective form of the new generation who turned their back on what they saw as the merely quotidian and banal.

At the same time, to the more intellectually demanding and self-consciously literary of this generation, the novel's very principles seemed untenable. Fictions that were to be taken as truth, arbitrary plot constructions masquerading as fate or destiny, contrived character traits laying claim to psychological depth and moral autonomy, extensive physical descriptions that gratuitously aped the contingency of the universe – all these simply ceased to command credence. Paul Valéry most famously – and persistently, in writings and comments cited with glee or consternation at the time and subsequently – embodied the reader who refused to be the passive subject of a vulgar enchantment. For this poet committed to the life of the spirit, the highest form of art involved the greatest degree of self-awareness and calculation: suspension of disbelief was out of the question, as was the sacrifice of beauty to realistic detail. The art of the novel was thus a contradiction in terms, and even when represented by Proust was 'presque inconcevable'.[1]

This degree of scepticism, restated over half a century later in the title of Nathalie Sarraute's volume *L'Ere du soupçon* (1956) – devoted precisely to a critique of assumptions underlying the form – has been a crucial concomitant in the novel's evolution throughout the modern era. Hostility to the novel's shortcomings has been instrumental in generating new developments. The 1890s and the early 1900s witnessed a first wave of extensive theorisation and the exploration of alternative prose forms and less familar genres such as *traité* (implying a didactic aim) and *sotie* (evoking the satirical element in medieval farce), the revival of the short story, publications such as allegedly posthumous notebooks of authors who died in the effort to write an impossible novel, and so on. Experimentation and innovation became a *sine qua non* of prose writers as the novel was effectively ruled out of bounds or proved out of reach. Valéry ostentatiously eschewed the genre in the prose meditations of *La Soirée avec M. Teste* (1896). Gide exploited the situation ironically in *Paludes* (1895), which consists of the diary of a writer whose aesthetic principles, he tells us, are opposed to the conception of a novel but who spends much of his time explaining to uncomprehending acquaintances the nature, significance and relevance to the everyday world of the precious symbolist fiction, entitled *Paludes*, which he is struggling with. This work-in-progress within a text which denies the possibility of a novel tellingly encapsulates the dilemmas facing artists in this climate: it would take Gide another thirty years to bring himself to give the label 'novel' to one of his works.

Those who could not reconcile themselves to merely repeating what their illustrious predecessors had done were reduced to speculating on the nature of the novel. Several sets of overlapping contradictions dogged their efforts. Firstly, should the novel address the external world or the internal world? Disciples of Zola opted for the evocation of physiological reality in human affairs; Bourget (*Le Disciple*, 1889, *Cosmopolis*, 1893) and his followers settled for psychological studies which were in their own way little less mechanistic. Secondly, should the novel be a work of art, sculpted and patterned, or did its vocation condemn it to be as shapeless as the world it existed to mirror? Finally, was it inescapably to be associated with the gratuitousness and contingency of its elements, drawing as it was bound to on the arbitrary facts of the real world? Or could it aspire to the condition of a poem, in which every element exists and is rendered necessary by virtue of its relations with all the other elements within the work? In Valéry's view, 'le monde du poème est essentiellement fermé et complet en lui-même' ('Hommage à Marcel Proust', p. 770) ['the world of the poem is essentially closed and complete in itself']. The poem *is* the sum of its parts: change a detail and the spell is broken. On the other hand, a novel is merely one artificial arrangement of any number of possible alternatives through which it could make the same point: there is no reason why the reader should not 'faire intervenir l'infini des possibilités de substitutions que tout récit admet sans altération de son thème' ['bring in the infinite possible substitutions that any narrative allows without impairment of its theme'].[2] Gide noted at an early stage of his career that the novel must shake off its flawed ancestry, based on the pursuit of verisimilitude, and aspire precisely to the higher aesthetic status of the poem: 'Le roman doit prouver à présent qu'il peut être autre chose qu'un miroir promené le long d'un chemin . . . Il faut que dans leur rapport même chaque partie d'une œuvre prouve la vérité de chaque autre' ['The novel must now show that it can be more than a mirror taken along a road. Every part of the work must prove the truth of every other part, by their very relationship'].[3]

In any case, it seemed to some that the French had always favoured a certain classical economy and harmony in the novel: a canon comprising *La Princesse de Clèves* (1678), *Manon Lescaut* (1731), *Adolphe* (1816) and *Dominique* (1862) gave pride of place to spare, short texts organised with the rigour of tragedy, focusing on a small group of protagonists whose feelings and experiences were evoked retrospectively in precise and decorous analytical detail. The more ambitious novels of Flaubert (*L'Education sentimentale*, 1869) are riven by the tension between the discipline of art and the sprawling nature of the real. Turn-of-the-century critics, trying to deduce the essence of the novel, found their surveys degenerated into a plethora of sub-categories including *roman de mœurs sociales, roman artiste, roman catholique, roman exotique, roman régional, roman collectif, roman lyrique, roman dramatique, roman synthétique*. When French writers looked at what happened abroad it was to wonder whether their literature had ever really envisaged the all-encompassing, expansive torrents of life presented in its full immediacy that foreign literatures called, simply, novels. Tolstoy, in *War and Peace* (1865–9), and Thomas Mann, in

Buddenbrooks (1901), ranged across several generations and numerous milieux; English novelists such as Dickens and George Meredith (whose *The Egoist*, 1879, was particularly influential) showed a striking disregard for the aesthetic scruples that tended to paralyse French novelists, and challenged the latter to rethink their conception of the genre. Such considerations were rendered the more urgent as the impact of Dostoevsky (*The Devils*, 1871, *The Brothers Karamazov*, 1880) began to be absorbed. Could the ample, leisurely attention to imaginative detail evident in the English novelists be reconciled with the geometrical spirit of the French and their aptitude for abstraction and deduction? Might Dostoevky's tumultuous complexities be accommodated within French notions of *bienséance* or artistic propriety?

Such creative experimentation as occurred was usually limited in scope, and none achieved the kind of prominence that could inaugurate a renascence of the genre. A telling instance is Edouard Dujardin's use of the interior monologue in his *Les Lauriers sont coupés* of 1888; it took the publication of *Ulysses* and James Joyce's acknowledgement of this as a source some thirty-five years later, in 1922, for the full implications of the device to be appreciated and exploited by many others. Another avenue which seemed more immediately to offer a way out of the impasse was the so-called 'roman d'aventure' which Marcel Schwob derived from the model of Robert Louis Stevenson as early as 1891, and which was taken up by others, notably Jacques Rivière. This form presented the prospect of a renewal of narrative impetus, at the same time as it pointed to a possible synthesis of subjective and objective reality in events and actions conceived as not merely features of the plot but as the embodiment of ideas and impressions: 'Je veux n'avoir affaire qu'à des événements' ['I want to deal only with events'] wrote Rivière in a 1913 essay.[4]

The two most significant practitioners of this form were Alain-Fournier, in *Le Grand Meaulnes* (1913), and André Gide, in *Les Caves du Vatican* (1914). In Alain-Fournier's hands, the *roman d'aventure* proves a vehicle for revitalising narrative through a tale of childhood memories and youthful dreams. The story hinges on a young man's attachment to the spell cast by a chance encounter with a beautiful woman in a strange château; the author achieves a striking blend of fantasy, poetry and realism in the depiction of this idyll and its sequel, succeeding in his stated aim of inserting the marvellous into the real. Not the least of Alain-Fournier's achievements is to have integrated a faithfully observed portrayal of day-to-day life in city and country with an archetypal dream-scenario echoing Maeterlinck's symbolist drama *Pélleas et Mélisande* (1893).

Gide's ambition was to attain a more panoramic, less ironic depiction of character and event than he had achieved hitherto, by featuring a criminal swindle from the 1890s. The resulting material, including a motley group of dupes or 'caves', a villain who is a master of disguise, and an ineffectual *naïf* who sets out on a lone crusade to put the world to rights, is the very stuff of a classic adventure yarn, into which Gide threads additional strands featuring his ideal of the youthful iconoclastic hero. Almost from the outset, however, the mixture can be seen to be over-rich; and with the introduction of a novelist planning a book about a motiveless crime, pastiche, satire and parody rise to the surface. The text's challenges to credibility are presented precisely in terms of traditional bids for verisimilitude – the claim that this truth is stranger than fiction. The ever-present influence of the criminal conspiracy, engineering encounters and overseeing events, becomes a metaphor for the author's extravagant plotting whereby characters' paths cross to melodramatic effect; and the portrayal of the novelist, spurning respectable literary accolades which have temporarily passed him by and ruminating on the possibilities of an altogether more scandalous aesthetic, provides a mirror of Gide's own concerns in his text. The motiveless crime is an attempt to engage with a Dostoievskian thematic, and the radical changes in outlook undergone by the central protagonists hint at an innovative mode of characterisation based, again like that of Dostoevsky, on contradiction and discontinuity. However, literary self-consciousness reasserts an ironic distance between author and text, and the writer's considerable narrative and stylistic verve culminates, effectively, in a spoof of the adventure novel. Gide applied the medieval label of *sotie* to *Les Caves du Vatican* in order, as he put it, to make clear that this work should *not* be considered a novel in the true sense.

What, then, *was* a novel in the true sense? Gide formulates his criteria thus: 'Le roman, tel que je le reconnais ou l'imagine, comporte une diversité de points de vue' ['The novel as I recognise or imagine it involves a variety of points of view'].[5] This stress on point of view as a crucial ingredient in the form is typical of a moment at which the influence of foreign novelists was again making itself felt, specifically in connection with technique. It was beginning to dawn on certain French commentators that a revival of the novel was not a matter of sensibility, intelligence or cultural particularities, but rather entailed a willingness to experiment with new forms and techniques. Already in the 1890s Marcel Schwob had pointed out how Stevenson presents two different narrators in *Treasure Island* (1883), and had commented on Browning's use of multiple narratives to present intersecting perspectives on a single dramatic event in *The Ring and the Book* (1872). Gide was to rediscover this latter work and apply its lessons as he wrote *Les Faux-Monnayeurs* (1926). Meredith's 'scenic method', revealing incidents through dialogue, had already challenged the narrative techniques that previously relied on an omniscient narrator to tell the story. The manner in which Henry James presents events strictly as seen or experienced by a specific observer or 'reflector', without narratorial commentary or explanation, notably in *What Maisie Knew* (1897) or *The Portrait of a Lady* (1881), was seen to have further creative implications across the range of narrative components: descriptive passages cease to be neutral but become bound up with the sensibility and state of mind of the perceiver; the selection, duration and chronology of events for narration relate equally to the protagonist's awareness; the entire organisation, articulation and rhythm of the narrative is inflected, not to say radicalised, by such considerations.

From 1913 onwards, Marcel Proust progressively published the seven volumes of *A la recherche du temps perdu*. In Proust's novel dramatic events tend to be eschewed in favour of the careful elucidation and poetic illumination of impressions arising from the everyday. Proust also opens the novel up to a wide range of other material such as art and literary criticism, extensive psychological analysis, and the skills of the essayist. The work immediately impressed through the discursive and poetic qualities of the writing; but gradually the novel revealed a complex, all-embracing architecture and a dense and purposeful textual patterning, features which were to become important elements in the modern novel's advance beyond story-telling to stake a claim as one of the highest forms of art. Yet the full measure of Proust's achievement was slow to emerge. In the first *Manifeste du surréalisme* in 1924 André Breton would initiate a series of attacks on the novelistic form. Quoting Valéry's declared inability to write a sentence of the kind 'La marquise sortit à cinq heures', Breton set out one of the most notorious challenges to the artistic credentials of the novel. It is true that the banal sentence incriminated here embodies two slightly different sets of shortcomings. For Valéry it exemplified a concern with the anecdotal trivia of character, event and chronology, infinitely substitutable by no less futile details and a world away from the rigorous necessities of true intellectual constructions which transcend the empirically observed. The crux of Breton's hostility, on the other hand, is that the novel as thus practised confines everyday life to its most mundane and insignificant ingredients instead of seeking out, triggering and celebrating 'le merveilleux' that lies hidden at the heart of things. For Valéry what is artistically worthwhile is the fruit of reflection, and in this connection the novel is far too casual and approximate. But the surrealists attach prime importance to inspiration and the untrammelled power of the imagination: for them the novel is not unfettered enough and too readily accepts the limitations of the real. Yet Breton accepts that the form is not beyond redemption if it is used to the right ends. The 'procès de l'attitude réaliste' ['putting on trial of the realist attitude'] which surrealism set out to accomplish involved both a destruction of conventional perceptions of the real and a liberation of the forces of the unconscious – which includes challenges to conventional psychology. The surrealists, like the symbolists before them, were therefore suspicious of contamination by or attraction to baser aspects of the novel. In this they were aided by the vigilance of Breton himself who discouraged novelistic dabblings. But extended works of prose were produced by leading surrealists, and in their efforts to break through to heightened levels of perception and experience they conceived new methods and techniques. Broadly, the surrealists challenged literature itself in the name of the truer insights they sought: their books therefore renounce the trickeries of fiction and flout the conventions of narrative. Above all, they assert the primacy of the imagination over the dictates of the material universe. This is clear in *Le Paysan de Paris*, which Aragon published in 1926. As the title suggests, Aragon here brings an outsider's eye – that of the surrealist poet – to bear on what he sees as he walks around Paris. Inaugurating a new spirit of place and a 'mythologie moderne' he seeks out 'le merveilleux quotidien' (Livre de Poche edition, p. 16) ['the marvellous in daily life'] and what he calls 'l'inconscient de la ville' (p. 170) ['the unconscious of the city']. Just as certain slips of the tongue provide vistas onto the repressed unconscious of the individual, so certain features of the urban environment offer glimpses of another reality, 'un grand secret dans un décor de lieu commun' (p. 25) ['a great secret in commonplace surroundings']. His method for unearthing this is a subversive recourse to description – not the banal, inert description of the realist novel, but the attentive scrutiny of everyday locations where he discerns the presence of 'serrures qui ferment mal sur l'infini' (p. 20) ['locks which fail to close out the infinite']. In the *Passage de l'Opéra* and the *Parc des Buttes-Chaumont* he focuses to unsettling effect on shop window displays and petrol pumps, for example, transfiguring the panoply of the modern urban environment by virtue of meticulous close-ups whose aim is to provoke a disquieting awareness of the instability of the real. The book has no narrative structure, comprising accounts of walks interspersed with poetic meditations and manifestos for surrealism. It is devoid of novelistic characters; such elements of story as are in evidence trace the evolution of a poetic temperament. But it offers radical innovations in the shape of the poetic 'event' and its defamiliarising descriptions of the modern.

A related sensibility predominates in *Nadja*, which Breton himself published in 1927. In a prologue the author inveighs against simple observation or invention and claims for his text the justification of particular kinds of authentic fact which plunge one into a different order of reality. The text recounts the author's relationship with Nadja, a mysterious woman whose words and presence seem informed by an other-worldly consciousness. There are hints that she may be mad, and Breton's innovation in this text is to adopt the tone of clinical observation while ruling out a psychological approach to her behaviour, presenting his account as a medical case-study which penetrates into a world set apart from the interventions of reason. The result is the creation of an atmosphere propitious to surrealist experience. The basis of the text is not fiction but life itself, which is presented as intrinsically fantastic; thus events, encounters, objects and conversations in the real world generate coincidence, strange juxtapositions of thought and incident – what Breton calls 'le hasard objectif' ['objective chance'] – and intimations of 'le merveilleux'. Eliminating descriptions, dismissed as redundant in his *Manifeste*, Breton substitutes photographs which, though connected to the narrative, are detached from their real context and thus signify differently, hovering between the actual and the virtual world of the imagination. Breton's techniques free his account from the determinisms of narrative and allow its elements to retain the sense of 'l'éventuel' ['the potential'] normally stifled by the structure of a novel.

If Breton and Aragon in their different ways sought to facilitate surreal experiences by their approach to the real, Michel Leiris, in his novel *Aurora* which was written in 1927–8 (though not published until 1946) provides direct access, as it were, to the strange landscapes and hallucinatory events of a surreal universe. This text more obviously adheres to the patterns of the novel: its rhetoric mimics sequentiality, it offers descriptions and incidents, and even stories within the story. But there the resemblance ends. In a preamble, the protagonist descends a staircase which is explicitly made a figure for the movement into the depths of the self, but psychological analysis and introspective meditation are absent. Like many surrealist works, this book is structured around the pursuit of an enigmatic female. Her name constitutes the title but it also features in anagrams scattered through the book, effectively associating her inspiring influence with the text's other manifestations of the spontaneous creativity inherent in language. The narrative is largely oneiric in character, the first-person narrator who initiates the story soon being eclipsed by a third-person account of bizarre dreamscapes and encounters and impossible surreal objects, which exist solely by virtue of the outlandishly precise detail, and the mock-solemn prose with its weird extended similes, in which their fantastic features are described. Allusions to occult patterns and evocations of cabbalistic practices suggest an underlying unity which can only be surreal – or textual, through the intermediary of mirroring devices (for which Gide had coined the term *mises en abyme*) such as a description of a volume of Paracelsus containing a 'schéma condensant la substance du texte' ['pattern condensing the substance of the text']. The form of the traveller's chronicle or the picaresque novel is drawn on, in effect, as a vehicle for depicting a world quite removed from that of everyday observation. *Aurora* is to the conventional novel what the paintings of de Chirico and Dalí are to figurative art: it uses the instruments and some of the conventions of the form to accomplish the replacement of material reality by the inventions of the imagination.

Narratives such as that of Leiris as well as other surrealist art show the influence of Freud, which began to make itself felt in France with the translation of his work in the early 1920s. Exposure to his theories of the unconscious gave renewed urgency to the search for techniques of characterisation that could convey the complexities of the personality: once again Dostoevsky's contradictory, unstable and inconsistent characters came to seem surprisingly modern and offered models to imitate. Gide, a long-term admirer of the Russian author, made what he called the 'inconséquence des caractères' a feature of his presentation in *Les Faux-Monnayeurs* of 1925. But the problem of point of view was equally important in this regard. In 1927 François Mauriac published *Thérèse Desqueyroux*, a novel in which a woman who has escaped prosecution for the attempted poisoning of her husband tries to understand what drove her to it. Mauriac struggles to reconcile the incompatible postulates of the approach he has adopted. On the one hand he relies on the lucidity of an intelligent, self-critical woman, backed up by the point of view of an omniscient narrator who intermittently espouses her perspective while also offering his own insights into her behaviour and character. On the other hand he needs to preserve the fundamental obscurity and complexity of impulses which if they are to be seen as authentic must remain impenetrable or inaccessible to the rational discourse of what remains essentially a *roman d'analyse* in the traditional mould. Merely hinting at hidden depths is an evasion of the issue, while bringing obscure motivations into the light of conventional narrative confers a misleading veneer of rationality upon them. Moreover, how authentic a portrayal of subjective reality can be achieved if a narrator's presence can constantly be sensed guiding the character's thoughts and shaping what we read?

Proust's novel graphically conveys the discontinuities of the conscious self, which for him is conceived as a mere succession of states of mind. If, going beyond this, the workings of consciousness in their vital immediacy and interaction with unconscious impulses were to become a focus of the novel's investigation, James Joyce's use of internal monologue in *Ulysses* appeared to some to provide the only appropriate model. Einstein's theories of relativity, percolating into cultural awareness at the same time as those of Freud, suggested also that an absolute perspective is impossible and that only subjective viewpoints on reality are available. The stream-of-consciousness therefore became one method, as Sartre was to put it, of moving the technique of the novel forward from the stage of Newtonian physics to that of general relativity. In Sartre's view this was a crucial matter since for him 'une technique romanesque renvoie toujours à la métaphysique du romancier' ['narrative technique ultimately takes us back to the metaphysics of the novelist'].[6] In 1939 he launched a scathing attack on Mauriac's narrative technique in *La Fin de la nuit*. He accused Mauriac of playing God in his novel, offering an all-embracing perspective, observing indiscriminately from inside and outside, mingling perceptions of the present with knowledge available only in hindsight, and thereby leaving no freedom for his characters to respond spontaneously to events through their free choice of actions.[7] For his own part, Sartre sought to develop novelistic techniques compatible with his theories on the existential freedom of the individual as well as his phenomenological analyses of the unstable, shifting structures of consciousness. His fiction presents virtuoso displays of formal experimentation inspired by his reading of Joyce and Virginia Woolf but also, in the course of the 1930s, of American writers such as Faulkner, Hemingway and Dos Passos. Never one slavishly to imitate, he adapted techniques to his particular needs. The interior monologue employed to depict the *mauvaise foi* of a self-deceiving woman in the short story 'Intimité' (in *Le Mur*, 1939) corresponds fairly rigorously to the phenomenology of consciousness developed in *L'Etre et le néant* (1943), as does his use of the device to communicate the estranged, hallucinating subjectivity of Roquentin in *La Nausée* (1938). In neither case is the individual perceived as locked into their subjectivity: on the contrary the stream of consciousness passes constantly, almost imperceptibly, between first-person and third-person narration in accordance with the endless projection towards the outside which is consciousness in the Husserlian perspective Sartre espouses. In *Le Sursis* (1945), the second volume of his unfinished trilogy *Les Chemins de la liberté*, Sartre borrows from the methods adopted by John Dos Passos in *USA* (1938) as a means of plunging us into the immediacy of the crisis that will lead to the Second World War. He depicts individuals who are at one and the same time isolated subjectivities but also anonymous participants in a collective social mentality and the movements of history. He does away with the techniques of retrospective recreation, remaining resolutely in the present, and he switches point of view with dramatic and sometimes unsettling abruptness, even in mid-sentence, from the perspective of one character to that of someone else at the other end of Europe, in order to convey something of the overall reality that is war, perceived simultaneously by a hundred million separate consciousnesses. The effect upon the reader of such devices is quite deliberately intended: it is to perceive as directly as possible the drama of consciousness coming to grips with a reality on which there is no omniscient perspective.

The intensely subjective vision, in any case apparently developed to its limit by Proust and Joyce, could however be construed as inappropriate in the face of great impersonal forces such as world wars and the rise of the mass mechanised society which arguably reduced human beings to little more than marionettes, flotsam on the surface of movements determined by history and economics. Some saw a more authentic portrayal of human reality in the 'behaviourist' techniques associated with Hemingway and Steinbeck, variants of which they discerned in the faceless heroes of Kafka. Albert Camus adapted this form in *L'Etranger* (1942), with the specific purpose of depicting a man apparently devoid of moral awareness and the normal social susceptibilities. Meursault, the first-person narrator of this novel, relates events in a flat impassive style, his use of the perfect tense and avoidance of causal explanations reducing action and incident to inert elements in an aimless sequence. Following a train of circumstances that ends with him killing an Arab, his arrest and trial serve as pretexts to contrast his vision of reality with the institutional narratives upon which society is built. Though the novelistic form adopted by Camus corresponded broadly to his conception of the absurd expounded in *Le Mythe de Sisyphe* (1942), he later claimed that he had used it for a particular purpose rather than endorsing the behaviourist novel in general. To borrow Sartre's terms, the metaphysic corresponding to this technique, its vision of human beings as automatons or purely instinctive creatures, was fundamentally uncongenial to Camus, and he was to repudiate it in *L'Homme révolté* (1951). This disavowal is actually inherent in Meursault's impassioned declarations at the conclusion of the novel; but it was the form of the first half which struck his readers most tellingly.

Nathalie Sarraute was among the first to highlight the contradiction at the heart of *L'Etranger* between its initial denial of any psychological depth to its hero and its ultimate vindication of his feelings in the face of the impersonal machinery of justice. In an essay on the subject she points to the continuing importance of Dostoevsky for the evolution of the novel and argues that depth psychology is an indispensable part of the genre: what is needed is a new form for exploring its hitherto neglected manifestations.[8] Sarraute herself seeks to depict the mental impulses and reactions she calls tropisms, which accompany day-to-day social interactions at a level just below consciousness. She gives the term 'sous-conversation' to the inter-subjective phenomena she charts. Her novels, such as *Portrait d'un inconnu* (1948) and *Le Planétarium* (1959) are given over to the depiction of the micro-events of mental life. She refines on free indirect speech and a form of stream-of-consciousness as her narratives gravitate among the inner lives of the characters. The latter are for the most part treated as virtually anonymous, unstable sites of tropistic activity: the language of the text seeps from one to the other as individual identities meet and blur in the commonplaces of experience, expression and opinion and the fantasies whereby one person projects into imaginary versions of another's point of view. Though dramatic incidents as such are not the stuff of her novels, the conflict that arises in human relationships emphatically is. The obsessions, paranoias, compulsions and manias through which the characters relate to each other are writ large in a language that draws richly on metaphor and mini-narratives of war, terror, humiliation and triumph that paradoxically (and satirically) charge her texts with an intensity belied by the usually trivial pretexts of such conflicts.

The first part of *L'Etranger*, just like certain pages of *La Nausée*, projected a vision of the external world strangely bereft of its familiar features, and reduced to a somewhat alien environment. Alain Robbe-Grillet was to highlight this aspect of the novels in his efforts to propound an aesthetic for the *nouveau roman*.[9] Critics writing of his first novels drew attention to the extensive, impersonal descriptions that featured in them, and which appeared to hold up the narrative to no discernible purpose. For Robbe-Grillet the point of such descriptions was that they restored to the world the strangeness which both Camus and Sartre had aimed at but failed to convey. Robbe-Grillet took issue with the meta-phorical elements in language which induced writers almost automatically to establish a complicity between the external world and the subjective experience of the human being: houses 'nestle' in valleys, and so on. He had determined to pursue objective, even geometrical language, purged of humanising adjectives and comparisons, in order to demonstrate that the tragedy and alienation that haunt human beings stem from a falsified sense of a relationship between people and things. There is no such relation-ship, just a gulf, he argued. By means of polemics such as these Robbe-Grillet prompted new insights into the role of description in the novel. When re-readings of *Le Voyeur* (1955) and *La Jalousie* (1957) revealed in their descriptive sequences significant instances of contamination by

anthropomorphic figures of speech, the author's response was to point out
that such passages reflect the obsessive psyche of the character through
whose eyes the perception of objects is distorted. Evocations of a piece of
string build into ongoing sado-erotic fantasies in *Le Voyeur*; repeated
descriptions of a tropical centipede and the stain it leaves when squashed
acquire a momentum paralleling the rising passion of a jealous husband in
La Jalousie. With *Dans le labyrinthe* (1959), the power of language to
engender secondary meanings through associations of ideas, word-play and
figurative off-shoots takes its place at the very heart of creative writing,
whose function henceforth is to build texts by exploring the material
language generates in this way. Thus the concern of the novel becomes, in a
telling formulation of the critic Jean Ricardou, no longer 'l'écriture d'une
aventure' ['the writing of an adventure'] but rather 'l'aventure d'une
écriture' ['the adventure of writing'].[10] Description can be not just a
catalogue of ancillary details to provide a background for the plot, but the
source from which all else springs. Such a transformation in the way novel-
writing is to be viewed (and performed) effectively calls into question the
function of all the elements traditionally associated with the form. A
common concern to challenge conventional expectations in this way was
a unifying principle linking the writers whose work was grouped under
the heading of the *nouveau roman*, and which includes Robbe-Grillet,
Sarraute, Butor, Simon and others. Sarraute's essay 'L'Ere du soupçon'
(published in 1950, it was to give its title to the later collective volume)
cites the scepticism of Valéry and goes beyond it to unpick the very concept
of characterisation; it will be recalled that her novels depart significantly
from notions of plot, character and psychological analysis. Butor addresses
Breton's strictures on description and confirms Robbe-Grillet's views on its
centrality when properly considered,[11] illustrating the point in his own
novels such as *L'Emploi du temps* (1956) and *La Modification* (1957) in
which description and narrative become the ground for mythological
patterns that structure the texts. In the essays published as *Pour un
nouveau roman* Robbe-Grillet further argues that the reality of subjective
experience is such as to require a drastic reconsideration, for example, of
narrative structures and representations of temporality: in *Le Voyeur* and
La Jalousie we cannot locate what we read in relation to any objective
chronology since it is impossible to distinguish the protagonists' perceptions as such from memory, fantasy and projections into the future.
Hierarchies of represented fact are superseded: 'le vrai, le faux et le faire
croire sont devenus plus ou moins le sujet de toute œuvre moderne' ['the
true, the false and the make-believe have more or less become the subject of
every modern work'].[12]

The trajectory of Claude Simon's career traces a similar path but with a less playful approach than Robbe-Grillet, and a more acute attachment to the kind of referential mission that Proust and Sartre pursued. His novels such as *La Route des Flandres* (1960) explicitly depict attempts to make sense of a reality – in this case the massacre of a cavalry detachment in the Second World War – that constantly eludes the grasp of protagonist and narrator (see chapter 10, pp. 176–7, for further discussion of this novel). Memory and speculation supplement but also distort the already fragmented nature of perception, producing at best a coherence which is misleading and is denounced as such, and resulting ultimately in a series of tentative hypotheses: 'Comment savoir?' ['How can one know?'] is a repeated refrain. Simon's style is characterised by huge sentences, vestigial punctuation, parentheses within parentheses and use of the present participle, to convey the stream of perception and speculation in its unending, inconclusive immediacy: the texts pose substantial challenges to the reader, casting radical doubt on patterns of intelligibility traditionally associated with the novel. With *La Bataille de Pharsale* (1969) his writing entered a phase where the proliferating creativity of language, highlighted by Robbe-Grillet and Ricardou, which had subverted the quest for referential accuracy, became the object and tool of texts which are increasingly devoted to an examination and exploration of their own workings. Later novels such as *Les Géorgiques* (1981) revert to the attempt to reconstruct history, memory and experience, but remain permeated by a deep pessimism about the prospects of success.

A loss of faith in literature's capacity to grasp reality is central to the history of the modern novel. It pursues the only authenticity it can claim in these conditions by openly conceding its limitations and by making of this problem a prominent theme. Moreover, as reality as such is seen to recede beyond reach, the novel devotes increasing space to reflections upon the workings of literature itself. Gide wrote *Les Faux-Monnayeurs* with the intention of dramatising the struggle between the real world and the representations we make of it, and included in his novel a novelist who manifestly fails to represent or understand in his *Faux-Monnayeurs* much of the reality in the midst of which he has lived. Sartre's protagonist in *La Nausée* denounces story-telling as a bogus interpretation of experience, asserting bluntly that 'il faut choisir: vivre ou raconter' ['you have to choose between living and telling']. The heroes of Samuel Beckett's novels, such as the narrator of *Molloy* (1951) or *L'Innommable* (1953), acknowledge as much but cannot shake off the compulsion to continue telling tales, their narratives becoming ever more incoherent, inconsequential and inconclusive – the very language they have recourse to being the chief cause of the dissolution they nonetheless seek to overcome.

Thus, the conventional patterns of plot, character and objective description are acknowledged to be irrelevant to a pursuit of the real. This leaves the novel two options. On the one hand, it can play with, mirror and mock its traditional ingredients in full knowledge that they are arbitrary constructions gratuitously elaborated. Elements of such ludic self-consciousness are features of many works by authors already considered in this chapter, from Gide to Robbe-Grillet and beyond.

On the other hand, in a category not always distinct from that just mentioned, the novel can seek to render something of the chaos and dispersion of meaning that characterises the real, by abandoning traditional sources of coherence and intelligibility. One type of illustration is produced by the quasi-schizophrenic narrator-protagonist duo Bardamu and Robinson in Louis-Ferdinand Céline's *Voyage au bout de la nuit* (1932), whose hallucinatory visions of the Great War are followed by apocalyptic perspectives on colonialism and modern industrial society. The attempt to register the experience of war is transcribed as chaos in Simon's *La Route des Flandres*; but in a sense it is merely a heightened instance of the universal fact of reality eluding the grasp of those seeking to impose meaning. This would include the nebulous entities who populate Sarraute's *Le Planétarium* as much as Jacques Revel, the narrator of Butor's *L'Emploi du temps*, striving for a form that will confer order on his experience of life in a foreign city. To varying degrees, all these novels and others like them confront the reader with a disorienting experience: a text which appears to proliferate without regard to conventional form. What is more, in the final analysis, the texts carry the implicit assumption that they are in fact separate from the reality they gesture at in such apparently disordered ways.

It is at this point that the novel, having broken free – or been wrenched free – from its traditional relationship with reality, is arguably in a position to assert its autonomy. That subordination to the real, which was alleged as the reason why the novel could never hope for true artistic merit, is now seen to be not intrinsic to the form but a mere effect of convention. And in this perspective, it becomes possible to speak of the novel and the poem in the same breath. Raymond Queneau, for example, after breaking with surrealism in 1929, defended the genre by tackling Valéry's arguments head on. Precisely because the content of the novel is arbitrary and gratuitous, it can aspire to the condition of a poem by virtue of a structure with its own internal patterns. Queneau speaks of 'rhyming' characters and situations as a poem rhymes words. Nothing is random in *Le Chiendent* (1933): the number of sections, the distribution of the text into passages of narrative or dialogue, all is worked out with the rigorous (often mathematical) precision of a sonnet. Symmetries between events and correspondences between people further highlight the importance of form. It was in the service of such structural rigour that Gide's term *mise en abyme* highlights those elements in the text which reproduce in miniature the work's overall patterns or themes. Hence, for example, the counterfeit coin in *Les Faux-Monnayeurs* sums up, mirrors and connects the various manifestations, metaphorical as much as literal, of trading in bogus currency that the novel charts. The device was to become a stock-in-trade of the *nouveaux romanciers*, whose subversive and slippery texts assert their shapeliness through multiple instances of internal mirroring and patterns of self-reflexivity. By this token the novel affirms itself as a tightly ordered literary artefact generating its own internal necessity in defiance of the haphazardness and contingency of the real. Jean Ricardou's analysis of *Le Voyeur* demonstrates that through its dense internal reworking and echoing of its own motifs the novel amply meets Valéry's definition of poetry.[13] For his part, Michel Butor, in an essay entitled 'Le roman et la poésie', argues against both Valéry and surrealism that the novel is the one form which can confer poetry on the whole of reality, allowing the real to 'prendre conscience d'elle-même' ['become conscious of itself'], through the powerful structuring dynamic of its formal devices.[14]

Butor's own novels, *L'Emploi du temps* or *Degrés* (1960), bear out this claim to artistic sophistication on the strength of formal integrity. Other examples can be cited of novels which seek to bring panoramas of experience within the purview of a unifying structure drawn extensively from cultural history and mythology. Michel Tournier, in *Le Roi des aulnes* (1970) and *Les Météores* (1975), creates characters who are themselves driven to perceive patterns, structures and parallels shaping their own lives and linking with the lives of others. Sometimes this is shown to lead to dubious results, as when Abel Tiffauges, in the former novel, sees himself as destined to achieve fulfilment among the Nazis (for further discussion of this novel see chapter 10, p. 176). But such obsessive readings of their own world by Tournier's protagonists place them at a distance from the actual reader and can engender fresh critical perceptions of habitual forms. Moreover, the text invites us in turn to seek patterns by hinting at religious or mythological keys to the character's story. In addition, the forms in which Tournier casts his narratives are deliberately imitated from traditional or cultural stereotypes and folk-tales, so that the reader is further encouraged to pursue the structuring impulse, encountering these narratives as if already at a second reading (e.g. in *Vendredi ou les limbes du Pacifique*

(1967), a rewriting of *Robinson Crusoe*), seeing them as saturated by half-glimpsed patterns. In this way formal innovation consists of making us re-read old forms with a measure of self-consciousness, using our recognition of them as a means of setting in motion the workings of intertextuality and prompting a dialogue between the different interpretations of reality that different structures propose.

Georges Perec inherits the ambitions of both the *nouveau roman* and the *Oulipo* group set up by Raymond Queneau to experiment with the creative potential of formal constraints in literature. After extraordinary achievements in gratuitous patterning such as an entire novel written without the letter *e* (*La Disparition*, 1969) and a palindrome of over 1,200 words, he published *La Vie mode d'emploi* (1978). This novel is the equal of Balzac or Zola in its encyclopaedic scope and the huge cast of characters whose lives are recounted in multiple narratives which intersect in a Paris apartment building. However, at the same time the immensity of the book's apparently sprawling substance is demonstrably structured to an unprecedentedly meticulous degree. Certain features, chiefly the life of Percival Bartlebooth its principal protagonist, highlight an intense self-reflexivity and a concern with problems of artistic representation present in many other modern prose works. More fundamentally, the chapters are ordered in accordance with the pattern of the Knight's Tour Problem in chess, and the content of each chapter is determined with reference to the orthogonal Graeco-Latin bi-square of order 10. Here, the rich novelistic content is recognisable as the recycling of more or less banal stories from the repository of human experience – though with an unusual fidelity to fine detail, at its most evident in extensive catalogues and meticulous transcriptions. At the same time, Perec seems to assert that the signature of human freedom as well as the mark of the highest art, lies in this commitment to observe, and to erase all evidence of, an almost insanely arbitrary formal discipline in the elaboration of the text. This work thus offers simultaneously the pleasure of traditional identification and involvement in the lives of fictional characters, places and objects, coupled with the allure of playful references to hidden patterns, culminating in intimations of an exceptional aesthetic rigour.

Perec's novel recapitulates the adventures in form which are a hallmark of the twentieth-century French novel. It reasserts the claim to take an imaginative hold on reality, tempering it with an acute consciousness of the characteristics, conventions and mechanisms whereby it does so. At the same time, its self-reflexivity, far from being a symptom of narcissistic introspection and flight from the chaos of the world, serves to celebrate its mastery of its vocation. By affirming the impulse to order and aesthetic patterning, it rises above the world and corrects the flaws in reality: which is perhaps the aim of all creative activity.

NOTES

1 'Hommage à Marcel Proust', in *Œuvres* (Paris: Gallimard, Bibliothèque de la Pléiade, 1957), vol. I, pp. 769–74.
2 Letter to Prévost, 16 May 1943, in *Œuvres*, vol. I, p. 1835.
3 *Journal 1887–1925* (Paris: Gallimard, Bibliothèque de la Pléiade, 1996), pp. 187–8, 19 October 1894.
4 Quoted in M. Raimond, *La Crise du roman, des lendemains du naturalisme aux années vingt* (Paris: Corti, 1966), p. 103.
5 'Projet de préface pour *Isabelle*', in *Romans, récits et soties, œuvres lyriques* (Paris: Gallimard, Bibliothèque de la Pléiade, 1958), p. 1561.
6 J.-P. Sartre, *Situations I* (Paris: Gallimard, Collection Idées, 1947), p. 71.
7 'M. François Mauriac et la liberté', *Situations I*, pp. 36–57.
8 'De Dostoïevski à Kafka', in *L'Ere du soupçon* (Paris: Gallimard, Collection Idées, 1956), pp. 14–66.
9 In articles subsequently published in the volume entitled *Pour un nouveau roman* (Paris: Minuit, 1963).
10 *Problèmes du nouveau roman* (Paris: Seuil, 1967), p. 111.
11 His critical essays were published in a series of volumes, *Répertoire I, II, III* in 1960, 1964 and 1968; a selection appeared as *Essais sur le roman* (Paris: Gallimard, 1972). The refutation of Breton's views can be found in 'Le roman et la poésie', pp. 21–47 of this selection.
12 'Temps et description dans le récit d'aujourd'hui', in *Pour un nouveau roman*, p. 163.
13 *Pour une théorie du nouveau roman* (Paris: Seuil, 1971), p. 86.
14 See above, note 11.

SUGGESTIONS FOR FURTHER READING

Brée, G. and M. Guiton, *An Age of Fiction: the French Novel from Gide to Camus* (London: Chatto and Windus, 1958)
Britton, C., *The Nouveau Roman: Fiction, Theory and Politics* (Basingstoke: Macmillan, 1992)
  Claude Simon: Writing the Visible (Cambridge: Cambridge University Press, 1987)
Burgelin, C., *Georges Perec* (Paris: Seuil, 1988)
Chénieux-Gendron, J., *Le Surréalisme et le roman* (Paris: L'Age d'homme, 1983)
Cruickshank, J., (ed.), *The Novelist as Philosopher: Studies in French Fiction 1935–1960* (London: Oxford University Press, 1962)
Dällenbach, L., *Le Récit spéculaire: essai sur la mise en abyme* (Paris: Seuil, 1977)
Heath, S., *The Nouveau Roman: a Study in the Practice of Writing* (London: Elek, 1970)
Hutcheon, L., *Narcissistic Narrative: the Metafictional Paradox* (London: Methuen, 1984)

Jefferson, A., *The Nouveau Roman and the Poetics of Fiction* (Cambridge: Cambridge University Press, 1980)

Matthews, J. H., *Surrealism and the Novel* (Ann Arbor: Michigan University Press, 1966)

Prince, G., *Métaphysique et technique dans l'œuvre romanesque de Sartre* (Geneva: Droz, 1968)

Rimmon-Kenan, S., *Narrative Fiction: Contemporary Poetics* (London: Methuen, 1983)

9

STEVEN UNGAR

Existentialism, engagement, ideology

'What should I do?' 'What can I do?' 'What will it mean for me?' Personal and urgent, these questions are at the core of story-telling and fictional narration cast in terms of plot and action as a thematics of difficult ('hard') choices. Scenes of men and women faced with such choices recur throughout the history of the novel in France, from Madame de La Fayette's *La Princesse de Clèves* (1678) and Balzac's *Le Père Goriot* (1835) to André Malraux's *La Condition humaine* (1933) and Annie Ernaux's *Une Femme* (1988). As a set, these scenes provide literary expressions to concerns with personal identity that vary over time more in detail and circumstance than in essence. For the novels mentioned, the decisions range from remaining in or retreating from courtly society (La Fayette) to moving with a spouse to another part of France or staying instead in one's native region (Ernaux). Both cases provide dramatic content for metaphysical concerns with existence set forth as a problematics of the individual in his or her world.

Parallel to the rise of nineteenth-century bourgeois capitalism, representations of individuals confronted with hard life-choices proliferated in the *Bildungsroman* typified in Stendhal's *Le Rouge et le noir* (1830) and Balzac's *Le Père Goriot* (1836) as a narrative of apprenticeship into worldliness and upward mobility. Well into the twentieth century, evolved forms of the *Bildungsroman* from Gustave Flaubert's *L'Education sentimentale* (1869) to André Gide's *L'Immoraliste* (1901) increasingly inscribed the thematics of decision and identity centred on the individual within issues of social involvement and allegiance to specific doctrines, world-views, and ideologies. Through the 1930s, this broadened sense of identity and apprenticeship remained integral to novels by established writers such as Gide, Marcel Proust and Roger Martin du Gard as well as those of a younger generation including Louis-Ferdinand Céline, Paul Nizan and André Malraux.

In a narrower sense, there are many readers for whom the thematics of decision and identity in twentieth-century France is inseparable from the name and writings of Jean-Paul Sartre. And this with good reason. For the crisis of Antoine Roquentin, the historian and would-be biographer portrayed in Sartre's 1938 novel, *La Nausée,* as slipping into mediocrity and loneliness, is a literary prelude to Sartre's sustained attempt in *L'Etre et le néant* (1943) to follow Martin Heidegger in *Sein und Zeit* [*Being and Time*] (1927) by analysing human experience as various ontological modes or ways of being in the world. Sartre's name also evokes the programme of committed writing ('littérature engagée') that he set forth in his 1947 essay *Qu'est-ce que la littérature?* as a means of overcoming an equation of literature and poetry that made language a barrier separating the writer from the world. The Sartre who founded the monthly *Les Temps Modernes* in October 1945 wilfully polemicised his position with a view toward exerting control over literature and the press in France following the 1940–4 German occupation. In so doing, Sartre's post-war programme of 'littérature engagée' equated commitment with political activism in the name of a just society over and above the preoccupation with personal identity he had portrayed a decade earlier in the fictional character of Roquentin.

Whereas *La Nausée* had shown in detail the estrangement and isolation of a male protagonist headed for mental breakdown, the solidarity that Sartre experienced during the months he spent in a German prisoner-of-war camp between August 1940 and early 1941 confirmed his growing sense of the need to relate the literary treatment of personal freedom to wider issues of individual and collective identity. By the time Paris was liberated from the Nazis in August 1944, Sartre's concerns had evolved towards a new emphasis on commitment. The expression of commitment in the plays *Les Mouches* (1943) and *Huis Clos* (1944), as in the fictional trilogy of the Occupation era, *Les Chemins de la liberté,* already pointed to the position on committed writing Sartre was to take in *Qu'est-ce que la littérature?* Between 1941 and 1947, what Sartre came to assert as the capacity of the committed writer to portray individuals confronting conditions of imposed freedom in specific circumstances led him to create fictional and dramatic characters concerned less with fashioning artistic solutions to metaphysical problems than with acting as directly as possible in and on history.

This evolved sense of literature's potential as a force for change and liberation also led Sartre to supplement the work of art in its own right with a view of the writer as a public figure responsible to speak on the social, political, or moral issues of his or her age. Without meaning to understate Sartre's contributions to existentialism beginning with *La*

Nausée, emphasis on the post-war period from 1944 up through Albert Camus's 1957 novel, *La Chute*, elides a substantial body of inter-war texts ranging from Roger Martin du Gard's *Jean Barois* (1927) to Nizan's *Antoine Bloyé* (1932) and Céline's *Voyage au bout de la nuit* (1932). It could even be argued that *L'Immoraliste* and the essays by Gide collected under the title of *Littérature engagée* (1938) exemplified varieties of committed writing that differed significantly from Sartre's post-war programme.

Militancy on the part of writers, artists and other intellectual figures is neither exclusively Sartrean nor exclusively post-war. In twentieth-century France, it extends back to debates surrounding the charges of treason for which Alfred Dreyfus was tried and imprisoned twice during the 1890s. Following the appearance of Emile Zola's 1898 manifesto, 'J'accuse', protesting the second conviction of Dreyfus, broader conceptions of 'littérature engagée' over the past century have diverged among those who, like Martin du Gard, believed that the artist should speak out only indirectly through the creative work and others such as André Breton and Simone de Beauvoir (as well as the more recent figures of Michel Foucault, Jean Genet and Bernard-Henri Lévy) who lent reputations as writers to petitions and manifestos in order to militate in favour of – and often against – specific causes.

The present chapter traces a shift in the thematics of existence, engagement and ideology in twentieth-century French fiction. It does so by approaching the novel between about 1930 and 1960 as an aesthetic and ideological entity. This shift is at its most acute in Sartre's post-war literary programme where the criteria for assessing engagement involve not simply what novels depict and how skilfully they depict it, but also the ends to which such depiction aspires. In this sense, the Sartrean doctrine of 'littérature engagée' is grounded in a view that the creative freedom of the writer is inseparable from a sense of social responsibility (see M. Adereth, *Commitment in Modern French Literature: Politics and Society in Péguy, Aragon, and Sartre*, p. 30). In order to assess the consequences of this evolution in the theory and practice of fiction between the 1930s and the decade following the 1944 liberation of France from occupation by Nazis, I want to explore how representations of choice and identity evolve in Sartre's *La Nausée*, Malraux's *La Condition humaine*, Nizan's *Antoine Bloyé* and Camus's *La Chute*.

La Nausée remains a dense and compelling novel open to a number of interpretations. For some, its format of fictionalised diary portrays in realistic detail several weeks in the life of Antoine Roquentin, a would-be biographer whose work on a minor eighteenth-century historical figure leads him to Bouville, a provincial port on the Atlantic coast of France. (The city name is invented and probably ironic. Bouville translates into English as either 'Mudville' [boue-ville] or – homonymically – as 'Endsville' [bout-ville]. As it appears in the novel, Bouville bears a strong resemblance to Le Havre, where Sartre lived on and off while teaching philosophy at the lycée du Havre between 1931 and 1936.) The diary recounts the routine of Roquentin's daily existence: his long days in the municipal library, his casual sexual encounters with the female proprietor of the café he frequents, and the rather fitful relations with someone he refers to only as the 'Autodidacte' ('Self-Taught Man') and with Anny, a former lover with whom he had travelled in Europe and Asia. As the novel ends, Roquentin has abandoned his historical biography and is waiting to leave for Paris where he hopes to write a book – perhaps a novel – whose steely beauty might make people feel as ashamed of their inadequate lives as he does, as he departs from Bouville after leaving yet another venture incomplete.

The ambitions that Roquentin projects onto the book he hopes to write once he leaves Bouville extend a behaviour pattern of deferral and displacement with which he wants desperately to break. This pattern is, in turn, marked by a series of failed ventures each of which culminates in the very kind of melancholy and depression whose onset he chronicles in the opening pages of his diary. While the brooding tone of the diary reflects Roquentin's temperament, it also points to Sartre's interest in Charles Baudelaire, on whom he was to write a study in 1947 in which references to Freudian elements of childhood trauma were countered by a distinctly non-Freudian emphasis on conscious decision. For *La Nausée* the relevant intertext was a series of disjointed reflections of the 1860s such as 'Hygiène' and 'Mon cœur mis à nu' published long after Baudelaire's death under the title of *Journaux intimes*. As in the Baudelaire texts, what counts in *La Nausée* is less a matter of truth or even versimilitude than the representation of intimacy bordering on confession. In fact, Sartre had first titled the novel *Melancolia* in reference to Albrecht Dürer's engraving in which a human figure surrounded by tools of reasoned and occult knowledge looks forlornly out toward the horizon while seated at the edge of the water. The melancholy and depression that Roquentin terms nausea is often linked to artistic temperament, the creative process, and to an aesthetic solution to issues of personal identity reminiscent of Marcel Proust's *A la recherche du temps perdu*. But where Proust's narrator redeems a wasted life by transposing its apparent failures into the material of a true novel, Roquentin's desire to resolve his identity crisis along similar lines looks very much like just another in a series of failed or abandoned ventures.

An alternative reading of *La Nausée* subsumes Roquentin's desire to exploit the creative potential of his nausea to what Sartre referred to when he conceived the novel in 1931 as a 'factum on contingency'. By which he intended to have Roquentin's identity crisis serve as an instance of the unstable ontological mode of existence that men and women try without success to transcend toward the more stable mode of being. While it is only several years later in *L'Etre et le néant* that Sartre analyses these ontological modes at length, *La Nausée* and the short narratives in *Le Mur* stage the ongoing tensions between the desire to attain being in the form of a stable identity and an understanding that this desire opposes what existence imposes as a burden of freedom on all men and women forced to make and remake themselves within the evolving circumstances of their lives. Freedom is understood less in an absolute sense as the total absence of constraint than as a condition of responsibility for one's actions in specific circumstances linked over longer duration to the variables of continuous flux.

In the light of what Roquentin acknowledges midway through the novel as the imminent collapse of his biography of the Marquis de Rollebon, he knows that he cannot avoiding confronting again the question of what to do with his life. For without an answer to this question, Roquentin cannot escape the fact that his existence is no more necessary than those of the lonely old bachelors and widowers who spend their days and nights playing cards to pass the time so as not to face the fact that they will most likely die alone and forgotten. As in the words – 'Some of these days / You're gonna miss me honey' – of the jazz tune that gives Roquentin momentary respite from his anxieties, he, too, wants to be missed, even if he knows all too well that nobody – except for Françoise and the Self-Taught Man – would notice his absence at all.

A third approach to *La Nausée* emphasises Sartre's transposition of philosophical concepts into fictional narrative. In such terms, Roquentin's bout with nausea stages an extended meditation on consciousness and identity whose self-consciousness borders on the pathological. Sartre makes Roquentin into a caricature of Cartesian introspection, a fictional character for whom thought stymies rather than promotes action once Roquentin sees that he is unable to control what distinguishes him as a thinking being from everything and everyone else in the world: 'Ma pensée, c'est *moi*: voilà pourquoi je ne peux pas m'arrêter. J'existe parce que je pense . . . et je ne peux pas m'empêcher de penser' (*La Nausée*, p. 119) ['My thought is *me*: that is why I cannot stop. I exist because I think . . . and I cannot prevent myself from thinking'].

La Nausée provides literary expression to a number of key concepts that Sartre was soon to set forth in his essay in phenomenological ontology,

L'Etre et le néant. Among these, the concept of bad faith ('mauvaise foi') dominates the novel from the start when Roquentin writes in his initial diary entry that it would be best to record events as they occur on an everyday basis. By so doing he hopes to see into them clearly without missing their subtleties and details, even if these appear at first meaningless. Moving from interpretation to perception, Roquentin adds that he must say how he sees this table, the street, people, his packet of tobacco, since *this* is what has changed. In fact, because Roquentin has already experienced the kind of change that he describes, the diary is less a full and honest account of this change than an attempt to master and overcome it through language. Self-deception, as the means to this end, involves the calculated attempt to write an account that attributes to other people and other things a change that – as the diary soon asserts – is located neither within or outside Roquentin, but instead in his interactions with people and things.

Roquentin's turn to self-deception is grounded in a fear that the imminent collapse of his biography of the Marquis de Rollebon will force him to contend with the effects of what Sartre analysed at length in *L'Etre et le néant* as the concept of contingency. Having sought to assert his difference from (and superiority to) those around him in Bouville by defining his identity in terms of his work, Roquentin dreads the thought of facing yet again the question of what to do with his life in the light of another failed attempt to give meaning to it. As Roquentin puts it midway through the novel after he has abandoned the biography of Rollebon, how could he have been foolish enough to believe that he might justify his own existence by saving from oblivion the life of someone who had been dead for well over a century?

An incident toward the end of *La Nausée* provides a supplement to Sartre's fictional portrait of the melancholic artist. On his last day at the municipal library in Bouville, Roquentin watches helplessly as the Self-Taught Man is humiliated by a library official who sees him unthinkingly stroking the hand of an adolescent boy seated next to him in the reading room. After the official makes a scene and punches the Self-Taught Man, Roquentin restrains him while the Self-Taught Man runs off. As with almost all aspects of the life in Bouville he depicts in his diary, Roquentin is so self-conscious and so ambivalent that when he finally acts, it is too late. This is as true when he follows his former lover, Anny, to watch her leave by train for England with another man as when he steps in to side with the Self-Taught Man against the library official.

Roquentin's estrangement from others and from himself perpetuates a behaviour pattern of self-consciousness and frustration. The more Roquentin thinks before acting, the more ineffective his action if and when he takes it. The result is a vicious circle of failure and inaction that Sartre continues to explore after *La Nausée* in *Les Chemins de la liberté* as a failure on the part of the thinking individual (such as Mathieu in *L'Age de raison*) to progress effectively from thought to action.

From Bouville to Shanghai and from Descartes to Pascal. Isolation heightens Roquentin's crisis to a point where even the simplest everyday encounter with other men and women brings on a display of paralysing self-consciousness. Linked to European modernist sensibilities of the late nineteenth and early twentieth centuries, Roquentin comes across as a composite character whom Sartre might have invented by setting the narrators of Descartes's *Discours de la méthode* (1637) and Fyodor Dostoevsky's 'Notes from the Underground' (1861) alongside the figure seated in lugubrious contemplation in Dürer's *Melancolia*. Much like Dostoevsky's Underground Man, Roquentin's loneliness leads him to seek out the company of others – Françoise, the Self-Taught Man – to whom he perceives himself superior. As a result, he falls into a no-win situation in which his options are either to befriend those he does not respect or remain more or less without significant human contact.

In contrast to *La Nausée*, André Malraux's *La Condition humaine* (1933) portrays men and women confronted with life-altering decisions amid upheaval caused by historical process of epic proportions. *La Condition humaine* chronicles several weeks during the spring 1927 breakdown of the revolutionary coalition of the Chinese Communist Party and the Kuomintang (People's Nationalist Party) led by Chiang Kai-Shek. Cast as a montage of scenes conveying the interplay of personal lives and historical processes, the novel focuses on members of a revolutionary cell involved in the ill-fated insurrection by Chinese Communists unwilling to follow party directives to let Chiang assume provisional control of Shanghai. Malraux portrays three central characters of the cell as distinctive revolutionary types. The first of the three is Kyo Gisors, a half-Japanese and half-French militant divided between his devotion to nationalist revolution and a strong compassion toward others. The second is Katov, a Russian whose lifelong commitment to revolution has made him into 'the perfect comrade'. The third is Tchen, the 'ecstatically suicidal terrorist' and only Chinese member of the group (see Douglas Collins, 'Terrorists Ask No Questions', p. 915). Surrounding these three are Gisors's wife, May; the international investor, Ferral; and Baron Clappique, the mythomaniac who gambles with his own life and with those of others.

La Condition humaine illustrates a literature of extreme situations by setting the kind of identity crisis portrayed by Sartre in *La Nausée* within a context where the individual is linked by circumstance to action as a test and/or trial of thought and will. Nowhere does Malraux convey this linkage as forcefully as in the novel's opening scene in which Tchen prepares to murder an intermediary in a gun deal in order to provide the insurrection with additional weapons. The novel begins intensely with two direct questions – 'Tchen tenterait-il de lever la moustiquaire? Frapperait-il au travers?' (*La Condition humaine*, p. 511) ['Would Tchen try to lift up the mosquito-net? Or would he strike through it?'] – whose brevity condenses the combination of anxiety and ecstasy that sets the action he is to execute at odds with the paralysing effects of thought that precede it.

So intent is Tchen on executing this murder that at first he registers the sound and light around him only as abstractions. When he realises that he does not know how hard he will need to stab in order to kill his victim, Tchen stabs his own left arm convulsively to test the resistance of the flesh. The gesture – unseemly, close to absurd, and almost laughable – measures an obsession with violent death that foreshadows Tchen's suicide in a terrorist act that turns out to be without practical value to the insurrection. Removed from those around him by a death drive he recognises only in part, Tchen is momentarily paralysed by the emotion he feels following the murder he has just committed: 'Ce n'était pas la peur, c'était une épouvante à la fois atroce et solennelle qu'il ne connaissait plus depuis son enfance: il était seul avec la mort, seul dans un lieu sans hommes, mollement écrasé à la fois par l'horreur et par le goût du sang' (p. 514) ['It was not fear, it was a dread at once horrible and solemn, which he had not known since childhood: he was alone with death, alone in a place without men, limply crushed both by horror and by the taste of blood'].

The opening passage 'stages the tensions that organise the novel in terms of plot, characterisation, and a discontinuous point-of-view narration akin to film editing' (Claude-Edmonde Magny, *The Age of the American Novel: The Film Aesthetic of Fiction Between the Two Wars*, p. 85). Tchen acts in the interests of the cell and – by extension – a vision of revolution increasingly opposed to the joint authority of the Chinese Communist Party and Chiang Kai-Shek. The passage also conveys a more intimate motivation that places Tchen at odds with the collective action imposed by revolutionary activity on the part of the insurrectionist cell. Where Malraux situates *La Condition humaine* at a specific moment of the Chinese revolution, Shanghai in the spring of 1927 serves largely as a particular site in which the individual tests the limits of life through what amounts to a series of encounters with death (see Gaëtan Picon, *André Malraux*, p. 22). This testing of limits is double in that while its extreme form is by necessity fatal, death acquires positive value as a measure of the risks with which the individual is willing to contend.

The vision of human existence conveyed in *La Condition humaine* by scenes of the 1927 Shanghai insurrection borders on the tragic understood less in ethical terms of good and evil than as the assertion of faith and/or value in the face of overwhelming uncertainty. This assertion varies from one character to the next. For Tchen, it occurs in his obsession to kill Chiang Kai-Shek even though the likelihood that Tchen's mission will fail reduces it to a glorious suicide. For Kyo and Katov who await death surrounded by some two hundred fellow Communists imprisoned in a converted school-yard, it is a matter of whether to swallow the cyanide they carry with them or share it with others in a final act of compassion and solidarity.

A passage from Blaise Pascal's *Pensées* (1670) quoted in the closing pages of Malraux's *Les Noyers de l'Altenburg* (1948) suggests the extent to which *La Condition humaine* inscribed the failure of the 1927 Shanghai insurrection within a vision that sought to convey the conditions under which human effort would have meaning in the face of inevitable defeat and death: 'Qu'on s'imagine un nombre d'hommes dans les chaînes, et tous condamnés à mort, dont les uns étant chaque jour égorgés à la vue des autres, ceux qui restent voient leur propre condition dans celle de leurs semblables, et se regardant les uns les autres avec douleur et sans espérance, attendent leur tour. C'est l'image de la condition des hommes' (cited in Malraux, *Œuvres complètes,* p. 1272) ['Imagine a large number of men in chains, and all condemned to death, every day some of them being butchered before the others' eyes, the remainder realising their own plight from the plight of their fellows . . . This is the picture of man's estate'].

Malraux's invocation of Pascal *also* links the types and degrees of commitment in the face of uncertainty embodied in *La Condition humaine* by Tchen, Kyo, and Katov to what Albert Camus was to explore in *L'Etranger* and *Le Mythe de Sisyphe* (1942) as the ontological category of the absurd. *La Condition humaine* portrays an atmosphere of political adversity in which the impossibility of victory precipitated by the betrayal of Kuomintang socialism by the conservative sector of the Chinese Nationalist Party forces Kyo and Katov to go against the Communist party authority in the name of a conception of human dignity that the party no longer upholds. This tension between Malraux's depiction of the cell members united in revolt and the fact that each of them dies alone tempers the imminence of defeat and death with a belief that certain kinds of political and ethical commitment can redeem the negative potential of the human condition.

The fact that *La Condition humaine* appeared five years before *La Nausée* reinforces the often overlooked point that Sartre's Roquentin was neither the first nor the only existential character-type portrayed in inter-war French fiction. Yet from the perspective of links between existentialism, engagement and ideology, *La Condition humaine* and *La Nausée* both portray commitment as grounded in concerns for personal identity prior to – and in Sartre's novel, apart from – ideology. This is not to suggest that identity, commitment and ideology are in each and every case at odds with each other. What counts among the variety of commitments portrayed in *La Condition humaine* is the assertion of value and self that the individual brings to his or her actions. As with Sartre in *La Nausée* (and later in the *Chemins de la liberté* trilogy), identity grows out of decisions made by the individual confronting circumstances over which he or she has only partial control. The sympathy that the reader may feel toward Kyo and Katov is grounded in a sense of their humanity above and beyond their commitment to the nationalist revolutionary cause. For Malraux, this sense of humanity is irreducible to ideology. Moreover, he conveys it as a prerequisite to identity that is lived and acted rather than simply contemplated.

The absence of a dominant ideological thesis in *La Condition humaine* illustrates the difficulty of equating engagement to a specific ideology or to political commitment in any absolute sense. The mix of values and motivations embodied in the novel's characters undermines interpretations that assert the priority of a single ideology over the broader human condition Malraux sought to portray in its complexity. Likewise, the reader who transposes the novel's portrayal of nationalist revolution onto the author's personal vision runs the risk of mistaking what Malraux conveyed as the necessity to contend with decisions imposed by circumstance for the illusion of arriving at a correct resolution. It is helpful here to clarify a major difference between Malraux and Sartre. Unlike the inter-war Sartre who wrote *La Nausée* as the portrait of someone unable to commit to anyone or anything in a sustained way, the wartime Sartre of *Les Chemins de la liberté* tended to link commitment to ideology much as thought extended to action. In *La Condition humaine* the links were multiple and the ideological message unclear even though Malraux seemed to privilege Kyo's and Katov's deaths among fellow insurgents over Tchen's isolated suicide in his failed attempt to assassinate Chiang Kai-Shek. By the time *L'Espoir* appeared in 1937, Malraux was less concerned with individual identity than with the potential for collective action in and on history (for a discussion of commitment and ideology in *L'Espoir*, see Susan Rubin Suleiman's perceptive study of the *roman à thèse*, in *Authoritarian Fictions: The Ideological Novel as a Literary Genre*).

The links between commitment and ideology portrayed in *La Condition humaine* vary as well among inter-war writers along the political spectrum from left to right. This variety holds true for Paul Nizan, Pierre Drieu La Rochelle and Robert Brasillach. Whereas Nizan rose to assume major duties in the French Communist Party until he resigned in the wake of the August 1939 non-aggression pact between Stalin and Hitler, Drieu and Brasillach wrote in active support of the Nazi cause during the Vichy regime. From another perspective, some committed writers such as Nizan, Drieu and Louis-Ferdinand Céline set fiction against genres of essay, pamphlet and newspaper article. Equating engagement with explicit political engagement seemingly privileges politics in general – and partisan politics, in particular – over commitment toward non-partisan causes such as pacifism. I am thinking here of Henri Barbusse's *L'Enfer* (1920) and secular movements such as the unanism portrayed by Romain Rolland. These exceptions notwithstanding, any survey of existentialism and commitment in inter-war French fiction should include the ideological novel understood in a strict sense that applies the fictional representation of identity and commitment to a discrete doctrine or cause.

Paul Nizan's *Antoine Bloyé* (1933) is a kind of negative *Bildungsroman*, a fictional case-study of a man destroyed by his attempt to rise above his class origins. As the life story of a petty-bourgeois recounted after his death from the perspective of his son, the novel is Nizan's fictionalised biography of his father. Bloyé's rise from scholarship student from the provinces through the ranks of the French railway system becomes little more than a vain attempt on the part of a 'dirty little peasant' to transform himself into a gentleman. The young Bloyé follows what he takes to be the rules of the game in order to attain respectability at work and at home. He studies hard at a state engineering school, goes where his job leads him, and even marries the daughter of one of his first bosses. Yet in so doing, he sacrifices himself to the illusions of a bourgeois decorum that cuts him off from the authentic origins of family, region and, especially, class. Only after it is too late does Bloyé realise that what he had taken for a life fashioned through freedom, effort and circumstance was an illusion perpetrated by the unforgiving machineries of the bourgeoisie and industrial expansion.

Antoine Bloyé provides an extended critique of class and social environment over two generations coinciding more or less with the first sixty years of the Third French Republic. The novel fulfils a critical function by denouncing bourgeois capitalism that Nizan conveys less in light of a realism adapted from Stendhal, Balzac and Flaubert than in view of the nascent populism announced in Eugène Dabit's *L'Hôtel du Nord* (1929) and the programme of proletarian literature undertaken by Henri Poulaille. This denunciation is conveyed first via the life and death of the central character and second through a series of propositions and judgements set forth throughout the novel as when, like others of his generation, Bloyé mistakes his seemingly open-ended future for the consequences of work and commitment whose limits he identifies only in middle-age after his career is ruined by a First-World-War scandal related to a consignment of faulty artillery shells for which he is made to take blame. Setting this corrected misperception into a mode of dramatic irony, Nizan's narrator comments that like other ambitious sons of artisans and minor function-aries of the period, Antoine was so caught up in entering the cabal of command that he failed to see he was a pawn in the huge game that the supreme masters of the French bourgeoisie were beginning to play.

The previous passage conveys the extent to which Bloyé's son sees in early adulthood what his father came to see only late in his life. The authority from which the narrator-son's perception derives is historical, both in the critiques of labour institutionalised in French Communist Party doctrine and in the broader dialectical sense of generational difference in terms of which children no longer repeat the lives of their fathers (see W. D. Redfern, *Paul Nizan: Committed Literature in a Conspiratorial World*, p. 49).

Few readers would question that *Antoine Bloyé* forcefully denounces the sterility of a petty-bourgeois existence for which the protagonist betrays his working-class origins, or that the novel's critique of degraded labour and the means of production linked to railway expansion during the Third French Republic falls generally within Communist doctrine. At the same time, the novel seeems to set concerns of class and critiques of labour against more metaphysical issues of identity, and this to a degree that tempers the novel's ideological vision with an existential discourse encoded in the central themes of sexuality, dreams and death (Michael Scriven, *Paul Nizan: Communist Novelist*, p. 124). A passage early in the novel describes the initial sorrow of Bloyé's widow, Anne, who begins to speak of her late husband only in the third person. The narrator-son comments on the transformation of a living being into 'un objet silencieux qui ne questionne plus, qui ne commande plus, qu'on n'interroge plus, qui ne répond plus *Je*' (Paul Nizan, *Antoine Bloyé*, p. 17) ['a silent object that no longer questions or commands, that is no longer questioned, that no longer answers *I*']. *Antoine Bloyé* fulfils only in part the ambitions of a revolutionary literature. For in denouncing the cultures of industrial expansion and petty-bourgeoisie that duped his father into betraying his class, the narrator-son who accuses and indicts fails to propose in practical terms how to transcend the conditions that led to his father's alienation. Alongside the figure of Karl Marx and his injunction in 'Theses on Feuerbach' to transform the world that philosophers had merely contemplated, it was almost as if Nizan sought to give Sigmund Freud his due by making *Antoine Bloyé* a study of alienation linked by class to the petite-bourgeoisie and at the level of individual pathology to the death-in-life of an unfulfilled existence. In this case, existential concerns such as dreams, sexuality and attitudes toward death mix with doctrine and ideology in what amounts less to a fully realised work of socialist realism than a forceful psychopathology of everyday life and labour.

Antoine Bloyé provides the example of a novel in which elements of existentialism, commitment and ideology allow the author – through the narrator – to assess and to critique after the fact the life of a man who recognised only in part and late in life that the identity he thought he had fashioned through will and effort was attained only at the cost of an authentic identity he believed he could do without. In terms perhaps more suitable to Sartre, Nizan's novel recounts the extent to which commitment to professional advancement and upward mobility is unfulfilling, in-authentic and mistaken. Yet in so doing, its critical portrait of a wasted life asserts only by implication what a fulfilled and authentic life might be. Along similar lines, the reactionary vision set forth in Pierre Drieu La Rochelle's 1939 *Gilles* belies assumptions that the thematics of identity and engagement devolve solely from the cultural left.

Inter-war novels by Georges Bernanos and François Mauriac provide alternative treatments of the themes of existentialism, engagement and ideology from the perspective of Catholicism. Less concerned with politics and history than with spirituality, both novelists asserted the ongoing presence of sin and evil in a material world where grace was continually under threat. As suggested by the titles *Le Nœud de vipères* (1932) and *Le Désert de l'amour* (1925), François Mauriac excelled at portraying the family unit as a viper's nest in which sin, estrangement and hatred flourished at the cost of love and communication. In *Le Journal d'un curé de campagne* (1936), Bernanos chronicled the frustration of a young unnamed priest whose encounter with estrangement, guilt and greed in the rural French Flanders parish to which he is assigned eats at his faith much as the stomach cancer that ultimately kills him. Cast in the form of a diary found after the priest's death by a friend and former seminary classmate, the novel ends with a brief letter from the friend in which he asserts the extent to which the priest's perceived failures were actually successes within a broad conception of grace that overcomes solitude, suffering and self-doubt.

Two decades after *La Condition humaine*, *Antoine Bloyé* and *La Nausée*, various *nouveaux romans* by Alain Robbe-Grillet, Michel Butor, Nathalie Sarraute and Claude Simon made metaphysical concerns sec-ondary to technical and formal experiments while Samuel Beckett and Raymond Queneau countered Sartre's austere vision of authenticity beyond despair in absurdist tones of paradox and irony that wavered between the tragic and the comic. A darker irony pervaded the disengaged perspective of Jean-Baptiste Clamence, the first-person narrator of Albert Camus's 1956 novel, *La Chute*. A self-avowed 'child of the mid-century' who practises his profession of duplicity in an Amsterdam bar with the curious name of Mexico-City, Clamence directs his monologue with calculation backward in time toward a grounding trauma linked to the Second World War. *La Chute* engages the Second World War and the Occupation period in terms that are all the more compelling because they are oblique. As Clamence recounts it with characteristic understatement, his pontifical adventures occurred in Africa where, thanks to a certain Rommel, war was waging. Clamence next admits that he wasn't involved in it, having dodged the one in Europe after being mobilised without ever facing action.

Clamence's admission that he dodged the war in Europe offers an initial sense of the ambivalence he shares with others who survived – as it were – because of their lack of commitment. Clamence explains that he arrived in the Southern Zone of France with the intention of finding out about the Resistance. But once there, he hesitated when he realised that he was temperamentally unsuited for activity: 'Il me semblait qu'on me demandait de faire de la tapisserie dans une cave, à longueur de jours et de nuits, en attendant que des brutes viennent m'y débusquer, défaire d'abord ma tapisserie et me traîner ensuite dans une autre cave pour m'y frapper jusqu'à la mort' (*La Chute*, p. 1539) ['It seemed to me that I was being asked to do some weaving in a cellar, for days and nights on end, until such time as some brutes should find me there, undo all my weaving, and then drag me to another cellar and beat me to death']. As Clamence concludes with brutal irony, he admired those who indulged in such heroism of the depths, but he could not imitate them.

An additional variant of the thematics of decision and identity in post-war fiction directs the identity crisis portrayed by Sartre in *La Nausée* and the literature of extreme situations in Malraux's *La Condition humaine* toward the act of writing itself. In the opening sentences of Maurice Blanchot's *L'Arrêt de mort* (1948), a first-person narrator recounts the circumstances bearing on what appears to have evolved into an obsession:

Ces événements me sont arrivés en 1938. J'éprouve à en parler la plus grande gêne. Plusieurs fois déjà, j'ai tenté de leur donner une forme écrite. Si j'ai écrit des livres, c'est que j'ai espéré par des livres mettre fin à tout cela. Si j'ai écrit des romans, les romans sont nés au moment où les mots ont commencé de reculer devant la vérité. (*L'Arrêt de mort*, p. 3)

[These events occurred in 1938. I feel great uneasiness in speaking of them. I have already tried to put them into writing several times. If I have written books, it is because I hoped by writing to put an end to all that. If I have written novels, the novels came into being at the moment when words began to draw back before the truth.]

For Blanchot's narrator, the act of writing is grounded in a conflict between his desire to reveal a hidden truth and his sense that it would be in the best interests of the truth for it to remain hidden. In keeping with the condition of irresolution that writing is meant both to resolve and to prolong, the identity of the narrator remains unstable. In such terms, *L'Arrêt de mort* returns uncannily to the act of writing to which Sartre's Roquentin had turned a decade earlier in hopes of committing himself to writing a novel that might provide him with a stable identity and draw him out of the shame of a wasted existence that plagued him. By contrast, Blanchot's narrator fashions a more tendentious self-presentation modelled on confession. Unlike Roquentin's metaphysical melancholy, Blanchot's narrator relates the onset of what plagues him to a specific period starting shortly after the September 1938 Munich agreements between Hitler, Chamberlain and Daladier. In so doing, *L'Arrêt de mort* is close in tone to the stance of ironic disengagement that Camus will embody a decade later in the elusive figure of Clamence.

In *La Nausée*, *La Condition humaine* and *Antoine Bloyé*, the fiction of decision and identity has been seen as evolving from assertions of engagement as a self-sufficient end and in the name of a cause or ideology toward the tendentious ironies set forth following the liberation in *L'Arrêt de mort* and *La Chute* as confessions of disengagement. Alongside this historicised thematics in the post-war novels by Blanchot and Camus, the cool detachment of the *nouveau roman* displaces the serious treatment of decision and identity in any sustained manner. (Claude Simon's 1960 novel, *La Route des Flandres* remains a forceful exception to this displacement, as Denis Boak will argue in the next chapter, pp. 176–7.) Subsequently, the thematics of decision and identity persists in the Francophone novel, in *l'écriture féminine* and in minority writings where it emplots stages of emergent identity asserted via nation, gender, class, religion and sexuality as specific forms of the metaphysical concerns that Sartre, Malraux and Nizan had addressed in their fiction of the 1930s.

SUGGESTIONS FOR FURTHER READING

Adereth, M., *Commitment in Modern French Literature: Politics and Society in Péguy, Aragon, and Sartre* (New York: Schocken, 1968)
Bauer, G. H., 'Melancholy of the Artist,' in *Sartre and the Artist* (Chicago: University of Chicago Press, 1969)

Blanchot, M., *L'Arrêt de mort* (Paris: Gallimard, 1948)
  Death Sentence, trans. L. Davis (Barrytown, NY: Station Hill, 1978)
Camus, A., *La Chute* in *Théâtre, récits, nouvelles* (Paris: Gallimard, Bibliothèque de la Pléiade, 1962)
  The Fall trans. J. O'Brien (New York: Vintage, 1956)
Collins, D., 'Terrorists Ask No Questions,' in D. Hollier (ed.), *A New History of French Literature* (Cambridge, MA: Harvard University Press, 1989), pp. 914–19
Magny, C.-E., *The Age of the American Novel: The Film Aesthetic of Fiction Between the Two Wars*, trans. E. Hochman (New York: Ungar, 1972; first edn 1948)
Malraux, A,, *La Condition humaine* in *Œuvres complètes* (Paris: Gallimard, Bibliothèque de la Pléiade, 1989; first published 1933)
  Man's Fate, trans. H. M. Chevalier (New York: Vintage, 1990)
  The Walnut Trees of Altenburg, trans. A. W. Fielding (New York: Howard Fertig, 1989; first published 1948)
Nizan, P., *Antoine Bloyé* (Paris: Livre de Poche, 1971; first published 1933)
  Antoine Bloyé, trans. E. Stevens (New York: Monthly Review Press, 1973)
O'Connell, D., 'Bourgeois Sin,' in D. Hollier (ed.), *A New History of French Literature* (Cambridge, MA: Harvard University Press, 1989), pp. 855–61
Picon, G., *André Malraux* (Paris: Gallimard, 1945)
Redfern, W. D., *Paul Nizan: Committed Literature in a Conspiratorial World* (Princeton: Princeton University Press, 1972)
Sartre, J.-P., *La Nausée*, in *Œuvres romanesques* (Paris: Gallimard, Bibliothèque de la Pléiade, 1982; first published 1938)
  Nausea, trans. L. Alexander (New York: New Directions, 1964)
  'What is Literature?' and Other Essays (Cambridge, MA: Harvard University Press, 1988)
Schalk, D. L., *The Spectrum of Political Engagement: Mounier, Benda, Nizan, Brasillach, Sartre* (Princeton: Princeton University Press, 1979)
Scriven, M., *Paul Nizan: Communist Novelist* (London: Macmillan, 1988)
Suleiman, S. R., *Authoritarian Fictions: The Ideological Novel as a Literary Genre* (Princeton: Princeton University Press, 1993)

10

DENIS BOAK

War and the Holocaust

Writing on war did not begin with the twentieth century. Far from it: the whole tradition of epic can be defined as, precisely, literature of war. Nevertheless it is only in our own century that it has expanded to become a major genre. There are of course nineteenth-century antecedents in French: best known, *La Chartreuse de Parme*, where Stendhal takes Fabrice del Dongo on a gratuitous excursion to Waterloo. But these pages, famous though they are, amount to less than a tenth of a very long novel. Zola's *La Débâcle* (1892) is the most important individual nineteenth-century novel devoted to the theme of war, taking in its sweep both the Franco-Prussian War and the Commune which followed. *La Débâcle* has acted as a seminal work, since many of the typical incidents of First- and Second-World-War narratives appear, if only in embryo, in its pages, together with the dominant theme of war as confusion, a humiliating shambles. And at the same time as presenting the war as experienced by individual characters, Zola succeeds in incorporating into his fiction a bird's eye survey of the conflict, almost from a historian's viewpoint, in a way no writer was to emulate until Jules Romains in the late 1930s. His description of the shattering defeat of the French armies at the hands of the Prussians prefigures, precisely, the even greater débâcle of May–June 1940.

However, in the twentieth century with two world conflicts in which millions of literate young men, and in 1939–45 women, took active part, with an impact on virtually the entire civilian population, war writing now takes in hundreds of titles in France alone. It has been not only a matter of experience viewed quantitatively, but also qualitatively. War (and revolution) have seemed to many to offer the keenest insights into the human condition, psychologically, politically, even ethically, with the notion of a 'literature of extreme situations' becoming a critical cliché. If war has caused millions of deaths and untold suffering, it has also often provided those who have lived through it with their most powerful moments of human experience. Intensity of experience is, of course, a Romantic criterion, a reminder of the continuing dominance of Romantic ideas over later attitudes and values.

Prose writing on war presents an immediate critical problem: how, indeed whether, to distinguish between the fictional and the autobiographical or documentary. For authors who have themselves been participants the distinction tends to collapse: both modes of representation are available, and the choice is not simply one between a supposedly aesthetically superior form (fiction) and an inferior one (reportage). Many, indeed most, writer/participants have felt that authenticity is paramount, that the industrialised slaughter in the trenches of 1914–18, or even more the experience of the concentration camp, was so uniquely horrifying that it ought to be narrated without the slightest distortion or inaccuracy, much less exaggeration; indeed, the veridical will be in the end more truly compelling. One might call this the 'mimetic imperative'. On this view, imaginative writing and therefore conventional fiction are thus excluded automatically. Others, no less sincere, have taken a different line, and considered that what mattered was not that some survived, but that so many did not. This being so, the appropriate end to a work ought to be the death of the principal character(s), which in the case of a first-person memoir by a survivor is obviously impossible. Referentiality is less insistent here, but remains, on a general rather than specific level. These two broad categories also imply two sets of evaluative criteria. On the one side, the veridical; on the other, conventional aesthetic standards of judgement, such as balance or form. It is however surprising how much formal preoccupations, such as patterning, can be detected in writers whose main concern seems to be the mimetic.

Given limitations of space, I refer to a relatively small number of works, all recently available, and I take a broadly inclusive view as to the fictional, especially since many of my titles have traditionally been treated as novels, whatever their autobiographical content.

The first works to appear in France during the 1914–18 struggle are today generally felt to be inferior, even unreadable. Some were of course naïvely patriotic novels, written by propagandising authors with no knowledge of actual fighting, in which the whole war was one long chuckle, a jingoist adventure broken only by flashes of selfless, suicidal heroism. But other, more serious, works are now also felt not easy to read. Partly for reasons of political correctness, by critics who believe that absolute pacifism was the *only* adequate reaction to the outbreak of war. In fact this attitude is not historically justifiable. Many of the French writers who would later bitterly criticise the war, Barbusse, Werth, Chevallier, were initially *volunteers* to fight. It is more that early novelists' narrative equipment was inadequate. John Cruickshank points out that they were those who recognised no need to invent new forms, and believed that 'unprecedented suffering could be satisfactorily expressed in terms of a traditional heroic and chivalric nineteenth-century rhetoric' (Cruickshank, p. 34). This is not simply a matter of ideological commitment: the same type of attitude which produced jingoistic nationalist rhetoric of the Right would later produce parallel rhetoric of the Left during the Spanish Civil War and in Russia between 1941 and 1945.

Behind the political issue lies an aesthetic one. On the one hand, the straightforward patriotic view was that nothing should be written, or at least published, which might weaken the national resolve, hence scenes of human suffering (by the French) or military incompetence should be suppressed, and the sordid sanitised. On the other hand, others felt that the true state of affairs should be publicised, and that incompetence and deficiencies could only thus be remedied, for the better prosecution of the war. Here we can detect a late stage in the quarrel about Realism: whether due decorum should be recognised in the choice and treatment of subject, or whether a principle of absolute veridicity should override all else. A third view, that of present-day political correctness, is that the whole war was not only unnecessary in the first place, but had degenerated into a murderous stalemate, with a negotiated peace (exactly how, not stated) the only possible outcome which would not utterly destroy Western civilisation. This third view is not necessarily present in, but can be inferred from, so-called 'works of protest'.

The two French First-World-War novels best known today, Henri Barbusse's *Le Feu* (1916) and Roland Dorgelès's *Les Croix de bois* (1919), are both now primarily assumed to be in this category, protest against the whole idea of war as well as against its innumerable idiocies at a personal level. However, Maurice Rieuneau, at the end of his monumental study, *Guerre et révolution dans le roman français de 1919 à 1939*, identifies four main categories: novels of testimony, initiation, historical reconstruction and commitment (Rieuneau, p. 533). On this basis, novels of protest would merely form part of the last category, thesis novels of commitment, a category they would incidentally share with very different works of jingoistic nationalism. Rieuneau admits that there is a good deal of overlap, and that it is difficult to place works of literary quality in any single category. Indeed, the very notion of literary quality may be connected with the ability to read these books on more than one level.

There is, moreover, a certain sameness in the best-known First-World-War accounts, largely imposed by the similarity of the experience: in nearly every case the trench war. Some critics have tried to assimilate this to a mythical pattern, such as Departure, Quest and Return (e.g. Cruickshank, pp. 45–6), although it seems more likely that this pattern necessarily follows from elements experienced in common: military induction and training, then departure to the line, initiation (first days under fire), travail (the grinding life in the trenches), ultimately followed by survival: the wounding and invaliding out of the hero, or in later works the final wearying outcome of the war.

The narrative of testimony was the one which exclusively interested the first systematic historian of French First-World-War narratives, Jean-Norton Cru. In *Témoins*, by far the most thorough survey, Cru, a Frenchman teaching in the United States who in 1914 went back to fight, examines 304 works by no fewer than 252 authors. He describes how, in 1914, the brutal shock of what modern war really meant in terms of death, maiming and destruction shattered his purely literary conceptions, and he uncompromisingly refuses to take into consideration any book not written by a participant: hence his title. Participants for Cru must, like himself, have been combatants, defined as soldiers having been under fire at the front. Of his 252 authors, only 49, incidentally, can be called novelists, and he comments that most of these wrote thinly disguised autobiographical accounts anyway (Cru, p. 11). Non-participants and works later than 1928 being excluded, this figure is smaller than it would otherwise be, but it is obvious even so that the vast majority of French writers who chose to write on 1914–18 opted against the purely fictional. Cru lists four genres: diaries, memoirs, letters and reflections. His criterion of quality is also rigorously based on factual accuracy, as far as he can determine it. He is indeed scathing about Barbusse and Dorgelès, whom he accuses of using personal experience less than their imagination, and exploiting sensation-alist myths with no basis in reality.

There is something in what Cru says. *Le Feu*, today, seems evidently superior to the jingoist accounts, but creaks considerably nevertheless, largely because it is itself just as much a thesis novel of another kind, its author preaching a hopelessly idealistic pacifism. Barbusse, an author with literary antecedents in *fin-de-siècle* decadence and pessimism – fascination with the morbid, death and the macabre – volunteered, over-age, for the infantry. His horror at what war actually meant led him to write *Le Feu*, which won the Goncourt Prize in 1916. Surprisingly, it was not censored, let alone banned (later works were not so lucky), and, despite Cru's strictures, it was the first book to give any real idea of the sordid and bloody nature of the war, the mutilated rotting corpses, the waterlogged trenches awash with filth. Narrated from the viewpoint of the private soldier, it is subtitled 'The Diary of a Squad': the squad being the minimal military unit, to which the individual fighting man's loyalties are by consensus primarily bound. Barbusse also devotes considerable space to the factual: descriptions of equipment, typical casualty statistics, types of shellfire. This documentary, informational function, sometimes deprecated as 'journalistic', is closely connected to the referential aspect felt so essential that, for instance, the initiatory experience of first exposure to fire is in almost all war narratives narrated in extensive detail.

As well as containing many incidents which would be repeated in dozens of accounts of this and later wars, *Le Feu* displays essentially literary techniques, such as the 'cultural' imagery later familiar in Malraux. Others, such as deliberately exaggerated macabre scenes, hark back to 'black' Romanticism. Thus the rotting corpse of a girl who had earlier been flitting through the trenches (why?) is found, and embraced, by a soldier who had been in love with her. This, and other implausibilities, such as a soldier who has made a private arrangement with the Germans (how?) to cross the lines and visit his wife in occupied France, do nothing for the novel and scarcely help Barbusse's thesis. Again, the use of vulgar language and slang is copied from Naturalism. Here Barbusse, like Dorgelès, avoids actual obscenity, using asterisks; later war writers, through the century, would move to completely unexpurgated language to represent the endless obscenity so familiar to anyone who has ever put on uniform.

Dorgelès's book, with the wooden crosses of its title acting as a compelling leitmotiv, had the advantage of using *Le Feu* as a model, it too showing the war from the viewpoint of a squad. Although also nominally a first-person narrative, it is more obviously fictional, its real protagonist being Gilbert Demachy, a former law student (and therefore educated) on whom most of the action is focalised. But Demachy is killed during a doomed attack near the end of the novel, and the actual ending switches to another soldier – about the only survivor of the original group – a proletarian called Sulphart, full of popular wisdom, who is wounded and invalided out: for Sulphart, victory means simply to emerge alive. Dorgelès, like Barbusse, indulges in deliberate, though effective, pathos, such as the troops moving up to attack past coffins prepared for their dead. He too includes scenes of which he had probably no direct experience, such as an execution for refusal to obey orders – a stock scene in protest novels. But Dorgelès does not preach, and his basic attitude is one of unproblematic patriotism, with occasional implausible heroics: but above all, the fighting troops deserve their sacrifices to be known and recognised.

A better example of the protest novel is *La Peur*, by Gabriel Chevallier. This work came out relatively late, in 1930, four years before Chevallier was made famous by his village farce, *Clochemerle*. It has been in the Livre de Poche catalogue, but is still not much read. Yet, as Rieuneau maintains, it is the ideal model of the novel of protest against the 'noble' vision of war (Rieuneau, p. 203). Although Chevallier's first-person narrator is called Dartemont, one can scarcely doubt that the general attitude to the war is his own. This is emphasised by a 1951 preface, in which Chevallier is proud to make the claim that he alone among First-World-War writers was prepared to admit he had been scared stiff. This is not entirely fair, but Chevallier goes further than others in communicating pure animal emotion, such as terror during an artillery bombardment.

La Peur is nothing if not an ideological statement, in which dialogue tends to the tirade, using liberal hindsight. The novel begins with general reflections on how the war began: 20 million civilised men, peaceably going about their preoccupations, were ordered to fight and kill, and, persuaded this was their duty, proceeded to do so. Dartemont is entirely pessimistic about humanity: men are stupid and ignorant, nor is he himself any better: at the start of the war, he saw no nobility in killing, but did nothing to avoid the draft. He is an anti-hero: not only does he never kill a German, he never even sees a live one. He takes part in only one scrappy skirmish, passing grenades he does not know how to throw, until he is wounded, apparently by one of these very grenades. Convalescent leave is a disaster of incomprehension, a frequent topic in war narratives. Dartemont's father is ashamed his son has received no promotion, his drinking cronies ask stupid questions about the good times he must be having. Yes, he retorts, every night we bury our comrades. On return from hospital he sees out the war as a company runner, though this means exposing himself under fire and is far from making him an *embusqué*, a shirker. The tone is consistently satirical: war is disorganised chaos, with superior officers – incompetent and often cowardly bullies – the real enemy. Majors and colonels are in a position to take decisions to help preserve their skins. The novel ends with Dartemont still surviving; yet victory infuriates his colonel as it prevents further promotion to general. Chevallier's book stands as a satirical monument, and some details are unforgettable, such as the scene of Verdun survivors talking of their only happy memory – the sight of three of their own military police hanged from a tree by angry French colonial troops.

Reflection on *La Peur* brings up some of the problems of uncompromising pacifism in protest novels. Such idealism left its holders in a complete moral vacuum two decades later, when they found no way of mentally coping with the incomparably more savage Nazi brutality then let loose. Partly at least as a result, during the Occupation some writers, such as Giono, were to adopt attitudes far from admirable. Applied to military strategy, the wish to avoid wholesale bloodshed at all costs was anyway to become an integral part of the purely defensive mentality which led to France's grimmest defeat and humiliation in 1940.

Giono himself published *Le Grand Troupeau* in 1931. Having spent most of the First World War in some of the bloodiest trench fighting, he wrote his novel, like Chevallier, whose taste for anarchism he shares, with a specifically pacifist intention. At the same time he had a second thesis, to propagate his idyllic dream of an ideal mystical/pastoral society. The war, apart from its general meaninglessness and horror, is a crushing denial of this ideal, and is given mythic status as the Beast of the Apocalypse. The flock of the title thus becomes heavily symbolic: of the men of Provence led to their death, and of the animals, now shepherdless and requisitioned for rations, forced down from their pastures to the abattoir. The parallel is insistent, and explains why, unlike other writers, Giono devotes only half his book to military scenes, alternating with descriptions of life continuing in Provence during the war years. This leads to an aesthetic weakness: since the pastoral scenes are obviously unrealistic, representing Giono's mystical fantasies rather than any true insight or observation, the reader may wonder why the battle scenes should be any more trustworthy. At the same time Giono achieves a high degree of lyricism and pathos in scenes of horror and in the contrast between industrialised war and idealised nature.

A fifth novelist who deserves a mention here is Léon Werth, whose *Clavel soldat* came out in 1919, only to be virtually forgotten except by specialists until republished in 1993. Werth was an intellectual and writer whose age placed him, like Barbusse, in a non-combatant role, but who in early enthusiasm volunteered for front-line service. And, like other volunteers, his disillusionment was all the more bitter: *Clavel soldat* is also a protest novel, informed by idealist anti-militarism and anger at the incompetence and petty injustice in the treatment of rank and file infantry. There is another aspect. Werth was Jewish, thoroughly assimilated into French life and culture – as he thought. Now antisemitism plays no role in French First-World-War narratives (nor in German ones). But Werth was still very much alive in 1939–45, and would write two books on it. *33 jours,* a manuscript admired by Saint-Exupéry, was an account of the exodus of 1940, as it affected Werth and his wife. Due to be published in the USA in the war, it in fact only appeared in 1992, together with *Déposition,* a new edition of Werth's Occupation diaries, a valuable documentary account first published in 1946. By this time Werth, as a Jew lucky to survive, had considerably modified his views of both pacifism and the secure position of assimilated Jews in French society.

The 1914–18 author considered by Cru as beyond dispute the best is Maurice Genevoix, who served as an infantry officer from the Marne to spring 1915, when he was badly wounded and subsequently invalided out. Without sharing Cru's uncompromising criterion of veridicity, I concur in this judgement. Genevoix wrote five war books in all, based on his own campaign diaries, starting early in the field with *Sous Verdun* (1916), followed by *Nuits de guerre* the same year, *Au seuil des guitounes* (1918), *La Boue* (1921), and finally *Les Éparges* (1923). They are now collected together as *Ceux de 14*. Not yet a professional writer like Barbusse and Dorgelès, Genevoix was at the Ecole Normale Supérieure when war broke out; he nevertheless knew what he was about. As part of his academic training he had written a thesis on Realism in Maupassant. The mimetic principle, including well-chosen detail, is his method. In a 1949 preface, he makes clear his stance, claiming that he deliberately avoided any imaginative rearrangement of his memories, since war provides such a powerful and special apprehension of reality that it imposes its own rules of veracity on the writer. Nor does he preach, allowing the human implications of the events he describes simply to emerge from a calm and seemingly objective, even understated, narrative.

As a platoon, and later company, commander, Genevoix has a wider perspective than Barbusse or Chevallier, though orders he has to transmit may seem no more sensible or rational to him than to them. He shows a gift for realistic dialogue – which certainly cannot have been remembered in toto – with an excellent ear for dialect and tricks of speech, and sketches in a large number of convincing subsidiary characters. As in any first-person memoir, unity is automatically achieved by the presence of the narrator throughout the action, with largely a single perspective. The book ends when the narrator is seriously wounded and evacuated, but there is a double climax, as the narrator's comrade-in-arms, with whom he has shared his entire war experience, has just been killed by shellfire, ironically when already wounded, but not fatally, awaiting evacuation in a field medical station.

Where Genevoix most closely follows Maupassant is in his use of the significant detail, the reality effect so decried by formalist critics, the memorable minutiae which add a symbolical dimension to an otherwise factual narrative. The main events are related in the dramatic present, that tense which has taken over French prose and is now predominant in media narrative, in which process factual war narratives have acted as a catalyst in the search to present experience with a minimum of aesthetic distance. Another device frequently employed, later to be taken up by Malraux, is the short, often verbless, elliptical sentence. *Ceux de 14* is probably too long ever to achieve the popularity of Barbusse and Dorgelès, but its quality is undeniable.

One of the finest treatments of the war is to be found in volumes XV and XVI of Jules Romains's fictional sequence, *Les Hommes de bonne volonté*, which must be the longest single novel ever published, with more than eight thousand pages in twenty-seven strictly structured volumes. His aim was to present a panoramic view of French life and covers the period from 1908 to 1933; naturally the First World War takes a central position. Individual volumes may be read and appreciated separately from the other volumes, although the recurring characters take on extra depth when seen in the perspective of the work as a whole.

Romains's situation was different from that of the other writers discussed. First, he had not been a participant. Unfit for active service, he served only as an auxiliary before being released in 1915. Second, he came late to the field, since his *Prélude à Verdun* and *Verdun* were published in 1938, the year of Munich, when another war was clearly inevitable. All this meant Romains could not use personal experience in his battle scenes, but had to rely on documentation, largely on narratives already published. To that extent, his volumes can be considered historical novels. But the twenty years which had gone by since the end of the war gave the opportunity for broader perspective and consideration of the causes and meaning of the war as a whole. His narrative technique, following the fates of (or focalising on) a large number of independent characters, meant that he could show various different aspects of the war, though the main theme of the two books is the mammoth struggle at Verdun in 1916. Some scenes are unforgettable, such as the description of a night march to relieve the threatened city. The fact that he had characters who had already appeared in fifteen volumes also meant that psychological depth could be explored. In most war narratives there is a certain shallowness of psychology, necessarily so, since a combatant can never really know much about the personal lives of comrades except where they impinge on his own military existence. Romains's reputation has unjustly declined since his death, but his two Verdun volumes, which much impressed Sartre when they first appeared, remain high achievements in the literature of war.

The finest book on war written in France this century deals with neither world war, but the 1936–9 Civil War in Spain, in which a Nationalist and Fascist uprising, actively abetted by Germany and Italy, finally crushed the elected Republican government after a bloody struggle. That book is André Malraux's *L'Espoir* (1937), written and published during the war, when its outcome was still far from clear. Malraux, who after the Nationalist rising immediately started to organise an air squadron to assist the Republican Government, uses his own experiences as makeshift aviator. But he goes far beyond what he could himself have witnessed, presenting a series of powerful dramatic scenes covering a wide variety of events. It is therefore not unreasonable to talk of epic sweep, in this, Malraux's longest and richest novel, moving from the suppression of the initial uprising in Madrid and Barcelona, to the unsuccessful siege of the Alcazar in Toledo and the subsequent retaking of that city by Franco's troops, bombing raids in Madrid, air crashes, infantry fighting in the Sierra – alternating with chapters of brilliant intellectual dialogue which supply a philosophical dimension. Here the metaphysical, historical and even aesthetic implications of events are discussed by various characters, all intellectuals: commitment as destiny, the psychology of fascism and revolution, the nature of human dignity and humiliation.

L'Espoir is also a *roman engagé,* the most effective novel of political commitment of our century. This inevitably implies a propaganda content. For Malraux, as for most Western liberals of the time, the Spanish Civil War was a simple moral issue: might versus right. But right by itself is not enough to win: our world is the construct of force, not of justice. 'L'Illusion lyrique' ['The Lyrical Illusion'] is the title of the first part of *L'Espoir*. Here illusion is the operative word, since the victory of the workers in Madrid and Barcelona proves hollow. At Toledo the Alcazar survives, and the worker militiamen flee the city without putting up any kind of organised fight. 'Organising the Apocalypse' is the keynote of the second part, with the antithesis between 'being' and 'doing'. Being right in the eyes of absolute humanist justice is not enough: the war will be won by action, by military efficiency. Few Nationalists or Fascists appear in the book, but those who do are just as courageous as the Republicans. And Malraux has to go further, because in the divided Republican camp, military efficiency means backing the Communist faction against anarchists and others. Now, over fifty years later, Spain's long dictatorship having evolved into what seems a relatively stable parliamentary monarchy, whereas Marxist regimes have crashed, the political implications of the Spanish Civil War look rather more complicated than they did in 1936. But for Malraux the War is 'us' against 'them'; which takes us back to the first generation of 1914–18 war narratives, where the patriotic imperative was never questioned.

When we come to consider French writing on the Second World War, we have two starting points. First, by common consent, the inter-war period saw one of the most brilliant blossomings of French literature. It was the age of Proust, Gide and Valéry, while the next generation of Martin du Gard, Duhamel and Romains was hard on their heels. Younger writers, born in the century, like Malraux, Prévost, Nizan and a newcomer, Sartre, showed brilliance or promise. Second, the defeat of 1940, followed by four traumatic years of German Occupation, was the most important, and potentially disastrous, historical event of the century, 'perhaps the most deeply humiliating and internally divisive episode in French history' (Flower, p. 47). How would this constellation of writers handle events?

They didn't. The established writers never really got to grips with the devastating experiences of 1939–45. Although Valéry's famous remark about the mortality of civilisations was certainly made more poignant, he himself was too old to digest, in writing, what had happened. So was Gide, who in any case took himself off to North Africa as soon as he could. Martin du Gard had good intentions in his *Colonel Maumort,* planning to review the events of the war against a lifetime of experience in his protagonist, a professional soldier. But most of what he did write of this novel is concerned with his hero's early life, well before 1914 let alone 1939, and what he had to say about the Second World War, if reflective and perceptive, never got beyond the stage of note-taking. Duhamel, who had so well captured the pathos of the maimed and dying in his sketches, *Vie des martyrs* (1917), had little to say about 1939–45, nor had Romains, in exile in North America. Nizan and Prévost were killed, fighting, in 1940 and 1944 respectively. Had they survived, no doubt they would have been heard from.

Malraux, who had written so impressively about Spain, placed the centre of gravity in *Les Noyers de l'Altenburg* (1943) in 1914–18 and the years immediately preceding. Post-war, to our loss, he had finished with fiction completely. Perhaps he, with his imaginative gifts and intellectual sweep, could better than anyone have handled the tragic and epic dimensions of war in full breadth and depth. Sartre's *Les Chemins de la liberté* (1945–9) was potentially the most ambitious attempt of all to deal with the Second World War; but he too could not bring his project to fruition, and as a result abandoned fiction no less definitively than Malraux. And Camus's *La Peste* (1947), taken by some at the time to be emblematic of the Occupation, now seems as an allegory distinctly hollow: both the bubonic plague and Hitlerism are scourges, but the second was man-made, creating questions of human responsibility and morality beyond the reach of this novel.

Now all this does not mean that the Second World War has been neglected in French writing (although no general critical overview such as Cru's or Rieuneau's exists). Far from it: it has provided an inexhaustible source of material for literary works and will no doubt continue to do so.

Unlike 1914–18 narratives, those of the Second World War can be divided into reasonably separate categories, based on the nature of the

French war experience itself. First the phoney war, the 'drôle de guerre'; then the débâcle of Summer 1940, and the exodus of fleeing refugees; the Occupation; the Resistance (not the same thing); the prisoner of war experience; deportation (again not the same thing); persecution of the Jews; Liberation. There is a certain amount of overlap, but the main distinctions are clear, and the immediate consequence is that there is much more thematic variety in Second-World-War narratives. Other categories could be argued for, in particular that of Collaboration, but in this area not too much has been published. Post-war themes, such as guilt (not too much of this either), self-disculpation (no shortage), disappointment and disillusionment, while providing abundant material for novelists, are not our concern here. The crucial difference from 1914–18 is the ethical dimension: after the shaming collapse of 1940 and the general acquiescence in a Fascist-type Vichy government only too willing to go beyond Nazi requirements in antisemitic persecution, what attitude should the French adopt? Between open collaboration at one extreme and defiant resistance at the other, there was an enormous grey area of moral ambiguity, a fertile source of literary potential.

It is a common critical view that 1939–45 did not produce literary works of the highest category, or indeed anything to be compared with the 'canonical' works of 1914–18. This is a view I do not share. Purely Resistance literature, the relatively few works written during the Occupation, is another matter. On the whole they have had a good airing, for propaganda reasons, which explains their prevailing weakness when read today, which is precisely that they are mostly propaganda. It is unfair to apply purely aesthetic criteria to works which were at the time a courageous call to arms, but fine sentiments do not make good literature – for once Gide was right – and the best-known of Resistance fictional narratives, Vercors's *Le Silence de la mer* (1942), has been, to my mind justly, attacked for gross psychological implausibility. Joseph Kessel's *L'Armée des ombres* (1945), written by a well-known journalist/novelist with the Gaullists in Britain, is in its way just as artificial a treatment, and impossibly idealistic into the bargain. Post-war, the fiction of a France almost entirely composed of Resisters was for twenty years the national myth: Kessel here provides one of its first literary embodiments. The Stendhalian pose of Roger Vailland's *Drôle de jeu* (1945) also makes Resistance activity seem far too facile, and it is moreover full of unacknowledged borrowings from Malraux; it tells us more about Vailland's pre-war preoccupations – drugs, alcohol, sex, literary surrealism – than it does about the Occupation. Vailland's political ideas, a simplistic belief in Stalinist Communism, obsolete on publication, now seem antediluvian.

Simone de Beauvoir's *Le Sang des autres* (1945) is also more concerned with her own preoccupations than with the Resistance, which occupies less than half the book, and that part decidedly the weakest. Her main interests are existentialist themes, specifically freedom and its relationship with responsibility and choice. Genuine active Resisters, such as Lucie Aubrac and Brigitte Friang, were less bothered with heart-searching, and went single-mindedly into action and danger. Nor did they have the leisure to set pen to paper until well after the end of the war; at the time, they had better things to do, as did one of the few French writers with any reputation to join the active Resistance. Jean Prévost would be killed in the Vercors uprising in 1944.

Two Goncourt Prize novels seek to isolate the occupation experience in a small provincial community. Jean-Louis Bory's *Mon village à l'heure allemande* (1945) has a brilliant title (the French had to put their clocks forward to German time); but its plot is implausible and its characters cardboard. Jean-Louis Curtis's *Les Forêts de la nuit,* (1947) is an altogether more solid work, which shows off well Curtis's chief literary gift, social satire. His fictitious Saint-Clar, a small town in the south-west, is intended to be typical of any small town in France. The novel begins in November 1942, at the moment of the Allied landing in North Africa, when most of the inhabitants of Saint-Clar have reconciled themselves to the German presence, and in many cases profited from it. Curtis shows a community where Resisters are few, far outnumbered by active, let alone passive, collaborators. By the end of the novel the young man who had been the leading Resister is dead, betrayed to the Nazis, while opportunists who have benefited from the Occupation are now set to profit equally from Liberation. Savage satire of black-marketing shopkeepers, who make a fortune under the Occupation and post-war successfully transfer their gains to social status and power, provides the dynamic for another memorable work, Jean Dutourd's *Au bon beurre* (1952).

As in the case of the 1914–18 conflict, the vast majority of the participants who came to write about the Second World War chose to cast their narratives in the memoir form. This is of course the easiest way of handling material anyway, as the inventive faculty need not be much tested, but it inevitably leads to limited perspectives, and there have been few attempts to place the events of the war in a panoramic overview, such as Romains attempted for 1914–18.

Women took no active part in the fighting of 1914–18; this being so, they could scarcely write about it, and the accusation that First-World-War writing is male chauvinist is pointless. On the other hand, their participation in the Resistance – a good deal more dangerous than 'regular' fighting

– meant that they too could now narrate their experiences, and indeed the best account of active Resistance activities, in my own opinion, is Lucie Aubrac's *Ils partiront dans l'ivresse* (1984), deliberately set in a symbolical period of nine months from May 1943 to February 1944. Aubrac's work is a memoir, only published forty years after the events, under the spur of the Klaus Barbie trial. It covers her actions in Lyons, where she has managed to spring her husband Raymond, a Resistance leader, from imprisonment; their reunion leads to the conception of a daughter, born in London when the couple have been safely airlifted out. In the intervening months Raymond has been arrested again, in company with Jean Moulin, and the central part of Aubrac's narrative is the description of how, heavily pregnant, she organises an interception of the prison van carrying her husband to Gestapo headquarters, shooting the escorts and freeing the prisoners. After this they have to hide out in the hills for months before a British plane can safely land and fly them out. This is a remarkable account of remarkable courage and initiative, coolly narrated by the schoolteacher who in 1944 became France's first woman parliamentarian.

Concentration camp narratives exist in hundreds, nearly all works by survivors so overwhelmed by their horrific experience that they felt an overriding obligation to bear witness. There are of course two different categories: accounts by Resisters who consciously risked arrest and deportation, and by Jews whose only offence was to have been born. But for both groups absolute veridicity is felt to be essential: the objective correlative for Auschwitz is Auschwitz. Some survivors, such as Charlotte Delbo, returned to the theme in several books, of poetry as well as prose; her works are now grouped together under the title *Auschwitz et après* (1970–1). Another survivor, Brigitte Friang, who post-war qualified as a parachutist and served as war-correspondent in two wars in Vietnam, wrote a lively account of her Resistance activities and deportation in *Regarde-toi qui meurs* (1970).

A number of the most striking deportation narratives are the work of non-French nationals who chose to pursue their literary careers using the French language, usually for idealist reasons: in particular Elie Wiesel and Jorge Semprun. Wiesel is now of course internationally known for his Nobel Peace Prize; his short account of deportation to Auschwitz with his family, *La Nuit* (1958), remains one of the best. Rumours of Nazi atrocities come to the Jews in Hungary, but they are ignored: such horrors could not happen to them. Wiesel's father, a respected man of substance, is even in a position to get his family away to Palestine, but rejects the opportunity. Then, in 1944, the whole community is marched to a train of cattle trucks and shipped to Auschwitz. Wiesel and his father survive the initial 'selection' by lying about their age, and are sent off to forced labour, temporarily reprieved; but his mother and three sisters are ordered to the gas chambers without even a word of farewell. Father and son are among the few still alive after the forced march which follows the evacuation of the camp in the face of the advancing Russian army, but the father dies of dysentery shortly afterwards. Some scenes presented are unforgettable, and Wiesel surely achieves tragic effect – if the term tragic cannot be used of the Holocaust, then it has truly lost all meaning – through careful selection of material and skill in presentation.

Semprun is not so well known. A teenage refugee (his father had been a leading diplomat of the defeated Spanish Republic; in 1988 he himself would return to Spain to become a cabinet minister), he took part in the French Resistance and was deported to Buchenwald in 1943. *Le Grand Voyage* (1963) is the account of his experience during Resistance and deportation, then liberation, all told in flashbacks and flashforwards, in the cadre of the four-day journey to Germany in a cattle truck. During this nightmare journey, a comrade known only as 'the lad from Semur', a decent, honest Resister obviously intended as a typical figure, gives the narrator sturdy support. But before the journey is over, this comrade is among those who have already died – of thirst, exposure, disease, shock, is not clear. It takes nothing away from the brilliance of Semprun's book to say that this narrative technique – non-linear but still firmly referential – probably owes something to Butor's *La Modification* (1957). There is, however, no question of Butor's second-person narrative; Semprun writes in the familiar first-person of the apparent memoir, though changing his own given name to Gérard. His account contains another element familiar among deportation survivors: bitter disillusionment at their reception on return to France. The returnees are presented with a 'repatriation indemnity': a 1000–franc note and eight packets of Gauloises. Not Semprun however – despite being a Resister, he was not a French national, so no money. He was allowed to keep the cigarettes.

For two million young men, war meant five years in the dispiriting monotony of prisoner-of-war camps, not on the face of it the most promising seeding-ground for literary works. But since many of these men were educated intellectuals, including professional writers, some sharply written narratives originated in this experience of captivity, for some prisoners of war the most powerful memories of their lives. The Jewish novelist Roger Ikor returned to this obsessive memory in a number of books, and specifically in his late memoir, *Pour une fois écoute mon enfant* (1975). Jacques Perret's *Le Caporal épinglé* (1947) crowns the monotony with excitement: Perret's protagonist succeeds in escaping back to France, hiding under a train. Few prisoners were so daring, or lucky.

There are exceptions to the prevailing realist technique in war narratives, but exceptions which prove the rule. Michel Tournier's *Le Roi des Aulnes* (1970) is one. In this novel, which some critics have found powerful but others pretentious, Tournier, soaked in German culture, though he himself seems to have taken no part in the war, uses Goethe's mythic figure of the Erl-King, the kidnapper of children, combined with that of the ogre of children's fairy tales. Abel Tiffauges, an oversized car mechanic with sado-masochistic tendencies and an unhealthy interest in young children, comes into his element as a prisoner of war in East Prussia, gaining the trust of his captors and eventually working in an SS military school. His job is to ride about the countryside recruiting children for the school, hence the title. At the end of the novel Tiffauges comes across a dying Jewish boy, Ephraim, and attempts to nurse him back to health. As the Russian army advances, Tiffauges, carrying the boy, attempts to flee through marshes, but both are swallowed up. *Le Roi des Aulnes* is a work of some imaginative power, usually described as 'disturbing'. The sado-masochism, overtones of homo-sexuality, and religious mysticism, all combine to form a deliberate attempt at creating myth, one that has been been attacked for presenting a picture of Nazi society in which fascination plays at least as large a role as repulsion. (See chapter 8, pp. 141–2, for further discussion of Tournier.)

La Route des Flandres by Claude Simon (1960) is another exception. Here the situation is complicated. Simon was early praised by avant-garde theorists as an exemplary non-referential writer. Yet much of the matter of *La Route des Flandres* is clearly inspired by a scene in the débâcle of 1940, a doomed cavalry sortie in which Simon himself took part. Some time after the novel was published, one of the author's former officers, a man incidentally satirised in the work, wrote to Simon praising the book for its historical accuracy in treating this episode, in which he himself had been involved (See A. Cheal Pugh, pp. 121–30). What is one to make of this information, as it were straight from the horse's mouth? One obvious answer is that the denial of referentiality, and the accompanying claim that there can never be any such thing as a coherent, conscious author accessible through writing, were themselves, never properly argued but stridently asserted, so much nonsense. Moreover, similar obsessive scenes recur in many of Simon's novels, and he has admitted their autobiographical basis. Simon, whose position in twentieth-century French literature has been firmly cemented by the 1985 Nobel Prize, is perhaps best seen as a post-Proustian (which is probably why he alone of the group so quaintly dubbed 'new novelists' seems to have some hope of a continuing readership); he uses war as he uses other experiential material, but without privileging it. His highly self-conscious narrative technique, with discontinuous sentences dotted with participles and Henry James-like qualifications of what he has just written, is not so much 'writing', somehow, like spontaneous combustion, generating itself. It can be seen as a deliberately 'chaotic' style: the term 'chaotic', along with 'baroque' and 'labyrinthine', being a favourite epithet applied to Simon. (See chapter 8, p. 139, for further comments on Simon as a stylistic innovator.)

Now the privileging of 'chaotic' style, or what I myself prefer to call the 'chaotic fallacy', though not necessarily limited to the question of form in purely war literature, has become widespread in recent decades. Its essence is the belief that because 'war is chaos', a view with which few participants might disagree, *therefore* its chaotic content can only be rendered by chaotic form. Or, in a weaker version, that it can best be rendered by chaotic form. The experience of war, especially of actual fighting, is shapeless, fragmentary, much of it incomprehensible, so work which attempts to reproduce or convey the experience of war must itself be shapeless, fragmentary or incomprehensible. Two – contradictory – factors lie behind this view. One is the American experience in Vietnam, a war which political correctness sees as not only chaotic and pointless, but also unforgivably wrong morally. The other is the popularised postmodernist view that *all* writing is nothing but empty rhetoric chasing its own tail; that this argument is self-refuting has not weakened its appeal. But in essence the chaotic fallacy is just an extreme form of photographic realism, and although often brilliantly effective in individual scenes – fragmentary experience – it is hopelessly inadequate as a general organising principle. That much more than an attempt to represent chaos by chaos is required in successful war narratives is surely confirmed by any examination of the works cited in this chapter, or by other writers in the field internationally admired, say Primo Levi or Solzhenitsyn.

Finally, many would deny war any connection with beauty. This is to take a narrow view, since it is a cliché in war narratives to contrast, say, the horror and filth of the trenches with a striking sunset or the song of a skylark above the lines, oblivious of the strife below. Nevertheless few war writers have found beauty a major preoccupation. An exception is Julien Gracq, who in *Un balcon en forêt* (1958) produced a remarkable novel which sets the first nine months of the war in a surreal context of undeniable poetic brilliance. Gracq's protagonist, a young officer called Grange, spends the phoney war in command of a small blockhouse in the Ardennes, enjoying a romantic idyll which as portrayed has as much to do with Shakespeare's Forest of Arden as with twentieth-century geography.

The German attack of May 1940 destroys Grange's idyll, and Grange himself, no less than it does the whole French army. But *Un balcon en forêt* is a *tour de force*; few war narratives are – or would want to be – on this plane.

SUGGESTIONS FOR FURTHER READING

On the First World War

Cruickshank, J., *Variations on Catastrophe* (Oxford: Oxford University Press, 1982)
Cru, J.-N., *Témoins* (Nancy: Presses Universitaires de Nancy, 1993; first published 1929)
Riegel, L., *Guerre et littérature* (Paris: Klincksieck, 1978)
Rieuneau, M., *Guerre et révolution dans le roman français de 1919 à 1939* (Paris: Klincksieck, 1974)

On the Second World War

Atack, M., *Literature and the French Resistance* (Manchester: Manchester University Press, 1989)
Flower, J. and R. Davison, 'France', in H. Klein (ed.), *The Second World War in Fiction* (London: Macmillan, 1984), pp. 47–87
Harris, F. J., *Encounters with Darkness* (New York: Oxford University Press, 1983)
Pugh, A. Cheal, 'Defeat, May 1940', in I. Higgins (ed.), *The Second World War in Literature* (Edinburgh: Scottish Academic Press, 1986), pp. 121–30

11

STEPHEN F. NOREIKO

From serious to popular fiction

It is almost trivially easy to distinguish between serious and popular fiction. We can do it on external criteria and rest safe in the assumption that anything published under, say, the Harlequin imprint, is unlikely to bring us new insights into the human condition. Previous generations have similarly turned to recognisable brand names. Around the time of the First World War, the titles in the 'Bibliothèque de ma Fille' announced themselves on the inside front cover as novels for young ladies. 'Les Romans Bleus' a generation later made the same claim more explicitly, asserting that they were for the (chastely) passionate young Frenchwoman of the day, modern, moral and respectable. Nor should it be assumed from the avowedly moralising character of these novels – irreproachable, upright and salutary as they proclaim themselves – that they are necessarily dull. Those who read (and still do read) them, read them avidly for enjoyment.

The term used for such enjoyment is 'distraire', and popular fiction is fiction that entertains and diverts. Guy Des Cars, in many ways a symbol of the popular novel in France today, claims no other aim: 'Je ne suis là que pour les distraire en leur apportant l'évasion' (*J'ose*, p. 57) ['What I'm here for is to entertain them by providing escape'], he says. An advertisement for one of his novels, quoted with extensive (and mainly disapproving) comments by Duneton and Pagliano (*Anti-Manuel de français*, pp. 127 ff.), states: 'Lisez par plaisir. Pas par devoir' ['Read for pleasure, not out of obligation'], implying and assuming the dichotomy between the serious (dull) and the popular (entertaining). Certainly, French writers appear to believe in the existence of a distinction between serious and popular novels, though they may not necessarily always use the same terms in the same way, nor even draw the dividing line in exactly the same place. Des Cars considers himself a *romancier* as opposed to an *écrivain*. For Patrick Modiano, the distinction is between *romanciers* and *intellectuels*.

But Modiano is published by Gallimard and a winner of literary prizes, including the Goncourt for *Rue des boutiques obscures* (1978). Such achievements can probably be taken as badges of seriousness – as much of it as is possible for a French author to attain while still alive. On the other hand, the interview in which Modiano draws the line and sets himself apart from the intellectuals is given in the postface to a popular book club edition of his 1981 novel *Une jeunesse*: the kind of bound edition (this one from Tallandier) complete with ribbon bookmark that is so obviously a packaging of literature as consumer object (collectible, unlike the consumable Harlequin). The highly commercial novelist Paul-Loup Sulitzer can also be found in the same kind of format. The distinction between serious and popular, easy enough to see where it is taken for granted, seems to attract more attention as it becomes blurred.

The epitome of facile, consumable, packaged mass-consumption literature today is the *bande dessinée*; a visit to the FNAC store in Paris's Forum des Halles, where adults and adolescents sit sprawled on the floor, enthralled for hours, reading before buying, is sufficient to convince anyone of the size and commitment of its following. But though *BD* in French is content with its original label even if the English equivalent tends more pretentiously to style itself 'graphic novel', the presentation of authors and artists and their works in the catalogue of Dupuis (one of the leading publishers in the genre) appeals to the same range of values as might be assumed to subtend serious literature: 'profonde humanité' ['profound humanity'], 'fouille jusqu'au cœur des êtres' ['goes to the heart of his characters'], 'fustige férocement le monde actuel' ['ferociously castigates the modern world']. Clearly, then, popular literature is not above taking itself seriously.

At the same time, serious fiction, at least fiction from a supposedly serious publisher – the Editions de Minuit for example – is now and then quite ready to borrow the apparatus of popular fiction. In *Cherokee* (1983), Jean Echenoz[1] has a character dressed in 'une cravate crémeuse sur une chemise en tergal chocolat, ce qui lui donnait une allure confuse de souteneur et de petit déjeuner' ['a creamy tie against a shirt of dark-brown terylene; it gave him a sort of in-between look: in between a pimp and a piping hot chocolate']. The garish clothes, the incongruity of the double comparison that yokes together a pimp and breakfast (which in France implies a different set of colour and culinary values), the mixing of menace and humour, are tricks found regularly in certain veins of popular literature, particularly in the mannered writing of thrillers. There are many such devices of the thriller to be found – self-consciously – in the novels of Modiano and Echenoz, among others.

There is cross-fertilisation between media as well as between genres high and low, particularly between word and image, though the relations are by no means symmetrical. Sulitzer's novels, announced as a whole 'new world' of *BD*, are recreated in graphic form. Radio and television, though they may consume serious or popular fiction for adaptations, do not feature largely in fiction, except possibly as sources of intoxication and noise pollution. Patrick Cauvin's novel *Haute-Pierre* (1985: see also below) is set in the world of television, but Cauvin deliberately avoids the glamour which other writers might seek with the evocation of film. Books, though they allude to and borrow from each other, seldom refer explicitly to other books: Jacques Poulin's *La Tournée d'automne* (1993), about a travelling librarian on the North Shore of the Saint-Lawrence, is one notable exception; another is Raymond Jean's *La Lectrice* (1986), ironically better known through Michel Deville's film; others will be examined later. In novels popular and serious, however, there are frequent explicit references to film. Cauvin, whose popular novels have been much adapted for film and television, calls on film-going for common cultural reference in *L'Amour aveugle* (1974), which recounts the affair between an ageing disillusioned schoolteacher and a blind though cinephile woman met in a cinema. Similarly explicit references to the 1967 John Bloomfield film *Point Blank*, with mention of the actors Angie Dickinson and Lee Marvin, are made by Echenoz in *Cherokee* (1983). What is low in one medium (Hollywood movie for example) may become high in another. Authors move between media; works can be recast. Modiano was co-author with Louis Malle of the film *Lacombe Lucien* (1974) and his 1975 novel *Villa triste* was turned into Patrice Leconte's atmospheric film *Le Parfum d'Yvonne* (1994). Claude Chabrol's 1993 film of *Madame Bovary* no doubt remains serious, but the lowest of all genres must surely be the popular and trivial *photo-roman*, or photo-novel, and it was in this format that the *Petit Echo de la mode* serialised Flaubert's novel in the 1980s.

How then are we to characterise popular fiction? Not simply by its sales figures: Victoria Thérame's *Bastienne* (1986) never topped any bestseller lists and yet this story of suburban love and violence is one to which I would attach the label popular. For its setting first of all: the action is situated in a squalid suburb on the fringe of Paris and its characters are the mixed bunch of out-of-work opportunists, downtrodden women, feckless or macho men – despairing, resigned, or earnest and ambitious – that one might well expect to find there. Not that the characters of popular fiction are necessarily of the people: often they are, of course, but the heroines and heroes of Des Cars or Sulitzer move far away and up from their humble backgrounds; the humble condition of the heroines in the novels of Delly is only an accident and the readers know that Hélène, Roselyne or Magali will in the end receive her reward or be recognised and restored to her heritage.

What the characters of popular fiction have in common is that they are types rather than individuals; archetypes or stereotypes, they are used for what they represent or for narrative facility. If we find serious writers attracted by the hackneyed and the popular, it is because of the fascination of reworking the instantly recognisable. And because popular fiction deals in types – even when not overtly didactic or moralising – it tends also to affirm, or at the least be a vehicle for, a set of values. The suburban low-lifers in Thérame's *Bastienne* are emblematic; she uses them because they illustrate and uphold her optimistic anarchism and the story she tells about them is constructed to justify her faith in her fellow-beings. And so her schematic characters are instantly recognisable types, and they do the right thing (or the wrong thing if they are villains), as Thérame hopes and her readers expect. Popular fiction – such is the law of the market – has to keep the customer satisfied. To an extent of course, all writers repeat themselves. 'Serious' writers claim that they attempt to avoid repetition, rewriting the same book in different ways. Popular writers have to fulfil the expectations of their readers, who demand from the names they know a recognisable product. Des Cars accepts (indeed boasts) that he is, like Delly and others, a product, the appearance of each new book an event awaited like the arrival of the year's Beaujolais nouveau.[2] Georges Simenon started by writing a kind of disposable popular fiction – short, lightweight romance or adventure novels, in small, cheap formats that have now all but disappeared. He then gained fame and fortune by making popular fiction almost respectable, and he has the distinction of two product names: for the enthusiasts, a 'Simenon' (without the famous detective) is one sort of novel and a 'Maigret' another.

To what extent the average reader looks for such brand names can be gauged by a visit to the second-hand bookstall in a local market in France. A glance across the boxes gives a fair impression of what the non-intellectual public at large is reading. The stock is sorted by imprint (Harlequin, Série noire, Le Masque), by genre (science fiction, western, espionage), by author (Cartland, Des Cars, Exbrayat); the miscellaneous box, where serious literature would end up if much of that were sold, is the smallest. When we read popular fiction, we like to know what we are getting, and we follow authors who flatter or confirm our assumptions.

The couple who collaborated under the pseudonym Delly were an author who confirmed assumptions. During the first third of this century they published some hundred titles, generally in the blue-covered collections described above and aimed at a readership predominantly female and initially young. And as I have already indicated, their purpose was avowedly didactic. The summaries on the covers reassured mothers that these gems of sentimentality had no other aim than to lift discreetly a corner of the veil on life and love, illustrating by their example the advantages of a loving family in a stable society. Though *Un Marquis de Carabas* (1935) begins with an apparent criticism of modern manners, the decadence that Delly's upright young people react against is of all time and no time in particular. War is generally only mentioned without details, as one of the ways, for example, in which Henry de la Rochethulac, hero of *La Chatte blanche* (1923), earned distinction. That passing allusion apart, there is little else in the novel that indicates when it is set. The war has not changed social structures: faithful old retainers are faithful to their old masters even in poverty, and scornful of upstarts and foreigners even when rich. The novels are not entirely without contemporary references: a Jesuit priest in *Magali* (1918) has been expelled from France by unjust laws; Magali calls herself reasonably feminist, though without excess, content to be able to earn her living, conceding the need for certain reforms while criticising excessive zeal. Not that Delly's heroines are submissive. But they know their place and Magali's pride prevents her from loving above what she believes to be her station, while Roselyne, the eponymous *Ondine de Capdeuilles* [*The Water Maiden of Capdeuilles*] (1921), limits her ambitions to what she believes she can obtain. With their resigned dignity goes courage: Yolaine in *La Chatte blanche* affronts danger, Magali stands up to injustice.

The heroes who win the hearts of these heroines are older, more experienced, learned or distinguished in some way. Though the women are devout, the men – while sparing them from evil influence – may be sceptical, even dangerously so like the satirical writer-hero *Gilles de Cesbres* (1930), though of course essentially virtuous. They are keenly conscious of the obligations of their position in society, and though they are usually noble and always wealthy, wealth and nobility eventually count for less than true love in a world where each knows their place and is happy with it. Magali herself repeats the point. Of course, since this is popular fiction, in the end the happy couples find they have both. After wrestling with his conscience, the Duke of Staldiff proposes to Magali before the secret of her noble birth is revealed. She of course only agrees after, when she can accept as his equal. Lorenzo Damplesmes proposes to the poor orphan Hélène while she still, like everyone else in Treilhac, believes him penniless. She loves him, they are both young and able to work for their living, she has no need of riches. Her reward for such selfless virtue is naturally to discover that her new fiancé, not long returned from Africa, did after all make his fortune out there.

Stern noble heroes, virtuous heroines moving unscathed through a world of temptations and remaining true to themselves: the world of Delly is a world without surprises. And if the world of Guy Des Cars is a little more sinister and dangerous, the surprises are still relatively few. Des Cars (his name sometimes parodied into 'Guy des Gares' for his reputation as purveyor of *romans de gare*, novels bought on station bookstalls) is another writer of the commonplace. Though he claims *Le Donneur* (1973) to be the study of a 'pathological case', the professional sperm donor of this supposedly scandalous story is ordinary, downtrodden and pitiable, dominated by the wife who launches him on his career. In spite of his multiple paternities he longs for unattainable women, and he is denied comfort in his own family after the revelation that his daughters were actually fathered by his best friend. The banality of the character, presented in the book as the most extraordinary feature of a remarkable story, in fact trivialises the events. Male readers can feel secure in their superiority to the inadequate Lucien Mardoux; female readers find confirmation of their ability to manipulate their men. The mechanisms of *L'Impure* (1946) are similarly transparent: Chantal, the heroine, is first seen on board a luxury liner as beautiful, elegant, enviable and mysterious. An orphan left to the care of the *Assistance Publique*, she has become a fashion model, thus demonstrating that one can attain worldly success from humble beginnings. The mistress of a rich banker (and mother of his child) she has also caught leprosy, thereby reassuring readers that there is justice after all and that beauty is fragile. She finds a fleeting dream of true love but – underlining her tragedy – sacrifices it to follow the chance of a cure. A reluctant member of a tropical island leper colony, she perturbs the Protestant pastor and destroys his daughter's sanity and happiness by stealing her doctor suitor, showing herself to be fickle, feminine and Parisian as ever. In the end, finding friendship and religion, she is cured and becomes a nurse herself to care for other lepers, thus proving that no one is beyond redemption. Her child meanwhile is entrusted to the father's widow and so set free from an unworthy mother and restored to good fortune. Chantal can hardly be called a consistent character and the novel is less a story than a sequence of situations, each of which is given the expected resolution. In other novels, a hero enigmatic but loyal defends France from drugs and the yellow peril (*La Vipère*, 1969); and a brave but over-trusting French officer is betrayed by a duplicitous woman (*Le Château de la juive*, 1958). Contemporary subjects may be touched on – sects for example in *La Coupable* (1980) – but despite the claim to be studying pathological or psychological cases, a claim repeated on the cover of several paperback editions and embedded in *Le Château de la juive*, the treatment is always facile.

The novels of Delly may be slight, but the readers know what they are getting, sensing from the first pages that the scheming temptress will be thwarted and that the obstacles separating hero and heroine will be swept away. Des Cars appears to promise more, but while flattering prejudices actually delivers a similar sort of recipe. With other novelists, the stock characters are used not for reasons of narrative facility or paucity of invention, but precisely because they are stock characters. Like the working-class heroines of Thérame, they are emblematic and thus the popular novel becomes a celebration and affirmation of popular values. Charles Exbrayat is one example. Though the name Exbrayat is for most French readers synonymous with detective fiction (some of it in provincial French settings), this author has also written regional and historical novels, starting with *Jules Matrat* (1942), and winning the Prix Ulysse du Roman Populaire in 1981 for *La Lumière du matin*. Whether the time is the aftermath of the Great War as in *Jules Matrat* or *Un matin, elle s'en alla* (1969), or the Napoleonic era of *La Lumière du matin*, the characters are less important as individuals than by their attachment to the land, the author's native Massif Central.

This celebration of regional identity is a broad seam in French popular literature. Beyond those authors – Ramuz, Giono or Genevoix, who have some degree of literary pretension and have achieved some recognition – there are others, such as the Burgundian railwayman Henri Vincenot or the Cévenol Jean-Pierre Chabrol, in whose works story, style and characterisation are often less important than the assertion of an identity by virtue of attachment to a *terroir* (a word with overtones of tradition, typicality and authenticity). The historical novels of Jeanne Bourin (*La Chambre des dames*, 1979, for example), or the *Rois maudits* cycle by Maurice Druon, in so far as they are perceived by the public to present types who have contributed to the identity of France, share this appeal. It is not belittling the Francophone literature of Canada to maintain that novels such as Antonine Maillet's Goncourt-winning *Pélagie-la-Charrette* (1979) (see chapter 13, pp. 220–1 for further discussion of this text), and others by by Réjean Ducharme or by Michel Tremblay, are excellent examples of literature which asserts and legitimates an identity. *Pélagie* the novel, Pélagie the character herself leading her people back home, and also Bélonie the old man who remembers the group's history, are all the signs of the vitality of a tradition and an assertion of the value of belonging to it.

In his first novel, *Banlieue sud-est* (1947), René Fallet celebrates (even more than he celebrates youth and survival amid the bombs that destroy the railway yards and burn the tenements) the inhabitants of a suburban town that lives by the railway. He returns to the same setting, a similar time and the same sort of characters, in *Il était un petit navire* (1962). But though the context is sombre in these novels set against the background of the Second World War, the Occupation, danger and deprivation, the overall tone is optimistic: the various characters are indomitable, with a vital spark which enables them to rise above the situation. *Il était un petit navire*, for instance, begins with the evocation of an exhibition of amateur paintings by railway workers; hungry, living on meagre wartime rations, they console themselves by painting richly Pantagruelian pictures of food. There is a certain note of pessimism in *Banlieue sud-est*, carried by the thread of cold lonely 'M. René Fallet' walking like a ghost through his own novel. His characters however rise above it and the contrast is great with, for example, Céline's *Voyage au bout de la nuit* (1932), which takes a much bleaker view of the industrial suburbs of Paris and the capacity of their inhabitants for survival. But Céline is not a popular author and he does not write to reassure; while popular authors assume working-class merit, he sees a black side; he challenges the assumptions that popular fiction vigorously confirms. Bardamu's Africa, therefore, is scarcely on the same planet as the Africa where the Lorenzo of Delly's *Marquis de Carabas* – published three years later – found his fortune, although Bardamu and Lorenzo might well have been there at the same time.

Apart from the conceit of including its own author, *Banlieue sud-est* is realistic, almost documentary. *Il était un petit navire* has a note of whimsy. In a number of other novels, from *Le Triporteur* (1951) to *La Soupe aux choux* (1980), the whimsy becomes progressively more predominant as Fallet proclaims more insistently the virtues of the honest peasants of the Bourbonnais, pickled in cheap wine and recalcitrant to progress. These are the novels Fallet considers to be Beaujolais-fuelled (he also claims another vein, whisky-driven, where the subject-matter is love). Goubi, the village idiot of *Un idiot à Paris* (1966), is lacking in intelligence but, attached to his roots, full of good sense. Juliette, who marries him and with her hard-earned money buys them both respectability, is a harlot with a heart of gold and a mania for agriculture. The mania for agriculture, in Paris and in her profession, is a handicap, but of course commendable and natural in the village of Jaligny-sur-Besbre. As for the heart of gold, it goes with her condition. Fallet writes a male universe where the place for women is small. The conviviality promoted as a supreme value in *Le Beaujolais nouveau est arrivé* (1975) exists among men and is disturbed by women such as Maman Turlutte or Debedeux's wives, mistresses and secretaries. Of the four friends, only Poulouc is young enough to have his mother still – but she is a prostitute and thus honourable. The polyandrous arrangement between the friends and Prunelle can work only as long as Prunelle remains, like Goubi, an innocent. Marriage and the respectability it involves are fled in *Le Triporteur* and when the dead Francine is resuscitated in *La Soupe aux choux*, her husband realises their total incompatibility. She goes away to live her new life, leaving him with his friend and neighbour. Paradoxically, the revelation of Francine's adultery with the neighbour only serves to bring the two men closer together; and a similar motif is used to close *Les Vieux de la vieille* (1958).

Facile and escapist, nostalgic and chauvinist, Fallet's novels appeal (and not simply to male readers) by the verve with which they articulate values which are felt to be typically popular and typically French. The opening pages of *La Soupe aux choux* are a roll call of emblems and evocative commonplaces: the village in its *terroir* with communal wash house and 'bistrot' – focal points of community life – the old trades and crafts, the Manufrance catalogue (an important strand in the cultural history of France and for years the source of whatever the inhabitants of far-flung villages could not provide for themselves), the postman and his glass of wine. Much the same cultural background in fact is portrayed in the 'petit village gaulois' of the Astérix adventures. The titles too are eloquent: *Le Beaujolais nouveau* in praise of wine; *Les Vieux de la vieille* evoking tradition and friendship; *La Soupe aux choux* signifying good traditional cooking; and *Le Triporteur* a pre-motorised age of skilled workers and apprentices running errands. *Banlieue sud-est* conjures up images of solidarity in working-class neighbourhoods, as does *La Grande Ceinture* (1956), which became René Clair's film *Porte des lilas* (1957).

Both veins of Fallet's work have given rise to films and Fallet himself was also a script-writer, as well as literary and film critic. The importance of film – evasion, inspiration and shared cultural reference – has already been touched upon. Patrick Cauvin was film critic for the magazine *Pilote* (a landmark in the history of *BD*) and, like Fallet in his whisky vein, he generally chronicles the loves and disappointments of middle-aged men (seriously for adult readers, humorously for children under his real name of Claude Klotz). Cauvin raises the question of French cultural identity in *E=mc² mon amour* (1977), which brings together two gifted pre-teenagers: Daniel, from the working-class suburbs of Paris and crazy about American films, and the rich American Lauren with her passion for Racine. And just as Cauvin's *Haute-Pierre* (1985) is a novel recounting a television script – a television script that depicts the characters of the novel, in what is basically the same device which sub-tends George Perec's monumental *La Vie mode d'emploi* – so all these novels have made films. They transfer easily, since they call on easily recognisable situations and a limited range of characters: Cauvin's warily ageing teachers or writers, with oversmart children to cut them down to size, or Fallet's peasants, or even the schematic and scheming heroes of Sulitzer who adapt so naturally to *bande dessinée*.

Paul-Loup Sulitzer is a commercial novelist in two senses of the term. In the sense first that his novels are bestsellers and designed to be such, but also in the sense that their subjects are commerce and finance. The significantly titled *Cash!* (1981) won the Prix du Livre de l'été, a prize whose title indicates that, as well as the decried *roman de gare*, French publishing also recognises a category *roman de plage* – usually massive enough to stop a towel blowing away, but not so demanding that it cannot be readily put down and picked up again. Protagonists and their immediate entourage are not stereotypes but on the contrary exceptional. This very fact does away with any need for description or analysis: they are 'prodigious' or 'extraordinary' and dazzling accounts of financial manipulation replace plot and character credibility. *Popov* (1984) is styled by the publishers 'the first novel of modern economic warfare'. In *Le Roi vert* (1983) a concentration camp survivor amasses vast wealth and builds a tentacular empire while himself remaining mysterious and unseen in the background. These are themes and devices familiar already in the nineteenth century (as David Coward has shown in chapter 5 of this volume), though Sulitzer's schematic annotations lack the verisimilitude of, say, Balzacian descriptions. Fabulously rich, the 'Green King' retains sympathy with the poor and downtrodden, using his financial dealings and speculations to buy and build a new country in the heart of the Amazon basin. From there, followed by supporters and citizens of his new country, he marches on the United Nations to demand recognition, fading away again when it is refused. *Hannah* (1985) and *L'Impératrice* (1986) follow the rising fortunes of Hannah from her Polish *shtetl* across the world as she builds up her cosmetics empire (the heroine and her story have more than a vague resemblance to Helena Rubinstein).

Popular fiction is essentially fiction for readers who want to know what happens next, turners of pages who, for this time at least, are reading in the mode of suspense.[3] The medium in which the story is recounted is not greatly important and the same story may be transposed to another medium to reach a wider audience. Michel Zévaco, the last of the *feuilletonistes* and a character as colourful as his heroes, was experimenting with cinema just before his death in 1918. The *Histoires extraordinaires* Pierre Bellemare told on the radio lack his portentous voice in their printed adaptations, but they are still the same stories. Greater exposure across another medium may in turn help sell more of the original. But the naïve reader is a fiction too, and popular fiction itself in whatever medium is not necessarily always limited to its face value. Drawing on commonplaces as they do, film, *bande dessinée* and novel come, in some cases, to exhibit a consciousness of the common stock in which they have their roots. The heritage of popular culture which writers and readers share becomes part, not of the matter, but of the texture of fiction and the naïve story is given another dimension by the manner of its recounting.

I have indicated that novels refer frequently to film. Films of course refer to other films and *Olé! San-Antonio* (1972), a *BD* version of the same story that appears in San-Antonio's *Viva Bertaga* (1975), cross-refers on its first page to another *BD*, the *Astérix* series (except that Obélix's menhir is a giant Coke bottle). San-Antonio, pseudonymous author and eponymous narrator of well over a hundred novels which might loosely be called crime fiction, is a quintessentially popular author, with an assured place in the history of popular culture in France. The sales are huge, the output is prolific, the plots are improbable, the characters are schematic. The impossibly good-looking chief inspector San-Antonio whom no woman can resist (but he loves his mother) is flanked by Bérurier, a caricature figure of Rabelaisian appetites, vulgar and ill-educated, and (though not as regularly) by Pinaud, hypochondriac and petty-bourgeois. Between them they incarnate and express a typically French set of prejudices, and through the pages of the novels there passes a procession of stock types: beautiful spies and sinister double-agents, devout provincial spinsters, impertinent urchins, earnest teachers, clod-hopping peasants and more. The gallery of portraits is close to that of Fallet and the intrigue in the early volumes, written in the fifties before the vein is well assured, is not far from Des Cars.

But this climate of shared assumptions is deliberately fostered by allusions and comparisons and above all by the linguistic verve. San-Antonio delivers essentially an authorial monologue that takes precedence over the narration and he is probably read chiefly for his derisive inventiveness and his idiosyncratic discourse. Quotation (and still less translation) cannot convey the total impression produced by the density of verbal invention, mixing of registers, amassing of references. The simple sentence 'Puis, c'est le jeu du serrement de paumes' ['And then, it's time for the handshake game'] is actually a rearranging of 'Serment du Jeu de Paume', the famous tennis-court oath sworn by the deputies on 20 June 1789.

However, though he pushes verbal subversion further than any others, San-Antonio is not the only popular author who adds deliberate linguistic embellishment, and Fallet is capable of the same kind of verve. 'Les contrevents s'ouvrirent en une volée de bois vert' ['the shutters flew back in a volley of green wood'] begins a bravura passage of similar type. Using the word 'contrevent' allows the author to delay the normal word for 'shutter', or rather its homonym 'volée' ('volley') to the expression 'volley of green wood'; shutters in France are of course generally painted green, but 'volée de bois vert' is in fact a fixed expression for a beating. The humour of this sentence consists in its engineering the appearance of a fixed expression in a context where it is appropriate (the shutters are green and they do fly open) in an unexpected way. The linguistic humour of the French, which is so much a part of their popular culture, works on this pattern and the culture of cliché out of which their popular fiction is made feeds on itself in the same way. Prolonged immersion in popular fiction provokes in certain subjects that third, or productive, mode of reading to which Barthes has referred.[4]

Daniel Pennac is an author whose work feeds on clichés even as it subverts them. His series of Malaussène novels moves from Gallimard's popular thriller collection, the 'Série noire', to their serious up-market 'Collection blanche' with the 546 pages of *Monsieur Malaussène* (1995), a move which acknowledges how serious popular fiction can become. The novels announce subversion in their titles. *Au Bonheur des ogres* (1985) recalls Zola's *Au Bonheur des dames* and is set, appropriately, in a Parisian department store. *La Fée Carabine* (1987) puts us in mind of fairy-tale Fée Carabosse though the connection between fairies good or bad and a little old woman with a pistol in her shopping bag is slight to anyone but a myopic child raised on the magic of stories. (In the opening chapter of the story, the old woman is crossing the road. Startled by the approach of a detective, she shoots first and asks no questions.) *La Petite Marchande de prose*, set in the world of publishing, reworks the French title of Andersen's little match girl. Only *Monsieur Malaussène* is not a deformation of an existing name or title; the subversion in this long-awaited sequel is more subtle, since 'Monsieur Malaussène' turns out in the end to be the name of the narrator's new-born son. The child continues the line of the narrator as *Monsieur Malaussène* concludes the narrative line.

Clichés are asserted, subverted, converted or inverted within the narration as well. Bernard Malaussène, the narrator, is a sort of single parent, brooding like a mother hen over his brothers and sisters. Neither detective, criminal, nor victim, Malaussène possesses the quality which most popular writers would wish in their readers: he *identifies* with all three. Julia (her real name is Julie: we may see here a reference to Queneau's Julia Julie Ségovie in the 1952 novel *Le dimanche de la vie*) is the intrepid reporter who returns from time to time to share his bed, the one fixed point in her roving existence. She is far removed from received ideas of femininity and so tough she can perform an emergency appendectomy on herself with a mirror. And though they are anchored in the Parisian village of Belleville, this twentieth *arrondissement* is firmly situated in a decidedly twentieth-century Paris. The friends and neighbours are Arab and Kabyle, black or yellow, and though there is conviviality to rival that of Fallet, it is cemented not with cabbage soup and Beaujolais but with red Algerian Sidi-Brahim and couscous.

What is more, these novels not only contain themselves – since Bernard (and then another character) recounts them to the assembled tribe each evening, with sister Thérèse noting them down and typing them up – but they are also a reflection on stories and the transpositions of stories. References to other stories and to the importance of reading abound. Popular fiction is the beginning of reading and the place where all readers start; some readers move on to other things, some stay or return to relish increasing depth in the supposedly shallow. *Monsieur Malaussène* shifts the focus from printed or spoken word to the moving image and deals with the last of the neighbourhood cinemas, the old dream machines. In this book, it is film which reflects the characters back at themselves. In all the books however, the constant underlying theme is the working of the imagination and its intertwining with the life we lead. So much so that Pennac's 1992 essay on reading, *Comme un roman*, does not seem to interrupt the series. It discusses, briefly, 'littérature industrielle' but Pennac says more on this subject, and says it more pertinently, in *La Petite Marchande de prose* where Malaussène is obliged to incarnate 'JLB', a doubly commercial author who bears a strong resemblance to Paul-Loup Sulitzer. But whatever criticisms can be levelled at the 'stereotype factory', Malaussène (and Pennac) must admit that no considerations of taste, no intellectual censorship, can stop his sisters (and others) reading and enjoying the novels it produces. And as Malaussène becomes JLB, the novels of JLB replace the adventures of Malaussène as the family's bedtime story.

But we are still in the realm of crime fiction and Malaussène, who is presented to the world as JLB, does not know that the JLB who wishes to hide behind Malaussène's person is not in fact the real author of the books. On his first public appearance as JLB, Malaussène is shot in the head by the real author, Krämer (which is the German for 'merchant'). The little prose-seller of the title is Isabelle the publisher; her love of literature does not blind her to the fact that a publisher needs to sell books and that the commercial fiction of the JLBs is what makes the rest possible. Pennac's books are popular literature and very enjoyable popular literature at that: they spin fascinating stories, yet even as they manage, in a serious vein, to reflect on literature, they are made of the stuff of popular fiction. As if to underline this point, Malaussène, plunged into a coma by Krämer's bullet and used as an organ farm by an unscrupulous surgeon, is in the end restored to life, his missing bits replaced by transplants from the dead Krämer.

The style of these novels suggests that all fiction is legitimate and that, if there is a hierarchy, then it is defined by the increasing consciousness of both writers and readers. For these two are inextricably linked – partners in crime we might say. Nor are such reflections anything new. Some of the earliest detective novels point out that of course events in detective novels happen differently. Des Cars occasionally uses the device of the documentary recorder, thus projecting his writing into the space of his fiction. And Jacques Laurent, fervent admirer, like so many, of Stendhal and author of *Le Roman du roman* (1977), was also the best-selling Cécile Saint-Laurent whose bodice-rippers subsidised Laurent's more serious work.

But the circles never quite close completely and that is much too convenient a place to stop. The field is vast, of course, since in the nature of things there is more popular fiction than serious literature. There is much more to be said about crime fiction, for example. Often formulaic, stilted, escapist fiction, it is true, but often also in modern France a vehicle for social comment and a genre which engages with contemporary life in a way other novels rarely do. Didier Daeninckx, for example in *Le Bourreau et son double* (1986) or *Meurtres pour mémoire* (1984), deals with the impact of the Algerian war on the young men of France. But Pennac, on the fringes of crime fiction, with his roots in omnivorous reading and his feet firmly straddling the imagined divide between serious and popular, points at another phenomenon, at a novelist who has, like him, come to find a home between Gallimard's serious white covers.

The opening of *La Petite Marchande de prose* finds Malaussène musing on a half-remembered sentence which comes back to haunt him. Though his novel is more concerned with the likes of Sulitzer, the attempts at attribution of this 'ready-made pronouncement', no doubt by 'a Frenchman trying to sound like an American', could be taken to indicate Philippe Djian. Best known for the film which Jean-Jacques Beineix made of his novel *37°2 le matin* (1985) – in English, *Betty Blue* (1986) – Djian is much given to portentous generalisations of the kind: 'The only ramparts a man can build around him are no higher than the sides of his coffin'; 'We were thinking all three of that Chinese proverb by which a man may avoid needless humiliation: "when he knows not what to do, the Sage will not wake his wife".' And apart from *Sotos* (1993), transparently placed in the Basque country where he in fact lived for a time, the setting of his novels is often a carefully ambiguous South-West which could be American. The cultural references too are predominantly American: Cendrars and Céline, but also Hemingway, Miller, Bukowski, Kerouac and Brautigan are named, over and again, as his heroes. And though film is not important for him, music is; scattered references indicate the importance he attaches to high culture and Bösendorfer pianos. There are however many many more to low culture: across the various books, Djian's narrator goes to see *Rambo* and remarks 'sod the avant-garde', whistles Bob Dylan, plays Willie Nelson, reveres John Lennon and Leonard Cohen. *Sotos*, his Gallimard début, is a more complex novel than his others, but the adolescent revolt of Mani is still sex, drugs and rock'n'roll. And of course Djian also writes lyrics for the popular singer Stéphane Eicher.

But for all that, Djian constantly proclaims himself a writer: the central narrator-character in most of his books is Djian the writer or one who closely resembles him. Djian claims moreover to be a classic writer and a master of style (even if this pretension apparently causes some flurries in the calm dovecotes of Gallimard). He is popular, a bestseller, a cult author despised by official critics, 'not much read by intellectuals' as a French intellectual once remarked to me. Delly or Des Cars make popular fiction out of a fanciful world they present as serious; Djian and to an extent also Pennac base their fictions on the realities of the resolutely popular, bohemian or working-class, worlds they live in. They show the popular and the serious turning back in on themselves and out to each other: what matters is less judgement and labels than reading and understanding and, above all, awareness of the whole body of literature as it exists and interacts.

NOTES

1 See chapter 15, pp. 256–8, for further remarks on Echenoz, and especially his novel *Nous trois*.

2 *J'ose*, pp. 199–200. The back cover of Delly, *Un marquis de Carabas* (1933) gives, as the highest praise of another novel by this author, *Ma robe couleur du temps*, 'C'est du bon Delly' ['It's good Delly'].

3 See chapter 1, p. 5, where Timothy Unwin outlines the three categories or modes of reading – 'suspense', 'desire' and 'production' – suggested by Barthes in his essay 'Sur la lecture'.

4 See note 3 above, and chapter 1, p. 5.

SUGGESTIONS FOR FURTHER READING

Des Cars, G., *J'ose* (Paris: Stock, 1974)

Duneton, C. and J.-P. Pagliano, *Anti-Manuel de français* (Paris: Editions du Seuil, 1978)

Pennac, D., *Comme un roman* (Paris: Gallimard, 1992)

Todd, C., *A Century of French Best-Sellers (1890–1990))* (Lampeter: Edwin Mellen Press, 1994)

12

FRANÇOISE LIONNET

The colonial and postcolonial Francophone novel

What is the 'Francophone novel' in relation to the 'French novel' and how do these two traditions form a continuum? This chapter will give an overview of French-speaking areas of the globe beyond Europe (excluding Canada which will be dealt with separately in the next chapter). It concentrates on those areas of *francophonie* that share a history of colonial domination: sub-Saharan Africa, the Maghreb, the Caribbean and the Indian Ocean, with brief mention of the Mashreq.

These locations have played a crucial role in the development of a specifically French *imaginaire* since the Renaissance. From Montaigne's cannibals to Montesquieu's Persians, from Baudelaire's exotic tropical islands to Flaubert's Egypt and Nerval's Orient, from André Gide's *Voyage au Congo* to Hergé's *Tintin au Congo*, the colonial encounter has marked the imagination of European readers, allowing them to project onto foreign lands and cultures an imaginary reality largely constructed through discourse. Written into Western narratives, the real human subjects of the French empire who were educated in the language and culture of the colonisers have been forced to negotiate with these representations of their identity. Their self-knowledge continues to be mediated by these discursive and literary examples, and many have reacted in strong opposition to these *Afriques imaginaires*.[1]

In the early 1900s, Picasso's discovery of the aesthetics of African sculpture revolutionised modern art, and in the 20s and 30s, American blues and jazz transformed Western musical tastes, while ethnographers Leo Frobenius and Maurice Delafosse's new perspectives on African culture were being read avidly by young African intellectuals. In Senghor's words, Frobenius 'revealed Africa to the world *and Africans to themselves*'.[2] The negritude movement owes its existence to this convergence of interests. Paris became a major cultural crossroads for intellectuals from the African diaspora. Manifestos and journals such as *La Revue du Monde Noir*, *Légitime Defense*, *L'Etudiant noir* brought together Francophone African and Antillean writers. Between 1941 and 1943, Aimé and Suzanne Césaire published *Tropiques* in Martinique. The journals were short-lived, but after the war, Alioune Diop founded *Présence africaine* which would have a major cultural impact (until Diop's death in 1987).[3] During the same period, Francophone writers discovered the Harlem Renaissance and expatriate black Americans like Langston Hughes, Countee Cullen and Richard Wright. Several Parisian 'salons littéraires', including the one held at René Maran's home around 1935, helped create the intellectual community that nurtured the beginnings of black Francophone literature.[4]

In 1921, Maran had published *Batouala, véritable roman nègre* (Paris: Albin Michel). It was the first novel to openly criticise European colonisation in Africa. A chronicle of daily village life in colonial Oubangui-Chari (now the Central African Republic) where Maran, a Martinican colonial administrator, lived for thirteen years, *Batouala* created a scandal and the author had to resign his post. The novel won the 1921 Prix Goncourt, but provoked violent reactions and was banned in all the colonies. For the new generation of African and Caribbean intellectuals, however, it marked an important beginning. It revealed the truth about colonial exploitation and showed the true feelings of the colonised: 'Nous ne sommes que des chairs à impôts. Nous ne sommes que des bêtes de portage' (p. 76) ['We are nothing but bodies for taxation. We are only beasts of burden'], exclaims Bataoula, as he recounts the events surrounding the arrival of the Europeans. The novel focuses primarily on the customs of the Banda people, but in his introduction, Maran validates the testimony of his protagonists and their complaints against the colonial regime. He denounces the cynicism of his fellow French administrators. His call for radical change would not be heeded by the colonial power, but it would have a profound effect on his successors, the major poets of negritude, Senghor (Senegal), Aimé Césaire (Martinique), Léon Damas (Guyana), and Jacques Rabemananjara (Madagascar), as well as novelists Camara Laye (Guinea) and Ferdinand Oyono (Cameroon). Each of these novelists develops one of the main aspects of Maran's novel: the representation of everyday life in a small African community and the denunciation of colonial injustice, respectively.

The use of the French language by writers from around the world requires brief discussion and historical perspective, since the language issue continues to remain central to the field of colonial and postcolonial studies. After the Revolution of 1789, a general language policy was established in France aimed at rooting out all dialects and regional languages. In the nineteenth century, linguistic imperialism became an integral part of the colonial project at home and abroad. At the height of colonial expansion, in 1880, the geographer Onésime Reclus coined the word *francophonie* in order to designate all French-speaking peoples, whether French happened to be their mother-tongue or a second language learned in school. The word and the reality behind it have now become institutionalised. But the term can mislead users into thinking that the 'Francophone' novel is a homogeneous category, whereas it is a vehicle of diversity that both reflects and records the traditions and transformations of many different localities.

For Senghor, poet, politician and member of the Académie française, 'la francophonie est un mode de pensée et d'action' (p. 80) ['a mode of thought and action'] (*Négritude et civilisation de l'universel*), that emphasises dialogue and reciprocity within a global community of French speakers and endorses a *civilisation de l'universel* which remains true to the ideals of the Revolution. By contrast, for the editors of the journal *Peuples Noirs, Peuples Africains*, 'Francophonie rime . . . avec hégémonie' ['Francophonie rhymes . . . with hegemony'], and reinforces élitism.[5] Despite these opposing views, which were also a matter of generational differences among writers, it is now clear, at the end of the second millennium, that the French language has been appropriated, africanised and creolised, enriched by a very diverse group of novelists, from Ahmadou Kourouma (Ivory Coast) and Axel Gauvin (Reunion) to Simone Schwarz-Bart (Guadeloupe) and Assia Djebar (Algeria), whose palimpsestic narratives reveal the multicultural sensibilities and the eclectic models they bring to the practice of French. As the late Tchicaya U'Tamsi (Congo) has proclaimed: 'La langue française me colonise, je la colonise à mon tour' ['If the French language colonises me, I'll colonise it right back'].[6] Local oral traditions, including the medieval African epic and the creole folk-tale, have become hybridised or braided with classic French realist or modernist narrative techniques. Languages such as Wolof, Malinke, Arabic or Creole have allowed the novelists who speak them to subvert French stylistics from within, performing a radical transformation of the standard written language.

In addition, English-speaking novelists – notably Emily Brontë, Jane Austen and William Faulkner – were appropriated by Maryse Condé (Guadeloupe), Marie-Thérèse Humbert (Mauritius), and Kateb Yacine (Algeria), respectively. The *real maraviloso* or marvellous real of the Cuban Alejo Carpentier and his Haitian contemporaries Jacques Roumain and Jacques-Stephen Alexis defines an important element of the theory and practice of what the Martinican poet and novelist Edouard Glissant has called 'le roman des Amériques' ['novel of the Americas'].[7] Finally, for many, autobiography and fictional self-portraiture continue to remain privileged narrative forms that allow the formerly colonised to come to terms with crucial questions of identity. This form has also provided intellectuals with a means of reflection on their work as academics, on the way knowledge is produced and consumed. Abdelkebir Khatibi does so in *La Mémoire tatouée* (1971), Assia Djebar in *L'Amour, la Fantasia* (1982), V. Y. Mudimbe in *Le Corps glorieux des mots et des êtres* (1994), and Réda Bensmaïa in *The Year of Passage* (1995) – a book notably translated into English and published in the United States first. Many prominent Francophone writers hold university positions in the United States, and the Francophone novel is more widely taught there than in France.

During the 1980s, the impact of Maghrebian and African immigration has resulted in a rich new concept: *francophonie* within France. The so-called Beur novel has acquired an important place in contemporary French writing with Leïla Sebbar, Azouz Begag, Mehdi Charef, Farida Belghoul and Nina Bouraoui. Calixthe Beyala now writes about African communities in and around Paris. The culture of the *banlieue* is represented in successful films (such as *La Haine*, 1995) which depict the contemporary explosion of plural horizons in France, and the uneasy relationship between mainstream French society and the minorities in its midst. Other authors whose cultural roots reach far beyond the French hexagon are Jean-Marie LeClézio, Marie N'Diaye, Kim Lefèvre and Linda Lê. They continually transform the idea of 'francité', giving new meaning to the adjectives 'French' and 'Francophone'. There is now a polyphonic French-language literature coming from all continents, and the modern novel is best understood when convergences as well as contradictions and conflicts arising from divergent aesthetic, thematic, cultural or political goals are highlighted or interrelated.

Although the African novel comes into its own in the 1950s and 1960s, a few titles appear before the Second World War, notably the Senegalese Ousmane Socé's *Karim* (1935) and *Mirages de Paris* (1937). After the war, the rise of nationalisms provides the ferment that will fuel independence movements across Africa. In the struggles for cultural liberation and political autonomy, the relationship of literature to society and the nation-state takes on a particular urgency. Many literary personalities play important public roles and influence the creation of new national identities. Some, like Ferdinand Oyono and Cheik Hamidou Kane, become diplomats or political leaders and give up writing altogether. Aimé Césaire's *Discours sur le colonialisme* (1955) and Frantz Fanon's posthumous *Les Damnés de la terre* (1962) remain two of the most eloquent and powerful manifestos of this period of struggle against external oppression. Other writers transform the generic codes of the colonial novel and create subversive representations of the colonial impact on indigenous cultures. Among those, four deserve special attention for their now classic texts that use techniques of realist representation in order to raise far-reaching issues.

Camara Laye's *L'Enfant noir* (Paris: Plon, 1953) attempts to represent a coherent cultural system with only marginal mention of the changes brought on by European penetration in Guinea. It has been criticised – notably by the Cameroonian novelist Mongo Béti – for its idealised portrayal of native traditions in an Africa apparently untouched by colonialism. Yet, the novel's structure duplicates and cleverly subverts traditional ethnography's tendency to freeze its subjects in a timeless dimension. Organised in chapters that cover the gamut of standard ethnographic narrative topics from belief and kinship systems to apprenticeship and education, religion and ritual initiations, habitat, food, sexuality and death, the novel is the moving self-portrait of a young boy caught in a transitional period, no longer fully cognisant of his father's rituals and traditions as a goldsmith ('Je l'ignore; j'ai quitté mon père trop tôt' (p. 11) ['I do not know; I left my father too soon']), and barely beginning to discover the West and its seductions. The last image of the book is a suggestive one. In an aeroplane, on his way to pursue his education, the narrator tries to control his emotions and his sense of being torn away. He suddenly becomes conscious of the map of the Paris Métro in his bulging pocket. This map is an interesting symbol of alienation: it plainly evokes the new spaces of his future, and suggests a new cartography as well as a mode of orientation in the world that relies on paper and printed material as opposed to the oral and mythic traditions he leaves behind. A 'roman d'apprentissage', *L'Enfant noir* is a widely read and popular novel because of the mythic quality of its narrative, reinforced by the repeated use of the phrase 'en ce temps-là', a device also used by oral story-tellers. The novel won the Prix Charles Veillon du meilleur roman français in 1954.

Ferdinand Oyono's *Une vie de boy* (Paris: Julliard, 1956) is a sharp critique of the colonial situation in Cameroon, of a young black man's illusions about the Europeans, and of the obscene and sadistic behaviour of French administrators. Here, the black and white worlds collide, and the exchange of ambiguous or penetrating glances between colonisers and colonised reveals the ironies of their respective situations. The houseboy Toundi has a crush on his 'patronne', the promiscuous wife of the Commandant. He comes to know too much about her daily life and incurs her wrath. Racial and sexual identity are constituted through the gaze, and the apparent naïveté of the narrator is a clever device that allows Oyono to satirise – in the tradition of Voltaire's *Candide* – the behaviour of the whites. Oyono also uses the convention of the 'found manuscript' to present an eye-witness account by Toundi, a Christ-like victim of the abuse of power. This novel is an allegory of an epistemological problem concerning the relative status of the visible and the invisible in the acquisition of knowledge. As Baklu the washman states, 'Il y a deux mondes . . . Le nôtre est fait de respect, de mystère, de sorcellerie . . . Le leur laisse tout en plein jour, même ce qui n'a pas été prévu pour ça' (p. 123) ['There are two worlds, and ours is one of respect, mystery and secret ceremonies . . . Theirs leaves everything in broad daylight, even what was not meant to be seen']. The eye and the ear, the known and the secret, observation and hearsay are subtly contrasted throughout the text, thus evoking a topic central to the understanding of modernity and the hegemony of vision. Read on this metaphoric level, the story of the demise of young Toundi, lured away from his village by the promise of a better life, becomes a parable and a cautionary tale that resonates with postcolonial preoccupations. Film-maker Claire Denis's *Chocolat* (1988) uses many of the same themes in her memoir of a Cameroonian childhood. Oyono's satirical tone is echoed by the Ivoirian Bernard Dadié's *Un Nègre à Paris* (1959), a humorous appropriation and reversal of Montesquieu's *Lettres persanes* and the genre of the travel narrative with its mock-ethnographic pretentions.

Cheik Hamidou Kane's *L'Aventure ambigüe* (Paris: Julliard, 1961 – awarded the Grand Prix littéraire d'Afrique noire in 1962) focuses on the different forms of knowledge that the Koranic school and the French school both impart to Samba Diallo, the young Senegalese protagonist. This novel contains many autobiographical elements. It is a lyrical meditation on the confrontation between traditional Africa and Western modernity, between religious beliefs and scientific or technical know-how. 'Mon pays se meurt de ne pas oser trancher cette alternative' (p. 128) ['My country is dying for want of decisiveness about these alternatives'], says Samba Diallo. His tragic end gives closure as well as mystical and symbolic value to the narrative. In a style steeped in Koranic prosody but also reminiscent of the *conte philosophique*, Kane writes an eloquent and sombre tale that stages lofty epistemological and cultural issues. The epic and aristocratic figure of the Grande Royale, the only female protagonist, plays a crucial role in this traditional Muslim society. She is a highly respected agent of change for the community, allowing Kane to show – idealistically perhaps – the central and active role that women could have within Islam.

Sembène Ousmane, a Marxist and *artiste engagé*, is one of Francophone Africa's most productive intellectuals. He has borrowed from Naturalism to shine a critical spotlight on the last years of the colonial period. *Les Bouts de bois de Dieu* (1960) focuses on the historic strike by the Dakar–

Niger railroad workers. In a famous scene reminiscent of Zola's *Germinal*, it stages the long march of the workers' wives from the town of Thiès to the bosses' Dakar office. The women represent a powerful vision of feminist and revolutionary struggles, their demonstration ending in bloodshed. Sembène is noted for his 'wolofisation of French': 'les bouts de bois de Dieu' is a direct translation of a Wolof phrase used as subtitle, 'banty mam yall'. Heeding the warning of critics of *francophonie*, Sembène has turned to film-making in Wolof in order to reach a wider Wolof-speaking public: *La Noire de . . .* (1966), *Le Mandat* (1968), *Xala* (1974) are adapted from his previously published Francophone narratives. When one considers the whole of Sembène's militant *œuvre*, his originality is striking. Unlike many of his contemporaries, he has found renewed inspiration at every stage of African history, and criticised colonialism as well as archaic traditions and the new societies emerging after independence. This critique has focused simultaneously on different historical and political themes and he has used tragic and epic modes to privilege the heroic actions of the social group rather than those of the individual. The film *Emitaï* (1971) allows him to question the existential logic of traditional societies and to show that the irrational and the religious are the main sources of human impotence in the face of political oppression. Influenced by the theatre of Bertolt Brecht and neo-realist cinema, he has developed a visual language all his own that rejects traditional or Hollywood narrative techniques. As he puts it, 'en Afrique, le cinéma marque plus par les images que par l'expression ou les gestes. Et le geste est plus important que le parlé. Le seul moyen pour nous d'avoir une dimension, c'est de trouver une voie qui nous est propre' ['in African cinema, images are more important than expressions or gestures, and gestures are more important than speech. The only way for us to have an impact is to find a way of our own'].[8]

The evolution of the Francophone novel as genre during this first period of its history can best be summed up in the gradual shift from an implied reader who is clearly external to the author's cultural milieu, as in *L'Enfant noir*, to one who shares the same local understandings as the narrator, as is evident in Sembène. After independence, the most influential novelists tend to focus less on the need to oppose colonialist ideologies than on the articulation of the concerns of a new generation anxious to free itself from the sterile illusions of authenticity or the myths of afrocentricity to which certain aspects of negritude had led their precursors. This generation innovates by appropriating and transforming generic codes along with language.

The Malian Yambo Ouologuem's *Le Devoir de violence* (1968) is an iconoclastic text that parodies and plagiarises Maupassant's *Boule de suif*,

Graham Greene's *It's a Battlefield,* and André Schwarz-Bart's *Le Dernier des justes.* The novel was awarded the Prix Renaudot in 1968 and translated into ten languages. Critiquing both the Europeans' attitudes in Africa and the Africans' own idealisation of their past, it was a *succès de scandale.* A pastiche of both epic and realist literature, it denounces domination in all its forms with a ferociously humorous prose that exposes both Islam's and Christianity's exploitation of the Africans. Its nihilism and copious use of sex and violence makes it controversial yet subversive. Its clever use of stereotypes has the effect of undermining the traditions it represents.

Ahmadou Kourouma's *Les Soleils des indépendances,* written between 1961 and 1965, was first published in 1967 in Quebec where it won the Prix littéraire de la francité, and in Paris in 1970 where it was awarded the Prix de l'Académie Française. The narrative presents itself as a modern African epic which ends tragically but captures the multiple facets of a society at a crucial phase of its evolution. An Ivoirian, Kourouma innovates by transforming standard French to make it conform to the thought processes and linguistic structures of the Malinke people. The chapter titles are particularly original and unsettle the French reader's expectations. Kourouma's style functions in between the two languages: he breaks up the syntactic codes; through lexical transpositions and translations, he creates original images; using a process of repetition and accumulation, he creates a distinct rhythm, closer to poetry and oral recitation than to Western prose. He makes his reader aware of the distinct Malinke world-view he embeds in language and narrative structure. This practice foregrounds the agency and creativity of African users of French who have made it a language of their own. Kourouma's only other novel *Monné, outrages et défis* (1990) is a brilliant fresco of a century of African history.

The Zairean poet, novelist, and philosopher V. Y. Mudimbe is a global intellectual, a rigorous thinker, and an influential scholar. He is noted for his portrayal of the difficulties encountered by ordinary men and women as well as intellectual and religious figures in the face of ideological and political turmoil. *Entre les eaux* (1973) and *L'Ecart* (1978) dramatise the crises of identity and the epistemological and political dilemmas of characters who are trying to understand what an African archeology of knowledge might look like so as to demarcate themselves from Western models, while *Le Bel Immonde* (1976) is a complex and multi-layered narrative that resists simplistic interpretation.

The first novels by Francophone African women are published in the 1970s and 1980s: in Senegal, Aminata Sow-Fall, *La Grève des bàttu* (1979), Mariama Bâ, *Une si longue lettre* (1979) and *Un chant écarlate*

FRANÇOISE LIONNET

(1981), Myriam Warner-Vieyra, *Juletane* (1982) and Ken Bugul, *Le Baobab fou* (1983); and in Cameroon, Werewere-Liking, *Elle sera de jaspe et de corail* (1983) and Calixthe Beyala, *C'est le soleil qui m'a brûlée* (1987) and *Tu t'appelleras Tanga* (1988). These writers successfully focus attention on complex gender issues, and now belong to the 'canon' of African women's writing.

Sow-Fall combines social analysis with a pointed critique of polygamy. *La Grève* focuses on the role of beggars in a society that relies on their presence to give itself good conscience. Bâ's work is self-consciously feminist without adopting a Manichean approach: after her husband's death, Ramatoulaye, the narrator of *Une si longue lettre*, who is a devout but emancipated Muslim woman educated in the French system, starts writing in a journal that she addresses to her childhood friend, Aïssatou. This tone creates a space of intimacy that draws in the reader: after thirty years of marriage, Modou had announced to Ramatoulaye his intention to marry Binetou, a friend of their daughter's. Profoundly hurt, Ramatoulaye remains faithful, accepting her fate in a polygamous society but exposing the pain and difficulties that this occasions for women in her situation. Awarded the 1980 Prix Noma, the book is noted for its continued 'best seller' status: it is the most taught Francophone African novel and has been translated into twelve languages.

Bâ's *Un chant écarlate* and Warner-Vieyra's *Juletane* share many themes: the mixed marriage, the Senegalese in-laws' rejection of the foreign woman, and the latter's slow descent into depersonalisation and madness. Bugul's *Le Baobab fou* stages the loneliness and pain of a female protagonist whose autobiographical narrative reveals her early separation from her mother, her father's indifference, and her exile to Belgium where she becomes addicted to drugs and attempts suicide. Beyala's *C'est le soleil* and *Tanga* are overtly feminist and represent without apology the exploitation and humiliation of black women by black men. Werewere-Liking's *Elle sera de jaspe et de corail* has the interesting subtitle: 'journal d'une misovire'. It is a lyrical and poetic novel which combines feminist critique with a rigorous reflection on aesthetics, the role of the writer in African society, and the need for new creative approaches.

The countries of the Maghreb (Algeria, Morocco and Tunisia) and those of the Mashreq (Lebanon and Egypt) have a long tradition of written literatures and multilingualism (classical and dialectal Arabic, Berber, French, Spanish and 'farabé', a creolised mixture spoken in North Africa). *Maghrib*, the 'West' in Arabic, is a designation given by medieval Arab geographers to distinguish it from the *Mashriq* or Middle-East. Islamic, Jewish and Christian traditions as well as Arabic and Berber expressions co-exist within the Francophone texts from these areas. Lebanese expatriates Andrée Chedid (*La Maison sans racines*, 1985) and Evelyne Accad (*L'Excisée*, 1980, *Coquelicot du massacre*, 1988), and Egyptian expatriates Albert Cossery (*Les Hommes oubliés de Dieu*, 1941, *Les Fainéants dans la vallée fertile*, 1948) and Edmond Jabès (*Le Livre des questions*, 1973) are the main prose writers of the *Proche-Orient*. Jabès and the Moroccan Edmond El Maleh whose poetic autobiography, *Mille ans, un jour* (1986), brings together many elements of the Arab–Jewish memory, are part of a small but significant Francophone Jewish diaspora, whose members include the Tunisian Albert Memmi and the prominent 'French' intellectuals Hélène Cixous and Jacques Derrida, both born and raised in Algeria.

The Algerian Mouloud Feraoun's *Le Fils du pauvre* (1950) is the first published autobiography in a corpus rich in this genre aimed primarily at the Western reader. Feraoun and Mouloud Mammeri (*La Colline oubliée*, 1952) both focus on rural Kabyle traditions and on the colonial malaise. Mohammed Dib publishes a trilogy (*La Grande maison*, 1952, *L'Incendie*, 1954, and *Le Métier à tisser*, 1957) which stages the emergence of nationalist sentiments in Algeria. After independence, Rachid Boudjedra's *La Répudiation* (1969) is a sharp critique of patriarchal power within the familial sphere, and Rachid Minouni's *Tombeza* (Paris: Robert Laffont, 1984) denounces the daily indignities of life for the poor and the powerless in contemporary Algeria: 'On ne peut pas compter sur un peuple dont on prend plaisir à bafouer la dignité' (p. 209) ['You cannot count on a people when its dignity is always being scoffed at'], he warns in a narrative that brings to the fore questions of democratic rights and political responsibilities at a time when such issues are no longer part of the public debate in the fundamentalist nation.

The two major Algerian writers are Kateb Yacine and Assia Djebar. Kateb Yacine's *Nedjma* (1956) interweaves four destinies and points of view (Rachid and Mourad from the city, and Lakhdar and Mustapha from the country) around that of a central female character (Nedjma or 'star' in Arabic) whose perspective remains absent. This novel is a poetic and mythic allegory of Algeria. Memory and history, the past and the present, interior monologues and realist descriptions alternate in a complex, open, narrative structure that produces ambivalence and makes linear time visible (there are frequent references to clocks) yet irrelevant. A difficult and polyphonic text, it shows the interpenetration of history and biography, while destabilising colonial models. Ambiguities and contradictions abound and are never resolved. The novel evokes referential discourses and identity-quests, but always transgresses these, focusing attention on the functioning of language and the movement towards an unrealised presence.

Nominated for the Prix Goncourt, Kateb was denied because of the political events surrounding the beginning of the war of independence. The novel should be read in conjunction with *Le Polygone étoilé* (1966) which prolongs and complicates the issues raised in it.

Assia Djebar's goal as a writer and film-maker has been to represent the perspective of women in relation to the Islamic past, the 1830 conquest, and the war of independence. A historian by training, Djebar is a would-be architect who has frequently stated publicly: 'Mon point fort, c'est la structure: je construis d'abord' ['My strong suit is structure: I begin by building']. These interests explain the highly structured form of *L'Amour, la fantasia* (1985). This complex self-portrait counters the ahistorical representation of women in Orientalism, ethnographies, military reports and historical chronicles. It combines an innovative approach to the articulation of time and space, and insists on the female subject's relationship to history. It is divided into three parts, the third 'musical' part comprising five movements that break up the initial binary structure in which alternating historical and autobiographical chapters are linked by either linguistic or thematic analogies. In the first two parts, women's bodies become metonymies for the figure of the Algerian nation conquered, violated, and dismembered. In the third, a multiplicity of voices narrate personal stories and echo the 'I' of the primary narrator. As these personal stories proliferate, they activate collective memory, pointing to the potentially liberating aspects of diversity. Memory renders the past visible in the present, and the lived experiences of women can now be heard and seen. This lyrical approach undermines the strategies of objectivity and closure central to traditional historiography, demonstrating that for the colonised, history has yet to be written. One of the novelist's responsibilities and contributions to knowledge thus becomes the imaginative reconstruction of the past. *L'Amour* is the first volume of a projected quartet which includes *Ombre sultane* (1987) and *Vaste est la prison* (1995).

Among Moroccan writers, Driss Chraïbi expresses revolt against the law of the father in *Le Passé simple* (1954). In *Les Boucs* (1955), he is the first novelist to expose the degrading and inhuman conditions faced by immigrant North African workers in France. Abdelkebir Khatibi's *La Mémoire tatouée*, published in 1971 with an afterword by Roland Barthes entitled 'Ce que je dois à Khatibi' ['What I owe to Khatibi'], and *Amour bilingue* (1983) are self-portraits that theorise identity, language, translation, culture, desire and writing. His texts are best understood in relation to his philosophical reflections on bilingualism and the 'double critique' published in *Maghreb pluriel* (Paris: Denoël, 1983): 'La langue dite étrangère ne vient pas s'ajouter à l'autre, ni opérer avec elle une pure juxtaposition: chacune *fait signe* à l'autre, l'appelle à se maintenir comme dehors . . . Toute cette littérature maghrébine dite d'expression française est un récit de traduction. Je ne dis pas qu'elle n'est que traduction, je précise qu'il s'agit d'un récit qui *parle en langues*' (p. 186) ['The so-called foreign language does not simply get added or juxtaposed to the other one. Each *signals* to the other, inviting it to maintain its exteriority . . . All of French language Maghrebian literature is a story of translation. I am not saying that it is only ['about'] translation, I am specifying that it is a narrative that *speaks in tongues*']. Khatibi's goal is to clear a space where differences (of language, of culture) interface without leading to either confrontation or reconciliation, dualism or fusion. He shows this postmodern problematic to be a historical ingredient of the postcolonial writer's psychic space and practice of writing. He continually questions the illusory opposition between identity and difference, and *Le Livre du sang* (1979) draws provocative parallels between androgyny, incest, bilingualism and textuality. These themes serve as correctives to the hegemony of the colonial *monolangue*. They also refer back to a turn-of-the-century figure, Isabelle Eberhardt, the Russian-born vagabond and nomadic cross-dresser who appropriated French and Arabic as elements of her polylinguistic creative matrix. She is considered 'an ancestor to at least three generations of Maghrebian Francophone writers'.[9]

Cross-dressing is the central theme of Tahar Ben Jelloun's *L'Enfant de sable* (Paris: Seuil, 1985), a haunting novel that graphically explores the problems of sexuality in the Maghreb. Ahmed/Zahra is the eighth female born to a Moroccan father who decides to disguise her and raise her as his son. He/she wields power through this simulacrum of virility. When the novel opens, Ahmed/Zahra is leading a solitary existence in a dark and quiet room, writing in a diary, sequestered behind the male mask. Her story, apparently taken from the diary, is told by multiple story-tellers in the crowd that gathers on the square in Marrakesh. But the story-tellers' versions are incompatible and their authority appears unreliable. One of those is different from the others: he is identified as 'le troubadour aveugle' ['the blind troubadour'] in the title of chapter 17 (p. 171). He is in fact a figure for the real-life Argentinian author Jorge-Luis Borges to whom Ben Jelloun pays homage. Ben Jelloun interweaves an important thematics of Borges's stories with his own: the visible and the hidden, appearance and reality, self and other, blindness and insight, the literary labyrinth and its bifurcations. *La Nuit sacrée*, Prix Goncourt in 1987, is its sequel. It thematises incest as a form of narrative transgression that apparently legitimises and renders visible – for the male narrator and his male reader – the desires of a hidden female body. These novels have made Ben Jelloun

an immensely popular writer, despite feminist concerns about his appropriation of the female voice. His themes and the narrative structures he uses
raise questions about knowledge and identity that seem to echo across
many different contemporary cultural arenas.

In Tunisia, the contrast between Albert Memmi and Abdelwahab
Meddeb allows us to conclude this discussion of African *francophonie* by
recapping its major themes. Memmi's autobiography *La Statue de sel*
(1953) is a paradigmatic text of the colonised's quest for identity. He uses a
confessional tone in the manner of Rousseau and André Gide to show the
alienation of the narrator; his sense of being torn between different
traditions, languages and ethnic groups; his fascination for the West that
rejects him; his inferior social place as a poor Jew within Islam and colonial
Tunis; and his status as a schizophrenic exile within his own country. The
narrative combines ethnographic description, social history and moving
personal experiences. *Agar* (1955) focuses on the failures of a mixed
marriage, and *Le Scorpion* (1969), taking a less referential tack, integrates
formal innovations and a multiplicity of narrative voices with traditional
Arab–Jewish story-telling techniques.

Abdelwahab Meddeb's more abstract concerns give us heterogeneous,
difficult and resolutely postmodern narratives. He explores interiority,
sexuality, social and religious taboos, Sufi mysticism and ecstasis, perception and memory, as well as the relationship between the body, writing and
death. His use of the French language has inspired Khatibi's theorisation of
the *bi-langue*. As Meddeb explains, 'L'écriture française nous livre à l'autre,
mais on se défendra par l'arabesque, la subversion, le dédale, le labyrinthe,
le décentrage incessant de la phrase et du langage, de manière que l'autre se
perde comme dans les ruelles de la casbah' (see Jean Déjeux, *Situation de la
littérature maghrébine de langue française*, pp. 103–4) ['Writing in French
surrenders us to the other, but we shall defend ourselves with the use of
arabesque, subversion, labyrinthine constructions, the incessant decentring
of the sentence and of language so that the other will get lost as in the
narrow streets of the casbah']. Meddeb's radically subversive poetics
functions as counter-discourse that turns the rules of European linguistic
hegemony against itself. His texts – like those of Kateb, Djebar and Khatibi
– make clear that deconstructive strategies and postmodernist techniques of
fragmentation owe much to postcolonial sensibilities and have been a
creative response to the impasses of various colonial legacies.

The history of the Caribbean and Mascarene (or Indian Ocean) areas
differs from that of Africa in several significant ways. The islands were
settled in the sixteenth and seventeenth centuries, Africa primarily in the

nineteenth. The traditions and languages of precolonial Africa, even when they were being destroyed by the colonial encounter, provided a substratum or cultural 'arrière-pays' that did not exist in the New World. The genocide of the Native American peoples and the Atlantic slave trade created an experience of complete dispossession, resulting in radical transculturation and in a special relationship to space and to the land.[10] Although the New World people's relationship to the past and their processes of memory are similarly transmitted through orality, their patterns of experience and their histories of decolonisation point to many local differences from those of Africans. Haiti was the first colony to proclaim its independence in 1804, and Mauritius, one of the last, in 1968. Martinique, Guadeloupe and Reunion have been 'départements d'Outre-Mer' since the 1940s and continue to be culturally subjugated.

Jacques Roumain, founder of the the Haitian Communist Party in 1934 and, with Jean Price-Mars, of the *indigéniste* movement in 1927, marked the Caribbean novel with his visionary perspectives. Roumain avoids the temptation of exoticism of his predecessors, creatively transposing peasant speech patterns into a sophisticated narrative technique that conveys a message of hope and liberation as Manuel, the hero of *Gouverneurs de la rosée* (1944), comes back home from Cuba ready to fight for social justice. The title of this internationally acclaimed text is a transcription of the creole *gouvéné rozé*: the name given in rural Haiti to peasants responsible for the irrigation of the fields. Like Sembène in Senegal, Roumain criticises superstitions and vodooist religious beliefs. His materialist ideology combined with his unique style gave birth to what Jacques-Stephen Alexis (*Compère Général Soleil*, 1955 and *Les Arbres musiciens*, 1957) would call 'le réalisme merveilleux des Haïtiens' in a famous speech to the first *Congrès des écrivains et artistes noirs* held in Paris in 1956. René Depestre, a poet and ardent critic of negritude (*Bonjour et adieu à la négritude*, 1980) whose *Hadriana dans tous mes rêves* obtained the Prix Renaudot in 1988, was, along with Alexis, active in the Communist Party and in the fight against Duvalier's dictatorship. Forced to leave the island in 1946, Depestre spent some twenty years in Cuba, after which he settled in France. Disillusioned by the failures of revolution and communism, Depestre has turned to a celebration of exoticism and eroticism that was praised by French reviewers but sent waves of consternation among some critics.

One of the most powerful novels about the way Duvalier has terrorised the people of Haiti is Marie Chauvet's *Amour, colère, folie*. In this trilogy, Chauvet exposes the condition of women under dictatorship, and the obsession with skin colour that plagues Caribbean societies. This caused a scandal in 1968: the book's distribution was blocked and it remained in warehouses. Chauvet went into exile in New York. The young Haitian-American writer Edwige Danticat published a novel in 1994, *Breath, Eyes, Memory*, which picks up the themes and tripartite composition of Chauvet's book, making Danticat an interesting case of cross-linguistic literary influence within the 'novel of the Americas'.

The women writers of the Caribbean have been successful in creating a tradition of their own, a fact acknowledged and confirmed by Maryse Condé's analysis in *La Parole des femmes* (1979). Early texts such as Michèle Lacrosil's *Sapotille et le serin d'argile* (1960) paint the pervasive alienation of women victims of the colour prejudice that persists in former slave societies. Simone Schwarz-Bart's novels are *Pluie et vent sur Télumée Miracle* (Grand Prix des Lectrices de *Elle* 1973) and *Ti-Jean l'horizon* (1979), and the co-authored *Un plat de porc aux bananes vertes* (1967) with her husband André Schwarz-Bart. *Pluie et vent* (Paris: Seuil, 1972) is in the tradition of the peasant novel started by Roumain. It transposes the creole vernacular and the style of magical realism to create a poetic female-centred narrative that imparts cultural and popular wisdom through the use of proverbs. Schwarz-Bart names the natural world, dwells on the economic exploitation and self-denials that blacks had to endure in 1930s Guadeloupe, and the resulting sense of doom and madness that plagues their lives. Emphasis on the characters' eyes is an important structuring device. The grandmother Reine Sans Nom lavishes affection on Télumée Miracle and communicates her love through a look that positively reinforces Télumée's emerging sense of identity. Reine Sans Nom's story-telling technique is an appropriate description of the author's own style: 'Elle sentait ses mots, ses phrases, possédait l'art de les arranger en images et en sons, en musique pure, en exaltation' (p. 76) ['She felt her words, her sentences, she knew the art of arranging them in images and sounds, in pure music and exaltation']. A haunting sense of mythic and circular time is reinforced by the first and last images of the book: Télumée is standing in her garden, a figure of female survival that some have criticised for its seemingly passive and apolitical stance; but as Condé has pointed out, 'Télumée, dépositaire de toutes les vertus de la dynastie des Lougandor, est un symbole. A travers elle, s'inscrit un hymne à la femme, à sa force, à sa richesse' (*La Parole des femmes* (Paris: L'Harmattan, 1979), p. 36) ['Télumée, a repository of all the virtues of the Lougandor dynasty, is a symbol. She is a hymn to woman, to her strength, to her richness']. An alternative gender trajectory in the Antilles of the 1930s is provided by the Martinican Joseph Zobel's *Rue Cases-Nègres* (1950), considered the chef-d'œuvre of the realist Antillean novel. Its linear composition underscores an ideology of progress: the narrator José Hassam is ensured a good education and escape from rural poverty thanks to his heroic and ambitious grandmother m'man Tine's hard work. This autobiographical novel was very successfully brought to the screen by Euzhan Palcy in 1983.

Maryse Condé's career now spans three continents and three decades. She is a prolific novelist. Also an academic, she has taught in France, Africa, and now in the United States. Her intellectual itinerary and the themes addressed by her books reflect broadly on the cultural evolutions of Francophone writers in general. She has moved from fictional autobiography in *Heremakhonon* (1976) to historical novels in *Segu* (1984 and 1985) and *Moi, Tituba sorcière noire de Salem* (1986), from family saga in *La Vie scélérate* (1987) to the fragmented realities of *Traversée de la Mangrove* (1989); she has staged the quest for historic Africa and the return to the Caribbean as well as the opening towards the American continent, North and South. In 1995, Condé published *La Migration des cœurs*, a Caribbean *Wuthering Heights*, explicitly dedicated to Emily Brontë. In *Traversée*, she juxtaposes the interior monologues of the inhabitants of a small village, Rivière au Sel, as they assemble at the wake of Francis Sancher, an ambiguous and mysterious figure. Like the Haitian novelists, Francis has lived in Cuba, only to come back home to attempt to write a novel which has the same title as Condé's. Echoes of Faulkner's *As I Lay Dying, Absalom, Absalom!* and *The Sound and The Fury* abound in this text which becomes a site of encounter and recognition for the diverse cultures of the Caribbean represented by the characters who are at the wake: a creole and an East Indian family, a story-teller and a healer, adults and children, men and women. Their monologues and stories do not add up to a clear view of Francis's past. Opacity and ambiguity remain even if Lucien Evariste searches for clarity and submits his interlocutors to an exhaustive interrogation. *Traversée* breaks away from the obsession with the past that has characterised much Antillean literature, although the painful legacies of the colonial past are embodied in both Sancher and Xantippe's persons. For the most part, it is contemporary events and everyday life in Guadeloupe that are foregrounded.

Opacity is the only possible response to the uncertain genealogies and bewildering nature of the New World, stresses Glissant in *Le Discours antillais* (1981). In *La Lézarde* (Prix Renaudot 1958) and *Le Quatrième siècle* (Prix Charles Veillon 1964) he articulates new relationships to space and memory by concentrating on the lives of two families and probing the experiences of a community made up of planters and their slaves, field workers and maroons. Although as politically active as other committed black writers of the forties, fifties and sixties, Glissant has steered away from reformist approaches and the literature of 'revendication' in favour of the exploration of 'la réalité dans ses moindres replis' ['the smallest knots and coils of reality'].[11] *La Lézarde* (Paris: Seuil, 1958) is divided into four sections whose poetic titles and densely patterned images challenge novelistic conventions. The meandering river Lézarde as it winds its way through hills and plains is the chief protagonist. Its journey is repeated in the lives of the main characters as they move from a landscape associated with freedom (the hill, the *morne*) to the more oppressive lower areas or plains. The river is also a figure for the narrative process itself and the limits of realism: 'Comme si les mots pouvaient être une rivière qui descend et qui à la fin s'étale et déborde. Comme si les mots pouvaient concentrer tout en éclair et le porter dans la terre propice . . . Comme si . . . les mots pouvaient conduire leur part de boues, de racines, de limon, jusqu'au delta et à la mer jusqu'à la précise réalité' (pp. 230–1) ['As if words could be a flowing river, spreading out, overflowing. As if words could concentrate things into lightning and carry them to fertile soil . . . As if . . . words could drive their share of mud, roots, silt all the way down to the delta and the sea: to reality in its precision']. To this 'reality', Glissant opposes a sense of the baroque anchored in the luxuriant diversity of the landscape. He emphasises discontinuity, uncertainty, elusiveness, openness and incompletion as ways of mirroring both the state of as-yet-unachieved 'nationhood' that characterises Martinique and the complexity of global processes of creolisation. In *Tout-Monde* (1993), Glissant puts into practice his *poétique de la relation*, a process of improvisation that celebrates diversity.

The Guadeloupean Daniel Maximin's *L'Isolé Soleil* (Paris: Seuil, 1981) is a lyrical and dream-like text that foregrounds the activities of reading and writing. Characters write letters, send clippings to one another, keep journals and notebooks, and converse with poets. This complex novel pays homage to Suzanne and Aimé Césaire, but especially to Suzanne, poet and essayist, who fell silent after the last issue of *Tropiques* was published. At the centre of the novel is a chapter titled 'Le Journal de Siméa', full of dense and allusive prose, that performs a textual *métissage* of voices. Quoting Césaire's 'Nous sommes les débris d'une synthèse' (p. 226) ['we are the debris of a synthesis'], Maximin creates an allegory of Antillean identity that stresses and includes those feminine components which continue to be ignored by many.

In 1989, the Martinicans Jean Bernabé, Patrick Chamoiseau and Raphaël Confiant published the manifesto *Eloge de la créolité* (Paris: Gallimard), demarcating a Caribbean multicultural reality but issuing controversial normative judgements ('La littérature antillaise n'existe pas encore' (p. 14) ['Antillian literature does not exist yet']), that remain blind to the accomplishments of women writers.[12] This aesthetics of *créolité* is developed by Chamoiseau in *Chronique des sept misères* (1986), *Antan d'enfance* (1990) and *Texaco* (Prix Goncourt 1992), and by Confiant in *Eau de café* (1988) and *Le Nègre et l'amiral* (1991) which chronicle diverse periods of recent history.

In the Mascarene islands, *créolité* has evolved somewhat differently.[13] Axel Gauvin published *Quartier Trois-Lettres* in French in 1980, and in creole as *Kartyé Trwa Lèt* in 1984. *Faims d'enfance* (1987) is his fictional diary of a young Tamil schoolboy that captures the particularities of a native *réunionais* consciousness. In Mauritius, women novelists have blazed an original trail in the lyrical representation of *métissage* and feminine subjectivity. Marie-Thérèse Humbert's *A l'autre bout de moi* (1979) is a fiction of the self with utopian overtones. It returns to the important sites of the colonial experience, thus reconstructing Mauritian insularities and identities in rich and evocative prose, whereas Ananda Devi's *Rue la Poudrière* (1988) plays with Western themes of urban, racial and gender degeneration. Both are grounded in a colourful and vivid cultural *imaginaire*.

In these creole-speaking islands, regional idiolects have exploded the constraints of French syntax. Local identities are now theorised in terms of *antillanité*, *créolité* and *diversalité* rather than negritude or other closed systems of representation. The novel constitutes a corpus that brings to the field of French literature a 'parole archipélique' (Glissant). The return to heterogeneity, the rehabilitation of narration, and the inclusion of a plurality of languages characterise a Francophone modernity which thrives on a proliferation of themes and registers, on a multiplicity of perspectives, and a veritable orgy of words that mirrors the Babel-like quality of postcolonial experience. As the dynamics between the insular and the global increasingly becomes the common denominator of our *fin de siècle* across continents and communities, Francophone novelists have much to teach us about the new cartographies of our imagination. They are renewing the novel in profound and lasting ways and bringing a never before seen cosmopolitanism to contemporary literature.

NOTES

1 See A. Wynchank and P.-J. Salazar, *Afriques imaginaires: Regards réciproques et discours littéraires, 17e–20e siècles* (Paris: L'Harmattan, 1995) and V. Y. Mudimbe, *The Invention of Africa* (Bloomington: Indiana University Press, 1988).

2 L. S. Senghor, 'Les Leçons de Leo Frobenius' (1973), quoted in C. Miller, *Theories of Africans: Francophone Literature and Anthropology in Africa* (Chicago: University of Chicago Press, 1990), p. 16.

3 See V. Y. Mudimbe, ed., *The Surreptitious Speech: Présence Africaine and the Politics of Otherness 1947–1987* (Chicago: University of Chicago Press, 1992).

4 L. Kesteloot, *Les Ecrivains noirs de langue française* (Brussels: Université libre de Bruxelles, 1963), p. 64.

5 Editorial, *Peuples Noirs, Peuples Africains*, 11: 59–62 (September 87–April 88), p. 6.

6 Quoted in J. Chevrier, 'L'écrivain africain devant la langue française', *Notre Librairie* 53 (1980), 45.

7 E. Glissant, *Le Discours antillais* (Paris: Seuil, 1981), pp. 254–8.

8 O. Sembène, quoted in *Jeune Afrique* 191 (27 January 1973).

9 H. Abdel-Jaouad, 'Isabelle Eberhardt: Portrait of the Artist as a Young Nomad', *Yale French Studies* 83 (1993), 117.

10 E. Glissant explains this 'dépossession', in *Le Discours antillais*, pp. 58–81. 'Transculturation' is a term coined by the Cuban intellectual Fernando Ortiz in *Cuban Counterpoint: Tobacco and Sugar* (1947), trans. Harriet de Onís (Durham: Duke University Press, 1995).

11 E. Glissant, 'Le romancier noir et son peuple', *Présence Africaine* 16 (October–November 1957), 31.

12 As Maryse Condé points out in 'Order, Disorder, Freedom, and the West Indian Writer', *Yale French Studies* 83 (1993), 121–35. See also R. Toumson, *La Transgression des couleurs: Littérature et langage des Antilles, 18e–20e siècle* vols. I & II (Paris: Editions Caribéennes, 1989).

13 See F. Lionnet, '*Créolité* in the Indian Ocean: Two Models of Cultural Diversity', *Yale French Studies* 82 (1993), 101–2, and 'Les romancières contemporaines des Mascareignes: lyrisme, témoignage et subjectivité féminine', *Notre Librairie* 118 (1993), 86–90.

SUGGESTIONS FOR FURTHER READING

Adotévi, S., *Négritude et négrologues* (Paris: Union Générale d'Editions, 1972)

Antoine, R., *La Littérature franco-antillaise: Haïti, Guadeloupe, Martinique* (Paris: Khartala, 1992)

Césaire, A., *Discours sur le colonialisme* (Paris: Présence africaine, 1955)

Condé, M. (ed.), *Penser la créolité* (Paris: Khartala, 1995)

D'Almeida, I. A., *Francophone Women Writers: Destroying the Emptiness of Silence* (Gainesville: University Press of Florida, 1994)

Déjeux, J., *Situation de la littérature maghrébine d'expression française* (Paris: Presses Universitaires de France, 1992)

Fabre, M., *La Rive noire: de Harlem à la Seine* (Paris: Lieu commun, 1985)

Fanon, F., *Peau noire, masques blancs* (Paris: Seuil, 1952)
    Les Damnés de la terre (Paris: Maspéro, 1961)

Gontard, M., *La Violence du texte: études sur la littérature marocaine de langue française* (Paris: L'Harmattan, 1981)

Hargreaves, A. G. and M. J. Heffernen, *French and Algerian Identities from Colonial Times to the Present: A Century of Interaction* (Lewiston: Mellen Press, 1993)

Hoffmann, L.-F., *Le Nègre romantique* (Paris: Payot, 1973)

Huannou, A., *Anthologie de la littérature féminine d'Afrique noire francophone* (Abidjan: Editions Bognini, 1994)

Joubert, J.-L. (ed.), *Littérature francophone: Anthologie* (Paris: Nathan, 1992)
Littératures francophones depuis 1945 (Paris: Bordas, 1986)
Littératures de l'Océan Indien (Vanves: Edicef, 1991)

Khatibi, A., *Maghreb pluriel* (Paris: Denoël, 1983)

Laronde, M., *Autour du roman beur: immigration et identité* (Paris: L'Harmattan, 1993)

Lionnet, F., *Autobiographical Voices: Race, Gender, Self-Portraiture* (Ithaca: Cornell University Press, 1989)
Postcolonial Representations: Women, Literature, Identity (Ithaca: Cornell University Press, 1995)

Lionnet, F. with R. Scharfman (eds.), 'Post/Colonial Conditions: Exiles, Migrations, Nomadisms', *Yale French Studies*, 82–83 (1993)

Mudimbe, V. Y., *The Idea of Africa* (Bloomington: Indiana University Press, 1994)

Miller, C., *Blank Darkness: Africanist Discourse in French* (Chicago: University of Chicago Press, 1985)
Theories of Africans: Francophone Literature and Anthropology in Africa (Chicago: University of Chicago Press, 1990)

Ngaté, J., *Francophone African Fiction: Reading a Literary Tradition* (Trenton: Africa World Press, 1988)

Pfaff, F., *The Cinema of Ousmane Sembène, a Pioneer of African Film* (Westport, CT: Greenwood Press, 1984)

Prosper, J.-G., *Histoire de la littérature mauricienne de langue française* (Rose-Hill, Mauritius: Editions de l'Océan Indien, 1994)

Rosello, M., *Littérature et identité créole aux Antilles* (Paris: Khartala, 1992)

Said, E., *Orientalism* (New York: Pantheon, 1978)

Senghor, L. S., *Négritude et civilisation de l'universel* (Paris: Seuil, 1977)

Yeager, J., *The Vietnamese Novel in French* (Hanover, NH: University Press of New England, 1987)

13

DENIS BOAK

The French-Canadian novel

Although in recent years French-Canadian writers, like their counterparts in other Francophone communities, have been energised by nationalism, the literary development of French-speaking Canada bears only a superficial resemblance to that elsewhere. Its conquest, by the British, goes back well over two centuries, but Canada has been politically independent from Britain since 1867, with Quebec as one of its founding provinces. What has happened there since has been the responsibility of its own citizens; and the fifty thousand French of the mid-eighteenth century, far from being swamped in a flood of English-speaking immigrants, have grown to seven millions. Montreal, a small, largely English-speaking town in the early nineteenth century, is now a vast metropolis, by far the biggest Francophone city outside Paris.

Formerly the term 'French-Canadian' was used to cover all Francophone Canadian literature; since the 1960s, it has been superseded by 'Quebec', 'québécois'. In some ways this term is less clear, even tendentious, since it sidelines writers from outside Quebec, such as Gabrielle Roy, from Manitoba, often considered Canada's greatest Francophone novelist, or Antonine Maillet, born in New Brunswick, the only Canadian Goncourt prizewinner. 'Québécois' also excludes Anglophone writers who draw their inspiration from the 'belle province', of whom the best-known is Mordecai Richler. Be this as it may, in French Canada we find the most vigorous of all non-French Francophone literary cultures, and from its rich stock of novels only a few salient titles can be cited. The present essay is of course written from the viewpoint of an interested Anglophone observer.

Literature developed slowly in Quebec, as it did in English-speaking Canada and indeed the United States itself. Early settlers, in a harsh environment barely providing the means of existence, had other things to do than write, and were probably largely illiterate. In any case no printing presses were permitted in 'New France'. Though the British conquest removed French political control for good, it left intact the other pillar of

French influence, the Catholic Church, which consequently grew more powerful still, untouched by developments in France such as the Revolution and its aftermath; it would be two centuries before its grip was weakened.

The 'quest for identity' has usually been seen as central in nationalist cultural development. This is not what happened in Quebec. By the nineteenth century, the cultural identity was already there. The emblematic motto of Quebec is after all *Je me souviens*, best translated as 'I shall not forget'. In fact the British intruders were perhaps not so much resented as ignored: in Anne Hébert's *Kamouraska* (1970) they are shown as irrelevant to the essence of Quebec life, while in any case, outside the centres of administration and commerce, they were rarely present. But Francophone Quebec, which already saw British rule as a betrayal, had also turned its back on 'godless' post-revolutionary France. The values instilled by such education as was available, firmly in the hands of the clergy, were the defensive ones of 'fidelity': fidelity to the patrimony, the French language and Catholic religion, in practical terms idealised in the figure of the hardworking and virtuous peasant with his dream of *défrichement*, the clearing of forest to put land to the plough, under the benevolent guidance of the parish priest. Sceptics might of course claim that this, and the similar notion of 'virgin soil' in the United States, were no more than a rustic adaptation of the ideal of the noble savage, agriculture proclaimed as the way of life most pleasing to God and transformed into a spiritual vocation. (The original noble savages, the Indians, received short shrift in both cases, steadily pushed to the margins when not eliminated.)

In this intellectual environment imaginative literature had a hard row to furrow. The Church saw its mission as to instil morality, and the novel as at best an idle diversion, at worst a dangerous corrupting influence. Nor were French models to be imitated: if the English were heretics, the French were now atheists. Balzac was on the Papal Index, with all its consequences of censorship, and there he would remain until its abolition in 1966. But at the same time the Church was the guardian of the French language. Ironically, the novel which perhaps best represents the mystical values of 'fidelity', *Maria Chapdelaine* (1916), and the first to achieve wide recognition outside French Canada, was not a local product at all, but written by a visiting Frenchman, Louis Hémon, who had the misfortune to die in a train accident in Canada. Although such edifying literature, not easy to read today, held the official field for decades, attitudes began to change, and in 1938 *Trente arpents*, by Ringuet (Philippe Panneton), subjects the pastoral ideal to devastating criticism.

By the 1930s, of course, all Canada was in the grip of the Great Depression, which hit as hard as in the United States, in some ways worse given the harsh realities of the Canadian climate (half the year is ice-bound winter). The Depression hit town and country alike, and slowed what has been the main feature of Quebec economic life in our century, its transformation into an industrialised urban society. This had been consistently opposed by the Church. From its viewpoint, rightly: accurately foreseeing that a move to the cities would – fatally? – weaken its influence, as peasants became proletarians and, worst of all, women deserted their hearths and families to join the workforce.

Problems of urban society in the Depression are central in Gabrielle Roy's *Bonheur d'occasion* (1945), the first French-Canadian novel to be a bestseller abroad and widely translated. Roy, a schoolteacher turned journalist, tempers observation on Montreal in early 1940 with considerable empathy, in a novel of some complexity though based on the single Lacasse family. The father, Azarius, has lost his job as a carpenter and works intermittently as a taxi-driver, but he is an incompetent dreamer, though indefatigable talker, as much as a victim of the slump. The real head of the family is his wife Rose-Anna, while their daughter Florentine, a waitress in a dime-store cafeteria, alone brings in a steady income. Her relationship with a socially ambitious young electrical technician ends in pregnancy and abandonment, then the marriage to another young man, an army volunteer, which gives the novel its title, 'Second-Hand Happiness'.

The feminine predicament is also crucial in the novel. What Church teachings on conception imply in practice is the pregnancy trap for both Florentine and her mother (the latter's twelfth, at nearly fifty). With neat symmetry, both Azarius and his son volunteer for the army, soldiers being at least relatively well paid, with family allowances. For Azarius, though, this is one more irresponsible evasion of his problems, rather than a conscious resolution of them. It is also no solution: the novel ends, just after the fall of France, with the troops leaving Montreal under looming storm clouds. Whether they will ever return we do not know, and the future is left open. Roy is particularly perceptive in scenes between characters, and in dialogue has a keen ear for convincing local speech. The deep humanity of *Bonheur d'occasion* does not blur into sentimentality, and transcends the historical context of the Depression, which has, with its grinding poverty, by now receded into folklore.

The irony of the war proving a kind of salvation – 'salut', Roy's own word – for the Lacasse family problems needs no stressing. Neither world war was particularly popular in Quebec, where isolationism tended to prevail. For most, Britain's quarrels were not Quebec's; nor were France's. Military conscription was a highly controversial issue in both conflicts, while in the Second World War there was even a certain sympathy in

Quebec with the Axis cause, via Church support for the 'Christian' (otherwise Fascist) dictators, Mussolini and Franco. In this atmosphere one would not expect the war novel, so strong in the United States, to attract much interest. There is nevertheless one striking Francophone war novel, *Neuf jours de haine* (1948), by Jean-Jules Richard, devoted to the year starting on D-Day, 6 June 1944, and ending precisely a year later. During that time a company of Canadian infantry, of mixed origins, have fought their way from the Normandy beaches across France, Belgium and Holland, to occupy Germany, and have run the gamut of experience from innocence to disillusionment. Richard's account, confined to nine crucial days during the year, provides an excellent, tough, crisply narrated action novel.

The same author's *Le Feu dans l'amiante* (1956) is a social novel based on a famous asbestos strike in a provincial mining town. Ecological overtones are present but not dominant, nor are they in two powerful novels by André Langevin. Metaphysical solitude is Langevin's main theme, used in an attempt to achieve tragic effect, in sordid small-town settings far from the pastoral ideal. In *Poussière sur la ville* (1953), a young doctor moves with his recently married wife, again to an asbestos town. Far from helping him establish a practice, the wife goes out to bars alone, and starts an affair with a young miner. Her husband, unable to cope with the situation, takes to the bottle, thus offending the townspeople. The local priest puts pressure on the miner, who is soon engaged to another girl; the wife vainly attempts to shoot him but succeeds only in killing herself. The backcloth of an ugly mining town in winter, where the pervading asbestos dust combines with driving snow in an update of the pathetic fallacy, a hostile nature reflecting the hopeless solitude of the characters. The only way to face this is gritty perseverance: the doctor, after his wife's death, will not move away from the town, but stay and attempt to recover his position and dignity.

Langevin's fictional universe is if anything even more negative in *Le Temps des hommes* (1956), another novel of atmosphere and crisis, set near a timber town with the alien name of Scottsville. The action takes place within a few days, among a logging gang holed up in a log cabin during a blizzard. The foreman has recently started an affair with the wife of one of his team, a jealous man with a revolver brought back from the war. Not one but three deaths ensue; and one of the survivors has frostbitten legs which seem to require amputation, although the ending is again left open. This man, a priest, has lost his faith in the Church as an institution, though not the humanitarian hope of becoming a lay saint, which is why he is working in the forest. But his fellow-workers, despising his unworldliness, ignore or exploit him, and his very attempt to help the murderer through some kind of spiritual human contact ends, melodramatically but ironically, in an involuntary killing. In this macho story there are only two women characters: the wife whose adultery triggers the action, and her sister, a good woman in love with the priest, who by definition cannot return her love. Langevin's fictional world is stark and grim, sordid both physically and morally, but paradoxically obsessed by the religion rejected. Social problems matter little in face of obsession with alienation and failure. Solitude and distress are man's lot, and critics have seen in Langevin echoes of French Existentialist preoccupations.

The 'révolution tranquille', the 'quiet revolution' of the 1960s, was primarily an overthrowing of the values of a reactionary provincial government, an attempt to change identities, one however which in literary terms was by then nothing new: fidelity to the rustic dream had long ago been abandoned. Resentment of the 'Anglos' had also lost its focus. The British themselves now scarcely mattered in Quebec. Anglophone Canadians, incapable of comprehending the separatists' passionate feeling of being exiles in their own land, were totally bemused by their linguistic nationalism (visiting French have been astonished to find that Quebec road signs read not STOP but ARRÊT), while Americans, in control of much of Canadian industry and not only in Quebec, were equally targets. Some nationalist grievances, such as the slogan 'White Niggers of America', now appear borrowed rather than genuine, even self-pitying, while the Marxist dynamic for subversion has also disappeared.

One important feature of the 1960s cultural ferment was the attempt at creating a genuinely local literary language, called *joual*, after the Quebec pronunciation of the word *cheval*, and originally a pejorative term. Spoken Quebec French is easily distinguishable from other French accents; indeed it became reasonably homogeneous long before metropolitan French (most nominal French citizens at the time of the Revolution could not speak the French language). It contains in regular use many words and expressions which have vanished in France itself (e.g. *itou = aussi*). *Joual* meant that a rough reproduction of demotic speech would replace classical French as a literary vehicle. Thus *à cette heure* ('now') was written *asteur*. More importantly, a vast stock of Anglo-Saxon borrowings in common use were also utilised, many not particularly elegant terms such as *la dompe*, 'dump', *une djobbe*, 'job'.

Joual as a serious literary language did not last long. Although it inspired colourful and inventive writing, such an attempt to abandon conventional French could only have one result: throwing out the baby with the bathwater by further marginalising a literature whose major problem was already that of finding an adequate readership. Few writers in Quebec (or anywhere else) want to limit their appeal to a narrow group, and they certainly do not want to exclude themselves from the French intellectual scene. (Quebec film-makers have encountered a similar difficulty with films only thought acceptable in Paris with subtitles.) Publishers in Quebec are prolific (listings of novels have quadrupled in two decades), but editions are small, often ephemeral, and the ideal for Quebec writers remains publication, and sometimes residence, in France itself. So after a flurry of *joual* activity in the 1960s, the use of demotic language returned to what it had been before, in novels such as *Bonheur d'occasion*, a valuable instrument for local colour, comic and satirical effect. Quebec writers continue to employ 'classical' French, however they may actually speak the language – which is, after all, what their counterparts do in France.

From the flurry of literary activity in 1960s Quebec, probably few novels will survive. This was the time of state-of-the-art literary experimentation, aesthetic anarchism and eroticism, with echoes of developments elsewhere, such as the curious but widespread belief that subversion in aesthetics is identical with subversion in politics. The novel as a literary genre may require a reflective mood that sits uneasily with political militancy. No subjects date as rapidly as the topical, while some writers celebrate an often gratuitous violence. Others, such as Réjean Ducharme, display scintillating powers of word-play and fantasy, even in the titles of his novels – *Les Enfantômes* (1976) or *Le Nez qui voque* (1967), punning on 'équivoque' – but appear unlikely to gain a wide readership.

Jacques Godbout's *Salut Galarneau!* (1967) contains elements which make it as good a fictional representative of this period as any other. Godbout's first-person protagonist Galarneau is an ambivalent figure: he has abandoned formal education and after a varied career as barman, building worker and shop assistant, has become proprietor of a fast food stand, *Au Roi du Hot Dog*, in the Montreal suburbs. He thus epitomises the difficulty of living in Quebec free of Anglo-Saxon influence. Galarneau has a broken marriage behind him, and when his new girlfriend leaves him for his brother, a radio writer, under severe mental strain he starts to wall himself up in his house, in another symbolic gesture. The overworked term of 'alienation' seems unavoidable, but Galarneau is redeemed by writing the story of his life, presumably the one we are reading, a typical use of the *mise en abyme*, the emblematic text within a text so popular in the 'new novel'. The book abounds with witty linguistic devices, puns, anglicisms and elements of *joual*, and Galarneau coins his own term for his aim in life, *vécrire*, an amalgam of *vivre* and *écrire*, living and writing simultaneously.

This character presumably means much to Godbout, a prolific novelist who as recently as 1993 published a sequel, *Le Temps des Galarneau*, in which picaresque elements run riot.

Anne Hébert came to the novel from poetry, and her masterpiece, *Kamouraska* (1970), belongs not to the Realist mode but to an essentially poetic universe of fable and mystery. Starting from a historical incident of 1839, a gory *crime passionnel* in which a young woman of good family provoked her lover to murder a drunken, brutal husband, Hébert creates a masterpiece of dramatic intensity which is at the same time a paradoxical amalgamation of the content of the gothic novel, appropriate to the early nineteenth century, and the techniques of the 'new novel'. The heroine, Elisabeth d'Aulnières, tempted by sensuality into a teenage marriage with the 'seigneur' of the manor of Kamouraska, takes a lover, an American doctor. Though a Catholic, he is an outsider in the community, and his idealistic struggle against disease is doomed in the general filth, superstition and malevolence. No idealised rustic paradise here. After the murder Nelson flees over the border, where he is safe from extradition; Elisabeth is arrested but soon released, to make a marriage of respectability with a Quebec lawyer to redeem her reputation.

The narrative consists largely of Elisabeth's hallucinated flashbacks during the hours of this man's lingering death from heart disease. Elisabeth's fevered mind, drugged by a sleeping-draught, re-enacts crucial events of her life, in particular the murder many years before. Basically melodramatic events, and supernatural elements such as sorcery, are thus rendered more acceptable. Elisabeth is at the same time a feminist heroine, an example of 'woman's condition' in the nineteenth century. Her *fureur de vivre*, rage to live a life of fabulous Romantic intensity, can find no channel but sexual passion, which proves as destructive to the men around her as to her own dreams. At the end of the novel she is left with an uncertain future – yet another open ending – but eleven children. The shattering of conventional narrative techniques through constant switches in narrative viewpoint and chronology, and the fragmented, often verbless sentences, fits what is more a stream of hallucination than of consciousness. *Kamouraska*, where the poet shows her presence in a flow of brilliant imagery, is a masterpiece of 'chaotic form'.

One of the features of literary nationalism, world-wide, has been the attraction of the historical novel, in attempts at self-legitimation through the deliberate creation of a myth of origins. In *Kamouraska* this is incidental rather than a primary aim. Antonine Maillet's *Pélagie-la-Charrette* (1979), the first French-Canadian novel to win the Goncourt Prize, is a Rabelaisian re-enactment of a mythical event in the history, not of Quebec but of

Acadie, what is now Nova Scotia. Under the leadership of Pélagie, a matron of indomitable personality, a group of Acadians exiled to Carolina travel back with her ox-cart all the hundreds of miles North to Acadie. The whole novel, a mock epic largely narrated in a lyrical reconstruction of pre-conquest French, is a joyous 'celebration of the tribe' with a vengeance, and, whether intended or not, as good an example as one could wish of the notion of the 'carnivalesque', in which the fabulous and fantastic merge with the subversive and supernatural in a world of wish-fulfilment.

It is sometimes said that a society has really come of age when it can satirise itself. Most of the 'subversive' works of the 1960s took themselves rather too seriously, though in *Salut Galarneau!* Godbout indulges in a light-hearted tone of mockery, at his own as well as others' expense. But it is with Francine Noël's *Maryse* (1983) that Quebec literature produced a brilliant satirical novel, set during the 'crisis' years of 1968–75, among a set of young Montreal intellectuals. Noël shows an infallible ear for spoken language, and a cruel nose for phoneyness and pretension. Her characters suppose themselves to be at the cutting edge of nationalist intellectual development, but use *joual*, stuffed with American borrowings, although it is officially despised as the *patois* of the ignorant. Their ideas are full of the -isms and -ologies fashionable in 1968 France, and their meeting-place is a 'Spanish' restaurant, *La Luna de Papel*. Women are not really accepted as card-carrying intellectuals, but are expected to live uncomplainingly with the men, doing the cooking and cleaning, again as in 1968 France: 'We men will make the revolution, you women can make the coffee.' Maryse herself (her real name Mary O'Sullivan), of Irish stock and genuine proletarian antecedents, is another outsider, patronised by her lover, under the skin an impeccable scion of the comfortable middle class. The plot of the novel is her successful struggle to become her own woman, or, to use the jargon, to move from object to subject. By the end she has broken with the lover and achieved a professional career as a university teacher, in 'literology' (one of the main targets of the satire is what passed at the time for a desirable higher education). This is a feminist masterpiece, its serious import reinforced by the fact that it is also that rarity, a genuinely very funny novel.

Although quantification is impossible, it seems that the proportion of significant French-Canadian writers who are women is as high as anywhere in the world. Why this should be so is not immediately clear: the traditional education system, and the values propagated by it, have not been particularly favourable to women's writing. Perhaps the best novel of education is to be found in an apparently autobiographical work by Denise Bombardier, *Une enfance à l'eau bénite* (1985), which portrays in detail the narrator's education during the 1950s. Treated schematically, one chapter to each school year, with therefore new teachers, mainly nuns, some doing their best to encourage intellectual development, others hidebound in narrow-minded piety and determined to do no more than produce good Christian wives and mothers, the book contains a remarkable analysis of the 'female condition'. The narrator's family situation is not happy either: her father is not local but French, a former ship's officer, an atheist, trapped in marriage to a conventional Montreal woman whose values and religious practices he cannot share. By the end of the book the narrator has broken free to the point of refusing to go to Mass, but she has had to take an uninspiring office job, her formal education for the moment blocked. However – and this is her final thought – at least she is now free, free to live her own life.

The future of the Quebec novel is bright, whether or not it is tied to nationalism, and whether or not this might bring fulfilment or a certain disillusionment. It seems inevitable that novelists will continue to look outwards as well as inwards as they carve out their creative space. Many of the novels discussed here can be related to literary movements or ideas elsewhere: *Bonheur d'occasion* to the social novel, Langevin to existentialism, *Kamouraska* to the 'new novel', while the intellectual restlessness of the 1960s was international, and feminism originally condemned as an Anglo-Saxon import. But all this is as it should be: surely in the contemporary world the idea of autarky, of complete self-sufficiency, listening to ancestral voices alone, is as outdated in the literary as in the economic world. Far from being doubly marginalised, French Canada's relationship to France on the one side and Anglophone America on the other makes its increasingly cosmopolitan culture doubly privileged, and its novels, while containing the unmistakable flavour and vitality of their own society, are international in scope and appeal.

SUGGESTIONS FOR FURTHER READING

Dorsinville, M., *Caliban Without Prospero* (Erin, Ont.: Porcépic, 1975)

Marcotte, G., *Littérature et circonstances* (Montreal: L'Hexagone, 1989)

Purdy, A., *A Certain Difficulty of Being* (Montreal: McGill-Queen's University Press, 1990)

Robidoux R., and A. Renaud, *Le Roman canadien-français du vingtième siècle* (Ottawa: Editions de l'Université d'Ottawa, 1966)

Shek, B.-Z., *Social Realism in the French-Canadian Novel* (Montreal: Harvest House, 1977)

  French-Canadian and Québécois Novels (Toronto: Oxford University Press, 1991)

14

JANE WINSTON

Gender and sexual identity in the modern French novel

Simone de Beauvoir's *Le Deuxième Sexe* (1949) soundly refuted the patriarchal myth of an eternal feminine nature which, until then, had provided poets and novelists with their most cherished topoi. The famous opening line of Beauvoir's second volume is considered the origin of gender construction theory: 'On ne naît pas femme; on le devient' (Beauvoir, *Le Deuxième Sexe* (Paris: Gallimard, 1949), vol. II, p. 2) ['One is not born, but becomes, woman']. Writing after the Holocaust, in the early days of France's colonial wars, at a time when Afro-American writer Richard Wright was in Paris publishing articles and excerpts from his novel *Black Boy* in *Les Temps modernes,* Beauvoir showed that patriarchy uses the eternal feminine to oppress women, precisely as antisemitic and racist systems of oppression deploy ideologies of the Black soul or Jewish character. *Le Deuxième Sexe* outraged French literary and critical establishments. Hostile articles and hate mail poured in. Even Beauvoir's friend Albert Camus castigated her for making French men appear foolish. But *Le Deuxième Sexe* also elicited letters of gratitude from female readers and stimulated a wealth of women's fiction in the following decade. It remains the intellectual cornerstone of twentieth-century Western feminism, the text with or against which feminist theorists and novelists have been writing for nearly fifty years.

Let us begin, then, with a brief survey of what Beauvoir challenges and enables and how, under her pen, issues of sexual identity and gender intersect with the writing of novels. Beauvoir opens her essay with seventeenth-century feminist Poulain de la Barre's claim that everything men have written about women must be considered suspect. She then makes two crucial moves. First she shows how patriarchal ideology underpins scientific, mythic, popular and literary representations of women and undermines their truth claims. Then she demonstrates that the patriarchal myth of feminine nature plays a fundamental role in the social construction and oppression of women. To explore that construction, she turns to women's accounts of their own lived experiences, especially first-person narratives and autobiographical novels. Despite her general view that women's literature tends to be less universal and thus less good than men's, she ends up convincing readers of the political value of women's writing as counter-representations to men's ideological fiction. The sort of novels Beauvoir encouraged has a great deal to do with her analysis of women's condition and views on writing. Beauvoir adopts an existentialist and sociological perspective to analyse women's oppression. Humans are primarily conscious beings, she holds, born empty of any pre-given content or essence into specific situations. Consciousness defines itself as a subject in relation to an 'other' and by its own transcendent activity. Patriarchy prevents women from taking up a subject position by casting them, *en masse*, as the other in relation to men. Born free, they are constructed as objects in a system designed to meet male needs and desires. As she becomes a woman, a girl thus becomes alienated from herself in a process that imposes objectified self-images on her and gets her to internalise them. Patriarchy arrests women in passivity and objectivity and makes them unable to reach out to the world, accept responsibility for their projects, and act authentically. Beauvoir does not explicitly extend these insights to the field of sexuality. She believes that the involuntary biological processes human reproduction forces on women render them slaves of the species and holds that patriarchy transforms this biological subordination into a permanent social, political and existential dependency and inferiority. To change their social situation women must reject marriage and maternity, attain financial independence, establish projects, and work toward transcendence.

Beauvoir considers writing one route to financial independence. Since they largely escape patriarchal domination, female intellectuals (like herself) are best positioned to elucidate the situation of 'woman'. Reading can raise a reader's awareness of her situation so that she might assume it and act authentically. It is thus essential that committed writers portray the world as it is in order to create the will to change it. Beauvoir does not propose that female writings transgress male and female sexual paradigms: she does not believe sexuality can be changed, nor does she appear to believe such a change desirable. She does not counsel formal experimentation either. In 1949, she considers language a transparent instrument used to communicate a message and tends to think of textual politics in terms of content. She neither argues for nor produces feminist utopian writing or heroic liberated female figures.

Beauvoir's novels often read like case-histories of the oppressive scenarios and woman-types described in *Le Deuxième Sexe*. *L'Invitée* (1943) worries about the restrictiveness of feminine social roles, while *Tous les hommes sont mortels* (1946) demonstrates women's historical marginalisation in patriarchy. Beauvoir is candid about this illustrative or cautionary nature of her writing, identifying, for instance, several fictional *amoureuses* – Elisabeth in *L'Invitée,* Denise in *Le Sang des autres* (1945) and Paule in *Les Mandarins* (1954). Beauvoir believes one of the greatest impediments to women's liberation is the fact that, living dispersed among men, we are unable to form a collective consciousness. She seems to hope that by reading Colette, Emily Brontë, Anna de Noailles, Virginia Woolf, Rosamond Lehmann, George Eliot, Clara Malraux or Katherine Mansfield we might recognise our shared conditions of oppression and begin to form a *nous* capable of thinking of itself in independent, collective terms.

Women published massively in the wake of Beauvoir. Editions Julliard had fifteen female writers in 1950; Plon had twenty-five by 1951. *Elle* magazine published a photograph of seventy women novelists and their children in 1954, eliciting Barthes's 'Novels and Children' article in *Mythologies* (1957). In 1952 the first French paperback appeared from Hachette and women began to dominate the pulp-fiction industry. René Julliard, the first publisher in France to deploy a heavy marketing campaign, was closely associated with women's pulp. Editions Julliard mobilised gender and sexuality in various ways to promote sales, printing young female authors' names on bands around their novels and placing their photos on book jackets. Julliard himself paraded around Paris with various young protégées, assuring them mass press coverage as well. Julliard writers sold well. Françoise Sagan's *Bonjour Tristesse* (1954) sold more than 840,000 French copies and 4,500,000 translations by 1962. Françoise Mallet-Joris's *Le Rempart des béguines* (1951) was translated into thirteen languages by 1953 and had sold 30,000 copies by the end of 1956.

The realist pulp of Sagan, Mallet-Joris, and the third of Julliard's 'trois F', Françoise d'Eaubonne (*Comme un vol de gerfauts,* 1950) dislodged the traditional construction of women as producers and consumers of sentimental fiction. Their anti-sentimental novels contested sentimentalism's themes, disrupted its family romance scenario, refused its happy endings, and flooded the French literary field with a new generation of independent-minded young heroines. Moulded in their author's image, these heroines assume the textual role of first-person homodiegetic (internal) narrator and look back a year or two to relate their own coming of age. As they take narrative power, these women transgress traditional boundaries separating fiction from autobiography. Many pulp tales are structured around the heroine's investigation, appraisal and rejection of patriarchal gender roles and her non-traditional sexual initiation. Anti-sentimental novels typically end with the heroine standing alone on the threshold of what one is left to surmise will be her active adult life.

But anti-sentimental pulp novels raise gender issues only to respond to them conservatively. One critic argues that 1950s pulp novels, authored mostly by privileged women like Sagan and Mallet-Joris, actually helped shore up France's emerging technocratic bourgeoisie (Kristen Ross, *Fast Cars, Clean Bodies: Decolonization and the Reordering of French Culture* (Cambridge, MA, and London: MIT, 1995)). Post-war France was moving rapidly from left-wing to right-wing political dominance. A conservative technocratic bourgeoisie was emerging around an ideology of happiness grounded in the privatised, consuming couple. The country was shifting to 'Fordist consumerism' structured around standardised housing, the woman's domain, and the automobile on which men spent their money. In 1945 De Gaulle called on French women to produce twelve million beautiful babies; in 1955 family subsidy laws were amended to provide bonuses for births in the first two years of marriage and allowances for women staying or returning home to raise children. Women writing realist pulp helped produce the myth of the car as an intimate domestic space. Consciously or not, some also aided attempts to coax women back home and into traditional feminine roles.

Mallet-Joris's *Le Rempart des béguines* thematises the lesbian relation of a fifteen-year-old girl and her father's mistress, but fails to analyse normative heterosexuality. It does not portray lesbian desire or pleasure and paints lesbian culture in unrelentingly negative, even homophobic, terms. What counts in *Le Rempart* is not lesbianism at all, but the interaction between an older and younger woman. Older Tamara is a clearly phallic-then-fallen Oedipal mother. She is phallic in her sadistic dominance of her young lover, Hélène; fallen when she has sex with a man and even more irreparably when she chooses the security of marriage to Hélène's wealthy father over freedom. Like the reader, Hélène is to watch and learn. She sees and experiences a woman's strength and glimpses a lesbian love once shared by Tamara and another woman. Yet lesbian sexuality remains too vague and distant to help this heroine. Mallet-Joris's neglect of female sexuality also constrains her own ability to envisage an active and fully sexual female subject. Like Beauvoir and for the same reasons, she can only imagine one possible first step toward liberation – financial independence. Symptomatically, she leaves her heroine right where *Le Deuxième Sexe* left off: poised for professional success, but in bed, and (like Renée Neré in Colette's 1906 *Vagabonde*) utterly alone. The sequel *La Chambre rouge* (1955) corroborates Mallet-Joris's impasse, as it leaves an even more isolated Hélène saved from dependence, from others and from herself, but lost to love.

In Françoise Sagan's *Bonjour Tristesse*, wealthy and motherless Céline refuses to identify with any of the substitute mother figures offered her. She detests the immanence of the bourgeois wife and mother. She goes so far as to force the suicide of independent mother-figure Anne, whose professional profile suggests that in rejecting her, Céline refuses the new technocratic bourgeois society and female model as well. But if Céline knows what she refuses, she has no idea of what she wants, other than a vague 'liberté de penser . . . de choisir moi-même ma vie, de me choisir moi-même. Je ne peux dire "d'être moi-même" puisque je n'étais rien qu'une pâte modelable, mais celle de refuser les moules' (Sagan, *Bonjour Tristesse* (Paris: Julliard, 1954), p. 4) ['freedom to think . . . to choose my life and myself. I cannot say "to be myself" as I was but mere modelling clay, but the freedom to refuse pre-cast moulds']. Céline's individualist revolt is tied to no collective struggle; *Bonjour Tristesse* in fact provides no social register outside the heroine's upper bourgeoisie and no historical context. Isolated, privileged and petulant, Céline fails to come of age: she remains a privileged *enfant terrible* – alone, projectless and in a state of complacent nostalgia for the patriarchal happy ending her own actions precluded. It is difficult to imagine who would be convinced by this novel to follow Céline's lead and reject women's patriarchal destiny.

Other women did pen sustained and convincing realist critiques of patriarchal gender and sexual identities. Two of them, Christiane Rochefort and Marguerite Duras, had manuscripts refused as too intellectual by Editions Julliard. A native of Paris's mixed fourteenth *arrondissement*, Rochefort indicts the alienation she considers fundamental to advanced capitalism. *Le Repos du guerrier* (1958) pits a philosophiser against a young bourgeois woman incapable of articulating her desires in his language, while *Les Petits Enfants du siècle* (1963) explores the alienation of working-class women under capitalism and patriarchy. Adolescent Josyane moves from a love of intellectual work to recuperation by a social order in which lower-class women like her serve solely to reproduce workers and consumers. Her sexual initiation with an older Italian migrant worker rings of medieval courtships, knights errant and pre-cultural nature, making it more promising as eventual daydream material for a depressed housewife than as a viable alternative to Joysane's bleak future. Raised in an HLM ('habitation à loyer modéré', or low-cost council housing), Joysane ends up pregnant, with her desires channelled into a thirst for consumer goods – washing machines, fridges and TVs. She looks forward not to freedom, but to life in the *grand ensemble* at Sarcelles where, in the early 1960s, France tried to contain its immigrants and working classes.

If Rochefort's portrayal of lower-class women forms a powerful reverse image of the élite heroines of Sagan and Mallet-Joris, her textualisation of immigrant populations gestures towards women's explorations of sexual identity and gender oppression in Francophone cultures (a theme which is developed by Françoise Lionnet in her discussion of the Francophone novel in this volume). One of the first novels to explore Francophone women's oppression and make the case for their liberation was the 1952 *Sommeil délivré* by Egyptian-Lebanese expatriate Andrée Chedid. Chedid tells of one woman's suffering and deadly revolt. Married at fifteen to an old man and victimised for her failure to produce a male child, the heroine finally kills her husband so that a young girl might live. *Le Sommeil délivré* prefigures 1970s and 1980s novels by Francophone women writers, especially Evelyne Accad's thematically similar but theoretically and stylistically more interesting treatment of the construction of female sexuality and women's oppression in the Middle East, *L'Excisée* (1982).

As for Rochefort, after *Les Petits Enfants* she worked more closely on sexuality and social change. *Une Rose pour Morrison* (1966) ironically casts the construction of female sexuality as a process that forces women to pass through prenuptial institutions where they learn to perform intercourse functions 'sans bouger', i.e. without moving. Despite her interest in sexuality and social change, Rochefort's understanding of the role language plays in forming and sustaining them lagged behind more experimental writings of the 1950s and early 1960s. Mid-century writers took a renewed interest in the Marquis de Sade and the sado-masochistic structures of the bourgeois patriarchal subject. In 1953 Editions Jean-Jacques Pauvert reissued Sade. In 1954 they published Pauline Réage's (Dominique Aury's) *Histoire d'O*. Pauvert also published Georges Bataille's *Bleu du ciel* (1956) and *Histoire de l'œil* (1967), whose title repeats and transforms Réage's. In his preface to *Histoire d'O*, Jean Paulhan claims the novel opposes female emancipation by establishing female subjugation as a matter of individual preference. Consistently, *Histoire d'O* has been widely read as a pornographic and misogynist work. More recently, however, Réage's novel has been seen to extend Beauvoir's analysis of the social construction of woman to the level of the body, showing in explicit detail that the structuration of the female subject begins with the inscription and organisation of the body. On this reading, O's violently physical assimilation into a network of prostitution (she is bound, whipped, raped, penetrated all the time, everywhere and by everyone) functions as an allegory of patriarchy's discursive territorialisation of the bodies which, duly mapped and charted, come to signify woman and female sexuality. Produced by a discursive network exterior to her and from which she is excluded, the signification inscribed on the woman's body and internalised by her to form a 'soul' is thereafter perceived, even by her, as a properly feminine interior or essence.

In the 1950s lesbian titles also increased. Three Nicole Louvier novels appeared in 1953 – *Chansons interdites, Qui qu'en grogne* and *L'Heure des jeux*. Julliard printed Simone Magny's *Présence* in 1954. Violette Leduc's *Ravages* (1955) explicitly portrayed lesbian desire and passion. Despite the authoritative support and protests of Leduc's friend and reader Beauvoir, Gallimard elided substantial sections of *Ravages* and expunged its prologue (which it published in 1966 as *Thérèse et Isabelle*). *Ravages* critiques heterosexuality and traces the heroine's journey from the heights of lesbian pleasure to extreme heterosexual suffering, including a late abortion that terminates the heroine's sex life as well. Splitting her narrative voice between an unconscious and conscious self, Leduc presents the inner conflict of a woman caught between shifting sexual desires and normative gender exigencies. Recalling the multiple sexualities in the writing of the first female Academician, Marguerite Yourcenar, Leduc refuses to reduce desire to one particular, fixed sexual orientation. Her desiring female subject is not merely lesbian, heterosexual or bisexual, but mobile and shifting.

Women's textual treatment of gender and sexual identity to the mid-1960s thus follows two main trends: realist accounts of gender oppression that maintain Beauvoir's view of committed literature, and explorations of sexuality and desire that extend her tentative deployment of Lacan's model of subject construction and engage in formal experimentation. Politics and collective concerns thus seem to gravitate to one side, personal narratives to the other. As Margaret Cohen shows elsewhere in this volume in her discussion of women and fiction in the nineteenth century, this division repeats the traditional distinction between the masculine novel's engagement with social, philosophical or political issues and the feminine rendering of personal suffering, sexuality and desire. As one critic put it, for a woman to treat anything but 'the personal, individual experience of women who live *hic et nunc*, their present boredom, their very personal hopes or despair . . . would mean writing science fiction or trying to imitate men' (Jacques Guicharnaud, 'Women's Fate: Marguerite Duras', *Yale French Studies* 27 (1961), 107). When post-war male critics did read women's novels, they were more alarmed by political themes than by transgressive sexuality. If some objected to women's textual sex on moral grounds, they did not seem to recognise its political potential. In any case they did not generally argue, as they routinely did against women's political narratives, that sexual explicitness makes women unfeminine or renders their novels unliterary. That such critics helped shape the production and reception of women's novels is borne out by Marguerite Duras's critical history, which began in earnest with the publication of *Un barrage contre le Pacifique* (1950).

Barrage was the first major novel in French by a woman writer to weave together a colonial context, a political narrative and the psychoanalytic portrayal of subject formation. Duras wrote it in the period framed by the May 1945 massacres of Algerian insurgents at Sétif and Guelma, the 1947 massacre of Madagascan insurgents, Ho Chi Minh and the Viet-Minh's attempts to reclaim Indochina from its French colonisers, and her own Parti Communiste Français activism. She situates her semi-autobiographical *Bildungsroman* in the Asian colonial context in which she came of age, thus broadening Beauvoir's bourgeois Caucasian account of gender oppression to include a cross-section of Francophone women – rich urban colonialists, prostitutes, rural Asian peasants, poor white French and a wandering lumpenproletarian girl-mother. Duras's treatment of these women remains within realist and engaged conventions; bearing witness to gender oppression across race and class, she is clearly out to educate readers and produce social change. At the same time, however, *Barrage* also engages with concerns that would characterise the 1950s *nouveau roman* (such as narrative form) and 1970s feminist novels (the relation between formal, social and subjective structures).

Barrage begins with an undefined third person plural 'ils', readily recognisable as an unusual Oedipal family comprised of an adolescent girl and her widowed mother, with the dead father's place taken by an older brother. The heroine's voice emerges from within that collective to chart, in the remaining 200 pages, her route to subjecthood. Her *Bildung* proceeds through a set of stages structured along the lines of Lacanian scenes of desire. In Lacan's famous account of the 'mirror stage', a child defines itself as a subject in relation to an image mediated by the mother and then in relation to paternal power. As it does, it enters the order of language and symbolism, where, Lacan says, the speaking subject is implicitly male and women are predicates. Duras appropriates and politicises Lacan's model. Infusing his scene with patriarchal colonialism's unequal relations of social, cultural, economic and political power, she sets the stage for the emergence of a political and sexual female subject that prefigures the subjects of later postcolonial and feminist writings. Sitting on multiple borders, her heroine hovers between colonial and indigenous cultures, torn by maternal and patriarchal power, trying to understand where she belongs in relation to established heterosexual gender positions.

Duras's most concerted efforts at textual and conceptual disruption engage the sex–gender link. She confuses traditional gender attributes, making her male lead physically and emotionally weak and her heroine emotionless, calculating and increasingly powerful. She denatures masculine power by detaching it from the male and objectifying it: her hero carries his power around in the comic, detached and transferable form of diamonds in his pockets. She correlates a diminution of male power with a rise in female sexuality, culminating in her heroine's subversion of the alignment of men, power and automobiles. Speeding around in her would-be lover's shiny black limousine, she dominates this man and the colonial streets: 'Au-dessus de la ville terrifiante, [elle] vit ses seins, elle vit l'érection de ses seins plus haut que tout ce qui se dressait dans la ville, dont c'était eux qui auraient raison' (Duras, *Un barrage contre le Pacifique* (Paris: Gallimard, Folio, 1991), p. 226) ['Above the terrifying city, she saw her breasts, their erections standing higher than everything in the city, and knew that it was they who would win the day']. *Barrage* ends after this girl takes her sexual initiation with a man of her choosing and refuses to marry him. She prepares to leave Indochina alone but in full possession of an active sexual identity and poised to engage her freedom in a revolutionary project: 'Il me faudrait entrer dans leur combine . . . pour mieux les tuer' (p. 275) ['I must enter their world . . . so as to kill them all the more efficaciously'].

After *Barrage*, Duras moved from realist accounts of female alienation like *Madame Dodin* (1954) and *Le Square* (1955) to formal experimentation. *Moderato cantabile* (1958) discards realist trappings, divests plot of all but essential details, slows narrative temporality to near stasis and bears in on the repressive structures of bourgeois desire. Her later works disrupt narrative linearity, foreground discursive gaps and silences, and efface genre boundaries, as in the text/theatre/film *India Song* (1973 and 1976) or exceedingly slim volumes like *L'Homme atlantique* (1982) and *La Pute de la côte normande* (1986). Duras's Prix Goncourt *L'Amant* (1984) carries no generic mark, while the equally autobiographical *L'Amant de la Chine du Nord* (1991) is labelled *roman,* dissolving the line between autobiography and fiction. In the 1991 novel as in *Agatha* (1981), Duras focuses on incestuous sexuality, while *L'Homme atlantique* (1982) textualises male homosexuality.

Duras claims her writing is of a piece with her revolutionary politics. Seen from this point of view, her work on linguistic and conceptual categories would represent an attempt to transcend rational structures of thought (see *La Douleur,* 1985) and the Western patriarchal social and economic system they subtend (see *Duras à Montréal,* 1981, and *Œuvres cinématographiques*, 1983). Yet few critics read Duras in Marxist terms or see *Moderato cantabile* or *Le ravissement de Lol. V. Stein* (1964) as studies of bourgeois women's alienation. They have tended rather to separate her novels and her politics and read the novels in terms of desire alone. This trend is reflected in the recent critical tendency to view Duras as the embodiment of *écriture féminine*, or feminine writing, and neglect those areas where she rejoins materialist feminist writers like Monique Wittig.

When Wittig's *L'Opoponax* appeared in 1964, Duras was being praised as a textualiser of Lacan's theories and spokeswoman for femininity. Duras praised Wittig, calling *L'Opoponax* a *chef-d'œuvre*, 'l'execution capitale de quatre-vingt-dix pour cent des livres qui ont été faits sur l'enfance' (in *France Observateur*, 5 November 1964) ['the complete annihilation of ninety per cent of the books heretofore written on childhood']. While Duras and Wittig might be seen to work towards a common end, Wittig's writing begins precisely where Duras's could or would not go: in the unwavering insistence that sexual differences are socially constructed. Like Beauvoir, Wittig compares the categories of sex to those of race, arguing that both were designed to isolate a group of human beings, construct them as different, and oppress them on the basis of what thereafter appear to be pre-social and essential differences. She describes woman like Beauvoir did, as an ideological and political myth used to form the socio-economic class women, whose individual members are negated as human beings and made to correspond body and soul to the myth of woman. Wittig labels woman the class enemy of women and argues that all heterosexual forms that support it, including linguistic, conceptual and literary structures (like the novel), must be destroyed and new ones created.

Wittig considers literature a battleground where attempts to constitute the subject compete and where s/he who defines the subject also determines social and economic meaning. To transform prevalent notions of subjectivity and help move humankind past the heterosexual paradigm, minority writers must transform their points of view into general models of subject identity. She believes sexism manifests itself in language by restricting minorities to the particular, making their experiences look like anomalies and perversions. They must reclaim the general, abstract and universal voice heterosexual men and Man currently monopolise. If universalising one's point of view is, as Beauvoir argues, the only way to write an important literary work, it is also, Wittig adds, the only political action a text can take. Wittig describes her texts as war machines designed to pulverise traditional narrative forms and conventions, destroy the signifying system structured around the phallus, and create a new one structured around the O. Of the many alchemical symbols in Wittig's work, the O, symbol of transformation, is most prevalent. It tends to change or transform its meanings constantly. At different times, it stands for the vulva, water (*eau*), the island of Lesbos, a mirror, the female breast, the sound of a siren, the mouth, or the *rien* (nothing, zero, o) of female sexuality in Freud. Wittig explicitly links her textual O to the O in Réage's *Histoire d'O*. Where Réage's O is the physical embodiment of the female human caught in the process of her social construction as woman, Wittig's O is a site of transformation, the place and means by which the mark of O's enslavement (O as woman and as branding ring inserted through her labia) is transubstantiated into the epic of female power and emancipation.

Wittig appropriates and rewrites specific literary genres. *L'Opoponax* attacks the humanist *Bildungsroman* and its tale of young love. *Les Guérillères* (1969) destroys the heroic male epic, myths and legends. *Le Corps lesbien* (1973) attacks pornographic literature, the heterosexual construction of female sexual identity, and medical and anatomical discourses of the female body. Suppressing gender, refusing the punctuation marks that divide heterosexual concepts and individuals, and subverting male authors' words, Wittig paves the way for a new subject identity. That new subject often seems to emerge from within the linguistic fabric she demolishes. Take for instance her neologistic *guérillères* (lesbian warrior/solders). To reverse patriarchy's valorisation of the masculine, the novel begins with only feminine characters and objects. This deconstructive strategy seeks to displace heterosexual binary thinking. By the novel's end it seems to have achieved that, for a new subject does emerge. It is identified by a new pronoun, an 'ille', formed of the gendered 'il' and 'elle' of the patriarchal social order. Wittig ironically implies that this 'new' subject has been with us all along, when she puts the *ille* before our eyes, or under our noses, from the novel's title on, as a still unrecognised route out of patriarchy.

Between *L'Opononax* and *Les Guérillères*, and between Duras's *Lol. V. Stein* and her own 1969 fiction-manifesto *Détruire dit-elle*, stands the student-worker revolt of May 1968. A year earlier, Claire Etcherelli's *Elise ou la vraie vie* (1967) had portrayed many of the social tensions that helped produce that uprising. Etcherelli's novel seems to take over where Duras's *Un barrage contre le Pacifique* left off by bringing racism home to Parisian streets and car factories. Much had changed between 1950 and 1967. Duras did not feel that she could identify her *Barrage* heroine's lover as Asian (she feared family reprisal, she said). Etcherelli foregrounds a white Frenchwoman's affair with an Algerian man. While Duras portrayed the author as something of a politically committed saviour, Etcherelli's characters no longer support such non-conflictual notions. They are not unified or in control of their actions and meanings the way the traditional humanist subject purports to be: indeed Etcherelli prefigures 1970s feminist writing by presenting identity as complex, contradictory and conflictual. Although she still relies on realist conventions, she is thus able to deploy the split autobiographical structure in new and exciting ways. Her first-person female narrator recounts her earlier coming of age as a political awakening, restaging the struggle to free her alienated self from patriarchal gender and racist positions. Appearing at a time when the influence of the left-wing revolutionary International Situationists was at its height, *Elise* shows how what Guy Debord calls the *société du spéctacle* alienates working-class women. So doing, *Elise* complements Beauvoir's study of the technocratic alienation of bourgeois women in *Les Belles Images* (1966). Etcherelli's females read the women's magazines Beauvoir's heroines produce and scan their pages for beauty and marital advice. They struggle to conform to the female images Beauvoir's women created and could alone afford. If Etcherelli's women suffer in the attempt, some are able to make light of the chasm separating their work-weary hands and bodies from those demanded of Woman. One even takes a clearly feminist and postcolonial step by aligning gender and colonial oppressions in her appeal to her husband, 'Moi aussi je suis ton Algérie' (*Elise* (Paris: Denoël, 1967) p. 55) ['I too am your Algeria'].

If French students and workers failed to bring down the French government in 1968, that was mainly because the French Communist Party rejected their unorthodox revolutionary methods. May 1968 thus taught the political left not to dialogue with the Party. Female radicals took away a second lesson: their male co-revolutionaries were as phallocratic as the bourgeois enemy. That summer, they set about forming women's groups in Toulouse, Paris and Lyons. In August 1970 Wittig and Rochefort brought feminism to the French front page in a pre-publicised event at the Arc de Triomphe, where they tried to place a wreath to the unknown soldier's less known wife. Borrowing a term from the USA, journalists reported the brief incarceration of members of the Mouvement de libération des femmes (MLF). This rubric was quickly adopted as an umbrella term by the disparate women's groups then meeting at the Sorbonne. Even though these groups rallied around the political goal of ending women's oppression, their political positions and analyses often brought them into open conflict. By 1970 the battle for dominance had been all but won by Antoinette Fouque and Psychanalyse et Politique (Psych et Po), while the radical Féministes révolutionnaires' Monique Wittig had moved to the United States.

Neo-Lacanian writers such as Hélène Cixous, Annie Leclerc and Chantal Chawaf were affiliated with Psych et Po. Theorists influenced by psychoanalysis, such as Julia Kristeva, Luce Irigaray and Michèle Montrelay were not. This is not surprising since Psych et Po were quite vocal in arguing that all theoretical work is hopelessly masculinist. Despite such differences of view, however, most neo-Lacanians share a certain amount of common analytic ground. They agree that when Lacan shows the speaking social subject to be an implicitly *masculine* subject, he simultaneously demonstrates that females are constructed as *objects* in both language (the symbolic) and society. This means, the neo-Lacanians continue, that the sexuality that would define any complete *female* subject is being elided in patriarchal linguistic and social systems. Some say that feminine sexuality (or 'libidinal economy') is repressed, forming an individual and social unconscious; others argue that it is absolutely excluded from both the individual subject and social system. To expand a bit, then, Lacan calls the patriarchal order of language 'the symbolic', and associates it with the father's law and the social order it structures. He calls the pre-social and pre-linguistic realms 'the semiotic' and associates them with the maternal function. Importantly, although he identifies the social and symbolic 'repressed' with feminine sexuality, Lacan emphatically does not believe that its repression could or should be avoided. Most neo-Lacanian feminists enlist and modify his model to study and *end* women's oppression.

Kristeva agrees with Lacan that one must be extremely cautious when it comes to overthrowing the existing order in favour of a fully fledged return of the repressed. Like him she believes that such a total revolution would abandon subjectivity altogether and precipitate humankind into violent and inarticulate chaos. Psych et Po writers disagree. Most of them want, precisely, to dislocate patriarchal language so as to define a fully sexed female subject. They believe that since language forms the subject and its reality, changing language can provoke revolutionary social change. To that end they work to dislocate the exclusionary subject–object relations that, in 1949, Beauvoir already identified with male dominance. They explore alternative subject–object relations and undermine the tools of conventional narrative coherence. They efface genre boundaries, use subject or object pronouns in plurivocal, inconsistent or otherwise confusing ways and reject narrative linearity, often in favour of seemingly endless digression. They use fragmentation, repetition, non-traditional syntax and punctuation, and elliptical or parenthetical phrases. They accentuate textual gaps and silences. They stress to varying degrees the political power of writing. Against Wittig's rejection of sexual difference and the myth Woman, many work on difference. Like Antoinette Fouque, they do not believe that 'women' – that is, female subjects in full possession of their own feminine sexuality – have ever existed. The goal of the women's movement must thus be to bring women and woman into existence. Many psychoanalytic writers appeal to women to write themselves, to invent Woman: Annie Leclerc's *Parole de femme* (1975), Benoîte Groult's *Ainsi soit-elle* (1975), Claudine Hermann's *Les Voleuses de langue* (1976), and Hélène Cixous's *La Jeune Née* and *Le Rire de la Méduse* (both 1975).

Women heeded this call differently. Even theorists whose research on psychoanalysis and women most influenced the course of the modern novel disagreed about the repressed and its relation to social change. In *Révolution du langage poétique* (1974), Kristeva talks of the pre-Oedipal 'semiotic', which she describes as the endless flow of rhythmic pulsions and which, with the 'symbolic' language, constitutes the signifiying process. Rather than gendering the semiotic, she warns against a too facile idealisation of it or of sexual difference. At the same time, she identifies poetic language as a privileged site of change and transformation and encourages its deployment to keep the subject mobile and perhaps productive of social change. In her work on women and gender, especially *'Stabat Mater'* (1979) *'Women's Time'* (1979) and *Histoires d'amour* (1983), she focuses on the mother–child relation as a promising form of subject–object relations. Motherhood, she suggests, is a mode of experience in which the child both is and is not the mother, in which the mother experiences a same which is not same, and which becomes, in the course of time, progressively but never entirely other.

Hélène Cixous defines patriarchy's repressed as the *féminine,* which she describes as a libidinal economy based on the relation to the mother and characterised by generosity, the gift, *dépense* with no thought of return. She tends to focus on internal rather than interpersonal difference. The *écriture féminine* she encourages is a *bisexual* writing that mobilises *'l'autre bisexualité* ... la présence ... des deux sexes, non-exclusion de la différence'* (Cixous and Clément, *La Jeune Née* (Paris: Union Générale d'Editions, 1975), p. 155) ['the other bisexuality, the presence of two sexes, non-exclusion of difference']. As Cixous describes it, feminine writing explores the other within. While Kristeva thinks the mother–child relation from the mother's perspective, Cixous approaches it from the daughter's. She describes writing as a process in which the self goes so close to the other as to be altered by it, while maintaining sufficient distance to avoid fusion. Her 1970s novels often trace the return to the origin of feminine writing, the mother's voice. These novels are dense dialogues between a mobile *je* and *tu* that attempt to free multiple and mobile selves. *Souffles* (1975) and *La Venue à l'écriture* (1977) explore the relation between writing, the maternal voice and the body. *La Missexualité, où jouis-je?* (1976) focuses on the ways in which the feminine economy of the gift can multiply the effects of desire.

In *Speculum de l'autre femme* (1974) and *Ce sexe qui n'en est pas un* (1977), Luce Irigaray argues that the path to a fully sexed female subject begins with the mother. The girl's desire for the mother is displaced to the father at the Oedipal stage, thus exiling her from her own sexuality. Excluded from male 'hom(m)osexual logic', objectified by male thought and gaze – 'specul(aris)ation' – she is unable to retrace her relationship to her origin, access her signifying or sexual pleasures, or achieve independence. Irigaray suggests the unconscious might be formed of repressed or foreclosed femininity; that is, of irrationality or madness, the child, the uncivilised and woman. Irigaray goes on to suggest that the unspoken in the relation to the mother is at the root of hysteria. The hysteric, she contends, speaks that repressed relation, albeit in a mode of paralysed gesturing or tabooed speech. Where Cixous conceptualises the connection between women in individualist terms, Irigaray explores dialogue *between women*, the spontaneous forms of speech she calls *parler-femme* ['women-speak'] as well as an exaggerated and ironic mimicry of male discourse.

As women took up pens to write themselves, they changed the face of autobiography. To them writing represented a process of self-birth aimed at defining new subject identities and social forms. Such self-birth often meant encouraging the return of the repressed. Many writers focused on the relation between madness, women and social change, while critics began to reinterpret women writers politically. Duras was suddenly read as a feminist, as her long-neglected lumpenproletarian 'beggarwoman' emerged from critical shadows to take up the place of Woman, excluded from patriarchal language, rational thought and society and forced to wander their multiple interstices. Psych et Po's publishing house, Editions des Femmes, printed works by ex-mental patients like Emma Santos's *La Malcastrée* (1975), *J'ai tué Emma Santos ou l'écriture colonisée* (1976), *La Loméheuse* (1978). Jeanne Hyvrard's *Mère la mort* (1976) exposed mental-home horrors. Chantal Chawaf's *Retable – La Rêverie* (1976) and Marie Cardinal's *Les Mots pour le dire* (1973) worked on the repressed relation to maternal origin.

Cardinal textualises her break with two origins, her mother and her native Algeria, and makes her recovery from hysteria dependent on coming to terms with both. In her work identity is seen as woven of cross-cultural and cross-class threads, including those involved in her relationship to her mother, who was also formed on multiple and conflicting socio-cultural, ethnic and historical intersections. Many other 1970s and 1980s Franco-phone women helped relativise hegemonic Eurocentric and bourgeois notions of women under patriarchy. Before discussing the ways in which these writers interrogate, expand or complicate the neo-Lacanian account of women's oppression, it is worth noting that some continental writers also reject the exclusively bourgeois model of female identity. Annie Ernaux's *Les Armoires vides* (1974) – to note an outstanding example – traces a white French heroine's sexual identity and oppression across the class divide in France. Assia Djebar's *Femmes d'Alger dans leur appartement* (1980) presents female identities within a rich North African collectivity: Djebar's women laugh and bath and suffer and die together. Individual subjects emerge ephemerally, then cede the place to others. In *Femmes d'Alger*, female identity is defined in relation to the larger group of women and children as well as to Algeria's colonial history and Algerian Islamic cultural tradition, including female circumcision (or female genital mutilation, FGM). For its part, Evelyne Accad's stunning *L'Excisée* (1982) forces readers to rethink the universalising pretensions of Irigaray's idealised two lips and Wittig's O, while Leila Sebbar's *Sherazade* trilogy (1982–91) portrays a young female Beur's effort to construct a viable identity in relation to other Parisian émigré adolescents.

Editions des Femmes also reissued lesbian classics like Liane de Pougy's *Idylle saphique* (1901) in the 1970s. Renée Vivien's *Une Femme m'apparut* (1904) and Natalie Clifford Barney's *Pensées d'une amazone* (1920) and *Nouvelles Pensées de l'amazone*, (1939) enjoyed enhanced readerships. Yourcenar's story of a bisexual seminarian condemned to burn at the stake, *L'Œuvre au noir* (1968), became her most popular novel. Women's heteroerotic novels also increased remarkably. Where *Histoire d'O* marked a certain feminist moment by presenting sado-masochistic violence from a victim's perspective, post-1968 writers often reject Sadean paradigms and focus on female erotics. Duras's *L'Homme assis dans le couloir* (1980) and *La Maladie de la mort* (1982) renounce traditional first-person erotic form for third-person objectivity. While such third-person efforts often result in an ambiguous identification of the narrator with the narrated female object, a more successful female erotic identity is defined in Xavière's *La Punition* (1971), whose first-person narrator traces her struggle and final victory over masochism. Benoîte Groult's *Les Vaisseaux du cœur* (1988) opened the heteroerotic scene to the evolution and agency of a female character. Unwilling to intellectualise her sexuality, her heroine recalls her life-long relationship with a man with whom she shares little but sexuality – he is a Breton fisherman, she a professor and both are married with children. Groult's concrete, detailed description of the desiring female and desired male bodies fills in the silences critics often label 'feminine' but leave abstract and empty. *Les Vaisseaux* resonates with laughter, which women writers from Duras to Irigaray have argued is profoundly disruptive of masculine rationality. Groult's version of the morning after: 'Tandis que j'étale une crème apaisante sur la région sinistrée je m'étonne que les auteurs érotiques ne semblent jamais tenir compte de cet accident du . . . plaisir. Les vagins de leurs héroïnes sont présentés comme d'inusables conduits . . . Quant au mien, c'est comme s'il avait été écorché vif' (Groult, *Les Vaisseaux du cœur* (Paris: Grasset, 1988), p. 221). ['As I spread a soothing lotion on the afflicted area, I am astonished erotic authors never seem to notice this accident of . . . pleasure. They portray their heroines' vaginas as indefatigable conduits . . . As far as mine is concerned, it feels as if it has been flayed'].

While Groult rewrote the desiring female subject, many gay writers were wrestling with the complex issues involved in writing AIDS (in French, *sida*). AIDS discourse was, from its beginning in the early 1980s, highly scientific and bound up in ideological attributions of blame, shame and high-risk. As one critic notes, AIDS 'had no poetic dimension, no literarity with which it entered the world of writing. The only name it had was the scientific one; it entered writing as a fact of life and a fact of death' (Lawrence R. Schehr, 'Hervé Guibert under Bureaucratic Quarantine', *Esprit Créateur* 34, 1 (1994), 73). The challenge, then, was to give AIDS a properly literary dimension. This effort was complicated by the etiology and dynamics of AIDS itself, which work to undermine the mental and physical boundaries of the inflicted writing subject/narrator. AIDS victims perceive themselves as inhabited, some say, by ghosts and memories of lovers past and now dead. Similarly, Hervé Guibert's *Le Protocole compassionel* (1991) portrays his AIDS-infected body as inhabited and sustained by the lost life of a gay dancer whose death alone made contraband medication available to Guibert. AIDS also blurs the boundaries between subject and virus. Uncannily recalling Kristeva's model of motherhood, the AIDS virus 'is both me and not me, different and the same . . . I am both it and not it' (Schehr, p. 81). Yet where Kristeva's maternity is pregnant with narrative and subjective possibilities, death-dealing, parasitic AIDS risks taking over the essential being of the subject and becoming the sole narrative signified. In other words, it threatens subject and narrative with aphasia.

In *Hotel Styx* (1988), Yves Navarre works to neutralise this narrative threat by integrating AIDS into the larger, more universal, story of human life and death. AIDS is but one reason for registering at his Hotel Styx, an idyllic last resort for those seeking a final exit. Navarre's postmodern pastiche paints a world of ever-changing subjects who arrive, emerge briefly into the reader's view, speak briefly of themselves or perhaps engage in last moments of *jouissance*, then disappear without a trace. Cyril Collard's *Nuits fauves* (1991) attempts to raise to the level of tragedy the story of a handsome young HIV positive man who willingly infects naïve adolescent girls. With its film version, *Nuits fauves* did manage to raise reader/viewer awareness of the risk of romanticising AIDS, thus enhancing public support for safe sex programmes in France. In a more interesting scriptural fashion, Hervé Guibert also textualises his battle with AIDS in *A l'ami qui ne m'a pas sauvé la vie* (1990), *Le Protocole compassionel* (1991) and the posthumous *L'Homme au chapeau rouge* (1991) and *Cytomégalovirus* (1992).

A l'Ami presents the early days of Guibert's battle with AIDS and the last of Michel Foucault's. Transcribing Foucault's deathbed admission that AIDS had rendered him speechless, Guibert takes Foucault's avowal as his textual challenge. He recorded and published an intimate account of Foucault's final days and insisted on writing his own AIDS narrative with maximum experiential transparency. Yet Guibert also recognised that a certain distance must be maintained between the writing subject and his AIDS-infected body, for that space alone can prevent the subject from merging with the dying body and permit him to transform AIDS into language. To that end Guibert enlists his experience as a photographer (for *Le Monde*) to write his body. Before his AIDS, in explicitly sexual works such as *Les Chiens* (1982), he focuses on the homosexual inscription of his and other desiring male bodies. From *A l'Ami* on, he works to write his body in pain, sick and dying. So doing, he reappropriates his body from the sole medical gaze and, as in a self-portrait, transforms it into the object and subject of his *sida* narrative as well. His latter novels thus familiarise readers with lexicological and experiential insights into the diagnosis and treatment of AIDS in France. But refusing to let AIDS function as his work's only meaning, he also emphasises the problematic intersections of pain and eroticism as well as of rough gay sex and violating medical AIDS testing procedures, and the power dynamics between medical personnel and *sida* victims. In *Cytomégalovirus* Guibert thematises his struggle against an opportunistic infection that threatened to blind him during his last months. This novel marks the late twentieth century as a time when, for many writers, issues of sexuality and gender seem less relevant and intersubjective relations are constrained by pain, fear and sheaths of rubber. Rather than redefining itself in terms of desire, the AIDS-infected writer traces his/her post-sexual, post-narcissistic path to fragmentation, dissolution and the silence or, as Guibert has it, blindness of death.

SUGGESTIONS FOR FURTHER READING

Nottingham French Studies: Hervé Guibert, Special Issue 1995 (vol. 34, part 1)

Apter, E., 'Fantom Images: Hervé Guibert and the Writing of "sida" in France', in T. F. Murphy and S. Poirier (eds.), *Writing AIDS: Gay Literature, Language, and Analysis* (New York: Columbia University Press, 1993)
Atack, M. and P. Powrie (eds.), *Contemporary French Fiction by Women: Feminist Perspectives* (Manchester: Manchester University Press, 1990)
Butler, J., *Gender Trouble: Feminism and the Subversion of Identity* (London and New York: Routledge, 1990)
Coquillat, M., *Romans d'amour* (Paris: Odile Jacob, 1989)
Durham, C. A., *The Contexture of Feminism: Marie Cardinal and Multicultural Literacy* (Urbana and Chicago: University of Illinois Press, 1992)
Fallaize, E., *The Novels of Simone de Beauvoir* (London and New York: Routledge, 1988)
  French Women's Writing: Recent Fiction (London: Macmillan, 1993)
Frappier-Mazur, L., 'Marginal Canons: Rewriting the Erotic', *Yale French Studies* 75 (1988), 112–28
Fuss, D., *Essentially Speaking* (London: Routledge, 1989)
Gallop, J., *The Daughter's Seduction: Feminism and Psychoanalysis* (Ithaca: Cornell University Press, 1982)
Hewitt, L., *Autobiographical Tightropes* (Lincoln: University of Nebraska Press, 1990)
Lévy, J. and A. Nouss, *SIDA-Fiction: essai d'anthropologie romanesque* (Lyon: Presses Universitaires de Lyon, 1994)
Lionnet, F., *Autobiographical Voices* (Ithaca: Cornell University Press, 1989)
Moi, T., *Sexual/Textual Politics* (London and New York: Methuen, 1985)
  Simone de Beauvoir: The Making of an Intellectual Woman (Oxford, UK, and Cambridge, MA: Blackwell, 1993)
Ostrovosky, E., *A Constant Journey: The Fiction of Monique Wittig* (Carbondale: Southern Illinois University Press, 1991)
Shiach, M., *Hélène Cixous: A Politics of Writing* (London and New York: Routledge, 1991)
Silverman, K., '*Histoire d'O*: The Construction of a Female Subject', in C. Vance (ed.), *Pleasure and Danger* (London: Routledge, 1984)
Stambolian, G. and E. Marks (eds.), *Homosexualities and French Literature* (Ithaca and London: Cornell University Press, 1979)
Whitford, M., *Luce Irigaray: Philosophy in the Feminine* (London and New York: Routledge, 1991)
Winston, J., 'Forever Feminine: Marguerite Duras and Her Critics', *New Literary History* 24 (1993), 467–82
  'Marguerite Duras: Marxism, Feminism, Writing', *Theatre Journal* 47 (1995), 345–65

15

JOHNNIE GRATTON

Postmodern French fiction: practice and theory

As several contributors to this volume have indicated, the modern French novel has shown a particularly strong capacity for questioning and redefining itself. This dynamic of constant self-renewal expresses the broader vitality of modernism at large, understood as a general ethos informing a variety of artistic movements since the 1880s, all bent on expanding, and in some cases exploding, a space of representation deemed to be unduly monopolised by codes inherited from the past. In the modern novel, as in the visual arts, the main codes under attack are those sustained by the orthodoxy of classical nineteenth-century realism, with the attack itself often being justified in the name of a 'higher' form of the same basic mimetic urge, such as 'psychological' realism, which prioritises the inner world of human subjectivity, or 'phenomenological' realism, which tracks the outer world as physically experienced by a human subject. Modernism, then, is characterised by a strongly felt need to effect a break with the past, which in turn generates a search, often conducted in an experimental spirit, for new forms and modes of artistic expression. In the twentieth century, this modernist logic of rupture and renewal, central to the very concept of an 'avant-garde', provides the framework within which most theorising about the novel has taken place.

But a growing consensus now exists to the effect that, under the sway of post-industrial society, even this modernist framework has broken down, giving way to a different cultural condition, loosely described as 'postmodern', and a different aesthetic project, loosely described as 'postmodern*ist*'. In this chapter I am mainly interested in the term 'postmodern', which I take to describe a broad new cultural sensibility, part mood, part ethos, marked by a loss of faith in the idea of underlying truths or overriding values. This sensibility breaks in particular with the modernist belief in progress, development, evolution. Abandoning the modernist contract with the future, postmodernism seeks rather to explore the possibilities of the present through a return to the past. Finally, more aware of the local and provisional nature of all intellectual endeavour, the postmodern sensibility encourages a new modesty within the humanities. Totalising theories are no longer considered tenable, and the perspective of the individual subject is correspondingly rehabilitated. As such, the postmodern sensibility reacts strongly against avant-gardism, shunning both its doctrinaire arrogance as a discourse and its very status as a future-orientated ideology. Indeed one aim of the present chapter will be to show how the French version of this sensibility helps explain what has become ever more evident over the last few decades, namely the fact that 'theory' in its most overt, avant-gardist form has ceased to accompany novelistic practice, giving way to an age of reticence, even as contemporary French fiction continues to demonstrate a high level of sophistication and self-consciousness.

My starting point, then, is the idea of a postmodern sensibility – which, I shall argue, can in the case of France be seen to emerge at a fairly precise historical moment. For this reason I am interested in identifying developments in French post-war fiction which are symptomatically and not just programmatically postmodern, trends which don't necessarily *think of themselves* as 'postmodern'. This also happened to be a necessary move in the French context, where right through to the early 1990s postmodernism has remained a largely unfamiliar concept. Indeed, despite Jean-François Lyotard's highly influential essay *La Condition postmoderne* (1979), French writers and critics have until quite recently regarded postmodernism as an essentially American, and therefore rather suspect, commodity. In the Anglo-American world, postmodernism as an area of study has gone from strength to strength: a phenomenon as yet without parallel in metropolitan France, where postmodernism has only recently been taken up as a serious issue in philosophy and the social sciences, while it has still barely emerged at all as a framework for literary studies.

In recent years the question of postmodernism has surfaced in retrospective assessments of the *nouveau roman*, the literary phenomenon which, more than any other, advocated theory as the necessary counterpart of novelistic practice. The *nouveau roman*, represented primarily by the fiction of Michel Butor, Alain Robbe-Grillet, Nathalie Sarraute and Claude Simon, first came to prominence in the 1950s. What bonded these new novelists together was their common desire to challenge the continuing hegemony of classic 'Balzacian' realism which, through its technical emphasis on plot and characterisation, they saw as drawing a falsely reassuring map of human experience. In rejecting a tradition which seemed to have survived the exemplary subversions of Proust, Joyce, Kafka and others, the *nouveau roman* met with the immediate approval of an influential young critic, Roland Barthes. Thus began an alliance which would develop through the 1960s into a prolonged and rewarding exchange between the practitioners of the *nouveau roman* and a new generation of literary critics steeped in structuralism, a cross-disciplinary intellectual movement which took meaning away from the domain of human agency, indeed away from single entities of any kind, and located it instead in the relationships between entities, seen now as nodal points holding together a 'signifying system'. By the 1970s, under the guidance of the critic and novelist Jean Ricardou, the *nouveau roman* had entered into a new phase, occasionally dubbed the *nouveau nouveau roman*. The ambiguity of certain early examples of the new novel – most famously, perhaps, Robbe-Grillet's *La Jalousie* (1957) – had encouraged readers to interpret them referentially, as subtle instances of psychological or phenomenological realism. Ricardou sought to eliminate such ambiguity, and with it the unquestionable fascination of a text like *La Jalousie*, by promoting a more radically intransitive fictional practice in which the productivity of language would take over as prime mover from the expressivity of a subject. To echo Ricardou's most memorable slogan, the 'new new' novel would reverse the writing of an adventure into the adventure of writing.

The case for regarding the *nouveau roman* as an instance of postmodernist fiction has been made most forcefully by Edmund Smyth.[1] Distinguishing three phases of development, Smyth places the first within the modernist paradigm in so far as it remains ambiguous in the manner just noted. The second phase corresponds to the ascendancy of the so-called *nouveau nouveau roman*, as practised by its strongest advocate, Jean Ricardou, and the two novelists most directly influenced by him, Robbe-Grillet and Claude Simon. It is at this point that for Smyth the 'new' novel appears to go 'postmodern':

> It would be difficult to find more suitable candidates for postmodern fictionality than the novels of Simon and Robbe-Grillet at this time. These plural, heterogeneous and non-totalized novels vividly proclaim their metafictional status, referring constantly to the processes of their own production. They would seem to demonstrate the proposition that a text can only ever designate its own activity, that textuality is inherently narcissistic. (p. 67)

Here Smyth identifies the postmodern turn mainly in terms of 'metafictionality', the condition whereby a text refers not beyond itself but to itself, in such a way as to exhibit the processes or ground rules governing its construction. Such a characterisation of the postmodern novel is, however, questionable. For one thing, at the level of literary history, the radical metafictionality under discussion here found its ultimate home not in the subsequent development of the novel but in the avant-garde experiment-alism of the *Tel Quel* group (led by Philippe Sollers), which was always far more preoccupied with exemplifying genre-free concepts such as *texte* and *écriture* than with renewing the tradition of narrative fiction, and which anyway came to a virtual dead end in 1983 when the journal which gave the group its name was dissolved. Furthermore, at the level of theory, Linda Hutcheon has argued that metafictionality on its own is a modernist phenomenon, not unlike abstract art, in that it doesn't so much 'transgress' codes of narrative representation as 'leave them alone'. The term post-modernism as applied to fiction, she suggests, should be 'reserved to describe the more paradoxical and historically complex form' she chooses to call 'historiographic metafiction'.[2]

Smyth himself clearly goes on to endorse this view as he proceeds to posit a third phase of the *nouveau roman* which he also wants to describe as postmodern, despite its retreat from the pure metafictionality advocated by Ricardou. This third phase, which began to have a major impact in the 1980s, is characterised above all by the emergence of an autobiographical dimension. Smyth is careful to point out, however, that, in texts like Nathalie Sarraute's *Enfance* (1983), Marguerite Duras's *L'Amant* (1984), Alain Robbe-Grillet's *Le Miroir qui revient* (1984), and Claude Simon's *L'Acacia* (1989), the element of autobiography does not go unproblema-tised. On the contrary, 'an examination of such works reveals a post-modernist contestation of the conventional boundaries between genres and an intertextual mixture of writings, of which the fragmented subjectivity of the writer was itself a discourse capable of being plundered in order to generate text' (pp. 71–2). Like history in Hutcheon's 'historiographic metafiction', subjectivity returns as something always already textualised, always found under a description, and therefore always more 'made' than 'found'. In fact one begins to find it regrettable that Hutcheon did not leave her definition of the postmodern novel more open, for the paradoxical/complex form we encounter most prominently in the contemporary French domain is not so much 'historiographic metafiction' (though Simon's novels come close to such a description) as a mode we could justifiably call 'autobiographic(al) metafiction'.

Moving beyond the confines of the *nouveau roman*, I shall now outline some of the broader cultural developments which need to be taken into account in any attempt to understand what postmodernism or post-modernity might be taken to mean in the French context. It is important to recognise that the emergence of an autobiographical dimension in the work of writers formerly associated with the *nouveau roman* is in fact part of a widespread phenomenon which came to be known in France as 'le retour du sujet', the return of the human subject as an active force with a legitimate perspective, itself part of an even more far-reaching process of change occasioned by the demise of the structuralist paradigm which had dominated French intellectual life from the mid-fifties through to the mid-seventies.

According to François Dosse, in his comprehensive history of the structuralist movement in France, structuralism entered into a period of decline from about 1967, before reaching terminal crisis-point in 1975.[3] The disarray of French left-wing politics around this time saw off any lingering attraction intellectuals might have felt towards the structuralist Marxism of Louis Althusser which, in its aspiration to become a science of history, had reduced the status of the human subject to that of a nodal point, a mere locus of conflicting social forces. According to Dosse, what lay more generally behind such abstraction was the ambition to unify the human sciences around a common method. But by 1975 a new eclectic and non-sectarian spirit was in the air. Thus a globalising ambition that had once looked laudable now appeared to be losing touch with the latest developments, as the dimension of the human agent was gradually reintroduced into academic disciplines throughout the human and social sciences. The human agent, the 'subject', was back.

In the French context, the idea often dramatised as 'the end of theory' derives from this waning of intellectual confidence in all-encompassing systems of thought such as structuralism and Marxism. In his highly influential study La Condition postmoderne, written just four years after the tide finally turned against Marxist-structuralist globalism, Jean-François Lyotard defined the postmodern attitude precisely as one of 'incredulity' towards 'metanarratives' or 'grand narratives' (métarécits/grands récits), that is, towards wholesale, overarching, grandiose theories of explanation which absorb smaller, lower-order narratives and claim access to their true meaning.[4] Retrospectively it is clear that such postmodern incredulity has resulted in a general 'return' to the subject. The dimension of personal experience has been restored as an important factor in numerous areas of academic and intellectual enquiry, not only as an object of study, but as a kind of methodological principle, while, in the domain of literary and cultural studies in particular, many researchers have been led to experiment with an overtly autobiographical style of critical discourse. French post-modernism, then, is not just about 'deconstructing' the subject, as often tends to be suggested; it is more properly about restoring the subject and, in the process, revising it.

Among the major figures associated with post-war French theory, Dosse singles out three – Roland Barthes, Tzvetan Todorov and Michel Foucault

– as the critics whose changing intellectual concerns most dramatically embody the return of the subject. I shall take this opportunity to focus on the case of Barthes, partly because his own return to the subject leads him irresistibly towards a literary practice.

An early exponent of structuralist analysis, but never a slave to method, Barthes is probably best known for his apocalyptic-sounding announcement of the 'death of the author' in 1968. As Barthes then saw it, the 'author' was little more than a glorified version of the subject as construed by humanist philosophy: a bountiful source of all kinds of initiatives. Against this he wished to promote an image of writing as the inscription of a 'champ sans origine',[5] a field without an origin, complemented by an image of meaning as a matter of negotiation between a text and its reader. And yet, within seven years, by the watershed year of 1975 in fact, Barthes had gradually come round to a position where he could produce a work whose title, *Roland Barthes par Roland Barthes* (Paris: Seuil, 1975), appeared, however ironically, to announce a self-portrait.[6] The text turns out, of course, to be no ordinary work of autobiography. On the contrary, it demonstrates all the 'complex' and 'paradoxical' qualities which Linda Hutcheon associates with the postmodern aesthetic. Composed of alphabetically ordered fragments, it is a consciously hybrid work, a patchwork. While shunning the narrative continuities of a life story, it is not averse to narrating moments of personal experience in short bursts. It juxtaposes essayistic snatches of critical and theoretical discourse with memories, photographic and other illustrations, and outbreaks of confessionalism revealing Barthes's desire to be a writer, and not just a critic or theorist. The inescapable paradox of this book is that it is at once a work of autobiography and one of anti-autobiography. The subject returns, but under suspicion, as Barthes's much commented epigraph, on the inside leaf of the front cover, indicates: 'Tout ceci doit être considéré comme dit par un personnage de roman' ['All this must be regarded as spoken by a character in a novel'].

There is no doubt, however, that in *Fragments d'un discours amoureux* (1977) and *La Chambre claire* (1980), the remaining works of his autobiographical trilogy, Barthes became progressively less guarded and ironic in his rehabilitation of the subject. Indeed the way he presents his investigation into the nature of photography in *La Chambre claire* as an extended sequential quest narrative, set out in chapters rather than fragments, suggests that his last work came close to being a kind of novel. At the same time, written in the shadow of his mother's death, this is Barthes's most deeply personal work, an ethical reclamation of the rights of individual experience, in which the still rather sober idiom of the 'subject' has been overtaken by an emotional concern for the 'truth' or 'essence' of identity. One is led to ask whether Barthes by 1980 had not already moved beyond postmodernism, or at least beyond the postmodern aesthetic as defined by critics like Hutcheon.

Barthes's writing during the late 1970s confirms A. Kibédi Varga's view that postmodern literature is based on the three-fold return of the subject, of ethics, and of narrative.[7] Indeed Barthes's 1975 self-portrait in particular was instrumental in bringing about this return in so far as it cleared a path later to be followed by the former *nouveaux romanciers*. However, the way Barthes's writing *evolved* over the 1970s signally fails to confirm Kibédi Varga's proviso that reconciliation with the 'narratable world' can only be achieved in an ironic mode (p. 16). On the contrary, it suggests that this three-fold return, once mobilised, may express itself across a much broader canvas than that covered by postmodern irony. As a general phenomenon, in fact, this return can be said to have created the conditions under which a number of novelists working well outside the catchment area of the *nouveau roman* came, from the late sixties onwards, to earn recognition from the critical and academic establishment. One thinks notably of Marguerite Yourcenar, Patrick Modiano and Michel Tournier. I shall now dwell briefly on Tournier, the most amenable of these three to evaluation as an author of postmodern fiction.

By the mid-1970s Michel Tournier's place as a major French novelist had already been firmly established on the strength of his first, and arguably best, three novels: *Vendredi ou les limbes du Pacifique* (1967), *Le Roi des Aulnes* (1970) and *Les Météores* (1975). Tournier came to fiction from philosophy. For a long time he saw himself as an intruder bent on rescuing the novel from itself, and more specifically from the *nouveau roman*, by employing traditional narrative forms to smuggle in far from conventional themes. If his fiction has a postmodern aspect, it is not so much despite its traditionalism as because of it. In stark contrast to the Balzac-bashing of Ricardou and Robbe-Grillet, Tournier's attitude towards the past is non-antagonistic. In recognisably postmodern fashion, Tournier treats the past as a kind of vast archive filled with a rich variety of narrative materials waiting to be recycled. His traditionalism leads him, then, not into a sterile reassertion of past forms and values but into a practice of rewriting. This is most obvious in the case of *Vendredi*, a rewriting of Defoe's *Robinson Crusoe*, whose very title, now highlighting the name of Man Friday, gives just one indication of the many shifts and reversals implemented by the novel. Beyond the rewriting of a specific text, Tournier's novel in fact engages with a range of past texts, from philosophical tracts to adventure stories. The novel thus strongly evinces another quality closely associated with the postmodern aesthetic, that of intertextuality, whereby the creation of fictional worlds is mediated, and in the process often problematised, by acts of reference to other texts.

The same general procedures are evident once more in *Le Roi des Aulnes*, a novel which, in tracing the career of one Abel Tiffauges between 1938 and 1945, draws upon a variegated intertextual archive of epic, fantastic, fairy-tale, philosophical and historiographic elements. The last element in this list denotes the fact that Tournier, in his concern for historical accuracy, carried out careful research into conditions and circumstances in Nazi Germany during the Second World War. But, like Yourcenar the historical novelist, refusing to get locked into an aesthetic of pure period reconstruction, like Modiano setting his otherwise hazy fictions in a Paris historically verifiable down to the smallest detail, Tournier in *Le Roi des Aulnes* includes realism only as part of his agenda. And it is above all the heterogeneity of that agenda, the astonishing mix of both narrative tools and narrative materials, which makes *Le Roi des Aulnes* worthy of inclusion in any history of postmodern fiction.

Published in 1970, *Le Roi des Aulnes* exhibits many of the features listed by Bruno Vercier and Jacques Lecarme as characterising the vitality of narrative writing in France throughout the rest of that decade: 'the end of the aggressively theoretical avant-garde, the emergence of minority voices ... a return to readability and representation, concern for the materiality of language, experimentation with parody and rewriting, a writing of the I which cancels the distinction between novel and autobiography.'[8] All of these features have at various times been claimed on behalf of the poetics of postmodernism, and in this chapter I have tried to demonstrate the particular importance of the first and last features for an understanding of postmodernism in the French context. In further exploring the question of postmodern narrative in France since 1975, I shall now return to the last of these features as my starting point for a discussion of the broader phenomenon of generic crossover.

The crossing of genre boundaries is part of a wider questioning of our fixed conceptions of borders, as found in philosophy (where deconstructionism, for instance, unsettles basic oppositions such as outside versus inside), at the level of scholarship in general (where interdisciplinary studies are changing the boundaries, identities, and methodologies of traditional subject-areas), or indeed at the level of socio-political reality (where the phenomena of multiculturalism and transnationalism make us constantly rethink our ideas about borders). When it comes to the literary field, generic crossover has been identified as a postmodern phenomenon by numerous critics, not least Linda Hutcheon in *A Poetics of Postmodernism*:

The borders between literary genres have become fluid: who can tell anymore what the limits are between the novel and the short story collection (Alice Munro's *Lives of Girls and Women*), the novel and the long poem (Michael Ondaatje's *Coming Through Slaughter*), the novel and autobiography (Maxine Hong Kingston's *China Men*), the novel and history (Salman Rushdie's *Shame*), the novel and biography (John Banville's *Kepler*)? But, in any of these examples, the conventions of the two genres are played off against each other; there is no simple, unproblematic merging.   (p. 9)

Can recent French literature boast a similar history of generic mixing? More importantly, can it match Hutcheon's list of generically mixed works in terms of quality? I think it can and in support of my belief I shall now highlight in turn two such works of exceptional merit, both published since 1975, Georges Perec's *La Vie mode d'emploi* and Marguerite Duras's *L'Amant*, following up each presentation with a brief survey of subsequent developments in contemporary narrative prose writing which the work in question might be said to have anticipated or encouraged. That neither work bears the official designation *roman*, and that I in turn am led to speak in terms of a generality ('narrative prose writing'), only serves to underline how the novel's famed capacity to absorb other genres may well be turning into a reverse capacity to be absorbed by other genres.

Published in 1978, but written over a nine-year period, Georges Perec's *La Vie mode d'emploi* sets out to describe in detail what would be revealed to the eye if a Parisian apartment block, in the manner of a doll's house, suddenly had its façade peeled away. Whence the novel's brilliantly realised merger of temporal and spatial coordinates into a 'chronotope', an overall unit of representation, a particular kind of narrative 'world', consisting here of a group of apartments, along with the various animate and inanimate objects visible inside them, all frozen in a single present moment, set just before 8.00 p.m. on 23 June 1975.

Among the many striking features of *La Vie mode d'emploi*, the one which most concerns me here is the peculiarity of the novel's dual status as both a descriptive and a narrative act (for comments on formal discipline and patterning in *La Vie mode d'emploi*, the reader is referred to David Walker's chapter in the present volume, pp. 142–3). The text sets out, as already mentioned, to be a global act of description. Its descriptive order is primary in that, most unusually in terms of fictional norms, it is not subservient to the act of narration. Within any given chapter, corresponding to any given room in the apartment building, the narrator as describer proceeds to draw up a dispassionate, often extremely detailed inventory of the objects visible to his gaze. Because these objects are all frozen in time, narrativity as such appears to be excluded. At best, certain characters are construed as being about to perform, or as having just performed, certain actions. Persons, moreover, are not necessarily foregrounded at the expense of inanimate objects. Indeed, the constant effect of flatness induced by the narrator's descriptions suggests strongly that he is engaged in representing not a reality but something which is already a two-dimensional representation – a painting, for instance. Collapse of depth in the representational field is reinforced by a loss of eloquence in the objects represented. Few manage to say anything of significance about their owners, and, more generally, very few are shown to bear any 'aura' of originality or authenticity. In this respect, the descriptive dimension alone would be enough to make Perec's text qualify as a distinctly postmodern novel.

But Perec's text is not just descriptive, for virtually every chapter finds a way of breaking into the narrative mode and generating an *histoire*, which may be the story of a past or present occupant of the room in question, but might equally be inspired by a painting on a wall. It is this profusion of micro-narratives which Perec signals when, to the title of his work, he adds the pluralised subtitle, *romans*. The novel, then, is also a collection of short stories of the kind often described as a 'framed miscellany', with the apartment block providing the frame. As Claude Burgelin suggests, Perec's models in this respect are the *Thousand and One Nights* and the *Decameron*, whose enclosed settings provide the ideal launching pad for the narrative excursions of the story-teller.[9]

Whereas modern short fiction has tended to invest more and more in a 'chronotope' characterised by reduced time-spans, delimited spaces, and the attenuated narrativity of a single incident or moment of experience, Perec's *histoires* recycle a more old-fashioned poetics based on the compressed life-story. Individual stories are recounted rapidly, with little concern for plausibility, in a zany picaresque style which brings their protagonists through successive episodes, stages, places and identities until inevitably they meet their death, often a violent one. Little concern is shown for subjective realism or psychological complexity. Most of the huge cast of characters put on display by Perec demonstrate the same core feature. Obsessively bent on having or knowing something, they dedicate their lives to an intense yet methodical and, for most, ultimately futile quest. As such, these protagonists hail less from the world of the modern novel than from that of the classical short story, where characterisation tends to be based on the exaggeration or magnification of a single defining feature. Like the text's descriptive order, then, its narrative order shows distinctly postmodern qualities, firstly by virtue of the way it revamps past narrative styles in order to produce splendidly inventive stories, and secondly by taking the form of a multiplicity of little stories rather than one continuous narrative.

This quality of narrative proliferation, reminiscent of the fictions of Salman Rushdie and Gabriel García Márquez, also brings the text into the hybrid domain of what has come to be known in French as the *roman-par-nouvelles*. In this respect, *La Vie mode d'emploi* may be said to have helped generate a new and vibrant direction in French fiction, as represented in more recent years by works like Paul Fournel's *Les Grosses Rêveuses* (1982), Didier Daeninckx's *Le Facteur fatal* (1990), Jean-Christophe Duchon-Doris's *Les Lettres du baron* (1994) and Gilbert Lascault's *Gens ordinaires de Sore-les-Sept-Jardins* (1994). The encyclopaedic spirit and sheer technical ambition of Perec's *romans* are also echoed in Olivier Rolin's impressive 500-page fiction, *L'Invention du monde* (1993), which tells the history of the world on a particular day, the spring equinox of 1989, through a host of factually based stories drawn from almost 500 newspapers published in thirty-one languages. Where Perec started with a single place, Rolin starts with a single day. But in each case the end result is a remarkable proliferation of stories and story-telling, an ebullient, postmodern *return* to narrative.

By the time she won the 1984 Prix Goncourt for *L'Amant*, Marguerite Duras was already a firmly established writer on the French, and indeed the international, literary scene. While some of her early writing was associated with the *nouveau roman*, much of her later work has been read by critics, occasionally with the author's own endorsement, as an instance of *écriture féminine*. By the 1980s, however, it had become clear that Duras's ultimate commitment was to the unconditional nature of writing. Writing as such could no more be tied to any preformed set of ideas outside it than it could be conveniently channelled into the mould of a single genre. Duras had moreover long since moved beyond the conventions of realism and psychologism. Increasingly intense, elliptical and rhapsodic, her writing continued to be drawn ineluctably towards extreme states of being: states of desire, passion and madness, always on the edge of non-being, always suspended between reparation and separation. Given such leanings, it was very unlikely that, in turning towards her own experience with unprecedented directness, Duras would produce anything resembling a straightforward work of autobiography.

L'Amant can easily be made to sound straightforward, as in the blurb on the back cover of the English paperback translation: '*Saigon, 1930s*: a poor young French girl meets the elegant son of a wealthy Chinese family. Soon they are lovers, locked into a private world of passion and intensity that defies all the conventions of their society.'[10] But this is to ignore the constant defiance of *narrative* conventions which here as elsewhere determines the character of Duras's writing. Early in the text of *L'Amant*, for example, Duras makes a statement which has since been read as articulating a key tenet of postmodern autobiography: 'L'histoire de ma vie n'existe pas. Ça n'existe pas. Il n'y a jamais de centre. Pas de chemin, pas de ligne. Il y a de vastes endroits où l'on fait croire qu'il y avait quelqu'un, ce n'est pas vrai il n'y avait personne' (*L'Amant,* p. 14) ['The story of my life does not exist. It does not exist. There is never a centre. No path, no line. There are great spaces where you create the illusion that there was someone. But it is not true, there was no one']. Life as such has no classical pattern. It is uncentred, non-teleological, and non-linear. The subject of experience is not necessarily the subject of a continuous, unfolding, life story. I can of course use the inaugural power of language to engineer such a story, but this would be to produce 'fiction' in a bad sense, fiction as pretence, creating the illusion that there was someone – myself or another? – when really there was no one. Instead, in order to respect a certain truth, or at least to challenge a certain untruth ('ce n'est pas vrai'), it becomes necessary to narrate according to a different temporal and thematic logic, one which incorporates displacement and digression, ellipsis and fragmentation. This said, it is important to add that Duras in *L'Amant* does give us a firm if intermittent sense of chronological and narrative progression, through which we see the relationship between a young European girl and her Chinese lover form and, even as it is crystallising, begin to move unavoidably towards the point of separation. This relationship occupies the focal space of the narrative, the essentially porous space of desire, whose textualisation will constantly open onto other spaces, and with them other times, such as that of the girl's family and – in the form of a kind of portrait gallery – that of other women.

The non-existence of my life story also makes it necessary for me to produce 'fiction' in a good sense: fiction as making and not just making up; fiction as the corollary of imagination, fantasy and desire; fiction as the supplement of memory (a supplement probably always already *in* memory). In short, fiction is coextensive with the idea of a performative dimension. It affirms the increasingly highlighted 'act-value' of autobiographical writing at the expense of its traditionally supposed 'truth-value'.

Among the many indications Duras gives in *L'Amant* of this shift from truth-value to act-value, the most striking lies in the way she handles the key motif of the 'image'. This refers basically to the self-image which formed in the mind of the fifteen-year-old protagonist at the moment she first met her future lover, while crossing the Mekong river on a ferry. From the very outset narrator and protagonist converge in this image inasmuch as it represents for both of them a source of narcissistic satisfaction. It is also a strangely temporal image, spread out over both the time of narrated experience – 'L'image dure pendant toute la traversée du fleuve' (p. 11) ['The image lasts all the way across the river'] – and the time of narration, where it is slowly built up, detail by detail. Beyond literal duration, the time of the image is the symbolic or mythical time of a crossing-over, a rite of passage: for the child, a passage towards womanhood, sexuality, knowledge of pleasure and death; for the writer, a passage towards her own past experience.

That the image proves to be not just empowering for the girl but enabling for the author in her role as narrator is confirmed in remarkable fashion when Duras, moving beyond psychologism, proceeds to compare what was initially a mental representation to a photographic image. A photograph might have been taken, we are told, but was not taken because only God could have foreseen such an important event in the girl's life: 'C'est pourquoi, cette image, il ne pouvait pas en être autrement, elle n'existe pas. Elle a été omise. Elle a été oubliée. Elle n'a pas été détachée, enlevée à la somme. C'est à ce manque d'avoir été faite qu'elle doit sa vertu, celle de représenter un absolu, d'en être justement l'auteur' (p. 17) ['That is why the image – things could not have been otherwise – does not exist. It was omitted, left behind. It was not detached or removed from the whole. And it owes its virtue – the virtue of representing an absolute, indeed of being its author – to the fact that it was never created']. The non-existent photograph, a direct analogue of the non-existent life story, asserts the absence for Duras of any possibility of simply or transparently re-presenting the past. Autobiographical writing cannot therefore be held within the economy of truth-value. Going a crucial step further, Duras even proposes that the image's power (now) lies in its not having been fixed like a photograph (then). It is on this condition that the image comes to represent an 'absolute'. It is not relative, not anchored to an origin, because its 'creator' – Duras herself uses the term *auteur* to forge this paradox of almost mystical status – is a failure, a lack, a non-event. The limited refiguring power of the photograph gives way to the more ample power of the virtual image, which is *con*-figurational in the sense that it summons together the acts of remembering, imagining and writing.

In France over the last twenty-five years, the entanglement of fiction and autobiography has proved to be an attractive and enduring mix. Among writers, its appeal has stretched far beyond those, like Duras, associated with the *nouveau roman*. Notable successes include Serge Doubrovsky's fascinating series of self-styled *autofictions* and Pierre Michon's remarkable *Vies minuscules* (1984). Using a blend of memory and imaginative projection, the narrator of Michon's text homes in on others he has known or met in the past. Transforming their existences one by one into 'lives', he gradually brings into focus the contours of his own wretched existence. The book can be read as a novel, a collection of short stories, a work of biography, and a work of autobiography. Its mixing of genres directly anticipates the creation in 1989 of the Gallimard series 'L'un et l'autre', whose programme, printed inside the back page of all texts in the series, constitutes nothing less than an agenda for postmodern biography:

> Lives, but as memory invents them, as our imaginations recreate them, as passions enliven them. Subjective stories, miles away from traditional biography.
>
> *L'un et l'autre*: the author and the author's secret hero, the painter and the painter's model, linked by a strong, intimate bond. Between the portrait of another and a self-portrait, where is the dividing line to be located?
>
> *Les uns et les autres*: not just those who have gloried in the limelight, but those who are present only on our inner stage, people or places, forgotten faces, erased names, vanishing outlines.   (My translation)

Presumably composed by the series editor J.-B. Pontalis, this programme could serve as a fitting introduction to many works written independently of the series, and even prior to it, such as Annie Ernaux's soberly impressive 'auto-socio-biographical' narratives, *La Place* (1984) and *Une Femme* (1988). Indeed, in its advocacy of creative subjectivism, in its vision of a dialogical relation between self and other across destabilised borders, and in its call for a return of the forgotten or repressed other, this condensed yet open text constitutes a key theoretical statement of the 1980s. The series itself, moreover, fuels a powerful trend in contemporary French literature, which, though it embraces the *romanesque*, ultimately threatens to absorb creative energies which might otherwise have gone into writing a *roman*. Interest among writers in autobiography, and not just biography, also continues to run high in the 1990s, as demonstrated not only by the quality of texts published in Gallimard's (originally Hatier's) important series 'Haute Enfance', but by the fact that so many of the contributors are relatively young. The risk to the novel is summed up in the fact that one of France's most gifted contemporary writers, Pierre Bergounioux, has, since the publication of *La Toussaint* in 1994, abandoned the use of the subtitle *roman*, a term which suggests, wrongly as he sees it, that what he has to tell exists only in the telling.

Alongside Michon, Jean-Loup Trassard, and to some extent Christian Bobin, Bergounioux belongs to a loose constellation of highly regarded authors who often explore rural or regional themes and who write correspondingly in the poetic and (auto)biographical margins of narrative fiction. These authors join the broader coalition I have just outlined, making it possible to assert that perhaps the most discernible trend in contemporary French literature is one which draws on the rich resources of the novel only all the more effectively to take leave of the novel.

This is not to deny the continuing variety and vitality of writing 'within' the contemporary novel. Indeed French fiction has become so diverse, and at the same time so theoretically reticent, that it is extremely difficult to map it in terms of significant tendencies. Keeping to my own perspective, and leaving aside potentially relevant areas covered in previous chapters, I shall conclude by highlighting two tendencies which exhibit in very different ways the increasing impact on contemporary French fiction of a postmodern sensibility.

The first takes the nowadays rare form of an explicitly defined tendency, as represented by a group of writers who in 1992 agreed to stand under the common banner of 'la nouvelle fiction' by appearing together in a collection of interviews and extracts edited by Jean-Luc Moreau.[11] What these writers share above all is a common return to the illusionism, mythical resonance and sheer inventiveness of stories, favouring narrative extravagance over psychological and historical realism. As so often since 1975, the degree of 'return' is measured directly in terms of a given writer's dissension from the overkill policies of the *nouveau roman*. Accordingly Moreau's preface-cum-manifesto invokes the ideas of Robert Louis Stevenson in what proves to be an awkward and unsuccessful effort to broach theory without lapsing into heavy theorism. The strongest theoretical insights are in fact found in the interviews, notably those with Frédéric Tristan, Georges-Olivier Châteaureynaud, Hubert Haddad and Marc Petit, all recognised in France as accomplished writers. It is Tristan, perhaps, who best sums up the significance of that postmodern return or reversal in which he as a writer feels directly engaged, and which I have sought to highlight throughout the present chapter: 'Modernity's great push towards wholesale desacralisation inevitably led to an emptying of narrative. Today, with the reversal of that tendency under what some call postmodernity, story-making [*le récit*] is called upon to reclaim its privileged role as a simultaneously mythifyng and demystifying agency' (p. 87).

The idea of regenerating the disenchanted world of modernity has an important place within the postmodern ethos, where it continues to exist, however, alongside a cooler, less vitalistic view of postmodernity. This is the view reflected in the work of a number of young writers, notably Jean-Philippe Toussaint, Jean Echenoz and Christian Oster, who, because their work seems to hark back to the *nouveau roman*, itself historically associated with their own common publisher, have been described as forming a new 'école de Minuit'. Using a mini-corpus made up of Toussaint's

L'Appareil-photo (1988), Echenoz's *Nous trois* (1992) and Oster's *Le Pont d'Arcueil* (1994), I shall now consider these writers as 'minimalists', another term sometimes used to describe them, in order to support my view that their novels offer the most direct literary response yet to the general phenomenon described by the philosopher-sociologist Gilles Lipovetsky as 'la désubstantialisation postmoderne' ['the postmodern process of desubstantialisation'].[12]

The notion of a minimalist aesthetic is validated at almost every turn in the work of these writers. The image of the subject is no longer galvanised by confrontational structures (self versus other, individual versus society). The individual subsists, but as a kind of spectre, distanced rather than alienated from its environment. In these novels, even first-person narrators come across as strangely anaemic individuals: reticent, amoral, dispassionate, indifferent. At the same time, making artful use of one of fiction's staple ingredients, each novel tells a postmodern love-story. Whereas Echenoz subordinates pathos to irony, Oster and Toussaint achieve a more balanced yet still unusual mix of these elements. Though Oster's narrator is distraught at being left by the woman he loves, his narrative tone remains disconcertingly unemotive throughout the novel. The mix is slightly different in Toussaint's *L'Appareil-photo*, where an impassive narrator finds himself being charmed by the irrepressible yawns of the woman he meets at the start of the novel. Indeed he soon comes to see her somnolence as constituting a worthy form of resistance to the bruising realities of everyday life.

Minimal love, minimal stories. Plot too has been devitalised in the work of these writers. One thing follows another without necessarily following *on* from it, while individual events are often non-events or ironisations of commonly represented types of event. The narrator of *L'Appareil-photo*, for example, spends forty-five pages quietly transforming the story of a car journey round the suburbs of Paris into a parody of past stories: part Grail quest (in which the occupants of the car seek to replace an empty gas cylinder with a full one) and part road-to-Calvary (in which the stations of the cross are replaced by *service*-stations). More spectacularly, in recounting a massive earthquake in Marseille, the narrator of Echenoz's *Nous trois* completely deflates his object by describing it in terms appropriate to a disaster movie. Here, as elsewhere in Echenoz's writing, one is inevitably reminded of Jean Baudrillard's explicitly postmodern theory of the simulacrum, the media-made simulation which replaces reality, the copy which has no original.

Finally it is at the level of setting that all three of the novels just mentioned most insistently register the postmodern process of desubstantialisation. As defined by the anthropologist Marc Augé, a 'place' is a communal space, one which invests its inhabitants with an identity, a basis for relating to others, and a connection to history. A space drained of such capacity to confer meaning is therefore a non-place, a *non-lieu.*[13] Augé basically argues that postmodernity, which he prefers to call 'supermodernity', is characterised by the production of non-places: temporary abodes ranging from refugee camps to luxury hotels, pseudo-gathering points such as supermarkets and suburban shopping centres, points of transit along the sprawling networks of interlocking transport systems, even the means of transport themselves, together constructing a sort of non-world, a world given over to solitary individuality, to being on the move, and to impermanence (p. 101). This is precisely the kind of world evoked in the novels of Echenoz, Oster and Toussaint, whose main characters are all remarkably nomadic: uncommitted travellers in an uncommitting world. To focus briefly just on *L'Appareil-photo*, we meet the novel's narrator on the day he decides to take driving lessons. Thereafter he spends his narrated time in cars, aeroplanes, trains, ferries, service-stations, railway stations and hotels. His 'home' is completely elided from the narrative. Instead he shelters from the outside world in the smallest of non-places, where he likes to lose himself in his own thoughts: first in a public toilet, later in a photo booth and, finally, in the last scene of the novel, in a telephone box at a crossroads surrounded by flat, deserted countryside. Here, paradoxically, and perhaps ironically, the isolated narrator experiences a moment of truth, a minimal 'epiphany' as James Joyce would have called it: 'I watched the dawn breaking and just thought of the present, the present moment, trying one more time to catch its elusive grace' (p. 127). The narrator's journey through the non-places of postmodernity has not been the pretext for a simple critique of postmodernity. On the contrary, the point he reaches, which is also the point reached in his love-story, seems to offer a possibility of reparation in the present. As Iain Chambers explains, in a postmodern meditation which chimes uncannily with the end of *L'Appareil-photo*, we may by now have lost the chance of 'going home', if by this we mean returning to an authentic past. It may rather be 'a question of seeking to be at home here, in the only time and context we have'.[14]

In this brief presentation of contemporary minimalist fiction, I have tried to suggest how the novel's relation to theory has become far more indirect than in the days of the *nouveau roman*. Theory no longer holds sway over fiction, and the novelist is much less willing to entrust his or her creative endeavours to the explanatory zeal of theoretical discourse. Such is the negative legacy of the *nouveau roman* and *Tel Quel* movements that this stand-off has left an especially deep mark on the postmodern French context. Fiction and theory do continue to interact, but at a distance and in unpredictable ways, through what Linda Hutcheon in *A Poetics of Post-modernism* calls 'overlappings of concern' or 'shared responses to common provocations' (p. 14).

As for the future of the French novel in general, that too is unpredict-able – which is not at all to say unpromising – for the contemporary and the temporary have never been more synonymous. If 'here' is the only time and context we have, then where we are now won't necessarily tell us what lies in store. At the moment the narrator of Toussaint's novel finds grace in the fleetingness of the present, the reader of that novel is already wondering what will become of him when he finally steps out of his phone-box. In asking an unanswerable question about the future of the narrator, are we not also asking an unanswerable question about the future of narration?

NOTES

1 E. J. Smyth, 'The *Nouveau Roman*: Modernity and Postmodernity', in E. J. Smyth (ed.), *Postmodernism and Contemporary Fiction* (London: Batsford, 1991), pp. 54–73.

2 L. Hutcheon, *A Poetics of Postmodernism: History, Theory, Fiction* (London: Routledge, 1988), p. 40.

3 F. Dosse, *Histoire du structuralisme*, 2 vols. (Livre de Poche, 1995; first published 1992). All references here are to volume II, subtitled *Le chant du cygne, 1967 à nos jours*.

4 J.-F. Lyotard, *La Condition postmoderne: rapport sur le savoir* (Paris: Minuit, 1979), p. 7.

5 R. Barthes, 'La Mort de l'auteur', repr. in *Le Bruissement de la langue* (Paris: Seuil, 1984), pp. 61–7, p. 64.

6 It is worth pointing out that in the same year there appeared Philippe Lejeune's *Le Pacte autobiographique* (Paris: Seuil, 1975), a seminal work which gave a new methodological basis and critical direction to autobiographical studies.

7 A. Kibédi Varga, 'Le Récit postmoderne', *Littérature* 77 (1990), 3–22, p. 16.

8 B. Vercier and J. Lecarme, *La Littérature en France depuis 1968* (Paris: Bordas, 1982), p. 189.

9 C. Burgelin, *Georges Perec* (Paris: Seuil, 1988), p. 174.

10 M. Duras, *The Lover*, trans. B. Bray (London: Flamingo, 1986). Originally *L'Amant* (Paris: Minuit, 1984).

11 J.-L. Moreau (ed.), *La Nouvelle fiction* (Paris: Critérion, 1992).

12 G. Lipovetsky, *L'Ere du vide: essais sur l'individualisme contemporain* (Paris: Folio, 1994; first published 1983), p. 23.

13 M. Augé, *Non-lieux: introduction à une anthropologie de la surmodernité* (Paris: Seuil, 1992), p. 100.

14 I. Chambers, *Border Dialogues: Journeys in Postmodernity* (London: Routledge), 1990, p. 104.

JOHNNIE GRATTON

SUGGESTIONS FOR FURTHER READING

Bertens, H., *The Idea of the Postmodern: A History* (London: Routledge, 1995)

Bertho, S., 'L'Attente postmoderne: à propos de la littérature contemporaine en France', *Revue d'histoire littéraire de la France* 4–5 (1991), 735–43

'Temps, récit et postmodernité', *Littérature* 92 (1993), 90–7

Compagnon, A., *Les cinq paradoxes de la modernité* (Paris: Seuil, 1990)

Henderson, M. (ed.), *Borders, Boundaries, and Frames: Cultural Criticism and Cultural Studies* (London: Routledge, 1995)

Sheringham, M., *French Autobiography: Devices and Desires* (Oxford: Clarendon Press, 1993)

Tilby, M. (ed.), *Beyond the Nouveau Roman: Essays on the Contemporary French Novel* (Oxford: Berg, 1990)

GENERAL BIBLIOGRAPHY

This bibliography supplements suggestions for further reading given in individual chapters of the volume. Although this is a general and selective list of standard reference works, the items cited here will lead the reader to many others in and around the area of the modern French novel. For more detailed bibliographical information, the annual MLA (Modern Languages Association) Bibliography (usually available on CD-Rom in University Libraries) is probably the most helpful single resource.

Manuals

Abraham, P. and R. Desné (eds.), *Histoire littéraire de la France,* vols. IV, V and VI (Paris: Messidor, 1972–82)

Ambrière, M. (ed.), *Précis de littérature française du XIXe siècle* (Paris: Presses Universitaires de France, 1990)

Borgomano, M. and E. R. Rallo (eds.), *La Littérature française du XXe siècle: 1. Le Roman et la nouvelle* (Paris: Armand Colin, 1995)

Didier, B. (ed.), *Dictionnaire universel des littératures,* 3 vols. (Paris: Presses Universitaires de France, 1994)

France, P. (ed.), *The New Oxford Companion to Literature in French* (Oxford: Oxford University Press, 1995)

Hollier, D. and R. H. Bloch (eds.), *A New History of French Literature* (Cambridge, MA: Harvard University Press, 1989)

Pichois, C. (ed.), *Littérature française*; vol. VI, *De l'Encyclopédie aux Méditations*; vol. VII, *De Chateaubriand à Baudelaire*, vol. VIII; *De Zola à Apollinaire*; vol. IX, *Du Surréalisme à l'empire de la critique* (Paris: Arthaud, 1989–90)

Robichez, J. (ed.), *Précis de littérature française du XXe siècle* (Paris: Presses Universitaires de France, 1985)

Studies

Alter, R., *Partial Magic: The Novel as a Self-Conscious Genre* (Berkeley: University of California Press, 1975)

Auerbach, E., *Mimesis: The Representation of Reality in Western Literature* (Princeton: Princeton University Press, 1968)

Bal, M., *Narratology: Introduction to the Theory of Narrative* (Toronto and London: University of Toronto Press, 1985)

Barthes, R., *S/Z* (Paris: Seuil, 1970)

'L'Effet de réel', in R. Barthes et al., *Littérature et réalité* (Paris: Seuil, 1982), pp. 81-90

Bersani, L., *Balzac to Beckett: Center and Circumference in French Fiction* (New York: Oxford University Press, 1970)

Booth, W. C., *The Rhetoric of Fiction* (Chicago: University of Chicago Press, 1983; first published 1961)

Brombert, V., *The Intellectual Hero: Studies in the French Novel, 1880-1955* (Chicago: University of Chicago Press, 1964)

Brooks, P., *Reading for the Plot: Design and Intention in Narrative* (New York: Knopf, 1984)

Butor, M., *Essais sur le roman* (Paris: Minuit, 1964)

Chambers, R., *Story and Situation: Narrative Seduction and the Power of Fiction* (Manchester: Manchester University Press, 1984)

Combes, D., *Poétiques francophones* (Paris: Hachette, 1995)

Culler, J., 'Poetics of the Novel', in *Structuralist Poetics: Structuralism, Linguistics and the Study of Literature* (London: Routledge and Kegan Paul, 1975), pp. 189–238

Forster, E. M., *Aspects of the Novel* (Harmondsworth: Penguin, 1990; first published 1927)

Fowler, R., *Linguistics and the Novel* (London and New York: Methuen, 1977)

Genette, G., *Discours du récit* in *Figures III* (Paris: Seuil, 1972)

Fiction et diction (Paris: Seuil, 1991)

Girard, R. *Mensonge romantique et vérité romanesque* (Paris, Grasset, 1961); trans. Y. Frecerro, *Deceit, Desire and the Novel: Self and Other in Literary Structure* (Baltimore: Johns Hopkins University Press, 1976)

Goldmann, L., *Pour une sociologie du roman* (Paris: Gallimard, 1964)

Iser, W., *The Implied Reader* (Baltimore: Johns Hopkins University Press, 1974; translated from the German)

Lukacs, G., *The Theory of the Novel* (London: Merlin, 1971; translated from the German)

Maugey, A., *Le Roman de la francophonie* (Montreal: Humanitas, 1993)

Peyre, H., *French Novelists of Today* (Oxford: Oxford University Press, 1967)

Prendergast, C., *The Order of Mimesis* (Cambridge: Cambridge University Press, 1986)

Prince, G., *Narratology: The Form And Functioning Of Narrative* (Berlin, New York and Amsterdam: Mouton, 1982)

Narrative as Theme: Studies in French Fiction (Lincoln: University of Nebraska Press, 1992)

Raimond, M., *La Crise du roman, des lendemains du naturalisme aux années vingt* (Paris: José Corti, 1966)

Le Roman depuis la Révolution (Paris: Armand Colin, 1967)

Le Roman (Paris: Armand Colin, 1988)

Ricoeur, P., *Temps et récit*, 3 vols. (Paris: Seuil, 1983–6)

Rougemont, D. de, *L'Amour et l'occident* (Paris: Plon, 1939)

Tadié, J.-Y., *Le Roman d'aventure* (Paris: Presses Universitaires de France, 1982)

Le Roman au XXe siècle (Paris: Belfond, 1990)

Tanner, T., *Adultery in the Novel* (Baltimore: Johns Hopkins University Press, 1979)

Wellek, R. and A. Warren, *Theory of Literature* (New York: Harcourt, 1956)

Zéraffa, M., *La Révolution romanesque* (Paris: Klincksieck, 1969)

INDEX

NOTE: In titles of works, any initial article (La, Le, Les, Un, Une) is transposed as in *Femme, Une; Douleur, La; Faux-Monnayeurs, Les*. Authors and titles are indexed as separate headwords as in 'Constant, Benjamin' under C; *Adolphe* (Constant) under A.

Duras, Marguerite 227, 229–32, 233, 238, 245
  autobiographical writing 250, 252–4
Dürer, Albrecht 151
Dutourd, Jean 173
Duvalier, Jean-Claude 207–8

E=mc² mon amour (Cauvin) 187
Eau de café (Confiant) 211
Eberhardt, Isabelle 205
Ecart, L' (Mudimbe) 201
Echenoz, Jean 180, 181, 256–7, 258
école de Minuit 256
Ecriture ou la vie, L' (Semprun) 13
Editions de Minuit 180
Editions Jean-Jacques Pauvert 228
Editions Julliard 225, 227
Edouard (C. Duras) 31, 36
Education sentimentale, L' (Flaubert) 5, 42–3, 46–7, 84
Egypt 202–3
Einstein, Albert 135
El Maleh, Edmond 203
Elise (Etcherelli) 233–4
Elle magazine 225
Elle sera de jaspe et de corail (Werewere-Liking) 202
Emery, Marie 86
Emile (Rousseau) 43
Emploi du temps, L' (Butor) 138
'end of theory' 246
enfance à l'eau bénite, Une (Bombardier) 221–2
Enfance (Sarraute) 245
Enfant de sable, L' (Ben Jelloun) 205
Enfant du carnaval, L' (Pigault-Lebrun) 76, 83
Enfant du faubourg, L' (Richbourg) 85
Enfant noir, L' (Laye) 198
Enfantômes, Les (Ducharme) 219
engagement theme in fiction 147, 154
Engels, Friedrich 5
enquiry category of reading 5–6
Entre les eaux (Mudimbe) 201
environment 40, 43, 44–5
Eparges, Les (Genevoix) 168
Epaulette, L' (Darien) 88
epistolary novel 10–12, 22, 66
Erckman, Emile 83
Ere du soupçon, L' (Sarraute) 127, 138
Ernaux, Annie 145, 238n 255
erotic writing 238–9
Espoir, L' (Malraux) 169–70

Etcherelli, Claire 233–4
Etranger, L' (Camus) 136–7, 153
Etre et le néant, L' (Sartre) 146, 150
Etudiant noir, L' 194
Eugène de Rothelin (Flahaut later Souza) 55, 57
Exbrayat, Charles 182, 185
Excisée, L' (Accad) 203, 238
existentialism 145–51, 154, 173, 218, 224
exotic fiction 78, 82, 207
experimental novel 46

Fabre, Ferdinand 86
Facteur fatal, Le (Daeninckx) 252
Faguet, Emile 68
Faims d'enfance (Gauvin) 211
Fainéants dans la vallée fertile, Les (Cossery) 203
Fairlie, Alison 46
Fallet, René 185–7
Family Romance of the French Revolution, The (Hunt) 33
Fanny (Feydeau) 81
Fanon, Frantz 197
fantastic fiction 89
Fantôme de l'Opéra (Leroux) 88
Far West fiction 82, 89
farabé dialect 202
Farrère, Claude 88
fascicules 74
Fausse Position, Une (Marbouty) 63
Faux-Monnayeurs, Les (Gide) 9, 130, 134, 139, 141
Féletz, Charles-Marie de 55
Felman, Shoshana 33, 51
feminine writing 236
  see also women
feminism 4, 234–5
Femme m'apparut, Une (Vivien) 238
Femme, Une (Ernaux) 145, 255
Femmes d'Alger dans leur appartement (Djebar) 238
Feraoun, Mouloud 203
Ferry, Jules 89, 109n3
Feu dans l'amiante, Le (Richard) 217
Feu, Le (Barbusse) 155, 163–5
Feuillet, Octave 81
feuilleton 75, 78, 81–2, 84, 87, 88–9
Féval, Pierre 82–3
Feydeau, Ernest 81
Figaro, Le 84, 107–8
Figures III (Genette) 8
Filles de Plâtre, Les (de Montépin) 84

Sein und Zeit (Sartre) 146
self-consciousness of French novel 13–14
self-portraiture in Francophone novel,
    fictional 196–7, 204
semiotic, pre-Oedipal 236
Semprun, Jorge 13, 174–5
Senancour, E. P. de 17, 20, 22, 23, 24
Senegal 195, 203
Senghor, L. S. 194, 196
sentimental novel
    anti- 225–6
    post-Revolutionary 54–65
    realist transformation of 60, 68–9
    Second Empire 82
separatism in Quebec 218
Sept Baisers de Buckingham, Les (Gonzalès)
    82
serialised novels 79
Série noire imprint 182
Settinia (Allart) 62, 63
Seuils (Genette) 10
sex and the novel 77–8, 80
sexism in language 232
sexual identity and gender 223–40
sexuality 51, 87, 97–8
    in African Francophone novel 205, 206
    in decadent period 98, 100-8, 102
    imbrication of narrative and 69
    in Proust 116–17
    transgressive feminine 65–6
short stories
    framed miscellany of 251
    replacing serialised novels 100
Silence de la mer, Le (Vercors) 172
Simenon, Georges 182
Simon, Claude, 139, 140, 157*n* 159, 176–7,
    244, 245
simulacrum, postmodern theory of 257
Sixtine, roman de la vie cérébrale (de
    Gourmount) 94
Smyth, Edmund 244–5
Socé, Ousmane 197
social, the (particular cluster of subject
    matter) 58
social conditions
    nineteenth-century 41–3
    sociology of the 'lowly' 40, 45, 52
social novels, sentimental 61–4
Societé des Bons Livres 86
society, changes reflected in novel 17
Soirée avec M. Teste (Valéry) 127
Soleils des indépendances, Les (Kourouma)
    201

solipsism and period of decadence,
    contemplative 101
Sollers, Philippe 245
Sommeil délivré, Le (Chedid) 228
sotie 130
Souday, Paul 112
Souffles (Cixous) 236
Soulié, Frédéric 78
Soupe aux choux, La (Fallet) 186–7
Sous Verdun (Genevoix) 168
sous-conversation 137
Souvestre, Emile 62, 80
Souvestre, Pierre 88
Souza, Adélaide de *see* Flahaut
Sow-Fall, Aminata 201, 202
Speculum de l'autre femme (Irigaray) 237
speech of characters in nineteenth-century
    novel 50
speed of narrative 48
spilt aristocracy and religion of Romanticism
    99–100
Square, Le (M. Duras) 231
Stabat Mater (Kristeva) 236
Stackhiev, Alexandre 23
Staël, Germaine de 21, 22, 24–7, 37, 55, 57
Statue de sel, La (Memmi) 206
Stendhal (Henri Beyle) 31
    Chartreuse de Parme, La 45, 51, 99, 161
    Racine et Shakespeare 38, 47
    Rouge et le noir, Le 36, 39, 40–1, 51, 52,
        58
    choices in 145
    hero and heroine 59, 60
    Vie de Henri Brulard 47
stereotypes
    in Francophone novel 201
    in popular fiction 182
Stevenson, Robert Louis 129, 130, 256
Stowe, Harriet Beecher 77
stream of consciousness 134–5, 137
structuralism 244, 245–7
student and worker revolt (1968) 233, 234
subject, postmodern return of the 246, 248
Sue, Eugène 32, 36, 79, 84
Suleiman, Susan Rubin 154
Sulitzer, Paul-Loup 188
surrealism 131–4
surroundings, detail of 40, 43, 44–5
suspense category of reading 5–6
symbolism 94, 96, 100, 102, 126
Symphonie pastorale (Gide) 99

Taine, Hippolyte 37